Voices and votes

Glenda Norquay here introduces a selection of literary texts from the early twentieth century, offering a new perspective on women's campaign for the vote in Britain.

Drawing on novels, short stories, poetry and autobiography, the anthology reveals the ways in which campaigners use literary forms to mobilise political ideas and challenge gender ideologies. The collection includes writing not only by the major figures in the campaign but also those who formed the rank-and-file, who opposed women's suffrage, or who simply observed the action. The excerpts are sufficiently long to enable the reader to become familiar with the diversity of voices and positions and to understand at first hand the issues that prompted the most passionate debates.

Following an introduction examining the sexual and textual politics of the writing, the extracts are organised around four key themes: conversion to the cause; suffrage militancy; the prison experience; and questions of identity. The book includes brief biographies of all the authors.

The anthology offers an essential collection of primary sources for undergraduates, postgraduates and teaching staff working in literature, history, women's studies and cultural studies.

Glenda Norquay is Senior Lecturer in Literary Studies at Liverpool John Moores University.

Voices and votes

A literary anthology of the women's suffrage campaign

Glenda Norquay

Manchester University Press
Manchester and New York
Distributed exclusively in the USA and Canada by St. Martin's Press

Copyright © Glenda Norquay 1995

Published by Manchester University Press
Oxford Road, Manchester M13 9NR, UK
and Room 400, 175 Fifth Avenue, New York, NY 10010, USA

Distributed exclusively in the USA and Canada
by St Martin's Press, Inc., 175 Fifth Avenue, New York, NY 10010, USA

British Library Cataloguing-in-Publication Data
A catalogue record for this book is available from the British Library
Library of Congress Cataloguing-in-Publication Data
Norquay, Glenda, 1958–
    Voices and votes: a literary anthology of the women's suffrage
campaign / Glenda Norquay.
        p. cm.
    Includes bibliographical references (p. 320) and index.
        ISBN 0–7190–3975–4 (hardback). – ISBN 0–7190–3976–2 (pbk.)
        1. Women–Suffrage–Great Britain–History–Sources.
JN979.N67   1995
324.6'23'0941–dc20   94–43134
                                                          CIP

ISBN 0 7190 3975 4 *hardback*
        0 7190 3976 2 *paperback*

First published 1995

99 98 97 96 95   10 9 8 7 6 5 4 3 2 1

Typeset in Great Britain
by Servis Filmsetting Ltd.

Printed in Great Britain
by Bell & Bain Ltd, Glasgow

Contents

Acknowledgements

My interest in writings on the women's suffrage campaign developed out of an interdisciplinary course on Women and Writing 1850–1930, which I taught with a colleague, the historian Timothy Ashplant. I am particularly grateful to Timothy, for his advice and enthusiasm for the subject, and to the many students over the years who have made thoughtful and provocative observations on the material. Janet Handley and Pam Morris both gave support and encouragement, as well as making helpful comments on the script, as did Anita Roy from MUP. Joe Sim helped with books and conversation, Elspeth Graham provided sympathy and advice, and Peter Childs obliged in tackling various computer problems. I am also indebted to the staff of several libraries: to Sheena Streather and other staff at Hope Street Library, LJMU; staff of the Sidney Jones Library, Liverpool University, and in particular librarians in the Special Collections unit who provided information on the invaluable Symie collection; the Picton Library, Liverpool; the British Library; Diane Atkinson and other staff at the Museum of London; and, above all, to David Doughan of the Fawcett Library, for his knowledge, courtesy and unfailing enthusiasm. Elizabeth Crawford of Women's Sphere Books also joined the search for material. Olive Banks, Brian Harrison, Peter Keating and Leah Leneman all responded promptly and helpfully to enquiries. Michelle O'Connell of MUP was of great assistance on the copyright front. Jean Burnett and Debbie Richardson of the MCCA Office, LJMU, carried out tedious tasks with good grace. Finally, thanks for his support go to Roger Webster who has lived with these women's voices for a considerable time, and to Annie Webster, whose voice has made its own particular contribution.

Every effort has been made to locate copyright holders of material included in the anthology, but if any have been omitted they should contact the publishers who will be pleased to credit them in any subsequent editions. I would like to acknowledge the following for permission to quote from copyright material: Mid-Pennine Arts for Ada Nield Chew's stories; Patricia Bower for excerpts from Cicely Hamilton, *William – an Englishman*; Aitken, Stone and Wylie for material from Annie Kenney, *Memories of a Militant*; Faber & Faber Ltd, for material from Hannah Mitchell, *The Hard Way Up*; Victor Gollancz Ltd, for excerpts from Emmeline Pethick-Lawrence, *My Part in a Changing World*; Mrs Mabel Smith, copyright holder for Elizabeth Robins, *The Convert*, published by The Women's Press Ltd, 1980, 34 Great Sutton Street, London EC1V 0DX; the Estate of the Author for J. S. Stainton, *The Home-Breakers*, published by Hurst & Blackett; Everyman's Library, David Campbell Publishers, for material from H. G. Wells, *Ann Veronica*; and Virago Press for material from Rebecca West, *The Judge*.

Chronology of the women's suffrage campaign

1847 Anne Knight, a Quaker and anti-slavery campaigner, issued leaflet on women's suffrage.

1851 Anne Knight and others formed the Sheffield Association for Female Franchise.

1865 Barbara Bodichon and others of her circle formed the Kensington Committee for Women's Suffrage.

1866 Kensington Committee became the London Committee for Women's Suffrage and drafted women's suffrage petition. J. S. Mill asked to present this to Parliament which he did in June. Manchester Women's Suffrage Committee launched by Lydia Becker in August. The National Society for Women's Suffrage (NSWS) formed by the London, Manchester and Edinburgh Committees.

1868 First ever public meeting in Britain on women's suffrage, held in Manchester.

1869 Municipal Franchise Act introduces municipal franchise for rate-paying spinsters.

1870 Lydia Becker and Jessie Boucherett started the *Women's Suffrage Journal*. Women's Suffrage Bill passed second reading in House of Commons with a majority of thirty-three, but rejected in Committee. Lydia Becker, Emily Davies, Elizabeth Garrett and Flora Stevenson are elected to the new School Boards.

1871 Women's Suffrage Bill lost on second reading in Commons, as were Bills in 1872, 1875, 1876, 1878 and 1879.

1882 Rate-paying spinsters allowed to vote for town councils.

1883 Primrose League for Conservative women founded.

1884 Women's suffrage amendment to 3rd Reform Bill is defeated by 136 votes.

1886 Women's Liberal Federation is founded.

1887 Through local government reform women were allowed to vote for, but not to stand as, county councillors.

1889 Women's Franchise League formed, with Emmeline and Richard Pankhurst as members. Campaigned for votes for all women qualified by rate-paying (married or not). The novelist Mrs Humphry Ward, and other prominent women (or wives of prominent men) published the 'Appeal against Female Suffrage'.

1890 Lydia Becker died and *Women's Suffrage Journal* ceased.

1893 Pankhurst family returned to Manchester from London and joined the Independent Labour Party in 1894.

1897 The National Union of Women's Suffrage Societies (NUWSS) founded by Millicent Garrett Fawcett.

1900 Emmeline Pankhurst, widowed in 1898, elected to Manchester School Board, and resumed ILP work in 1902.

1901 Christabel Pankhurst, inspired by Eva Gore-Booth, joined North of England Society for Women's Suffrage.

1903 Women's Social and Political Union (WSPU) formed by Emmeline Pankhurst; first meeting 10 October. Lancashire and Cheshire Women Textile and Other Workers' Representation Committee formed.

1905 Bamford Slack Bill on Women's Suffrage talked out on second reading in Commons. Christabel Pankhurst and Annie Kenney interrupted Liberal political meeting in the Free Trade Hall, Manchester, 13 October, and were accused of 'assaulting' a policeman. In court next day they were offered the choice of fine or arrest and chose imprisonment.

1906 Liberals came to power under Campbell-Bannerman as Prime Minister. WSPU moved its activities to London. Term 'suffragette' first used in *Daily Mail* 10 January. First women's march to lobby Parliament organised by WSPU in February. Emmeline Pethick-Lawrence becomes treasurer of WSPU. WSPU demonstration in lobby of House of Commons, leading to ten arrests and imprisonment in Second Division. Attempts by Christabel Pankhurst to disengage WSPU from its Labour connections.

1907 NUWSS held its first outdoor procession. WSPU held 'Women's Parliament' at Caxton Hall, followed by march on Parliament and fifty-one arrests. Women's Suffrage Bill talked out on second reading. WSPU formed many provincial branches. Emmeline and Christabel Pankhurst resigned from Independent Labour Party. Emmeline and Christabel Pankhurst and the Pethick-Lawrences overturned the constitution of the WSPU and cancelled forthcoming annual conference, in an attempt to maintain control. The Women's Freedom League (WFL) was formed as a separate organisation by opponents of the Pankhursts and Pethick-Lawrences, with Charlotte Despard as President. *Votes for Women* newspaper founded as monthly organ of WSPU.

1908 Asquith became Liberal Prime Minister (and expressed opposition to votes for women). WSPU held Women's Parliament, lobbied the Commons, organised a meeting of over seven thousand women in the Albert Hall and a massive demonstration in Hyde Park. First window-breaking took place in 1908 when Asquith refused to receive WSPU deputation and massive demonstration was held in Parliament Square. Large demonstrations took place outside London. At Christabel Pankhurst's instigation, WSPU attempted to 'rush' the House of Commons; she and her mother imprisoned.

1909 Agitation increased, including window-breaking. Largest march yet on Parliament on 29 June. First hunger strike started by Marion Wallace Dunlop on 5 July (released after four days), followed by others. Forcible feeding for hunger-strikers introduced.

1910 General Election, Liberals returned with reduced majority. Suspension of militant tactics continued until November 1911, except for week in November 1910. 'Conciliation Bill' introduced to give women a limited franchise, but effectively killed by being referred to Committee of whole House. Black Friday (18 November): WSPU deputation to Parliament met with increased police brutality.

1911 Liberals returned to power. Truce of militancy for Coronation. Forty thousand women stage Coronation procession. Asquith announced that a manhood suffrage bill will be introduced the following year and that a women's suffrage amendment would be possible. WSPU decided to resume militancy.

1912 Large-scale window-smashing and arrests, including Pethick-

Lawrences. Christabel Pankhurst fled to Paris. WSPU's first serious arson attempt in July. Pethick-Lawrences ousted from WSPU in October, retaining control of *Votes for Women.* Christabel and Emmeline Pankhurst launched *The Suffragette.* Sylvia Pankhurst campaigned in East End of London, and built up branches of WSPU there into semi-autonomous East London Federation. WSPU members began to attack post in pillar boxes.

1913 Speaker of Commons ruled out of order amendments to enfranchise women. Concerted campaign against public and private property begun by WSPU. Emmeline Pankhurst sentenced to three years for incitement. Growing concern over forcible feeding. 'Cat and Mouse' Act (Prisoners Temporary Discharge for Ill-Health) introduced in April, allowing hunger -striking prisoners to be released until they regained health, then recalled to prison. Emily Wilding Davison threw herself at the King's horse in Derby and died of her injuries. Christabel began moral crusade with 'The Great Scourge and How to End It', a series of articles on effects of prostitution and venereal disease. WSPU no longer willing to co-operate with men supporters. Forcible feeding re-introduced in October.

1914 Christabel broke with Sylvia Pankhurst and East London Federation (ELF) became an independent organisation. Sylvia launched *The Workers' Dreadnought. Rokeby Venus* slashed by Mary Richardson in National Gallery. New organisation, The United Suffragists, established in February, open to men, women, militant and non-militant members. WSPU demonstration at Buckingham Palace. Asquith received deputation from ELF. First World War broke out, Christabel returned to London, militancy suspended. Emmeline and Christabel supported the war effort.

1917 Representation of the People Bill clause to give women the vote carried by 387 to 57.

1918 Representation of the People act gives vote to women of thirty and over who were householders, wives of householders, occupiers of property worth £5, or university graduates – a total of 8.5 million women. Countess Markievicz elected for Dublin constituency but as Sinn Fein leader refused to take her seat.

1919 Lady Astor became first women MP to take her seat.

1928 Equal Franchise Act granted vote to all women of twenty-one and over. Emmeline Pankhurst died.

1929 General Election: women formed 52.7 per cent of electorate.

Women's suffrage organisations and journals

NUWSS: The National Union of Women's Suffrage Societies. United all previous suffrage organisations in 1897, under the leadership of Millicent Garrett Fawcett. A democratic organisation, committed to constitutional and non-militant means in approach. Campaigned for franchise for women on same terms as men. Elected president and national executive committee. Its members are referred to as 'suffragists'.
Membership: 1909: 13,161 members; 1914: 53,000+ members
Newspaper: *The Common Cause*
Colours: red and white until 1908, with green added in 1909.

WSPU: The Women's Social and Political Union. Founded by Emmeline Pankhurst in 1903, this was the militant arm of the suffrage movement. Broke from Labour movement in 1905. In 1907 Pankhurst/Pethick-Lawrence leadership cancelled annual conference to keep control of organisation. Pankhursts split with Pethick-Lawrences in 1912, and retained control. Its members are referred to as 'suffragettes'.
Membership: total membership not divulged but estimated new members: 1909: 4459; 1912/13: 2380; first eight months of 1913: 923
Newspapers: 1907–12 *Votes for Women*; 1912–15 *The Suffragette*
Colours: purple, white and green.

WFL: The Women's Freedom League. Founded as a break-away from the WSPU in 1907. Leading members included Charlotte Despard and Teresa Billington-Greig. Committed to a more democratic organisation than the WSPU and favouring tax protests.

Membership: 1908: 53 branches; 1914: 4000 members
Newspapers: 1907–9 *The Women's Franchise*; 1909–13 *The Vote*
Colours: green, white and gold.

East London Federation of the WSPU. Founded in May 1912, and went through various names: East London Federation of the Suffragettes (1914–16); Workers' Suffrage Federation (1916–18); Workers' Socialist Federation (1918–24). It was run on democratic lines and with working-class women. Sylvia Pankhurst was the key figure. Links with socialist and syndicalist organisations.
Membership: 1917: branches in East London and elsewhere in London, and twenty-four provincial branches.
Newspapers:1913–17 *The Women's Dreadnought*; 1917–24 *The Workers' Dreadnought*
Colours: purple, white, green and red.

VWF: Votes for Women Fellowship. Founded by Pethick-Lawrences after split with the Pankhursts in 1912.
Newspaper: *Votes for Women*
Colours: purple, white and red.

WWSL: The Women Writers' Suffrage League. Founded in 1908, with various well-known writers, including Olive Schreiner, Eizabeth Robins, Cicely Hamilton, Sarah Grand, Evelyn Sharp, May Sinclair and Edith Zangwill amongst its members, the League expressed itself as 'strictly neutral in regard to suffrage tactics'. Produced various publications, organised booksales etc.
Colours: black, white and gold.

Men's Political Union for Women's Enfranchisement. Formed in 1910 to support the WSPU and closely tied to that organisation until the split with the Pethick-Lawrences and increasing antipathy towards male suffragists in 1913. Until then the WSPU had included among its supporters Israel Zangwill, Laurence Houseman, Henry Brailsford and H. W. Nevinson, who had all contributed material to *Votes for Women* and spoken on WSPU platforms.

National League for Opposing Women's Suffrage. Formed in 1908 as the Women's National Anti-Suffrage League, with a separate Men's Committee for Opposing Female Suffrage. Collected 337,018 signatures in anti-suffrage petition in 1908. Amalgamated in 1910 as National League for Opposing Women's Suffrage. Marshalled a range of arguments against women's suffrage, although female members were opposed to platform speaking and women's public demonstrations. Its membership, often accused of being aristocratic and plutocratic, included Lord Cromer, Lord Curzon, Lady Jersey, The Duchess of Atholl, Mrs Humphry Ward, Mrs Frederic Harrison.

Membership: 1909: claimed to have 9,000–10,000 members; 1913: 255 branches in England.

Newspaper: 1908–18 *The Anti-Suffrage Review*

Colours: white, pink and black.

Note: in general women are referred to either by their full name or by the names they were known by in the various organisations.

Sources: Garner, Harrison, Rosen, Stanley, Fulford, Tickner – see Bibliography.

1

Introduction

An act that will be marked by woman's seizing the occasion to speak, hence her shattering entry into history which has always been based upon her suppression. To write and thus to forge for herself the anti-logos weapon. To become at will the taker and initiator, for her own right, in every symbolic system, in every political process.

It is time for women to start scoring their feats in written and oral language.

Hélène Cixous[1]

'A Lost Opportunity'

Others there were who spake with fire and art;
   I stammered, breaking down beneath the weight
Of that great store that lies upon the heart
   When with one passion all my nerves vibrate.

Little I said, who had so much to say -
   This is the memory that sears and stings,
My soul was fire, my thoughts were clear as day,
   Yet had my soul no wings.

No matter, when that force beyond control
   Sweeps on one side the cobwebs of the brain,
In broken stammers speaks the inmost soul . . .
   Nor shall her passion smite the air in vain.

Eva Gore-Booth[2]

The hand has touched the figure and passed it and the speech goes on. Edith has not spoken. She has failed; utterly and miserably failed. Her throat was dry and hard; her voice would not come; because, as she tells herself in agony, she is a coward, has failed for very fear. . . .

How dry her throat was! Her tongue seemed fast to the roof of her mouth. Could she ever manage to get out the sentence that her comrade had not been able to finish? Yes, for the power that had forced her here was paramount now, and her voice came to her and rang out clear: "The women of England demand the vote."

Gertrude Colmore[3]

Long, long – we in the past
   Cowered in dread from the light of heaven.
Strong, strong – stand we at last,
   Fearless in faith and with sight new given.
Strength with its beauty, Life with its duty
   (Hear the call, oh hear and obey!)
These, these – beckon us on!
   Open your eyes to the blaze of day.

E. Smyth[4]

The literature of the women's suffrage campaign

This anthology is about women who raised their voices in demand for a place in the political process. Speaking out was for most a difficult and a transgressive act. Even now, more than sixty years after the gaining of the vote, many of their voices are still unheard, although their concerns – the battle for equal rights, the questioning of gender roles, the challenge to limiting representations of femininity – expressed with such power in the early years of the twentieth century, continue to engage feminists today. In presenting a selection of literary texts about the suffrage campaigns my aim is to give the modern reader access to some of those raised voices. The collection will, I hope, offer an insight into the concerns and literary strategies of the writers who addressed women's struggle for political representation. By introducing a range of hitherto neglected texts, it may also alter existing maps of women's writing.

Excellent histories of the suffrage campaign itself now exist, and are supported by valuable collections of documentary material. The work of feminist biographers has done much to make the lives of many suffrage activists accessible to us. The lively drama produced during the fight for the vote has been reprinted. The powerful visual images, pageantry and spectacle of the women's struggle have been the subject of fascinating critical analysis.[5] The novels, short stories, poetry and autobiographies surrounding the campaign have, however, received far less attention. Much of the material contained in this book is out of print and extremely difficult to obtain. In putting this volume together my intention has been to add another dimension to our understanding of the battle for women's suffrage and broaden our definitions of textual politics.

For readers interested in women's struggle for political rights, the writings contained here reveal the different strategies employed by activists campaigning for the vote. They also show, through the inclusion of anti-suffrage literature, the arguments and opposition these women faced. As the writers challenge and negotiate possible meanings attached to the term 'woman', we can learn much about the general debates over femininity and its representation taking place at the time. In addition, the texts force us to think about one aspect of women's writing that has, I believe, been neglected in the late twentieth century. With the changing focus of feminist literary criticism, first on the experience of women as represented in literary texts, then on the experimental and subversive nature of women's writing, we may have lost sight of what it means to write as a direct intervention in public and political debate. In contrast to the notions of women's literary production as bound by domesticity and interiority or limited to the marginal and experimental, the novels, short stories and poetry presented here are, by the very nature of their subject matter, located in the public sphere. Created to convince the reader of their arguments, aimed at altering the structures of society, these texts contain voices which demand to be heard. Heated, committed, often unsubtle, the arguments that play across the pages still have the power to hold our attention, forcing us to question our own position on issues central to feminism today.

In understanding what writing as a form of public intervention might mean to women in the early twentieth century it is important to place their activities in the context of the previous century. Throughout the second half of the nineteenth century women had been negotiating for a place within the public domain, moving from the so-called private sphere of the home into the professions, chal-

lenging the legal system which supported the economic and domestic subservience of their sex, claiming recognition of their place in
the work force, demanding unionisation, and taking part in social
reform of various kinds. The right to vote meant the right to participate in legislation, to articulate opinions in public, to be part of
the processes of government. For those campaigning for female suffrage it also represented women's proper place within the public
sphere. By making the claim upon a public space and a public voice
the literal and symbolic centre of their cause, the suffrage campaigners chose to build upon the advances made by their sisters in the
nineteenth century. Through large public meetings and well-organ-
ised demonstrations, by speaking in parks and selling papers at
street corners, through disruptions of male political arenas where
female voices were not heard, and in the literal and metaphorical
shattering of boundaries between public and private spaces, the suffrage campaigners demanded recognition in the wider world.

The textual productions of these women were likewise characterised by the claim upon public space. Just as postcards, banners,
posters and pageants characterised their artistic production, so
speech-making, polemical tracts, newspaper articles, letters to those
in power and to the public, were the dominant forms in their
writing. From such material, to be found in anthologies and discussed by historians, our images of the suffragists and suffragettes
have been constructed. Of the more conventional literary forms that
have survived to interest later generations, drama, the most public
genre, has received the greatest attention from historians, critics and
publishers and been recognised as central to the movement. The suffrage campaigners, however, were prolific in all areas of creative
activity: musicians, artists, poets, playwrights and novelists were
found within their ranks and, in several cases, formed explicit sub-
groups such as the Women Writers' Suffrage League and the
Actresses' Franchise League. In some instances those involved had
already entered the precarious and radical world of the female artist
and were therefore inclined to sympathise with the feminist
demands of the campaigners; in other instances it was involvement
with the cause itself that liberated women into new spheres of activity. The suffrage campaigners, as I hope this volume will demonstrate, also drew skilfully upon the more conventional literary
genres of fiction, poetry, the short story and autobiography.
Occupying a position on the boundaries between public and private

worlds, such areas of literature had become increasingly acceptable as a sphere of female activity in the previous century. By writing novels, poetry, and autobiographies, suffrage women were perhaps making a less radical entry into a masculine domain than in their striking public and polemic textual productions. Nevertheless, within established literary forms the campaign for the vote was also vigorously conducted and fought over.

I would suggest that until we recognise the significance of these literary writings our picture of the suffrage movement will remain incomplete. It is the aim of this volume, therefore, to bring together extracts from the conventional literary forms of the time, and in particular fiction and poetry, so that they may be read alongside the public documents of the campaign. In this respect, the book makes space for a kind of writing that has been marginalised in histories of the movement. I hope these extracts will lead the reader to examine the literary qualities and characteristics of the writing produced around this crucial issue, and that this process will in turn raise larger questions about the relationship between literary form and political intervention which occupies a central place in feminist literary theory and practice.

To date this subject has received little attention from critics, although some groundbreaking work was carried out by Elaine Showalter in *A Literature of their Own*[6] and by Wendy Mulford in her short essay "Socialist-feminist criticism: a case study, women's suffrage and literature, 1906–14".[7] Sandra Gilbert and Susan Gubar also explore early feminist writing in *No Man's Land,* but focus on sex-antagonism and utopian fiction at the turn of the century.[8] Until now, however, the main difficulty for anyone interested in exploring this area has been the inaccessibility of the material itself.

Much work also remains to be done on the circumstances of production and reception surrounding the texts. Some publications were clearly intended for an identifiable and sympathetic audience: the Women's Freedom League was responsible for the publication of Gertrude Colmore's collection of short stories *Mr Jones and the Governess,* while Evelyn Sharp's collection *Rebel Women* was brought out in a second edition by the United Suffragists. The Women's Press was also a valuable outlet for supporters of the cause, but tended to concentrate on non-fiction. Although commercial publishers approached Arnold Bennett's novel *The Lion's Share* with caution, viewing it as too contentious, the response in most cases appears to have been determined by the reputation of the writer or the handling of material. *Outlawed* by Charlotte Despard and Mabel Collins, and *A Fair Suffragette* by Adrienne Mollwo, were both marketed as popular romantic fiction, while Constance Lytton, H. G. Wells and Rebecca West had little difficulty in finding established publishing firms interested in their work. With poetry, it was not unusual for individuals such as Elizabeth Gibson to publish their own slim volumes themselves. The serious press, however, gave the literature about the suffrage cause little attention. One of the few reviews of suffrage fiction was a mocking account by Lytton Strachey in *The Times Literary Supplement* of J. S. Stainton's novel *The Home-Breakers*.[9] Middle-brow writers such as Gertrude Colmore and Edith Zangwill did receive obituaries in *The Times*, but neither paid much attention to the writers' suffrage activities.[10] With the paucity of publishers' records and the obscurity of many of the writers, it is, however, extremely difficult to ascertain how successful different publications were and the opinions and constitution of their readership.

Selection and organisation of material

This book offers a range of writings about the campaign for women's suffrage but concentrates on novels, short stories, poetry and autobiographies. Drama has not been included, partly because, as I have argued, it occupied a rather different place in the public sphere and its importance for the suffrage movement has already been acknowledged but also because many of the best plays are available in Dale Spender and Carole Hayman's collection, *How the Vote was Won*. Likewise, the public form of journalism has been well represented in other publications; this volume concentrates instead on literary pieces from magazines and newspapers, such as the short stories, satires and cameos of Ada Nield Chew and Rebecca West. Autobiographies dealing with the campaign have also received critical attention, partly because they tend to be pro- duced by figures who have attained wide public recognition but also for their usefulness as documentary sources. The autobiographical writings included here have been selected for their interpretations of particular issues, not the fame of the writer. Indeed, it often seems the case than those with a lower profile in the movement enjoyed a greater freedom in retrospectively assessing their involvement than well-known leaders with specific political agendas.

The volume primarily draws upon material produced by suffrage campaigners but it also provides a range of writings by women (and some men) who appear to have had no discernible link with the suffrage movement but operated within the popular fiction market and found the cause a suitably dramatic subject for their pens. The work of writers such as Adrienne Mollwo or J. S. Stainton, now disappeared from all literary histories, provides fascinating insights into contemporary presentations of the campaign. While the former's novel *A Fair Suffragette* appears neutral on the political issue at stake, interested instead in the romance of the situation and the personal and social tensions it creates, Stainton's novel *The Home-Breakers* is actively hostile to the campaign, ridiculing its aims and participants.[11] Yet these texts are also important objects of study, not only for their contributions to the range of public opinion at the time but also as demonstrations of the shared literary characteristics to be found across a range of opposing political perspectives.

The material in this volume is organised into four key areas: *conversion*; *militancy and militarism*; *the prison experience*; and *questions of identity*. While these categories cover only a part of the suffrage experience, they represent arenas in which central issues of the struggle – both practical and theoretical – were played out. They also reveal the deployment of particular textual strategies and indicate debates pertinent both to the women involved and to contemporary historians and critics. Each section enables the reader to hear contrasting voices on a particular subject, to compare the treatment of an issue during different stages of the campaign or in retrospect, to engage with writers of conflicting opinions, and to consider a range of literary forms. In the collection of material on the prison experience, for example, the reader can find an excerpt from a pro-suffrage novel, *Suffragette Sally*, written during the campaign, alongside a retrospective account by a working-class suffragette, Hannah Mitchell.[12] A range of defiant and inspirational poetry written within Holloway prison can be compared with an extremely negative portrayal of imprisonment in the anti-suffrage satire *From Hampstead to Holloway*.[13] Each text places its own interpretation and value upon both the practical and symbolic aspects of imprisonment.

In terms of its historical focus this volume concentrates on material from the period 1906 to 1914 when agitation for the vote was at its strongest and literary engagements with this at their most immediate. It also includes, however, certain novels written after the war but before the gaining of votes for all in 1928, selected on the grounds that those active in the campaign were still very much concerned with the wider issues it had raised. Literature written after the 1914 watershed often points to important questions about the significance of the vote for feminism and its future developments. It also allows for a retrospective evaluation of the tactics utilised in the campaign by those involved: Rebecca West's novel *The Judge* admires its young heroine's enthusiasm for the cause but is also able to present a psychological analysis of her motivation in a way that might not have been desirable when real political gains were at stake.[14]

Each piece of writing is prefaced by a brief introduction. Unlike mainstream literary texts, details about books, writers, publishers, and readership are often unavailable, but I have tried to provide some kind of context wherever possible. The volume also contains a brief chronology of events, although the reader seeking further historical information about the various stages of the campaign, its shifting groupings and the political context of the day is directed to the various historical accounts now available.[15] Likewise, the biographical reference section at the end of the book aims to give such details as are known about the writers and campaigners mentioned. Further information, on the major figures in particular, is easily to be found in biographical dictionaries and histories.[16] A striking feature of this period is how much is known about women such as the Pankhursts but how little can be found out about their lesser-known supporters.

In selecting material for inclusion in the volume I have tried wherever possible to give a reasonable length of excerpt from novels and autobiographies, and to present poems and short stories in their entirety. This should allow the reader to get to know the voice and texture of the writing and to gain some sense of the internal contradictions and textual dynamics of each piece.

Texts and voices

By focusing on specific aspects of the campaign and examining a range of representations on each point, we can see how the texts themselves construct historical experience for us, defining the terms in which we understand the suffrage campaign. The range of perspectives presented on each issue also allows the reader to consider her own position for if, as Jane Marcus argues in her introduction to *Suffrage and the Pankhursts*, the dominant histories of the campaign have long forced the woman reader to engage in a test of her political and sexual orientation, the material here also demands that we should interpret, evaluate and define ourselves in relation to its competing discourses.[17]

If any one aspect of suffrage literature can be identified as its key feature it is this element of dialogue. The texts themselves are full of discussion and debate; the novels packed with reported speech, the poetry full of declamation. As the characters in novels discuss their position on enfranchisement, the writers of autobiographies defend their views, and the poets proclaim opinions to their audiences, the clash and clamour of many voices is inescapable. It is no surprise that one of the first novels to be reprinted with the resurgence of feminist publishing houses in the 1970s was *The Convert* by Elizabeth Robins, an author far better known as a playwright; the novel itself originated in her short play *Votes for Women!*[18] The public and political sphere of debate determines the subject matter of fiction and poetry, offering a significant departure from the domestic and introspective features conventionally attributed to such forms.

The texts, however, do not only contain dialogue and dispute but are, structurally and thematically, quite clearly in dialogue: the shape of their narratives, the discourses drawn upon, the symbolism used and the political positions adopted all sustain a debate with the dominant ideologies of their time and frequently challenge other texts. This feature could be described as a kind of public intertextuality. All the texts contained in the volume, even those present in forms traditionally directed to the private realm of reading, speak aloud. Even the most monologic take their stance in relation to a range of other voices, participating in a wider political argument.

Finally, the texts are in dialogue and debate with themselves. Although frequently radical in its politics, suffrage literature is obviously influenced by the dominant ideologies of the day. This leads to some fascinating contradictions within the material. In the novels, for example, a conventional and heterosexual romance may be offered as a reward for the heroine's feminism. Poetry stressing women's solidarity in prison often draws upon noticeably masculine discourses of fellowship; symbols of the struggle are taken from established military iconography; the literature of political protest falls back upon anti-industrialist rhetoric. Language itself is strikingly unstable, with the struggle to define and redefine terms such as 'womanly', 'martyrdom', and even 'the vote' a central feature of every text.

Equally conspicuous is the extent to which pro- and anti-suffrage writings draw upon the same scenarios, plots and characterisation. In *Ann Veronica* by H. G. Wells we see Ann Veronica's relationship with her scientific mentor and lover superseding her temporary interest in suffrage, whereas the heroine of Edith Zangwill's novel *The Call* becomes increasingly involved in the cause following her exploitation by a paternalistic scientist and would-be lover.[19] *Delia Blanchflower* by Mrs Humphry Ward and *Suffragette Sally* by Gertrude Colmore both focus on the strength of female friendship, but the latter presents it as a source of strength within the movement while the former depicts it as a sinister diversion from 'normal' womanly activities. Although the components and results may differ, many novels are structured by the idea of choice between conflicting desires. Involvement in the cause as a source of female adventure is used both positively and negatively in many instances. And the motif of battle – on behalf of women, with other women, against unwomanliness even – is to be found throughout. By bringing together a wide range of texts, differing in opinions and forms, the tensions and contradictions of the time are not only demonstrated but enacted, as each piece of writing itself becomes an arena of external and internal contestation.

The battle of representation

The women (and some men) who debated the suffrage cause in their writing had two main aims: to provide a representation of the movement and its participants, and to persuade readers into sharing the writer's opinion on its issues. In the writings in this collection we can see how these dual aims of representation and persuasion determined the focus, structure and form of their work.

All the texts here aim to show what the women who campaigned for the vote were like and why their cause might merit support or disapproval. The representation of women in art, literature, film, and other media has become a central feature in feminist criticism, revealing the dominant images of femininity in circulation, challenging those images, and demonstrating the cultural construction of gender. On the question of the vote, however, it may be argued that the concept of representation gained another dimension: in this context women were also seeking political representation – wanting to speak for themselves, to be heard, to be present in the political processes.

How women were depicted was of central importance in assessing why they should or should not be given the vote. To fight for political representation, women had to do battle with existing systems of representation. For the suffrage campaigners their struggle was inextricably linked to nineteenth-century gender ideology and in particular to the contested concept of the 'womanly woman'. The legacy of this debate over what constituted the true nature of 'woman' and how it structured feminist and anti-feminist thinking of both the nineteenth and twentieth century is an important factor in understanding the tactics adopted by the suffrage campaigners to challenge the stereotypes of femininity prevalent at the time. It also throws light on the strategies adopted by suffrage artists and writers seeking to undermine these dominant images. The process, however, was a complex and often contradictory one. An attack on one stereotype could often mean the unwitting embrace of an equally restrictive image. Delicate negotiations had to take place, for example, between the depiction of women's oppression and the well-established representation of woman as victim. Likewise, an insistence upon the centrality of 'woman' to the political process might be read as playing into the hands of sexual conservatism with its insistence upon 'woman' as a separate category.

For writers in this arena, then, the whole issue of representation was complex, potentially perilous and extremely important. The depiction of women is an important issue in many kinds of writing but patterns emerging from suffrage literature indicate a particularly fierce fight in the battle over 'woman'. In these texts misrepresentations and misrecognitions of 'the suffragette', for example, are frequent: the pretty women whom the male spectator cannot believe is a suffragette; the woman who surprises herself by sudden allegiance to the cause; the secret sympathiser jolted into action by the treatment of other women; the strident public campaigner revealed as gentle and diffident in private. Through such devices a writer could challenge critical stereotypes and make readers reassess their own preconceptions. In other texts strikingly negative images are found: the hitherto caring wife and mother ruining family life by her involvement with the suffragettes; the lonely spinster seeking solace and fulfilment; the natural 'fanatic', a crazy gleam in her eye, who happens to have fixed on the suffrage movement. In each case the cause is presented as bringing about a distortion and diminution of 'womanly' qualities. On such a battleground, how women 'appeared' – how their faces, clothes, bodies, voices, actions, lives were depicted – could not be read as neutrally descriptive. The authors were, after all, making conscious choices in their intervention into the political arena.

The significance of representation does not, however, stop with the conscious creation of the authors, for in examining representations of femininity we can also discern the dominant cultural constructs of the time, challenged in some instances, affirmed in others. Although the writers consciously sought to project particular viewpoints they were still working within the circulation of dominant ideologies, within established definitions of female experience and identity. And these images might not be contested in the campaign for the vote. If some myths of femininity were challenged, others passed undetected. While challenging women's political oppression, many writers presented an image of the suffragette in terms of physical beauty and a noble, self-sacrificing nature, quite in accord with the domestic ideology of the previous century.

Finally, within the complex redefinitions of 'woman' taking place within these texts, attention must also be given to areas of silence: to that which is unrepresented. Questions of free love and female sexuality strongly emerging themes in fiction of the 1890s, are largely absent. Passion, when it occurs, is presented as a reward for the woman who has achieved fulfilment within an approved context – either found in the cause itself or through marriage. Expressions of emotional fervour directed towards other women, as striking instances in *Suffragette Sally* and *The Call* show, were represented in terms which emphasise their spiritual and political dimensions and play down the personal.[20] Explorations of motherhood and childrearing, a significant element of many women's experience and a genuine constraint for women without child-care facilities who wanted to campaign, were likewise scarcely evident in suffrage literature. Class differences, although signalled as an issue in some of the pro-suffrage literature, were rarely explored with any complexity. Any conflict of social hierarchies was usually represented as being resolved by the common adherence to a shared cause. Although campaigners often argued that they wanted the vote in order to address the problems of working-class women or unmarried women, the efficacy of their campaign depended upon the campaigners themselves being presented in positive and socially-acceptable terms.

By putting themselves upon the public stage and, literally, the platform, women lost the 'protection' of their sex and became fair game for comment and ridicule. As a story such as 'Patrolling the Gutter' demonstrates, the campaigners were keenly aware of ways in which their appearances might be interpreted.[21] Within suffrage literature the writers were equally alert to constructions that might be placed upon their fictional characters and took extreme care in the facets of femininity they presented. The 'representation' of women, in both political and textual senses, is therefore a crucial issue in all the material in this book. In the four sections that follow this introduction the complex questions and delicate balancing of images with which the writers struggled in representing their cause are evident, although the central issues take on different forms.

Conversion

In the section on conversion to the cause we can see how a key development in the individual life carries a range of implications and interpretations. Both as a theme and as a goal, conversion is all about transition and transformation from one state to another, from one perception to another, from an old mind-set to a new world view. As the texts demonstrate, it can be brought about and represented in many ways. Pressure of circumstances or a change of context may force a new outlook. In *Ann Veronica* we can see both, when the combination of the heroine leaving home and her ill-treatment at the hands of a male friend make her involvement with the cause practically and emotionally inevitable.[22] In its structure, such a narrative of conversion offers parallels to working-class autobiographies where writers demonstrate that a move away from their original lifestyle was inescapable and echoes the plot found in much nineteenth-century fiction where a woman's isolation or misfortune liberates her into unconventional or unexpected behaviour.[23]

In other texts a less secular model is adopted, with the moment of conversion being likened to spiritual transformation. A sudden moment of *éclaircissement* is reached – and described with religious fervour. Depicting the conversion of Sally, for example, Gertrude Colmore employs the imagery of a bird taking wing in Sally's breast, allowing her to ignore material and physical constraints and conveying the power of her new vision.[24] Similar representations occur outside fiction: Annie Kenney, for example, adopts a tone of involuntary ecstasy in her account of hearing Christabel Pankhurst speak for the first time.[25] While these emotive narratives appear very different from *Ann Veronica*, it could be argued that both Wells and Colmore – and, to an extent, Kenney – go some way to removing agency from the converts: an external force leads or drives them without any clear act of will on their part. If textual strategies of this kind are in any sense aimed at converting the reader, it is on an emotional and sympathetic level. We too are drawn into an imaginative inevitability, unresistant to the forces operating upon us.

Other narratives engage more specifically with the politics of conversion, showing the effects of successful propaganda or creating scenarios in which conversation and debate lead to a new intellectual understanding. *The Convert* is, as the title might suggest, a text in which such processes of conversion are depicted in detail; as a result it is a novel packed with argument. Several autobiographers also reveal their conversation to be on an intellectual level, brought about through debate. In such instances the fight for suffrage is often presented as an extension of previous political activities. Helena Swanwick goes to some lengths in *I Have Been Young* to emphasise the range of her radical interests prior to women's suffrage and Emmeline Pethick-Lawrence shows how her organisational abilities, demonstrated elsewhere, led the suffragettes to recruit her to their side.[26] Converts of this kind also tended to maintain their life in the public sphere in one way or another after the vote was won. Where the political nature of conversion is acknowledged, an explicit engagement with agency is more evident: the convert is given detailed justification for her beliefs. Such texts, although they lack the emotion or plot-driven involvement of other texts, could still convince readers through intellectual propositions in favour of the vote.

A third model of conversion might be termed the dramatic: conversion through witness. Again and again narratives describe atrocities to women as seen in demonstrations, in court, even in private life. In each case this brings about the realisation that if women are to be protected by the law, they themselves must be able to legislate. Witnessing bravery in other women campaigners is also a popular catalyst for conversion, and often combined with the atrocity theme. Ideally suited to vivid retelling, this fusion of courage and atrocity is clearly illustrated in *The Call* but occurs elsewhere in both fiction and autobiography, frequently in association with depictions of militant acts. As a conversion tactic it offers emotional and intellectual appeal, combined with the dramatic impact of shocking spectacle.

Lastly, these texts depict conversions through force of personality. In *Suffragette Sally* the romantic figure of Lady Henry Hill draws both middle- and working-class women into her vision; through rhetoric and example she sustains their fervour. The enigmatic character of Mary Blake likewise confirms Ursula's dedication to the cause in *The Call*, while in *Delia Blanchflower* the heroine's 'fanatical' friend, Gertrude Marvell, is shown to exploit Delia's love for her in order to push militancy to further extremes.[27] Friendship or adulation of role models were, of course, powerful forces in the suffrage movement, with the cult of personality being strongly criticised from some quarters. Emmeline Pankhurst, Christabel Pankhurst and Emmeline Pethick-Lawrence have all been described as mesmerising audiences and inspiring passionate devotion in their followers. From an early stage in the campaign, however, this emphasis on personality within the WSPU was seen as dangerous not just to the organisation's democracy but also in its effect on young minds. Teresa Billington-Greig, writing in 1911, is scathing about this calculated emotionalism: 'The leaders impose a yoke of emotional control by which the very virtues of the members are exploited; they produce a system of mental and spiritual slavery.'[28] Although it might be exploited by Pankhurst dominance, emotional interaction between women working together was clearly a significant factor in drawing converts to the cause. The moment at which Ursula comes to Mary Blake in *The Call* is presented as one moment of symbolic beauty and release; the paper flowers Mary is making fall dramatically to the floor when Ursula enters.[29] Madeleine Rock's short poem beginning, 'And the words, the words she said' also creates a specifically female passion which brings her into the cause.[30] Female friendship in such writing appears not only to offer a reworking of role models and a recontextualising of the convert in a female community but also implicitly to challenge heterosexual social structures. For this reason, it could also be presented as a threat to 'natural' womanly emotions, as the anti-militant novel *Delia Blanchflower* demonstrates. In pro-suffrage texts considerable care is taken to avoid such accusations: the spiritual purity of relationships is stressed and devotion to the cause is emphasised as a determining context for the passion experienced.

Conversion through friendship is arguably the most radical of textual strategies and one that speaks directly to the female reader. In contradiction of Virginia Woolf's claim in *A Room of One's Own* that female friendship remains silenced in fiction – 'And I tried to remember any case in the course of my reading where two women are represented as friends. . . . But almost without exception they are shown in their relations to men' – these texts set women in definitional relationships with each other and explore the emotional and political impact one woman might have upon another.[31] While the choice between a man and the cause is a plot device in several novels – especially the anti-suffrage fiction – even 'the cause' has an inescapably gendered identity, bringing with it a body of women whose power cannot be ignored. And in other texts, such as the pro-suffrage novels of Colmore, Robins and Zangwill, all the most fully characterised relationships are between women. In the creation of a woman-centred fictional world, the text could awake the consciousness of the woman reader, offering an insight into the freedom felt by many women when they moved into the predominantly female community of the suffrage cause.

Militancy and militarism

In popular images of the suffrage campaign, militancy – as expressed in acts of disruptive political violence – occupies a central place in the struggle for the vote. At the time, however, it was a deeply divisive strategy and its political efficacy and symbolic significance have been energetically debated in subsequent interpretations of the women's movement. Militarism – the adoption of military ideas, vocabulary and imagery – on the other hand was only one of a range of discourses available to the campaigners who also drew on religious iconography, the politics of space, the construction of sexuality and representations of femininity in order to convey their point of view. A militarism of metaphor and organisation is present from fairly early in the campaign, and particularly evident in the structures of pageants, processions and rallies. Militancy in action emerged only at a later stage, most notably from 1912 onwards, and was specifically associated with the activities of the WSPU. But whereas militarism could offer an imagery and rhetoric outside militancy, militancy itself was never perceived in isolation. The actions of the militant were carefully selected not only in terms of the potential disruption but also for their symbolic power.

The relationship between the discourses of militarism and militancy of deed is complex and contested, but plays an important part in suffrage systems of representation. In many of the accounts presented here, the rhetoric of war and the sense of fighting within a unit offer a disciplining structure in which women could contextualise their commitment. It allowed them unity and identification when in opposition to society and provided them with a vocabulary of courage and heroism. It is, however, debatable whether this rhetoric represented any real engagement with the practicalities of war. As the poems and songs included here reveal, much of the imagery simply imbues combative figures drawn from women's history with mystical significance and employs a high-flown rhetoric of battle and sacrifice – as in Emily Wilding Davison's poem, 'L'Envoi' or Ethel Smyth's famous song, 'The March of the Women'.[32]

Nevertheless, the fiction in particular shows a concern with the extent to which a discourse of battle meshes with deeds of militancy. In *The Call* Ursula is shown to dismiss the military metaphors of the leader, only to be confronted by the evidence of battle:

But for one item in the programme Ursula could feel nothing but an amused scorn. The Leader . . . was to decorate each hunger-striker with a medal 'For Valour'. The Leader herself in her speech had referred to the women in a way that the girl had felt pitifully theatrical. 'Oh, God of Battles, steel my soldiers' hearts,' she had cried amid a tumult of applause. Suddenly she found herself staring, shocked, aghast. She wanted to cry out, and at the same time, she could not cry out. For this was not theatrical. . . . These women looked tortured.[33]

Here apparently empty words acquire a new and horrible force, moving beyond rhetoric. Mrs Pankhurst herself, on whom 'The Leader' in *The Call* is modelled, was frequently represented during

the campaign as uniting rhetoric with action, drawing upon powerful images of battle in her speeches but in her physical frailty presenting   striking   evidence   of   male   brutality   and   female
determination.

In the battles of words and deeds, ill-treatment by police of the
various women's deputations to Parliament, and in particular the
incidents of Black Friday, have often been identified as a point of
transition in militant tactics. When peaceful demonstration was met
with a brutal response, militant action became the recourse. In the
many fictions and autobiographies which depict these scenes of
violence, one image recurs: the small, white-haired old lady who is
thrown to the ground and trampled by the crowd or police. In every
instance this is presented as a catalyst for the spectator and the
reader. The figure of the old lady, abused in her frailty and femininity, exposes the vacant rhetoric of masculine chivalry in which age
and sex are supposedly objects of reverence.

It is not only the transition from a militarism of approach to a militancy of action that is explored in these writings. In the fiction we
can find a sophisticated consideration of the justifications and
limitations of militarism in relation to militancy. A short story by
Evelyn Sharp, 'The Women at the Gate', enacts a long and articulate debate between various spectators with different fields of experience: glorifications of 'war' are qualified by the military
onlooker who redefines and reinforces the heroism of the women.[34]
With a more critical perspective, Cicely Hamilton in *William – an
Englishman* shows a suffrage militant horrified by the actual experience of war.[35] In a startling attempt to reveal the limitations of
suffrage militancy and its misapprehension of the nature of violence,
she is brutally mocked and eventually raped by German soldiers
before dying of her wounds and her shame. Here too relationships
between deeds and words are explored. In both texts, although
aiming at very different ends, metaphors of militarism are tested by
superimposing them upon realities of action. In the short story, the
exposure of war as messy and unheroic becomes an ironic means of
justifying the women's struggle, whereas the novel suggests that
while militarism might function as a discourse of rebellion in peace-
time, it has little connection with the actualities of war and appears
trivial by comparison.

In contrast to the complex explorations of militarism as a discourse, texts dealing with militancy in action appear more

straightforward. In general the element of adventure is stressed, with the central participants shown as young women of courage and high spirits. Negative representations of militancy are equally one-dimensional. In the anti-militant novels *The Home-Breakers* and *Delia Blanchflower* activists are presented as dangerous fanatics, whose actions lead to the degradation not just of themselves but of those whom they suck into the cause.[36] Judgements against them are rendered more convincing by coming from male onlookers who have experienced 'real' battle.

With less antipathy to the cause and in more sophisticated terms, women who campaigned vigorously for the vote also expressed disquiet with militancy. Even someone as closely involved with the leadership of the WSPU as Emmeline Pethick-Lawrence attributed Mrs Pankhurst's support for attacks on public property to a worrying aspect of her personality: 'Excitement, drama and danger were the conditions in which her temperament found full scope.'[37] Helena Swanwick offers a more damning indictment in her autobiography, attacking the attention-seeking 'martyrdom' of militant tactics as dishonest and cynical.[38] Teresa Billington-Greig was again fierce in her criticism, stating: 'I do not believe that the best emancipation for women is through emotionalism, personal tyranny, and fanaticism.'[39]

Going far beyond the physical manifestations of militancy, such women confronted and debated its symbolic and discursive power and contested its practical usefulness, an issue still debated by historians today. Some would argue that the power of militant action lay in its symbolism, as women entered male space and broke down barriers between public and private space.[40] Others believe that militancy alienated potential supporters but had little political impact in any other respect.[41] Echoing opinions expressed by women at the time, it has also been suggested that militancy was a reactive phenomenon, a response to male violence upon women, and was not always fully controlled by the leadership of the WSPU.[42] The argument that involvement in militancy diverted the attention of women away from the wider goals of feminism has also been voiced.[43]

The debate over militancy, in conclusion, represented a political and strategic conflict at the time and has caused further contention in subsequent assessments of its efficacy. What the writings included here demonstrate is that militancy was perceived as a challenge to established gender boundaries, a recognised transgression of women into the domain of physical force and a subversion of prevalent discourses of womanliness. The strength of feeling apparent in the writing on the subject also indicates that for some women at least this was a problematic strategy and that for all women involved in the campaign it involved a constant reassessment of their beliefs and commitment.

The prison experience

It was not only the large numbers of women involved and the publicity gained that makes the prison experience such a central part of suffragette consciousness. Prison came to have a much wider significance within the movement's ideology and iconography. Imprisonment served several purposes for the suffrage campaigners. Initially it offered them access to publicity and a public platform in court, then permitted them the creation of educative female communities within prison. For many women it was also the point at which estrangement from family and friends became inevitable; it was therefore seen as a test of allegiance and a rite of passage. On a more abstract level, prison bars provided a potent symbol of women's confinement in society, while the incarceration of their bodies offered a recognisable form of physical sacrifice. Within this arena women could enact in microcosm their battle with government and authority, exploiting the symbolic significance of a politics of space.

Arrest and imprisonment left an indelible mark on both the public record and the public mind. It allowed articulate and hitherto respectable women to break into the public space of the court-room, a useful venue for airing of suffragette opinions. Using their defence to make a case for the validity of their arguments, they could display their own wits and abilities, often at the expense of figures of the male establishment. Imprisonment of 'respectable' women also forced patriarchal authority into revealing its oppression, making explicit the forces through which women were kept in place. Yet imprisonment was not without its negative aspects: apart from the physical hardship endured, the value of prison experience was the subject of debate between suffragettes and suffragist, highlighting differences in class and domestic background and, as with militancy, dividing women on grounds of tactics.

If imprisonment served a symbolic function in publicly imaging women's oppression and confinement, for the campaigners themselves it often represented a testing of their courage and the threat of the unknown. In their accounts of the prison experience included here it is the physical conditions and the alien environment that feature most strongly. Again and again the practical details of clothes, bedding and food are enumerated, although, as the rather different accounts by Hannah Mitchell and Constance Lytton reveal, the response to such conditions was also shaped by class background.[44] Indeed, for some many women, incarceration carried little symbolic significance. As Ada Nield Chew's commonsensical character Mrs Stubbs points out in her critique of militancy: 'What good does it ever do anybody t'goo to prison . . . ? Tha rowins thi own 'ealth, an' tha owds wimmin up for a spectikkle.'[45] She proceeds to argue that prisons themselves are man-made, and that getting put into them is neither difficult nor special. Apart from such strategic qualifications, practical considerations also carried weight. Emphasising this point in her autobiography, Hannah Mitchell comments on her husband's need to bail his wife out of prison in order to have someone to cook his meals for him. The loss of a female wage-earner often meant a significant difference to the family economy and women from such backgrounds also found it difficult to afford alternative means of child-care. Such concerns were less likely to determine the decision of unmarried or middle-class women to face imprisonment. Therefore, although in writing about prison suffragettes might stress the opportunity it created to meet and sympathise with women of different classes, the 'freedom' to enter its gates was itself determined by class and circumstances.

But to the militants prison became yet another space that they could enter and appropriate. On a simple level, they made it their own by seeing it as an honour to be part of the sisterhood who had gone to prison. Within prison walls they could set up an alternative social structure and a centre of feminist education, from which women 'graduated' with their own honours and medals. A brooch with the suffragette colours, designed by Sylvia Pankhurst, was given as a badge of honour to those who had been to prison. Former prisoners were given the place of honour in processions and demonstrations; and poetry written from within Holloway describes the elite band who are the FHG: the Fellows of Holloway Gaol.[46] Welcoming committees were organised for women coming out of prison and these often took extravagant forms. The breakfast banquets to greet the returning prisoners became as much part of the ritual as arrest and court. In May Sinclair's *The Tree of Heaven*, Dorothy recognises there is no escape from this final ordeal.[47]

Within the female community of prison women could develop a new self-awareness and some found the experience liberating. Indeed, the historian Martha Vicinus argues that going to prison became a self-transforming act: 'In prison each woman made "a larger world of freedom" for herself and other women – even as the public space of the male world was denied them, women found inspiration in creating freedom and space within the prison.'[48] Liberation within this new space could take the form of activities – reading, talking, even jogging – or could emerge in transgressive relationships.[49] In her account Constance Lytton describes the earnest attempts she made to befriend the wardens in each prison.[50] Forms of resistance could even lead to appropriation of space itself.

Subversion of authority, through making the physical space imposed upon them their own, is best represented by the experience of Emily Wilding Davison who protested against forcible feeding by barricading herself in her cell. As Gertrude Colmore depicts the scene in her biography, she not only used the furniture but also such 'feminine accoutrements' as her slippers and hairbrush to jam the door.[51] Through her actions the authorities were forced into the demeaning role of pleading with her for entry to the cell, while she had become a figure of strength and authority. When the hosepipe is turned on her, the text depicts her as a little child who doesn't want to 'be good', emphasises the bullying behaviour by the warders. A final irony emerges when, the water treatment failing, '. . . the door must be burst open. But if it fell, it would fall on the prisoner: the men outside knew it, so did the woman within.' Here too an inversion has been effected: it is those outside who are breaking into a controlled space, bringing violence and destruction, rather than suffragettes forcing entry into male space through the window-breaking.

The most horrific details of prison life, however, were reserved for hunger striking, for it was here that women made their most painful protest at male violation. If prison buildings came to represent a contested space, the battle for the bodies of the suffragettes was waged with even greater vigour. To women who had already suffered physical assaults when storming Parliament, the desire to retain control over their own bodies was powerful, enabling them to undergo brutal and humiliating treatment at the hands of the prison authorities. Again this is vividly detailed in fiction and auto-biography.

Hunger striking clearly acquired a deep symbolic significance for the women involved, although – as with militancy – others have since questioned the emphasis they placed upon this. While hunger striking could be interpreted as a powerful means of resistance, and even a symbolic refusal of maternal nurturing, it has also been argued that to place bodily sacrifice at the centre of female martyr-dom was reinforcing well-established images of women's victimisa-tion.[52] Here too conflicting representations of politicised femininity created divisions between women and continue to be debated today.

Imprisonment nevertheless created opportunities for publicity, rebellion and reclamation of space. For literature about the cam-paign, it not only provided a dramatic plot event and a cathartic nar-rative experience but, in the poetry in particular, offered a structuring metaphor with which to explore fellowship, spirituality and self-awareness. The collection of poems in *Holloway Jingles*, published by women imprisoned in Holloway in April 1912, is typical in this respect. From the rousing 'There's a strange sort of college' to the enigmatic and meditative 'To D. R. in Holloway', these writings operate through inversion of establishment defini-tions of prison. Whether using prison as a symbol of liberation or simply reversing the idea of prison as a place of silence and isolation by complaining of the noisiness of life in Holloway, these poems challenge our expectations.

Holloway Jingles is also characteristic of prison literature in that part of its appeal lies in the unexpectedness of articulate voices emerging from so base a situation. The suffragettes maintained a strong sense of the inappropriateness of prison for their deeds and conveyed this to their readers at every opportunity. Whether detail-ing the strange incidents and circumstances of prison life or describ-ing the spiritual insights derived from the experience, the material on this subject maintained a curious duality, stressing on the one hand the common and unifying aspects of imprisonment as suf-fragettes tread a path well-worn by fellow campaigners and other suffering women, but emphasising on the other hand horror that society could place them in such an anomalous situation. This duality draws the reader into a sense of the alien and inappropriate nature of the prison experience, while reinforcing a sense of solidarity. While the political value of imprisonment might have divided women it gave them a new vocabulary of resistance and remains a powerful symbol of the suffrage campaign.

Questions of identity

The fourth group of writings in this book does not focus on a specific issue within the suffrage movement but brings together a range of texts that explore the theme of female identity. If the suffrage campaign began as a battle for the vote, it also became an arena in which women could redefine the self. Moving into new spheres of activity and experience, they both created and were given alternative narratives of their selves and their femininity. In their writing women's own sense of their expanded horizons, their discovery of new selves, and their challenges to existing definitions of femininity, are expressed with excitement and power. Juxtaposed, however, with this awareness of selves newly authenticated through the cause is a resistance to other definitions of suffrage identity in public circulation. Another battle is thus enacted between conflicting definitions of self, as the writing draws upon competing discourses surrounding women's social and psychic identity. The curious result of this is a literature apparently intent on establishing specific formulations of identity, yet underpinned by an awareness of the shifting nature of subjectivity and the potential instability of representation.

Certainly for many women the campaign allowed them to find a voice, to explore new ideas and to redefine both internal and external images of themselves. Two important aspects of this, foregrounded in the literature, are the educative experience of campaigning and the entry into the public sphere which it facilitated. Emmeline Pethick-Lawrence's image of the movement as offering 'education into living identification of the self with the corporate whole' finds a more practical echo in Margaret Haig's assertion that her involvement led her into a whole new world of ideas and books.[53] For women who had struggled so hard in the nineteenth century to gain access to education this concept of their own educative community, dedicated to a shared aim, was strongly attractive. Of Haig's educative experiences, however, it is her development as a public speaker that she singles out as the major transformational feature of her suffrage years.

Of continuing concern to women today, entry into the public sphere forms a recurring theme in fiction, autobiography and poetry. As Hélène Cixous writes: 'Every woman has known the torment of getting up to speak, her heart racing, at times entirely lost for words, ground and language slipping away – that's how daring a feat, how great a transgression it is for a woman to speak – even just open her mouth – in public.'[54] The terror and physical sensations she is described as undergoing are repeated throughout suffrage accounts of breaking that public silence: 'It seemed to Ursula that everyone in the room was looking at her. Her heart began to thump. She felt sick. It was the first time she had ever been called upon to speak in public.'[55] A similar trepidation is felt by Evelyn Sharp in *Unfinished Adventure* where she describes being ejected from a meeting as almost a relief when the moment came.[56] In speaking out women were transgressing their confinement to the private domain and to domestic discourses. But in presenting themselves to the public, they were also crossing boundaries of the body. Once upon that public platform their morality and sexuality were no longer protected by their silence and anonymity.

Although newly acquired identities might bring with them fears and exposure to ridicule, much of the writing offers a positive representation of the newly discovered self as a challenge to dominant constructions of femininity. Gertrude Colmore's short story ''Ope', in which a drunken woman, famed for her crude impersonations of 'the suffragette' gains a new dignity and identity through a genuine alignment with the cause, demonstrates a belief in the power of woman to transcend imposed social identities.[57] Other fictional and factual accounts of militancy allow the writers to redefine the qualities associated with woman. In Evelyn Sharp's 'Rebel Women' and Emmeline Pethick-Lawrence's description of militant action, women are described positively in terms of their coldness, calmness and fixity of purpose in the midst of action, testament to a new definition of courage.[58] The sacrifice of self and ideals of selflessness, traditionally linked with conventional images of Victorian femininity, are also reappropriated by suffrage activists. While embracing these images could be damaging, reinforcing notions of female sacrifice, it also indicates an awareness that new spheres of action demand new forms of rhetoric.

Inevitably some representations of the new self to be found

through suffrage campaigning are less positive. In its psychologising of the suffrage fanatic Gertrude Marvell, *Delia Blanchflower* suggests that an inadequate family life and social isolation might force a woman into the movement. Other narratives by pro-suffrage campaigners also express some reservations about new identities, in particular about the mass spirit demanded by the WSPU. Some, fearing a diminution of self when used as an instrument for the cause, or a loss of individuality in the collective whole, see the roles it offered as limiting. While relocation within a new structure of identity could be liberating, the emotional and political effects may also be dangerously overwhelming.

All the writers who stress the positive side of transformation share a sense that the newly discovered self is not only more fulfilling but also more 'authentic'. Yet ironically, for both writers and campaigners, this is predicated upon a strong sense of the instability and fluidity of identity. An engagement with shifting identities had a political rationale within the campaign, where a battle of images over both 'the suffragette' and woman herself was being conducted. To contest the stereotyped association of feminism with masculinity, found at its crudest form in *From Hampstead to Holloway* in which a suffragette is depicted in pin-striped suit and bowler hat, members of the WSPU took great pains with their appearance.[59] Hannah Mitchell ruefully observes her own dowdy appearance in comparison to their finery on several occasions, while Cicely Hamilton offers a more specific analysis:

There was no costume-code among non-militant suffragists, but in the Women's Social and Political Union the coat-and-skirt effect was not favoured; all suggestion of the masculine was carefully avoided, and the outfit of a militant setting forth to smash windows would probably include a picture-hat. This taboo of the severer forms of garment was due, in part, to dislike of the legendary idea of the suffragette, as masculine in manner and appearance – many of the militants were extremely touchy on that point.[60]

This manipulation of appearances found its literary parallel in the repeated theme of misrecognition. Gertrude Colmore in particular returns to this idea with great frequency. Characteristic in this respect in her short story 'Pluck', in which two different definitions of woman – an angry suffragette and the brave rescuer of a drowning child – are initially placed in irreconcilable opposition by a young man, before both are superimposed upon the dignified young woman he is watching.[61] Also from a male perspective, although with less positive ends in mind, *A Fair Suffragette* depicts the male hero attracted to a young woman and unable to believe her appearance as being consistent with a commitment to women's suffrage. Even more negative representations are to be found in *The Home-Breakers* in which the cause is shown to force women to go against their 'natural' feminine instincts. In all these texts both opponents and supporters attempt to redefine femininity and female identity.

One curious aspect of the potential fluidity of a suffrage identity emerges in the autobiographies dealing with the campaign. All the women who were active in it were born in the nineteenth century, a fact which appears to have structured their self-perception in particular ways. Margaret Haig writes: 'My experience is perhaps in one sense typical of that of many women of my generation who, born into a Victorian world, passed into an Edwardian and thence, through the kaleidoscope of the war, into a neo-Georgian one, adapting as best they could as they went along.'[62] Haig was indeed typical: several autobiographies emphasised the writer's own sense of being a transitional figure. Through this narrative device the writer might wish to explain changes in their lives, or justify their radicalism. It could even be read as a characteristically 'feminine' apology for any perceived lack of coherence in the narrative. But if understood as an expression of the writers' sense of their subjectivity, it would appear that instability of identity was a concept they grew up with and one that may have helped in challenging existing gender boundaries.

For a challenging of boundaries – physical, political discursive and ideological – lay at the heart of the campaign. Although 'questions of identity' occupy a separate section in this book, issues concerning the self are also explored in conversion narratives, in accounts of female friendship, in the discourses of militancy and in the reworking of prison imagery. In demanding the vote women were rewriting and reassessing their political and personal selves. In their textual tactics adopted, in the exploration of alternative symbolic systems, and in the debates over political strategies, they were engaging with issues of representation that still divide and unite women today.

Strategies of persuasion/questions of form

If representation is a key feature within these texts, the desire to convince or convert the reader is an equally significant structuring
element. All the writers here seek to persuade the reader of the validity – or of the dangers – inherent in the suffrage cause. The process
of conversion is, as I have suggested, a dominant motif in many of
the texts. The point of reversal, of transition, of *éclaircissement*, at
which a recognition of the rights (or wrongs) of the suffrage movement is brought about, offers a key moment in autobiographies,
fiction and drama. It also plays a significant role in establishing the
particular value systems within that text. Conversion as a theme
therefore has a section of primary text material devoted to it in this
book. But conversion as a central textual objective also carries significant implications for the form and structure of suffrage literature.

As interventions in a public debate, with specific political
agendas, all the material included in this anthology was aimed at
converting or persuading the reader. With this in mind it was essential that texts were accessible and spoke a familiar language,
whether it be that of those inside or outside the suffrage movement.
The texts included here reveal the array of tactics adopted. Writers
drew upon a range of techniques, from humour (satire, parody,
irony, even slapstick) to rigorous intellectual debate. They made
appeals to common sense, justice, religion or a sense of Englishness,
offered adventure, hagiography, romance and pathos, and were
skilled in rhetorical strategies that might make readers reassess their
own positions. A writer like Gertrude Colmore is adept at taking a
concept such as 'pluck' (in the short story of that name) which
carries with it connotations of British masculinity, and then demonstrating its appropriateness when applied to the suffragettes, or of
showing, as in *Suffragette Sally*, that concepts of womanly sacrifice
are not confined to the 'angel in the house' but may be better suited
to the suffragette in prison. In her fiction she works with a discourse
and value system familiar to her readers but recontextualised in a
way that might lead them to review their opinions.

In their attempts to convert, many of the pro-suffrage writers
offered a challenge to established gender ideologies and contemporary definitions of 'woman'. But, as with any kind of writing, they
also faced the constraints of literary conventions and genres. Given

their subject matter, innovations in form might be expected in these texts, but their function within the public sphere also limited experiment. Radicalism in writing, the unfamiliar in form and technique, was hardly likely to attract the wide readership or audience these texts sought. Rather, then, writers worked within the dominant literary conventions of the novel, short story, poetry and autobiography. In each of the literary genres we can see writers utilising established forms but also, in some instances at least, manipulating them to serve their purpose.

In particular the novels written about the cause illustrate this stylistic and structural conventionality in the predictability and closure of their conclusions, although there are some exceptions. Rebecca West's novel *The Judge* might be usefully contrasted with *The Call* in this respect.[63] The latter, published in 1924, appears to have been little influenced by modernism but instead adopts the form of earlier 'naturalist' fiction. Although it explores a range of contradictory roles and conflicting emotions which might be experienced by a woman of the period, any possibility of the suffrage heroine leading a life of continued unconventionality, or taking further the female friendships forged within the campaign, is precluded by the return of the masculine hero after the war, in need of her feminine attentions. Inevitably this leads to a resolution in which marriage and 'mutual respect' dominate. As such, the text remains 'closed' in both form and content. West's novel, partly because the suffrage cause is only one element within its concerns, displays a greater ambiguity. The first half of the novel does indeed end with the suffrage heroine's engagement, but the second half follows her relationship with the hero and his mother in a situation of psychological intensity where the complexities of female sexuality and the social constraints surrounding it are more fully addressed.

The question of an ending was, of course, a particular problem for fiction written before the vote was gained; no clear political resolution could be offered and the degree of commitment to the cause as a subject was often revealed by the kind of ending adopted. Thus, *A Fair Suffragette* ends with a wedding-bells scenario as its resolution, whereas the conclusion of *Suffragette Sally* involves the death of the eponymous heroine. The former novel, in which the lives and romances of the leading character are its main focus, is content with a neatly closed ending, whereas the latter's openness reflects its central concern with an ongoing political struggle, explicitly acknowledged in a final Author's Note: 'This is a story which cannot be finished now.'[64]

Another problem for novelists, as *The Judge* illustrates, lay in finding a 'plot' that would allow the writer to address wider feminist concerns. It is noticeable that several of the suffrage novels – and indeed autobiographies – use the experience of trial or imprisonment as a means of commenting on the misfortunes of other women encountered in an unfamiliar context, where the usual moral and social boundaries are crossed. One such instance occurs in *The Call* when Ursula is led to contrast the sentences meted out to the suffrage women with that of a child-abusing pimp. Other novels incorporate different devices: *Suffragette Sally* uses the central figure's class background to give some indication of the ill-treatment of women in the labour market, while *The Convert* brings in a rather creaky seduction and abortion plot to demonstrate the double standard of morality for men and women. Balancing the central suffrage story with other concerns can, however, lead to shaky plot structures and sudden shifts of direction. Charlotte Despard's *Outlawed*, written with Mabel Collins in 1908, and advertised as based upon the author's experiences of prison, offers a striking example of this.[65] Only through a melodramatic plot of mistaken identity, murder, seduction and wrongful imprisonment does the heroine come to fight for suffrage, which is described with extreme brevity at the end of the novel.

Even more destabilising than this uneasy dependence on plot was the hybridity of form in the novels, a characteristic of Edwardian fiction attributed to the influences of journalism and social investigation.[66] Novel writing of this time has been seen as transitional, juxtaposing different kinds of fiction within the same text and displaying an uncertainty of direction and genre. As other critics have noted, this appears particularly true of suffrage fiction.[67] Again *The Call* illustrates the point. It opens with a fairly humorous account of Ursula's attempt to become a woman scientist and be taken seriously by the male scientific establishment, then shows her conversion to suffrage – largely through the strong emotional attachment she forms to a leading campaigner – which constitutes the central theme in the novel. Meanwhile, it sustains a subplot in which Ursula is almost seduced by her plausible but married science tutor, before realising that her true love lies in the heroic soldier, Tony. The novel ends with Ursula and Tony together after the First

World War, in which one of Ursula's inventions played a vital part. In the different elements of this text we can discern: an opening akin to 'New Woman' fiction, in which the heroine is trying to make her way in the world in the face of peer and parental opposition; a subplot of seduction and romance; the rhetoric of heroism and deeds of military adventure; and, as the main body of the text, a detailed account of the suffrage campaign with an analysis of women's oppression. In the title itself, with its multiple significance of 'the call' – military, feminist, vocational, emotional – the different strands are brought together in a fragile web.

The Call is not unusual in this respect. Looking across the range of novels included in this volume it would appear that the mixing of forms is a central aspect of the writing. Traditions of political satire, of romance, of science fiction, of polemical poetry, of working-class autobiography and spiritual confession are all utilised in different combinations in order to attract and convince the reader. It is in the cohabitation of popular, if ill-matched, genres that the 'experimental' nature of such writing lies. Two areas of popular fiction in particular – romance and adventure – demonstrate the ways in which writers drew upon, but adapted, familiar fictional motifs and forms. In the manipulation of such popular genres we can see how the battle for representation and the struggle for conversion had formal as well as thematic implications.

Romance, whether on heterosexual terms with the inevitable wedding-bells conclusion or the more unusual form of an intense friendship with another woman, is an important structuring element in many of the texts. Love triangles, between 'woman, man and the cause', 'woman, man and another woman', or 'woman, the cause and family', are frequent. This issue of choice is central to plot development, drawing the reader into an evaluation of conflicting opinions before reaching a conclusion which will reinforce one particular position. In the anti-militant novel, *The Home-Breakers* a contrast is drawn in the resolution between Louie, the half-hearted suffragette who settles for happiness with the man she loves and Elinor, the fanatic, who – at great personal cost – tells her would-be suitor: 'There is no room in my life for you or any man.'[68] Through the comparison with other characters in the novel, however, her choice is also presented as an indictment of the demands made upon women by the militant movement. A 'happier' solution may be found in *A Fair Suffragette*; here a compromise is reached whereby

Gipsie, on her marriage, will be permitted to continue in the campaign to an extent, but agrees, with womanly submission, to abandon the battle for married and working-class women's votes: "'I give you my vote," she said softly, "as I give you my love and my life."'[69]

At the time of the suffrage campaign, marriage carried more significance than romantic daydreaming. It was still an economic imperative for many women, seen as an institution increasingly under threat but central to the future of the English race and nation. For a writer to place the cause in opposition to marriage meant playing upon such anxieties, whereas a reconciliation of personal and political commitments was infinitely more reassuring. For women attempting to stress the value of their potential contribution to national life, images of spinsterhood were best avoided. If a novel could combine commitment to the cause and to a man in its heroine, then it would offer a reassuring emotional, political and racial image to the readers. Unsurprisingly, the most virulent anti-militant fiction combines attacks on suffrage with depiction of threats to national as well as family values. In *Delia Blanchflower* even the ancient homes of the English countryside are at risk, both externally and from within, by the 'poison' of suffrage fanaticism. By working within a familiar ideological context, and activating a strong emotional response, the romance plot was useful to both pro- and anti-suffrage writers seeking to persuade the reader of their argument.

Another area of popular fiction that provided a rich resource was the adventure novel. While this genre changed and developed within the period, the empire epic and the action adventure were still widely popular. Militancy in particular, with its emphasis upon deeds not words, allowed writers to create exciting scenarios in which women, too, could achieve the heroism of male adventurers through their wit and courage. Indeed, such actions were often presented as an outlet for a frustration deeply embedded within the Englishwoman's psyche: Gipsie, in *A Fair Suffragette*, longs to follow in the tradition of her father – a British Officer who dared and died: 'I wish I were a man that I could do something as brave and as glorious but I am only a stupid girl, and girls can never do such things.'[70] Isolation from family and friends, created by involvement with the campaign, could also be given popular appeal through the image of the lone hero(ine) battling against the odds for a just cause. Alternatively, the suffrage fighter could be presented in images made popular in both adventure fiction and in school stories: the small figure struggling against a bullying and tyrannical system or the team player who cares little for personal glory but will perform for the greater good. Building upon these motifs, writers could draw upon a frame of reference that gave positive and recognisable meanings to the suffrage fight.

Writers taking an anti-suffrage perspective, however, also found useful material in images of adventures and deeds of empire. In particular they played upon the fear of invasion, of the threat to English values, and the degeneration of the race, found in popular action novels of the time. In *Delia Blanchflower*, the threat is epitomised in plot terms through the dangers of a militant attack on the Elizabethan country home of Sir Wilfred Lang, an opponent of women's rights. Even those sympathetic to the cause see this action as an affront to English culture and history, an act of desecration with no justification but with obvious symbolic import for the future of Britain were women to gain the vote.

Romance and adventure were two areas in which suffrage writers manipulated literary conventions in the attempt to convert their readers, but in looking through the material in this book the reader will find other instances in which established forms are redirected towards political ends. And while the fiction may initially appear unadventurous, it forces us, I think, to reassess what we mean by the politics of literary form when writing is engaging directly and specifically with public debate about existing structures of government.

While novelists struggled to find a convincing voice, the short story offered a form ideally suited to suffrage propaganda, attracting some of the most skilled exponents of women's rights. Many of the short stories by writers such as Evelyn Sharp, Gertrude Colmore, Ada Nield Chew and Rebecca West appeared first in newspapers and magazines, and are often little more than cameo sketches. Nevertheless, they succeed in exploring an issue – usually a specific aspect of the campaign – with immediacy and confidence. Within the shorter form there is less need to resolve a complicated plot: the conclusion may make a simple point through neat denouement or ironic comment. Humour, more evident here than any other form except drama, can be sustained with greater dexterity, emerging in linguistic play and point of view rather than in plot-driven incidents.

Brevity of form may also account for the immediacy and power of some of the stories. Worth singling out in this respect are Gertrude Colmore's ''Ope', a strikingly concentrated tale of transformation, and the more complex story by Evelyn Sharp, 'The Women at the Gate', which offers both a dramatic and theoretical enactment of militancy.[71] Accessible to a range of readers, immediate in its impact, and less demanding of the writer's time, the short story provides some of the liveliest writing in this anthology.

A considerable amount of poetry was also produced during the campaign, much of it highly predictable and of limited literary merit. Some previously published poets were, of course, campaigners – Eva Gore-Booth is a prominent example. Other writers such as Josephine Gonne and Elizabeth Gibson published slim volumes of poetry through private means. The most obvious opportunities for publication, however, were in the suffrage papers. A glance through any edition of *Votes for Women* or *The Common Cause* reveals the kind of poetry that was popular. Much of the material is humorous and satirical, exposing public attitudes and the short-sightedness of opponents. Rousing calls to battle are also frequent, as are eulogies to inspirational females from the past and mystical visions of a woman-centred future. 'Woman', in the abstract, tends to dominate. Like the fiction, this poetry is fairly conventional in structure, imagery, language and substance but also quite clearly and intentionally accessible. Poems foregrounding 'difficulty' in the manner of modernist writing would lack the immediacy necessary for propaganda purposes and might alienate readers. The most 'accessible' writing of this kind, of course, was that used in the protest songs and marches in which military imagery and sturdy rhythms suited communal renditions on large demonstrations. Perhaps the most interesting poetry of all, however, is that which followed the tactics of the campaign itself by making symbolic the everyday experiences of the suffrage fighters. Most notable here is the poetry in *Holloway Jingles* in which images of space and enclosure offer metaphors suited both to the cause and to wider questions of female emancipation. Even the foreword to the collection could be read as a microcosmic example of suffrage discourse, moving from the language of comradeship to that of natural imagery and regeneration, then drawing on images of spiritual fertilisation within the walls, and closing with an evocation to the inspirational effect of suffering.[72]

Autobiographies by women involved in the campaign have less of a specific agenda in converting readers to the cause, as most were written some time after the vote was won. These life-stories nevertheless continue to interpret and debate aspects of the campaign, emphasising the writer's stance on key issues. In the autobiographies written by the leaders of the campaign, there is an almost complete identification with the cause and a strong desire to convince the reader of the validity of their actions. Of more interest in some ways are narratives by women who were less prominent, or who maintained a range of concerns and activities outside suffrage. The autobiographies of Helena Swanwick, Hannah Mitchell and Margaret Haig provide a range of perspectives on suffrage activities and leaders, but also display a broader understanding of their own development into a pro-suffrage position and combine that with a discriminating assessment of its advantages and disadvantages. By placing their suffrage activities within a wider life they allow the reader to identify with their sympathies, yet also reveal much about the minds and situations of women who were brought up in Victorian Britain but helped to change its face in the twentieth century.

In each of the literary genres included in this anthology different strategies of representation and persuasion emerge. In all the material, however, it is the textual choices made by the writers which determine our understanding of the suffrage conflict today. And while the vote may have been won, issues raised by the cause are still alive. In reading through this volume contemporary readers may begin to understand the women involved, and the complexities of identity and identification surrounding their struggle. The excitement and commitment of their voices will also, I hope, alert us to the continuing relevance of their concerns.

Notes

1 'The laugh of the medusa', *Signs* Summer 1976, tr. Keith Cohen and Paula Cohen, reprinted in *New French Feminisms*, ed. E. Marks & I. de Courtivron, Brighton, 1981, pp. 250–1.

2 *The Agate Lamp*, 1912, in *Collected Poems*, London, 1928.

3 *Suffragette Sally*, London, 1911; reprinted as *Suffragettes*, London, 1984, pp. 232–3.

4 'The March of the Women', WSPU, London, 1911.

5 For collections of documentary material see Jane Lewis (ed.), *Before the Vote was Won*, New York & London, 1987, and Jane Marcus (ed.) *Suffrage and the Pankhursts*, London & New York, 1987. Dale Spender and Carole Hayman's collection of plays, *How the Vote was Won*, London, 1985, offers a good introduction to suffrage drama, and Lisa Tickner's book *The Spectacle of Women*, London, 1987, contains a fascinating analysis of suffrage visual imagery. For details of biographies and biographical dictionaries, see Biographical details, pp. 306–19.

6 E. Showalter, *A Literature of their Own*, London, 1977, chapter VIII.

7 W. Mulford, 'Socialist-feminist criticism: a case study, women's suffrage and literature 1906–1914' in P. Widdowson (ed.), *Re-reading English*, London, 1982.

8 S. Gilbert and S. Gubar, *No-Man's Land: the place of the woman writer in the twentieth century*, Vol. 1, *The War of the Words*, New Haven & London, 1988, chapter 2.

9 *The Home-Breakers by a Looker-On*, *The Times Literary Supplement*, 23 October 1913, p. 469.

10 'Mrs Gertrude Baillie-Weaver', *The Times*, 27 November 1926; 'Mrs Israel Zangwill', *The Times*, 8 May 1945.

11 A. Mollwo *A Fair Suffragette*, London, 1909; J. S. Stainton, *The Home-Breakers*, London, 1913.

12 Colmore, *Suffragette Sally*; H. Mitchell, *The Hard Way Up*, London, 1968; 1977.

13 W. Burton Baldry, *From Hampstead to Holloway*, London, 1909; N. A. John (ed.), *Holloway Jingles*, Glasgow, 1912.

14 R. West, *The Judge*, London, 1922; 1980.

15 For further reading see: R. Fulford, *Votes for Women*, London, 1957; L. Garner, *Stepping Stones to Women's Liberty*, London, 1984; L. Leneman, *A Guid Cause*, Aberdeen, 1991; J. Liddington & J. Norris, *One Hand Tied Behind Us*, London, 1978; M. Mackenzie, *Shoulder to Shoulder*, London, 1975; M. Ramelson, *The Petticoat Rebellion*, London 1972; A. Rosen, *Rise Up Women!*, London, 1974; S. K. Kent, *Sex and Suffrage*, Princeton, 1987.

16 See Biographical details, p. 306–19.

17 J. Marcus (ed.), *Suffrage and the Pankhursts*, p. 6.

18 E. Robins, *The Convert*, London, 1907; 1980; *Votes for Women!*, London, 1907.

19 H. G. Wells, *Ann Veronica*, London, 1909; E. Zangwill, *The Call*, London, 1924.

20 Colmore, *Suffragette Sally*; Zangwill, *The Call*.

21 Evelyn Sharp, 'Patrolling the Gutter', *Rebel Women*, London, 1910; 1915.

22 Wells, *Ann Veronica*.

23 B. Sharratt makes this point in *Reading Relations*, London, 1982. C. Bronte's *Villette* (1853) is a striking example of this pattern. Lucy Snowe denies all volition for her bravery in setting out for a new career in Europe, but presents herself as driven by circumstances.

24 Colmore, *Suffragette Sally*.

25 A. Kenney, *Memories of a Militant*, London, 1924.

26 H. Swanwick, *I Have Been Young*, London, 1935; E. Pethick-Lawrence, *My Part in a Changing World*, London, 1938.

27 Zangwill, *The Call*; Mrs H. Ward, *Delia Blanchflower*, London, 1915.

28 T. Billington-Greig, *The Militant Suffrage Movement: emancipation in a hurry*, London, 1911, p. 115.

29 Zangwill, *The Call*.

30 M. C. Rock, *Or in the Grass*, London, 1914.

31 V. Woolf, *A Room of One's Own*, London, 1929; Grafton, 1977, p. 79.

32 E. W. Davison, *Holloway Jingles*; E. Smyth, 'The March of the Women'.

33 Zangwill, *The Call*, p. 164.

34 E. Sharp, 'The Women at the Gate', *Rebel Women*.

35 C. Hamilton, *William – an Englishman*, London, 1919.

36 Stainton, *The Home-Breakers*; Ward, *Delia Blanchflower*.

37 Pethick-Lawrence, *My Part in a Changing World*, p. 278.

38 Swanwick, *I Have Been Young*.

39 Billington-Greig, *The Militant Suffrage Movement*, p. 3.

40 See M. Vicinus, *Independent Women*, London, 1985, chapter 7, 'Male space and women's bodies: the suffragette movement'.

41 See A. Rosen, *Rise Up Women!*

42 See A. Morley with L. Stanley, *The Life and Death of Emily Wilding Davison*, London, 1988.

43 See B. Harrison, 'The act of militancy: violence and the suffragettes, 1904–1914', in *Peaceable Kingdom*, Oxford, 1982, chapter 2.

44 H. Mitchell, *The Hard Way Up*; C. Lytton, *Prisons and Prisoners*, London, 1914.

45 A. N. Chew, 'Mrs Stubbs on Militancy', *The Common Cause*, 20 August 1913.

46 See E. A. Wingrove, 'There's a strange sort of college', in *Holloway Jingles*.

47 M. Sinclair, *The Tree of Heaven*, London, 1917.

48 Vicinus, *Independent Women*, p. 274.

49 Laura Grey, the author of one of the poems in *Holloway Jingles*, is described in one account by M. E. and M. D. Thompson, *They Couldn't Stop Us!*, Ipswich, 1957, as jogging round the prison yard. Other accounts describe amateur theatricals, story-telling sessions and the sharing of food parcels.

50 C. Lytton, *Prisons and Prisoners*.

51 G. Colmore, *The Life of Emily Davison*, reprinted in A. Morley & L. Stanley, *The Life and Death of Emily Wilding Davison*.

52 See Harrison, *Peaceable Kingdom*, Marcus, Introduction to *Suffrage and the Pankhursts*, and Vicinus, *Independent Women*, for conflicting interpretations.

53 E. Pethick-Lawrence, *My Part in a Changing World*, p. 215; M. Haig, *This was My World*, London, 1933.

54 H. Cixous, 'The laugh of the medusa', p. 251.

55 Zangwill, *The Call*, p. 23.

56 E. Sharp, *Unfinished Adventure*, London, 1933.

57 Colmore, ''Ope', *Mr Jones and the Governess*, London, 1913.

58 E. Sharp, *Rebel Women*; E. Pethick-Lawrence, *My Part in a Changing World*.

59 W. Burton Baldry, *From Hampstead to Holloway*.

60 H. Mitchell, *The Hard Way Up*; C. Hamilton, *Life Errant*, London, 1935, p. 75.

61 G. Colmore, 'Pluck', *Mr Jones and the Governess*.

62 M. Haig, *This was My World*, p. vii.

63 R. West, *The Judge*; E. Zangwill, *The Call*.

64 A. Mollwo, *A Fair Suffragette*; G. Colmore, *Suffragette Sally*.

65 C. Despard & M. Collins, *Outlawed*, London, 1908.

66 For further discussion of this see S. Hynes, *The Edwardian Turn of Mind*, Princeton & London, 1968; J. Hunter, *Edwardian Fiction*, Cambridge, Mass., 1982; and P. Keating, *The Haunted Study*, London, 1989.

67 Mulford, 'Socialist-feminist criticism: a case study'.

68 Stainton, *The Home-Breakers*, p. 338.

69 Mollwo, *A Fair Suffragette*, p. 258.

70 *Ibid.*, p. 138.

71 See pp. 259 and 96.

72 Teresa Gough, introduction to *Holloway Jingles*; see p. 172.

2

Conversion

Women were drawn into the suffrage cause for a range of reasons and by many different means. For some, such as Emmeline Pethick-Lawrence and Hannah Mitchell, the movement represented an extension of their previous involvement in politics, while for the Lancashire mill-girl Annie Kenney conversion to the cause and friendship with the Pankhursts offered a whole new way of life. Her enthusiasm was immediate, whereas Constance Lytton, later so prominent in her support, arrived more slowly at commitment.

Whatever the process of conversion, it represented a key development in the individual life. Each of the pieces included in this section offers an interpretation of that transition. Some texts emphasise the intellectual arguments behind conversion, others stress the power of particular role models or the attractions of female friendship. Several accounts are couched in mystical or religious terms. In some narratives, such as *The Convert* and *The Call*, a developing sense of injustices against women also plays an important part. A sudden moment of *éclaircissement* may be found in several texts, but ironic accounts of a subtle change of heart, with the convert almost unaware of the process, are also characteristic. Eva Gore-Booth's short poem 'The Street Orator' shows the public speaker, who is seeking converts, herself undergoing a spiritual transformation.

If all the accounts here depict conversion as a theme, those written during the suffrage campaign itself also had the conversion of the reader on their political agenda. Gertrude Colmore's short story 'Mr Jones and the Governess', Elizabeth Robins's novel *The Convert*, and Kathleen Roberts's semi-fictional account, *Pages from the Diary of a Militant Suffragette*, aim to bring in new supporters and reinforce the commitment of those already involved. Indeed the suffrage campaigners were adept at propaganda, and recognised the role of the arts in this process. Postcards and posters celebrated individual figures amongst the leadership and in song, drama and pageant the campaign was promoted. The existence of The Women's Press, run (until 1912) in close co-operation with the WSPU, and of the Women Writers' Suffrage League, founded in 1908, indicate the importance of literature in the process of recruitment.

M. C. Rock, 'And the words'

Madeleine Caron Rock appears to have been an active suffragette. An 'M. C. R.' was a contributor to *Holloway Jingles* and, in details of her arrest given in *Votes for Women*, she is described as a poet and regular seller of the paper. This short poem, taken from her collection *Or in the Grass*, published in 1914, describes a moment of conversion with passion and excitement.

– And the words, the words she said
Wandered lightly o'er my soul,
But they left a track of flame,
Left the white fire burning there.
So I rose and followed her,
So I set my face for freedom.
O! I dared and I will dare –
I am fearless! who of old
In the flickering of the firelight –
　　Hid my face and was afraid.

E. Zangwill, *The Call*

This pro-suffrage novel, published in 1924, was written by Edith Zangwill, an active suffragette and wife to Israel Zangwill, also a leading figure within the men's campaign for women's suffrage. Daughter of an eminent electrical inventor, Sir William Ayrton and his first wife, Dr M. C. Ayrton a pioneer of women in the medical profession, Edith Zangwill was also step-daughter to Hertha Ayrton, a prominent women scientist and campaigner. The scientific background she chose for this novel was therefore a familiar one. In the novel, Ursula, an aspiring scientist, is initially interested only in her career but limitations imposed upon her as a woman combine with the injustices she sees elsewhere to persuade her into the suffrage cause. As these passages depicting her slow conversion indicate, an important contributing factor is her admiration for the charismatic Mary Blake. Three pieces from the novel are included here. The first shows Ursula's familiar social world disrupted by the presence of the suffragettes, the second depicts her growing but still detached interest, and the final passage paints a vivid picture of her decision to participate in the movement.

A shot was heard; it meant the start of the race. Everyone gazed up the course. After what seemed a long time, but was really a very few minutes, a boat was seen rounding the bend. The cox was not in the Eton blue. But there was the nose of the second boat. It was barely a length behind. Yes, and it seemed to be creeping up. It *was* creeping up. Balestier and Cartwright began to shout – indeed there was a roar of cheering. The two boats were almost level as they passed. 'Well rowed, indeed,' came from all sides. Before the boats disappeared round the bend, Eton was leading.

The finish at this point was almost a foregone conclusion. But by how much would they win? Presently the official tug came along. 'Eton two and three-quarter lengths' – there was a gasp of astonishment. No one had expected more than a length. '*Floreat Etona*,' Cartwright yelled. Both he and Tony Balestier looked as though they had come into a fortune.

Ursula had been caught up in the general enthusiasm, but now she felt a little contemptuous. How absurd it all was! Why did the Englishman take his sport – and nothing else – seriously? She remembered a Russian scientist she had known, who had been invited to some meet. 'What a great organization!' he had said to her afterwards, laughing aloud in his amusement, 'and all for the capture of one so small an animal that my little boy of twelve could readily shoot it!' Ursula had stared for a moment in genuine horror; then she, too, had laughed. 'We call that vulpicide in England,' she explained. 'It is a great deal more reprehensible than killing all your relations!' And now again, she reflected, was not Henley 'so great

an organization' for 'so small' an end? What did it really matter
which of the two boats was a few yards ahead?

Jack Cartwright had meanwhile been untying the painter and
they were again moving. Keeping watch for her mother distracted
Ursula's thoughts, but she saw no sign of her until the appointed
lunch place had been reached. There was the little canoe already
established in the best nook under the overhanging trees. 'Oh, there
you are at last, you naughty people,' Mrs. Hibbert called out gaily.
'I am absolutely starved! Wasn't it too lovely, those darling boys
winning after all? I can't understand anyone not sending their sons
to Eton – the blue is too sweet.'

It was while they were having lunch that a little craft passed
unlike any that they had seen before. It was carrying a large white
notice stretching from bow to stern with purple and green lettering.
The legend was at that time too indented on the public consciousness for it even to be necessary to read it. 'The ubiquitous suffragette,' Mr. Balestier murmured with a slight air of disgust.

'What can be the point of their coming to Henley?' Mrs. Hibbert
observed. '*Boats* for Women?'

'My aunt, that's a thunderingly pretty girl!' The interruption came
from Jack Cartwright, who had parted the overhanging willow
boughs to get a clear view of the suffrage skiff. 'Shouldn't mind
being the bobby who runs her in!'

'Oh, those Pankhurst people are quite clever enough to pick out
a good-looking girl to send here.' Mrs. Hibbert's tone was a shade
acid. She put up her lorgnettes, but as the canoe was on the inner
side of the double sculler, her vision was rather blocked. 'Well, I
can't see your siren very well but she doesn't strike me as so wonderful.'

'Yes, Mother, she really is. She is extraordinarily pretty – look,
that one in the bows.' Ursula, too, had been peering out between the
branches. Her praise, though decided, was surprised. This, as far as
she knew, was her first introduction to the redoutable 'militants.'
She was not quite sure what she had expected them to look like, but
certainly not like this! The 'siren' might be an exception, indeed,
such beauty could not fail to be, but the four other occupants of the
suffrage boat all looked refined and ladylike; indeed, they were quite
indistinguishable from other girls in other boats. Was it possible that
these were the raging viragoes of whom the papers were full?
Besides, the 'siren' was not only lovely; she impressed Ursula as

being the most ethereal-looking creature she had ever seen. Yes, there was something flower-like about the slight figure, the pure, pale face with its tranquil expression – or was saint-like the truer description? A little smile was on the girl's lips as she sat trailing one white hand in the cool, green water. She was evidently quite unconscious of the scrutiny to which she was being subjected.

Ursula Winfield sat back with a jerk. The suffrage boat was moving away and she felt suddenly that she had been rude; she ought not to have stared. Still when people came to Henley in a craft plastered all over with huge notices presumably they expected starers. She realized with surprise that Captain Talbot was enunciating quite a long sentence: 'Biggest crowd I ever was in, by Jove! Even if they'd only come for a rag, they had come, what? Men shovin' and singin' all round the Pankhurst girl's stand. Thought the whole caboodle would be over, but she never turned a hair. Some nerve, what?'

'The whole business is detestable – it degrades women.' Mr. Balestier was speaking. Perhaps he thought that such seriousness verged on bad form, or perhaps he was merely bored with the subject for he abruptly changed the conversation.

The afternoon passed very much as the morning had done. Ursula began to get rather tired of it all. A Henley day was so excessively long, and doing nothing so extremely exhausting. She would not have felt nearly as tired had she been working in her laboratory for the same length of time. They had arranged to leave by a seven o'clock train, but Ursula was not at all sure whether her mother intended to catch it. Mrs. Hibbert had perfected the plausible missing of trains into a fine art, although nothing annoyed her more than other people's inopportune unpunctuality. Mr. Balestier had now taken Captain Talbot's place in the canoe, and Ursula's heart sank as she saw that her mother was evidently appreciating his conversation after her previous escort's heavy, if admiring, silences. The girl found, however, an unexpected ally in Mr. Smee, who was also anxious to get home in good time, and even inquired about the possibility of catching an earlier train. Between them they managed to hustle Mrs. Hibbert on to the platform just as the guard was preparing to blow his whistle.

Ursula sank into her seat rather breathless. It was a good thing that Mr. Smee had hurried on ahead and found places. As it was, he had only been able to secure three, each in a different compartment, but she supposed that the other men of the party had managed to crowd in somewhere. How hot it was in this packed carriage! Apparently her neighbour also felt it so, for she half rose to take off her cloak. Ursula glanced round carelessly. A tri-colour suffragette scarf flared on her vision. Yes, and there was the 'siren' sitting beyond in the corner. What an odd coincidence!

As the journey went on, Ursula could not help overhearing a good deal of the suffragettes' conversation. It was amusing to get a view of Henley from this totally different angle. The races seemed to play an even less important part in their thoughts than in her own – indeed, she began to wonder if they knew that there had been races! They were talking about the owner of one of the houseboats they had boarded. 'She really seemed impressed,' the girl next to Ursula declared triumphantly. 'If only she keeps her promise and comes to Queen's Hall on Monday! She's quite important, you know, and very rich.'

The 'siren' gave a tired sigh – her real name was Mary Blake, Ursula had discovered. 'One is glad to do it, of course, but Henley is horrible. All those staring men!'

'That is because you are so pretty.' The friend's tone was calmly impersonal. 'But it's awfully useful really.' Whether she was referring to Miss Blake's appearance or to the visit to Henley, Ursula could not determine. 'Anyway, it was pleasanter than a raid!'

'I don't know.' Ursula looked up involuntarily at Miss Blake's words. 'At a raid one can just think of the Cause and forget oneself.'

'Well, I can't!' The other suffragette laughed. 'Not when a mounted policeman's horse is prancing on my toe. Why, aren't you black and blue all over after a raid?'

'Oh yes, of course, but I meant –' Miss Blake's voice trailed away. She seemed too tired to explain, too tired to speak at all. She began languidly drawing out her hatpins, and took off her hat, revealing masses of pale golden hair coiled round her head. Presently, as she leant back in her corner, her white eyelids began to droop.

Ursula felt interested; she was also puzzled. So these suffragettes really did not enjoy the publicity they courted; they seemed positively to dislike it. And how unpleasant it must be to find oneself 'black and blue all over!' They genuinely were doing these outrageous things for the sake of 'the Cause,' as they called it. How could anyone feel that a vote was worth it? If it had been a question of sacrificing themselves for some scientific work, for the furtherance of a discovery, then she could have understood it. But if these girls were nice, as they seemed, it made it all the more tragic that they should be thus mistakenly lowering themselves, lowering the whole of womanhood by their antics. Involuntarily Ursula's gaze wandered back to Mary Blake. She appeared to be asleep, and she looked even lovelier than before. The peaceful purity of her clear-cut pale face, the curve of her lips, the long dark lashes curling on her cheek, quite took Ursula's breath away. Once more she sat staring at this girl.

Suddenly Mary Blake's eyes opened. She did not seem to resent the stranger's gaze, perhaps because she was still hardly awake. Her hand wandered to a large, limp whitish canvas bag that lay on her lap. 'Have you seen our last number?' she said, pulling out a copy of the well-known suffrage organ. 'It is the only one I have left.'

Ursula took it reluctantly. She could hardly refuse, but she disliked being even associated with the movement to this extent. 'I never see your paper; I am not a sympathizer,' she said curtly.

Mary Blake smiled. 'Perhaps if you did see it, you would be,' she suggested gently.

'I hardly think so.' Ursula felt irritated by the girl's calm assurance. Perhaps something of the age-long antagonism between science and religion, between fact and faith, was rising in her. 'Still, I will try,' she added with an effort at fairness. The little paper was, perhaps, better written than she had expected but it did not impress her much. Its arrogant tone of confidence was simply exasperating. And the way in which it acclaimed the suffragettes in gaol as heroines and martyrs. It was too ridiculous! Why these women had only to promise to behave themselves for twelve months and they could all walk out. As soon as she decently could, Ursula folded the paper and handed it back with a bold, 'Many thanks.'

'One day' – there was a curious light in Mary Blake's eyes, a rapt note in her voice – 'one day you will come to us.'

. . .

After that Ursula bought the paper regularly. Much of its contents still struck her as high-flown trash, but she also came across some arresting facts. The experiences of one woman in particular were profoundly impressive. For this lady belonged to a famous English family, a family which even Mrs. Hibbert could not look down upon. Indeed, although the lady in question had been extremely gracious on the one occasion that Ursula had met her, the girl had a suspicion that such people looked down upon the Hibberts and all the rest of the former Marlborough House set. And now Ursula read, to her amazement, of this aristocratic, delicate-looking woman taking part in a suffragette row, being arrested, imprisoned, on hunger-strike. After two days she was discharged without being forcibly fed. They could not do it, the prison doctors said; her heart was not sound. A cheap martyrdom, Ursula felt scornfully.

A few weeks later she came across more news. The same lady had again been arrested, but it had been in the guise of a working girl. None of the prison authorities had recognized her. She had again hunger struck. This time she had been forcibly fed. No one had troubled about her heart. The greatest roughness and indignity had been shown her. One day her real identity leaked out. The result was immediate discharge.

It was disconcerting. Clearly her stepfather was wrong. Forcible feeding was not employed to make things easier for the suffragettes. On the contrary it seemed to be used to make things harder. And poverty increased your punishment. If this was the celebrated English justice there might be some grounds for women wanting the vote!

Early in December a suffrage meeting was to be held at the Albert Hall. The huge notice outside had already caught Ursula's eye. Her new indignation decided her to attend. As instructed by her *Votes* she wrote to headquarters for a ticket. She was a little surprised at being required to send half-a-crown, particularly as she had heard that there was to be a collection. Surely this was unusual at political meetings. These suffragettes must be very ardent to be willing to pay for the privilege of paying again.

The evening was fine – did not the militants boast that the weather was always on their side? – and Ursula was glad to walk the short distance to the meeting. But how ridiculous it was, she mused, for these WSPU people to have taken the largest hall in London. Probably it was done for effect; it was impossible that they could fill it. As she got nearer and found herself in a dense hurrying throng, she wondered if the impossible might, after all, be possible. Her seat was reserved, and as it was still fairly early, she halted on the main pavement in front of the hall to watch the incoming crowd. The motor 'buses were stopping just in front of her, each in turn discharging almost its entire freight; while near by a continuous stream of private carriages, cabs, and taxis were turning up towards the chief entrance. Ursula was rather surprised; she had not known that the Cause counted so many of the well-to-do class among its adherents.

More interesting than the vehicles were the actual people all around her. The great majority were naturally women – women of curiously diversified strata. There was a large element in so-called artistic attire, rather untidy, rather attractive – at least Ursula found them so, although she could not help remembering the well-known quip, 'Oh, Liberty, what crimes are committed in thy name.' There was another numerous and distinct contingent, probably ladies from Suburbia, the mammas stout and unintellectual looking, the daughters slight and equally unintellectual looking, but all alike wearing the then fashionable large hat and long coat, the latter usually of a deplorable cut. Under it Ursula divined a fussy white silk blouse, for on the rare occasions when Mrs. Hibbert insisted on her daughter's presence at a theatre party, the girl, looking round at the pit and the upper circle, had seen them filled with women of this type, rows and rows of them. Another distinct class was present with which Ursula was less familiar, poorer women with sensible, worn faces and toil-coarsened hands. She guessed them rightly to be the wives of working men, probably mothers of large families. There were also a sprinkling of working girls, more noisy and even smarter than the young ladies from Suburbia – perhaps hailing from East End factories. But in all these varying kinds of womanhood there was one similarity. As the girl stood there, she could not help noticing a certain enthusiasm, a certain uplift in all the faces around. There must be something in a cause that gave people that expression, she reflected.

Although men were in a minority, a certain number went by, and these Ursula studied with an even greater interest. For they were of a type quite strange to her; more unconventional in appearance than either her mother's friends or her own scientific acquaintances; more interesting – she could not but admit it. But how queer their loose tweed overcoats and soft felt hats looked in town! A small, middle-aged man, who now got out of a 'bus, was, however, irreproachably clad; indeed, Ursula would never have remarked him, with his spectacled, amiable face, but for several eager ladies who immediately rushed up to him. From their excited questioning he was evidently someone of importance in the suffrage world. 'Did he think the Government had really paid Mrs. Pankhurst's fine?' 'What chance was there of turning Winston out?' Queries such as these reached

Ursula's ears from the circling feminine throng. The driver of the halting 'bus was, like Ursula, watching the scene. 'Now then, Solomon, ain't you a-going it?' he suddenly shouted. There was a general laugh in which the victim joined.

Time was now getting on and Ursula thought she had better go in. At the chief entrance the official, an elderly man in semi-evening dress, was opening and shutting the glass door, apparently in a state of frenzied indecision. As Ursula, with some difficulty, struggled up the crowded steps, he suddenly called out that everyone was to go round to the other entrance and definitely shut the door. There were protests, tickets were held up displaying a printed 'main entrance' but in vain. 'I thought the "General" was organizing this meeting,' a surprised voice, near Ursula, observed. 'Oh, that idiot of a man goes with the hall,' another feminine voice replied. 'Yes, he has lost his head badly, poor dear. I must get a message round to the "General."' At this moment a short, stoutish woman in the tricolour sash was seen through the glass talking to the agitated official. Apparently she soothed him, for the door was again opened.

It was the only hitch in the perfect organization. Indeed, but for this, Ursula might not have realized that there was any organization – everything ran with such automatic smoothness. Girlish stewards posted at frequent intervals piloted her through the confusing circles of the hall to her seat. Placed on it was a little donation card with a green pencil suggestively attached.

Ursula looked round curiously. There were more empty gaps than she had expected, for it had been announced that every seat was sold. A woman sitting next to her explained that the empty places belonged to lifeholders. At other political meetings these people were willing to give up their seats – 'but they won't let *us* have them – the brutes!' the woman exploded. However, despite these blanks, the great hall was a wonderful sight with its solid human floor ringed with rising circles of faces. Above were the tiers of bursting boxes and finally the unreal, doll-like band of figures in the top gallery. These had come, Ursula supposed, to see, for they could not possibly hear.

A tremendous roar of applause announced the arrival of the leaders, applause that burst out again and again during the speeches that followed. Frankly, Ursula thought it undeserved. The speeches were good, but not great as she had expected. Then she realized that the fact of being able to move ten thousand people to a frenzy of emotion without supreme oratory was in itself greatness.

But for one item in the programme Ursula could feel nothing but an amused scorn. The Leader – so the announcement ran – was to decorate each hunger-striker with a medal 'For Valour.' The Leader herself in her speech had referred to the women in a way that the girl had felt pitifully theatrical. 'Oh, God of Battles, steel my soldiers' hearts,' she had cried amid a tumult of applause. Nevertheless when the white-robed procession crossed the arena towards the platform, natural human curiosity impelled Ursula to look round. Suddenly she found herself staring, shocked, aghast. She wanted to cry out, and, at the same time, she could not cry out. For this was not theatrical. As at the raid she had come across something that was real, horribly real. It was not so much that the woman looked ill – though they did look ill. Ursula had seen illness before. No, these women with their straight, colourless faces, with their straight, angular figures looked – looked – she did not know how to express it. Then the word came to her, a word that she had always scoffed at the suffragettes for using. But it was the only word. These women looked tortured.

The strange row of white gowns and grey faces was meanwhile moving along towards the platform. As each woman received the trumpery decoration, the chairman announced her name. 'Mary Blake,' Ursula heard suddenly. She stared still harder. Where was Mary Blake? That could not be she, that girl who was getting a medal. Why she was not beautiful. She was almost ugly. Now she was moving away. The new Mary Blake had caught hold of the back of a chair; she was hardly able to walk.

'That's Miss Blake.' It was Ursula's neighbour who was speaking. 'She has been forcibly fed a hundred and forty-two times. Her release was really due last week, but they kept her until this Tuesday to pay her out for hunger-striking. And they knew her mother was dangerously ill. Aren't they beasts?'

Ursula did not reply. She, too, was filled with a sort of rage, but not so much against Mary Blake's gaolers as against Mary Blake. How dared the girl thus have misused herself! How dared she have spoilt her wonderful beauty! It was wicked, criminal! And when her mother was dying – but perhaps she had not known about the mother. Of course it was rather amazing that Mary Blake, that all these women, should be willing to go through such suffering. In a way it was fine, even although it was insane.

To Ursula the rest of the meeting seemed of small importance, but probably most of the audience found in the collection their central moment. Indeed, it could hardly be called a collection – there was no need to collect. Money flowed to the platform, the incoming cheques being thrown so rapidly into the large waste-paper basket that several fluttered to the ground. The amounts themselves were scored up by slipping cardboard figures into a huge frame, such as is seen on a football field; at the end it showed a two with three figures to follow. Ursula had not meant to contribute – she was not sure enough about her attitude – but she found herself scribbling a promise for ten pounds. How could she do less when that band of white-gowned, grey-faced women, who had already given so much, were now giving money as well?

And yet, when she got home, the girl regretted her gift. For although she might admire, she still did not approve. What need was there for these extreme measures, for all this noise and violence? Woman Suffrage would surely come with the gradual emancipation of women. Where was the hurry?

. . .

Ursula's face was white. It grew whiter as the case went on. She sat there frozen and sick with horror. She had known that prostitutes existed. But she had not known that men could live with prostitutes and upon their shameful earnings. The prisoner was such a man. Lily Smith herself had denounced him. 'You had had a quarrel, I suppose?' the magistrate suggested carelessly.

A clerk sitting at the table just below the bench here rose and said in a low tone that the quarrel was connected with the second charge. The magistrate, putting on his pince-nez, turned to his notes. 'Er, yes, I see – criminal assault. Yes. That will do' – this was to Lily Smith – 'I will now take the child's evidence. I suppose she is in Court.'

A little girl of nine or ten was sitting on the front bench not far from Ursula. An usher now approached her and said something that Ursula did not catch. The child burst into tears and clung to the woman beside her. 'Mother, don't let him take me! I don't want to tell them.' The magistrate was again conferring with the clerk. 'All women to leave the Court,' came the peremptory order.

There were two ladies sitting near whose suffrage badges had already attracted Ursula's attention. At this decree they grew excited. 'Monstrous!' one of them shouted. 'It's the men who ought to be turned out, not women!'

The magistrate looked annoyed. 'Silence in the Court,' he said severely.

A burly policeman appeared magically beside each suffragette, and shepherded her, still shrilly objecting, out through the swing doors. Ursula followed them. All feeling had been lost in a state of dazed incomprehension. Why was the little girl crying? What could she have to do with it?

In the outer hall the two indignant ladies were standing, still talking violently. Some remarks reached Ursula as she passed – 'having to give her evidence alone before all those men, poor little thing. It's time we did have the vote!'

Ursula's one idea had been to get out, out into the fresh air, away from all this filth. Probably only a sense of physical numbness had kept her in her seat so long. But now she hesitated. A scientific training is not conducive to leaving problems half-solved. 'Excuse me.' She went up to the irate ladies. 'I do not understand. What is the matter with the little girl?'

The required explanation was given, indeed, given with alacrity. The suffragettes were too accustomed to speaking on these subjects to realize the feelings of the girl who had questioned them. Details were elaborated; one of the ladies knew the child's mother – 'such a nice woman, absolutely heart-broken.'

No, no, it was impossible! Although Ursula stood there silent and motionless, her whole being was crying out in revolt. This was a nightmare, not reality. Such things did not happen, not to-day, in England. They belonged to savage countries, to history books. 'But you can not be certain; children romance,' she stammered at last, white now to the lips.

'Physical facts do not romance.' The suffragette gave a semi-hysterical laugh. 'There is a house near here –' Further searing revelations followed. '"Fallen children," they call them,' she concluded bitterly. 'And then they wonder that we are militants!'

Ursula turned away blindly. She must sit down; she was trembling all over. Why, this was the same bench on which she had sat earlier this morning. Was it only this morning? Then the world had been a clean and pleasant place of healthy men and women. Now it had become rotten, crawling with obscene abomination. These suffragettes talked of the vote – as though the vote could help! If people were so vile and bestial, nothing could help, nothing! It was all horrible. She did not want to live. Science was dead, futile. Everything was tainted – even Tony.

After a while she grew more rational. After all, whatever the suf-fragette ladies might say, it was not certain that the man was guilty – at least, not of that ultimate horror. The case was still *sub judice*. She would wait and hear the verdict. Until then she could keep the last hope.

Presently, as she sat there, she became conscious of a sound, which up till then, she had been too overwrought to notice. Someone, not far off, was weeping. Leaning forward, she saw Lily Smith sitting on the other bench, her face buried in a handkerchief, her body shaken with sobs. Her friend, the bold-looking girl, was patting her shoulder in a not untender attempt to comfort her.

Ursula stared for a moment and then sank back into her corner. Her emotions seemed exhausted. She could only feel numbly that life was beyond her. She recalled the particulars that she had heard in Court. Lily Smith herself had denounced the prisoner. The quarrel had been in connection with the second charge. It flashed through Ursula's mind that a prostitute must then also have a moral code. Lily Smith apparently drew the line at assaulting little girls. But why, if she denounced the man, should she now be crying heart-brokenly? Was it conceivable that she could care for him, for that vile brute who had lived upon her shame? If she did care for him, then was not that just a little redeeming? And he, to have made her care, must surely have some spark that was not utterly evil. Indeed, was 'evil' the right word at all? Ursula wondered suddenly. Such a man seemed too incredibly wicked to be wicked. The thought brought comfort. He was insane.

There was a sudden emergence through the swing doors. The case was over and the men, who in virtue of their robuster sex, had been allowed to stop and listen, came pouring out. They were laughing and talking over the spicy details they had heard. At another time Ursula would have been revolted by their attitude, but now her only thought was of the verdict. She got up and went forward. 'Is he guilty?'

The youth, whom she had accosted, leered unpleasantly. He prob-ably was going to say something familiar, or even indecent. But Ursula's aspect, her set, grey face, seemed to check him. Instead he answered, civilly enough, that the prisoner had been found guilty on both counts – 'three months for each to run consecutive.' Jerking his bowler awkwardly, he passed on.

Ursula remained staring. Even horror was lost in amazement.

This man who assaulted little girls, who lived on a prostitute's earnings, had got three months imprisonment – not even years – months!
After three months he would again be at large. Why, it was not safe
when the man was insane! And if he were not insane, then it was
still less safe. Did they think that three months' imprisonment would
terrify, or reform him into morality? Twenty-three imprisonments
had not reformed that other man even of stealing boots. And the
other man had been given twelve months! The magistrate must be
insane too! They were all mad together!

The two suffrage ladies, who were still lingering in the lobby, now
learnt the verdict. 'Three months – that's all they think a little girl is
worth. I'd like to kill the brute,' one loudly exclaimed. 'We'll expose
it in *Votes*. Let us go round to Clement's Inn at once,' the more composed friend suggested.

How absurd they were! Still, Ursula felt it must be a comfort to
take any active step. If only she could do something. It seemed
impossible to go back and work in her laboratory in this new world
of enlarged maniacs and crazy magistrates. But, after all, was it the
magistrate's fault? He only administered the law. Probably the punishment for such an offence was specified. Certainly it had not been
the magistrate, but the law, that had dragged poor old Mrs. Bennett
to prison. Then it was the law that was insane, or rather the law-
makers. Yes, and Mrs. Bennett's starvation wages had been paid for
Government work. The suffragettes were right. There was some
connection between such things and the Vote.

The policeman in the Strand gave a weary smile at Ursula's
inquiry for Clement's Inn. She was too intent to notice it, too intent
to be surprised at the size of the suffragette headquarters. It was
uncertain whether the Leader could be seen. Would she wait in
there. A door was opened for her.

The room was large with a window at the farther end. The sunshine, streaming through it, fell upon a girl in blue, who knelt, surrounded and half-hidden by a surging mass of open, white
umbrellas. What could she be doing? The girl now rose. It was Mary
Blake, but the hunger-look had been wiped away; she stood there
serenely beautiful. Her hands were filled with short, bright-coloured
strips; doubtless to keep them from falling, she had clasped them to
her breast; the white cloud-shaped umbrellas seemed to billow at
her feet. There was a moment of silence. Then came Mary's gentle
voice. 'Do I know you?' she asked.

Ursula pulled herself together. 'Yes, that time in the train. You lent me *Votes*. You told me that one day I –'

A sudden transfiguring radiance shone in Mary's face. She held out her white hands, showering to the ground their gay, trivial contents. 'And you have come,' she said.

G. Colmore, 'Mr Jones and the Governess'

Typical of the many pro-suffrage short stories written by Gertrude Colmore, an activist, novelist and biographer of Emily Wilding Davison, this tale was first published by the Women's Freedom League. Like all Colmore's work, it is lively, accessible and, characteristically, depicts the reversal of initial impressions.

'Women indeed!', said Mr. Jones. 'I call them hussies.'

The three little girls, who had round, well-fed faces like their father's, looked up; the governess, who was pale and rather small, looked down, and continued to eat her stewed fruit and milk pudding.

'Papa dear,' said Dorothy, 'what is a hussie?'

'A hussie is a – is a – a – a woman who, instead of being womanly, is a forward minx. Am I not correct, Miss Taylor?'

'I cannot be certain that that is Johnson's definition,' answered the governess, 'but I will look it up after lunch.'

'Oh, hang Johnson!' said Mr. Jones. 'Do you agree with me or not?'

'Certainly; I should say that hussie and forward minx are fairly synonymous terms.'

The rubicund face of Mr. Jones took on an expression half irritated, half puzzled; he knew the point on which he wished to have the governess's opinion – possibly the governess knew it too – but he could not succeed in putting his questions so as to draw that opinion forth.

He was not good at putting things. The late Mrs. Jones had responded to what he meant to say rather than to what he said; the governess – confound her! – responded to nothing except inquiries as to the children's progress. He had understood the late Mrs. Jones

– or thought he had; he was hanged if he understood the governess. But he had perseverance, and he tried again.

'To be pestered in the streets by hussies and minxes, some of them mere girls, to buy their outrageous paper – I call it derogatory to womanhood.' He felt that he had come upon an oasis of language in a desert of inexpressible ideas, and repeated the happy phrase. 'Derogatory to womanhood. I feel sure, Miss Taylor, that you don't approve of such conduct.'

Miss Taylor approved of nothing which was derogatory to womanhood; or to manhood either, she added, as she folded her table napkin. She had a decided way of folding her table napkin; it was as though she said: 'Lunch and my conversation with my employer are at an end. My duty now is concerned solely with my employer's children.'

Mr. Jones felt – somehow she made him feel it – that it would not be the thing to detain her further; and as 'the thing' was the practical embodiment of that which, on an anti-Disestablishment platform, he would have described as the God of his fathers, he could not persist in the conversation.

Left alone, doubt rose in his mind; it had risen before, but he had quelled it; he tried to quell it again. It was impossible that Miss Taylor should be a – a –.

When asked by his brother-in-law what the governess was like he had replied that she was not pretty – which, of course, was unnecessary in a governess; but very feminine – which was supremely important. She *was* feminine; he didn't care; he knew a womanly woman when he saw her. It was quite impossible that she was a – a –. He struck a match. His little motherless girls – puff, puff – were quite safe. He had always been a judge of character – puff, puff; he was sure she was not a – a –. And the cigar was a deuced good one.

Mr. Jones was in his study; it was half-past five o'clock. Miss Taylor went at half-past five, after the children's tea; he heard her step now upon the stair; a step that stopped this evening when it reached the study door.

She was standing before him. Thank you, she would rather not sit; she had come to say that she must give up her post.

Why – surely – what fault had she to find?

No fault, but she was quite strong now, and fit to take a hand again.

Mr. Jones begged her pardon; he didn't understand; a hand at what? What had been the matter with her? Tuberculosis flashed into his mind, and he tried to recall the latest scientific pronouncements on it. Did you get it from milk or from other people – or was it rats? He couldn't for the life of him remember. Anyhow, it was very deceptive of Miss Taylor – not at all the thing –

'I was knocked up after prison and the forcible feeding.'

His two questions and all his doubts were answered at one fell swoop. He nearly choked. 'Do you mean to tell me that a – that you – that I – my children in the care of a – a –?'

'You need not be afraid. I have treated them as shamefully as even you could desire; I have left them in complete ignorance of our movement and what it means.'

She was gone. Mr. Jones sat helpless; it was far, far worse than tuberculosis. That would not have been at all the thing; but this – that she was, after all, a – a –. He could not bring himself even now to say the horrid word; she had *seemed* so feminine.

It was some months before he saw her again; there had been no occasion to see her, since, as she had intimated to him, she was not going governessing any more, and was consequently in no need of a reference.

It was in November that he ran across her; in the evening, towards eight o'clock, when right-minded women were safely sheltered in the home; and in the neighbourhood – God bless his soul! – of Piccadilly. He felt bound to stop and tell her that she had no business to be where she was.

On the contrary, the little ex-governess told him, in just the same quiet voice in which she had spoken of Johnson's dictionary, and with just the same modest eyes, on the contrary, she had very important business; not in this particular street, but within a short distance of it.

'Do you not realise,' said Mr. Jones, 'that it is not the – er – the thing for you to be here?'

'The thing that I am here for,' she replied, 'makes my presence imperative.'

'At – a – at this hour – getting on to to –.'

'The hour and the woman are necessary the one to the other,' said Miss Taylor.

'There is but one kind of woman –,' began Mr. Jones.

'Oh, don't be afraid! We Suffragettes are at the other end of the pole. We are out for the salvation of women, not for the vices of men. Good-night, Mr. Jones.'

She had no shame, he told himself. To dare to mention –! And all the time to look and speak so unlike a – a –.

It was a tremendous crash. Mr. Jones, in common with many another, wondered what on earth had happened; in common with many another, rushed towards Piccadilly Circus to find out. He was in time to see his ex-governess led away by two policemen amidst an excited crowd. There were other women, escorted in like manner, but Mr. Jones saw only one.

That one did not see him. Did she see anybody, anything? He wondered. The eyes he had thought modest looked, if they looked at all, at something far away, something – the thought flashed into the mind of Mr. Jones – something beautiful. The thought flashed like lightning in a dark place, and, like lightning, in less than a moment, was gone; it was followed by a thunder of disapproval that roared and rolled all the way home, that rumbled and muttered all the evening through. She had looked modest, she had spoken quietly; and she – she – had attacked – actually attacked – oh, shade of 'the thing'! – *property*.

She got six weeks, with hard labour. Serve her right, said Mr. Jones, and told himself and everybody he came across that she richly deserved it; only in speaking to the many who agreed with him, he put her in the plural and called her 'those women.' Somehow he could not bring himself to single her out for condemnation; grossly as she had deceived him, hussy and minx as she had proved herself to be, he did not speak her separate name either at dinner tables or in smoking-rooms.

He told his brother-in-law that he was ashamed to think he had ever had such a woman in the house; he told himself that prison was the only place for women like her, and that he was jolly glad to think of her being there.

Somehow he thought of her a good deal as being there. In one way it didn't seem altogether suitable, for he would have taken his oath she wasn't strong – But she deserved it; false as well as degraded, as she had shown herself to be, it would do her a thundering lot of good. It was a bore that the thought of her in a cell was apt to come when he was halfway through his cigar; but all the same, to say that prison was rough on refined women – why it was her – their own fault if she – they went there.

He was walking down the Strand, past the place where many months before had occurred the experience that had caused him to break forth at the luncheon table into a diatribe against women paper sellers. There was a woman there now selling papers, a woman young and pretty, a mere girl, and, as Mr. Jones passed her, she asked him, as the other woman had asked him, to take a paper.

On that former day he had pushed the seller and her paper aside; to-day he hesitated, stopped – and took it.

'Thank you. It's only a penny.'

Mr. Jones put his hand into his pocket and brought out, he hardly knew why, a half-sovereign.

'Thank you.' The girl looked down at her hand. 'Oh, thank you! You are a friend, then, of the Cause?'

Mr. Jones did not answer: he hurried on; he was half ashamed of what he had done, half surprised that he had done it. He had acted on an impulse that sprang he knew not whence, been moved by a feeling rooted in he knew not what; and he was hardly aware that he had given his gold penny, neither to the Cause nor to the girl who represented it, but to a pale little governess in prison.

E. Pethick-Lawrence, *My Part in a Changing World*

> Emmeline Pethick-Lawrence's autobiography, published in 1938, describes her upbringing, involvement with her husband in the leadership of the WSPU, and their eventual expulsion from that organisation. Here, in an early section of the work, she traces her initial experiences of the WSPU.

The days when woman's suffrage was a live issue were over before my time began. The story of the betrayal of the suffrage movement by Parliament, and of the death-blow given to it by Gladstone, has been told to weariness. The young do not waste time by sitting upon graves.

I must go back to the days of my youth and make it clear, if I have not already done so, that my early enthusiasms were aroused not by ideas of political democracy but by dreams of economic and social deliverance of the toiling masses of the people. This was true not only of myself but of all those of my own generation with whom I was in association.

I have already alluded to the influence upon us of the-end-of-the-century poets, Whitman, Morris and Carpenter, and of the way in which their idealization of the craftsman and the labourer had redirected our reaction towards the social environment of our time, thus driving a wedge between our idealisms and those of the generation which preceded us. The Churches had been quick to seize upon the new conception of 'Fellowship'. Pamphlets and essays defining new ways of social living were eagerly read by the young. A new biography of St. Francis by Sabatier had been translated into English, and this book had created an emotional excitement in my circle of friends, so that we all began to think and talk about simplicity of life and the sharing of all we possessed. There was something of religious fervour in the way we embraced these ideas. Later on, these somewhat dreamy sentiments took more definite form and shape in the new, Independent Labour Party founded by Keir Hardie, but the franchise question did not occupy our attention. Political interests were subordinate to our fervent desire to bring about an amelioration of the social conditions of the workers. Nothing less than this absorbing interest could have made me indifferent to the question of woman's franchise. I was convinced that all injustice and wrong would come to an end if a system of socialism could supplant the old capitalist regime.

I had yet to be awakened to the fact that a system of socialism, planned by the male half only of humanity, would not touch some of the worst evils that were engendered by a politically and socially suppressed womanhood. Although I had never met the Pankhursts or the Kenneys or any of the other members of the little group in Manchester, I found later that they had passed through the same transition as myself, and had been occupied with the same ideas, which had come to some of them through somewhat different channels, through the *Clarion*, for example, the weekly paper edited by Robert Blatchford, author of *Merrie England*, and through their association with the Independent Labour Party, in which Mrs. Pankhurst had played for some considerable time a prominent part. It was as an outcome of their socialistic fervour and of their concern for the welfare of the working woman in the North that a new demand for women's enfranchisement arose and latent feeling blazed up in the stormy scene of the Free Trade Hall which launched the revival of the old cause under the new cry: Votes for Women! The demand in 1905 was the same as that of 1867, that the word 'man' and 'person' used in the Franchise Acts should include both sexes, so that the vote should be granted to women on the same terms as it was, or would be, granted to men. On this demand every section of the suffrage movement, old or young, was united.

Mrs. Pankhurst called on me in February 1906, because Keir Hardie had told her that in me she would find a practical and useful colleague who could develop in London the new society which she had founded in Manchester – The Women's Social and Political Union. She went back to Sylvia disappointed. 'She will not help,' she said, 'she has so many interests.' Then Annie Kenney was sent to me by Keir Hardie. She burst in upon me one day in her rather breathless way and threw all my barriers down. I might have been a life-long friend by the complete trust in me that she showed and by the conviction that she expressed that the only thing needed to bring the movement to complete and speedy success in London was my co-operation.

There was something about Annie that touched my heart. She was very simple and she seemed to have a whole-hearted faith in the goodness of everybody that she met. She told me her version of what had happened at Sir Edward Grey's meeting in the Free Trade Hall, for it was she, with Christabel Pankhurst, who had made the scene which had shocked and horrified the conventional world. She went on to tell me that because Christabel could do nothing further for the suffrage movement until she had obtained the LL.B. degree, Annie herself felt that she must leave Manchester and come to rouse London, as she herself expressed it. The education authorities of Owen College had threatened to expel Christabel after her prison experience and had finally made it an absolute condition that she should take no further part in political action until after she had completed her period of studentship. So the Pankhursts and a few working women in their little group had amassed the sum of £2 and had given it to Annie for the purpose of her campaign. I was amused at Annie's ignorance of what the task of rousing London would involve, and yet thrilled by her courage. 'How do you want me to help you, Annie?' I asked. 'Mr. Keir Hardie told me to ask you to be our national treasurer,' said Annie, speaking as if by rote. 'Your treasurer'! I exclaimed. 'What funds have you?' 'That is just the trouble,' said Annie, simply. 'I have spent the money already and I have had to go into debt. I do not understand money, it worries me; that is why I have come to you for your help. You need not decide at once,' she went on hastily, no doubt seeing my lack of enthusiasm for the job. 'We have a committee at Park Walk to-morrow, and you will meet Sylvia Pankhurst, the honorary secretary, and the others, and will hear a lot more about it then. You will come, won't you?' I gave my promise because I could not repulse her wistful eagerness.

After she left me I did not feel quite happy about my promise to attend the committee. To tell the truth, I had no fancy to be drawn into a small group of brave and reckless and quite helpless people who were prepared to dash themselves against the oldest tradition of human civilization as well as one of the strongest Governments of modern times. I asked my lifelong friend and colleague, Mary Neal, to go with me, as I wanted to have the reinforcement of her extremely shrewd judgment and common sense.

We went together to Park Walk and found the small house where Sylvia Pankhurst lodged. Gathered round the table were six people; Sylvia Pankhurst, Mrs. Rose, her landlady, Mrs. Clarke, her aunt, Annie Kenney, Miss Fenwick Miller, and Mrs. Martel, an Australian woman.

How it happened, I hardly know, but that evening with Mary Neal and myself, we formed ourselves into a Central London Committee of the Women's Social and Political Union, and I was formally requested to become the honorary treasurer. I consented to accept this office on condition that my old friend, Alfred G. Sayers, a chartered accountant, would accept the position of honorary auditor. He inaugurated the system on which the books were kept, a system which won the tribute of the prosecuting Counsel when all our books, with our banking account, were seized by the Government for the purpose of the Conspiracy Trial in 1912. He was my unfailing good adviser in all the circumstances that attended my office as treasurer.

It was by a very extraordinary sequence of incidents that I, who am not of a revolutionary temperament, was drawn into a revolutionary movement like the Women's Social and Political Union. The first thing that drew me to it was the story of the imprisonment of the two girls who had raised the suffrage issue at the memorable meeting in Manchester. Then I was touched by the appeal of Annie

Kenney and made the promise to go to this pathetic little committee that talked so bravely of their plan to rouse London but seemed
so helpless.

In reply to my question I found that there was no office, no organization, no money – no postage stamps even. The honorary secretary looked over-burdened and distraught, as well she might be, for,
as she has told us in her own story *The Suffragette Movement*, her
financial position just then was desperate. It was not without some
dismay that it was borne in upon me that somebody had to come to
the help of this brave little group, and that the finger of fate pointed
at me.

I found Sylvia Pankhurst, whom I met for the first time at the
inauguration of the Central London Committee, a baffling personality. She was the impersonation of what I had imagined those
young Russian students to be who, in the last decades of the nineteenth century, had given up career and status to go amongst the
masses of the people in order to instruct them, and so to prepare
the ground for the revolution which they believed would some day
take place. There was a certain infantile look about her, because
her face had the roundness and smoothness of a child. In contrast
to her childlike face was the outer hardness of her character, the
hardness of finely tempered steel; she had a strong will, trained to
endure.

This impression of her character was as far as I was able to get at
the first interview. It has taken me more than thirty years of close
association to penetrate to other layers of her complex character. I
know now that under that outer coat of mail there hides the sensitive and tender child that corresponds to her appearance, still youth-
ful in spite of the many tragic experiences that she has gone through.
Quiet and shy in those days, she had surprised her friends by one
brilliant success after another. She did it first when in 1901 she
obtained the Lady Whitworth Scholarship awarded to the best
woman student of the year at the Manchester School of Art,
although she had only put in part-time attendance, devoting half her
day to taking her 'share in the disagreeable work' of the small business run by Mrs. Pankhurst. She did it again in 1912 when she won
the National Silver Medal, the Primrose Medal, and the highest
prize open to students of both sexes at the Manchester School – the
Proctor Travelling Studentship – a vacation scholarship entitling the
holder to study abroad. The expression of Sylvia's real self was to

be found in her creative art and in the depth of her emotional attachment to a very few persons.

I did not meet Christabel until some months after I had been working with Sylvia and Annie. Christabel, in her self-confidence, struck the major note. She was the embodiment of 'Youth knocking at the Door'. She was cut out for public life. Her chosen career, that of Barrister-at-law, had been checked by the refusal of the Benchers at Lincoln's Inn to admit a woman as a student, so that the career of a political pioneer offered to her the finest kind of self-expression. She possessed the gifts necessary to success. Like all the Pankhursts she had great courage. She had a cool, logical mind, and a quick, ready wit. She was young and attractive, graceful on the platform, with a singularly clear and musical voice. She had none of Sylvia's passion of pity – on the contrary, she detested weakness, which was discouraged in her presence.

Although to all the Pankhursts the cause of woman suffrage was a religion that demanded from them everything that they had to give, the approach of each one was different. As to Sylvia, her passion for beauty, great as it was, had to yield in the end to her passion of imaginative pity. She entered into the humiliations and sufferings of the great company of over-worked and poverty-stricken people, especially of overworked mothers. She has never wavered in her loyalty to the victimized and the oppressed in every part of the world. Although, in comparison with many who took the lead in the suffrage movement, she was not considered as conspicuously popular or conspicuously effective, yet she, with her devoted following in the East End, was the first (in 1914) to break Mr. Asquith's resistance and to win from him the admission that the vote must be granted to working women like those she had sent to him as a deputation. (That story belongs to a later chapter.) To her, the Vote meant the amelioration of the lot of the workers.

Christabel was inspired not by pity but by a deep, secret shame – shame that any woman should tamely accept the position accorded to her as something less than an adult human being – a position half way between the child and the citizen. Christabel cared less for the political vote itself than for the dignity of her sex, and she denounced the false dignity earned by submission and extolled the true dignity accorded by revolt. She never made any secret of the fact that to her the means were even more important than the end. Militancy to her meant the putting off of the slave *spirit*.

To Mrs. Pankhurst the appeal was different again. She was, as she instinctively knew, cast for a great rôle. She had a temperament akin to genius. She could have been a queen on the Stage or in the Salon. Circumstances had baulked her in the fulfilment of her destiny. Married as a young girl to an older husband whom she adored, left a widow with a family to educate in straitened circumstances, the fire in her had been damped down. But the smouldering spark leapt into flame when her daughter Christabel initiated militancy. It was fed by a passion for her first-born. Once years later her habitual reserve broke down when, on a future occasion, she and I were walking round the exercise yard in Holloway Prison. She dwelt upon the name of her daughter 'Christabel the Anointed One', the young deliverer who was to emancipate the new generation of women. Mrs Pankhurst was driven on by her 'daemon' to fulfil her destiny and to provide herself, as she said, with a 'niche in history'.

Annie Kenney made the family party four-square. Her strength lay in complete surrender of mind soul and body to a single idea and to the incarnation of that idea in a single person. She was Christabel's devotee in a sense that was mystical; I mean she neither gave nor looked to receive any expression of personal tenderness: her devotion took the form of unquestioning faith and absolute obedience. St. Paul says that the truest freedom is to be the slave of Christ. I understand that to mean that in absolute obedience there is no division of will and therefore no sense of external discipline. Just as no ordinary Christian can find that perfect freedom in complete surrender, so no ordinary individual could have given what Annie gave – the surrender of her whole personality to Christabel. That surrender endowed her with fearlessness and power that was not self limited and was therefore incalculable. She was lit up with a spiritual flame. The visible Annie was rather a moving person, at any rate to me, but it was the invisible Annie that possessed world-moving power; I felt it the first time I met her. I did not understand the secret of it then. It has taken me many years to come to a satisfactory understanding of these four gifted people who influenced my fate.

K. Roberts, *Pages from the Diary of a Militant Suffragette*

Kathleen Roberts (possibly a pseudonym) created two semi-fictional accounts based on her own experience of militancy, both published during the campaign. From this excerpt it would appear that they were primarily directed at impressing the reader with justifications of the cause and thus recruiting members.

February 4th, 1909

While I was out this morning doing some shopping, I met a Suffragette! It is the first time that I have seen one, owing to the fact that I have been living abroad; but, of course, I have read about them in the papers. This one was not one bit like what I should have expected.

Obviously a lady, and most becomingly dressed in a white costume with a green hat, and wearing a large bunch of violets at her waist, she was standing at a corner of the street in the busiest part of the town endeavouring to sell papers to the passer-by.

'She's a Suffragette,' said a small boy beside me, in tones of contemptuous scorn, to a still smaller companion.

There was a slight drizzle of rain, and I noticed that most of the people to whom she offered the paper brushed it angrily on one side and walked on. Being greatly impressed by her cheerful indifference alike to the state of the weather and the attitude of the public, and marvelling much that any woman should have so much moral courage, I paused for a moment to look at her.

Instantly she walked up to me. 'You are wearing our colours,' she said, smiling; 'Are you interested in our Cause?'

I happened to have on a green coat and skirt with a white blouse and a purple motor scarf. 'What are your colours?' I asked.

'White, Purple, and Green. They stand for purity, courage, and faith.'

'I did not know,' I replied; 'and I am not particularly interested in the Cause. However, I am extremely interested in you. I want to know why you are doing this. I would not be in your place for thousands of pounds.'

The Suffragette laughed. 'Will you buy one of our papers?' she suggested. 'When you have read it you will understand why. Later on perhaps you will be doing it yourself.'

'Never,' I replied, 'that I can guarantee; but I will buy a paper.'

On my return home I read it straight through with the greatest interest. It is a weekly paper, called *Votes for Women*, and costs one penny. I have said for years that women ought to be allowed to vote if they want to, just as I think they should do any other thing they like, if they are able to. It is ridiculous to debar a person from any sort of profession or occupation, which she is capable of pursuing, simply because she happens to be a woman, as if that in itself were any disqualification; but what I fail to understand is why they want a vote. Personally I have no desire for one, and cannot see what advantage it would be. However, there must be some reason, so I have decided to investigate the subject without further delay. I see in this paper that there are weekly At Homes here, so I shall certainly go to the next one, and hear for myself their side of the story.

February 6th

I managed to find my way to the Suffragettes' At Home this afternoon, and am extremely glad that I did so. I have never heard such good speeches, or been so much entertained before. It is not my intention to write a dissertation on Woman's Suffrage, but I wish to record in my diary the fact that I have made three discoveries to-day.

(1) That this is not a sex war. The woman who are members of this Union have no desire, I find, to neglect their homes, or to become like men; they are simply fighting against an overwhelming force of prejudice to bring in what to them seems the biggest reform of modern times. Moreover, I am convinced that they will succeed, because they are fighting with the weapons of loyalty, faith, and love for humanity, and the best men in the country are on their side. They realise, as Tennyson has said, that

'Woman's cause is man's; they rise or sink
Together, dwarfed or godlike, bond or free.'

(2) I have discovered why they want the vote. They look upon it merely as a symbol of citizenship – in other words a latchkey, which will open a very big door. It seems a small and insignificant thing – a latchkey – but when one considers that there is no other way of getting into one's house, *i.e.*, of bringing in certain reforms, which,

in their opinion, are of vital importance to women, except through political power, one begins to understand why they go through so much to get it.

My third discovery is that I have been a Militant Suffragette all my life and never realised the fact until just now.

C. Lytton, *Prisons and Prisoners*

A well-known aristocrat and campaigner, Constance Lytton is perhaps best-remembered for disguising herself as a working-class woman, Jane Warton, in order to reveal the treatment meted out to less well-connected campaigners when in prison. This incident is referred to in *The Call* and Lytton is used as the basis for one of Gertrude Colmore's characters in *Suffragette Sally*. A whole chapter of her autobiography, written with extreme difficulty because of the ill-health she experienced subsequent to imprisonment, is devoted to 'My Conversion'. The following pages are only part of that description.

It was in August–September, 1908, at 'The Green Lady Hostel,' Littlehampton, the holiday house of the Esperance Girls' Club, that I met Mrs. Pethick Lawrence and Miss Annie Kenney. I was two or three days in the house with them without discovering that they were Suffragettes or that there was anything unusual about their lives. But I realised at once that I was face to face with women of strong personality, and I felt, though at first vaguely, that they represented something more than themselves, a force greater than their own seemed behind them. Their remarkable individual powers seemed illumined and enhanced by a light that was apart from them as are the colours and patterns of a stained-glass window by the sun shining through it. I had never before come across this kind of spirituality. I have since found it a characteristic of all the leaders in the militant section of the woman's movement, and of many of the rank and file. I was much attracted by Mrs. Lawrence, and became intimate with her at once on the strength of our mutual friendship for Olive Schreiner. We had, besides, many other interests and sympathies in common. The first Sunday that we were together, the girls of the club were asked to come in early that evening, so that Jessie

Kenney, Annie Kenney's sister, who had only recently been released from Holloway, might tell them of her prison experiences. I then realised that I was amongst Suffragettes. I immediately confessed to them that although I shared their wish for the enfranchisement of women, I did not at all sympathise with the measures they adopted for bringing about that reform. I had, however, always been interested in prisons and recognised from the first that, incidentally, the fact of many educated women being sent to gaol for a question of conscience must do a great deal for prison reform, and I was delighted at this opportunity of hearing first-hand something about the inner life of a prison. I listened eagerly and was horrified at some of the facts recorded. Amongst these I remember specially that the tins in which the drinking water stood were cleaned with soap and brick dust and not washed out, the tins being filled only once or at most twice in twenty-four hours; the want of air in the cells; the conduct of prison officials towards the prisoners.

Having betrayed my disapproval of the Suffragette 'tactics,' which seemed to me unjustified, unreasonable, without a sense of political responsibility, and as setting a bad example in connection with a reform movement of such prominence, there was naturally something of coolness and reserve in my further intercourse with Mrs. Pethick Lawrence and the Kenneys. But before their brief stay at the club came to an end, I achieved a talk with each of the leaders.

One evening, after incessant rain, Annie Kenney and I marched arm-in-arm round the garden, under dripping trees. I explained that though I had always been for the extension of the suffrage to women, it did not seem to me a question of prime urgency, that many other matters of social reform seemed more important, and I thought class prejudice and barriers more injurious to national welfare than sex barriers. I was deeply impressed with her reply. She said, in a tone of utmost conviction: 'Well, I can only tell you that I, who am a working-class woman, have never known class distinction and class prejudice stand in the way of my advancement, whereas the sex barrier meets me at every turn.' Of course, she is a woman of great character, courage and ability, which gives her exceptional facilities for overcoming these drawbacks, but her contention that such powers availed her nothing in the face of sex prejudices and disabilities, and the examples she gave me to bear out her argument, began to lift the scales of ignorance from my eyes. She was careful to point out that the members of her own family had been remarkably free from sex prejudice, and her illustrations had no taint of personal resentment. She explained how the lot of women being not understood of men, and they being the only legislators, the woman's part had always got laid on one side, made of less importance, sometimes forgotten altogether. She told how amongst these offices of women was the glorious act of motherhood and the tending of little children. Was there anything in a man's career that could be so honourable as this? Yet how often is the woman who bears humanity neglected at such times, so that life goes from her, or she is given no money to support her child. I felt that through Annie Kenney's whole being throbbed the passion of her soul for other women, to lift from them the heavy burden, to give them life, strength, freedom, joy, and the dignity of human beings, that in all things they might be treated fairly with men. I was struck by her expression and argument, it was straightforward in its simplicity, yet there was inspiration about her. All that she said was obvious, but in it there was a call from far off, something inevitable as the voice of fate. She never sounded a note of sex-antipathy; it was an unalloyed claim for justice and equity of development, for women as for men.

Then Mrs. Pethick Lawrence and I, during a day's motoring expedition, achieved a rare talk out. She met all my arguments, all my prejudices and false deductions with counter-arguments, and above all with facts of which I had till then no conception. I trusted her because of what I had learnt of her personality, her character, mind, wide education and experience, and was to a certain extent at once impressed; still I only half believed many of the things she reported, the real purport of her statements did not yet sink into my soul as they were soon to do, fact upon fact, result upon result, as I found out their truth for myself.

During my stay at Littlehampton I witnessed a scene which produced a great impression upon my conscience. One morning, while wandering through the little town, I came on a crowd. All kinds of people were forming a ring round a sheep which had escaped as it was being taken to the slaughter-house. It looked old and mis-shapen. A vision suddenly rose in my mind of what it should have been on its native mountain-side with all its forces rightly developed, vigorous and independent. There was a hideous contrast between that vision and the thing in the crowd. With growing fear and distress the sheep ran about more clumsily and became a source of amusement to the onlookers, who laughed and jeered at it. At last it was caught by its two gaolers, and as they carried it away one of them, resenting its struggles, gave it a great cuff in the face. At that I felt exasperated. I went up to the men and said, 'Don't you know your own business? You have this creature absolutely in your power. If you were holding it properly it would be still. You are taking it to be killed, you are doing your job badly to hurt and insult it besides.' The men seemed ashamed, they adjusted their hold more efficiently and the crowd slunk away. From my babyhood I have felt a burning indignation against unkindness to animals, and in their defence I have sometimes acted with a courage not natural to me. But on seeing this sheep it seemed to reveal to me for the first time the position of women throughout the world. I realised how often women are held in contempt as beings outside the pale of human dignity, excluded or confined, laughed at and insulted because of conditions in themselves for which they are not responsible, but which are due to fundamental injustices with regard to them, and to the mistakes of a civilisation in the shaping of which they have had no free share. I was ashamed to remember that although my sympathy had been spontaneous with regard to the wrongs of animals, of children, of men and women who belonged to down-trodden races or classes of society, yet that hitherto I had been blind to the sufferings peculiar to women as such, which are endured by women of every class, every race, every nationality, and that although nearly all the great thinkers and teachers of humanity have preached sex-equality, women have no champions among the various accepted political or moral laws which serve to mould public opinion of the present day.

Nothing could have exceeded the patience, the considerate sympathy even, with which both Annie Kenney and Mrs. Lawrence endured my arguments, arguments, as I now realise them to have been, without any genuine element, stereotyped and shallow. Before we parted, Mrs. Lawrence said to me, and it was the only one of her remarks which savoured in the least of the contempt which my attitude at that time so richly deserved, 'You are sufficiently interested in our policy to criticise it, will you be sufficiently interested to study its cause and read up our case?'

For two months I 'read up' the subject as I had never read in my life before; I took in the weekly paper *Votes for Women*, the only publication which gave events as they happened, not as they were supposed to happen. I attended as many meetings as I could, and the breakfasts of released suffrage prisoners, whereat the spirit behind this movement, its driving force, seemed best exemplified. Above all, I watched current politics from a different point of view. I still held back from being converted, I criticised and argued at every turn, over every fresh demonstration of the WSPU, but I began to realise of what stuff the workers in the movement were made; what price they paid for their services so gladly given; how far removed they were from any taint of self-glorification, and how amazingly they played the game of incessantly advertising the Cause without ever developing the curse of self-advertisement. I have never been amongst people of any sort who were so entirely free from self-consciousness, self-seeking and self-vaunting.

G. Colmore, *Suffragette Sally*

Gertrude Colmore's novel, written during the heat of the campaign, compares the suffrage experience of three women from very different backgrounds: the maid, Sally, whose conversion opens the novel; the inspirational and aristocratic Lady Geraldine Hill; and middle-class Edith, of suffragist and liberal sympathies but initially opposed to militancy. Readers in 1911 would, no doubt, have recognised prominent campaigners in the fictional characters, but the three women also typify the range of support for the cause. In the two short chapters here both Sally and Edith are drawn into the movement.

Chapter II: A song of freedom

'It takes a soul
To move a body.'

E. B. Browning

Sally did not go to bed. She put out the candle, for Mrs. Bilkes had a way of coming to see if any light crept out from under her door; then she sat on the edge of her bed and looked out through the square of window in the sloping roof, out into the darkness. Darkness was the next best thing to a fire; it shut out immediate surroundings.

Sally's window looked on to a space of roofs, grey, smoke-begrimed, and dreary in their sameness, and beyond the roofs could be seen, when it was light enough to see anything, the upper windows of a large, dark-walled building, Holloway prison. It was not a cheerful view; the darkness was better.

It was cold in Sally's room, and Sally's body grew chilled while she left it sitting on the bed, and went away into the new country which had opened out before her that afternoon.

A large hall in the West End of London, and people streaming into it, people of all kinds and classes; ladies, regular swells, richly dressed; 'toffs' in overcoats and tall silk hats; girls who might have come, as Sally had come, to this part of London, just to have a look at the splendid fashionable shops. It was not dark any more, but daylight, the lifeless daylight of a London winter's day.

''Ave yer got to pay?'

'Pay? Lor' no. Ain't yer never 'eerd 'er? Come along in along of me.'

No more dull daylight, but the radiance of electric lamps; crowded benches; a platform with fine ladies and gentlemen upon it. One of them was speaking, one of the gentlemen; he was going to say but a few words, he said, but to Sally it seemed that he said a great many. She could not follow him; it was like preaching, only that there was no mention of God or heaven or hell; she began to fidget and to wish she had stuck to the shops. And then – Then came the beautiful lady – whom the gentleman called upon. 'I will now call,' he had said, 'on Lady 'Ennery 'Ill' – or, that, a least, is what to Sally's ears he had seemed to say.

She heard him say it again, as she stood, far away from that shivering body of hers on the bed, stood in the lighted hall. She had stood most of the time that the lady spoke, for she had been in the last row of all, close up against the wall, so that it had been possible to stand, and all the hats and heads between her and the platform had been more than her interest and her patience could bear. She could listen better when she could see uninterruptedly, and once the tall lady with the brown hair and the clear voice had begun to speak, Sally wanted to listen.

She forgot the shops and forgot the time; she only wanted to hear; to hear, and – how she wanted to ask questions, to understand! To understand it all, just because she understood a part; because the wonder of it and the strangeness of it were not completely strange, entirely unknown; because, in some queer way, some unknown thing in herself seemed to have a dim knowledge of the things the lady said. It seemed to Sally as if there were some bird within her, fluttering, moving its wings, longing to fly towards the platform and join in the song that Lady 'Ennery 'Ill was singing. It was not a song of course, but a speech; she was only speaking; and yet, in some odd way, it seemed to Sally that there was a sort of song in what she said. A song of freedom it was, a song which told that women, however poor, however put upon, had a right to have a say in the things which mattered most to them; that it was unjust that a human being, whether rich or poor, married or not married, should go without the rights that were given to human beings, just because she was a woman; that justice was stronger than any other force, and that justice was bound, in the end, to be given to all. Sally could not remember the leaping sentences, could not recall the words, the meaning of many of which was naught to her. But the general meaning of Lady Henry's speech had, at the time at least, reached her understanding. As she said to herself, 'She put it so plain.'

The plainness seemed to go out of it when Sally had left the hall, and to give place to a confusion of swarming ideas which were yet stimulating in their force and novelty. And through them all went the song; yes, and the battle-cry. For there had been a call to arms – was it only in the voice, or in the words too, of the speaker? – a call to all women; to stand together; to be full of courage; to fight for themselves and for each other; most ardently for the poorest, the most oppressed of all. To stand together; she and Lady 'Ennery 'Ill! To stand up for all the women that were put upon! She hardly knew for what she was to fight; what was the liberty, what the rights, of which the speaker spoke. But the bird in her breast knew.

The wings of that bird fluttered all the way from Regent Street to Holloway. She had bound them fast for a while, with steak and onions and cheese; but now they were free again, and wafted her far away from Brunton Street, through dim regions which opened out from that large lighted hall far away to the south-west of her window. Then, at last, the wings quivered and drooped, and Sally was back on her bedside, staring out into the darkness, chilled and tired and hungry, for in her absorption she had found no time for her usual evening meal.

She crept into bed quickly, quietly; her limbs were cold, her head ached, but her heart was aglow.

Chapter VIII: Red in the mist

'Far and near
The grey mist floated, like a shadow-mere,
Beyond hope's bounds; and in the lapsing ways,
Pale phantoms flitted, seeming to my gaze
The portents of the coming hope and fear.'

John Payne

The next morning was overcast; a sea mist hid the sun and damped the atmosphere. Would Lady Henry Hill keep the tryst, or did she perhaps only care to walk when the weather was clear and bright?

'It's next door to raining, child. You're surely not going out in such an atmosphere.'

'Why yes, Aunt Elinor, it's just the day one wants exercise, and you know I go out in all weathers at home.'

'Which is one of the things I should not allow if *I* were your mother.'

'I daresay it will clear. In any case I shall be back in plenty of time to go out with Uncle Beauchamp.'

'I doubt whether your uncle will go out on such a day. I shall be very vexed if you catch cold and have to be nursed.'

'I never catch cold, at least it's the rarest of rare things, and I promise you I won't to-day. Good-bye, Aunt Elinor.'

'Humph!' said Aunt Elinor.

'Would she be there?' Edith hastened, searching amongst figures in the foreground for a little bit of blue.

She was there, beyond where the visitors congregated, standing by the breakwater where yesterday Edith had left her. But there was no blue scarf to-day. She was all in brown, with a close-fitting cap that made the brown of her hair look golden.

'It's too damp to sit,' she said, 'and chilly. Besides, I always walk to begin with, and should miss the exercise. You like walking, don't you?'

'Yes, I walk a good deal.'

They moved on; the mist was like a screen about them, shutting them into a space of wet brown sand, with grey intangible walls that shifted as they advanced. Always afterwards, when Edith thought of the militant movement, she saw it take its rise with just such a mist about it, and heard faintly, beyond the voice beside her, beyond the many voices, the plash of tiny waves. Many voices; for

Geraldine Hill had the gift, in narration, of calling up the scenes of which she spoke; and Edith Carstairs had the faculty which can see intangible forms, and hear speech independently of actual utterance: and so it came to pass that on the solitary sands that day, where, as it seemed, only two women walked, there was enacted a drama which had been played for the first time nearly three years before; had been cut on the heart of history; and in history's repertoire must ever find a place while the world remains the stage of human action.

The 13th of October, 1905, and the Free Trade Hall at Manchester filled to overflowing.

All through the country there had been a stir; a thrill of unrest and expectation: the power of one party was on the ebb; change and a new order showed, full of hope to some, and to others darkly, on the verge of the political horizon. The Liberals were marshalling their forces, rousing their followers, and in the great Hall of Manchester, one of the Liberal leaders told in glowing words what his party was prepared to do if the people would put it into power. Fine prospects and great promises, splendid reforms; the speaker spoke magnificently of the improved conditions, the fuller liberty to come; and, as he ended, applause broke out; cheers, and the clapping of a multitude of hands.

Far away from that Hall and from that hour, Edith yet heard the applause ring out, and through and beyond it, the plash of tiny waves.

Then, in the body of the Hall – or out of the mist, was it, in the way that those phantom friends of hers came to her in the lane? – a form arose, slight and small enough almost to be that of a child, but a woman's nevertheless; the form of Annie Carnie, the mill hand, who had worked since she was ten years old, had come to the meeting to ask what the Liberal Government would do for working women, and who stood now, holding up a little white cotton banner with black letters on it, spelling 'Votes for Women.' Standing there, but little taller on her feet than the seated figures around her, she put her question, and hardly was it out of her mouth when around her there were other questions; questions from men; questions to which were given immediate replies. But the woman's question remained unanswered.

Again she rose, but there were men beside her; Edith was no more conscious of the sands or of the sea, as she saw them pull the woman down and force her into her seat, while one of them, a steward, pressed his hat over her face.

'Sit down!'

'What's the matter?'

'Let the lady speak!'

Cries and counter-cries.

Geraldine paused, and two women stood on a still morning, far away from crowds and the cries of crowds. For a minute they walked on, side by side in that grey silence: the cheeks of the one were flushed; the other had grown paler.

'And then – did they answer her?'

'Then Christina got up and asked the question that Annie Carnie had asked; and the men shouted as before, some in favour of giving her a hearing, some trying to shout her down. The Chief Constable of Manchester came down from the platform and made his way to her and promised that if the question was written down, he would see that it was answered.'

'That was fair.'

'Oh, quite fair. Well, it was written down, and Annie Carnie wrote in addition, that she was one of ninety-six thousand organised women cotton workers, and for their sakes earnestly begged for an answer.

'The Chief Constable took it back with him to the platform and gave it to the principal speaker – the one who had spoken so splendidly of liberty and the relief of the oppressed. He took the paper, read it, and smiled; then passed it on; and it went from hand to hand till it had gone the round of the platform.'

'And then –'

'Then?' Lady Henry shrugged her shoulders. 'Oh, then it was laid on the table and no more notice was taken of it.'

'But that wasn't the end?' said Edith, after a moment's waiting.

'No, it was the beginning – of the militant movement.'

The mist had lifted a little; Edith could see now the tiny advancing waves, and dimly, the smooth bosom of the sea.

'There were votes of thanks, of course, praise of the speaker, and applause, and his reply. The meeting was pretty well over, the chairman thanking for his vote of thanks, and people beginning to go. . . .'

Through the voice beside her, Edith heard again the mill hand's voice, the woman who had worked since she was ten years old and who wanted an answer to take back to the ninety-six thousand other women who were waiting for what she had to tell them. A small woman not easily to be seen in the crowd; but she can stand upon a chair.

'Will the Liberal Government give working women the vote?'

She was the first wave of the in-coming tide, the first to break, and to be broken, on the rocks.

At once and all around her the men who had cheered in praise of liberty and progress were shouting, gesticulating, crying out upon the woman who had dared to speak. The girl beside her – the girl whom Lady Henry had called Christina – put her arm round the little woman's waist, her one arm round her waist to strengthen and support her as she stood; with the other arm, she parried, or tried to parry, the blows that the men were striking; striking at them both.

There is red now in the mist; no, not in the mist, but in the great historic Hall which stands on the site where Peterloo was won. Blood was there on that day, and blood is there again; blood that runs down from Christina's torn hands on to the hat that Annie Carnie had taken off and laid on the chair by her side.

But the girl's voice is calling still: 'The question, the question. Answer the question!'

Six men to seize and drag out one girl. But there are so many men! No need to stint in numbers, either with one woman or the other. Christina goes first, and then the mill hand, the spokeswoman of thousands of working women like herself.

The people at the back of the Hall cry 'Shame!' but the ticket-holders are shouting 'Throw them out!' and on the platform the future ministers look on and say nothing.

Silence. In the Hall? No, the Hall has gone; with the cessation of Geraldine's voice. Silence of the sea and sand, broken only by the in-coming waves.

'Shall we turn?' Geraldine asked.

'I – didn't know.'

'No; most people don't. The Press boycotts us, or puts in garbled versions of our doings, versions which we are given no opportunity to contradict.'

'There *was* a report. I remember reading – But they were arrested, I thought?'

'Yes, outside, because they tried to hold a meeting in the street, where there was a crowd ready to listen to them; arrested for obstruction, and Christina was charged further with assaulting the police. From the report that *I* read, you would have thought they had behaved like wild beasts. Yet, if one of the men who asked a question that night had been set on and mauled by the others, it is the attackers and the maulers who would have been called wild beasts. But still the tide comes in. And the calling of names won't stop it. In fact' – Lady Henry's tone changed, and she smiled – 'vile names are the concomitants of all causes, and the finer the cause, the viler the names.'

The mist was lifting more and more; the sea carried silver gleams and the sun showed red.

'I believe it's going to be a lovely day after all,' said Lady Henry. 'We ought to have left our walk till later.'

Walk! And Uncle Beauchamp? He had completely evaporated from Edith's consciousness: he loomed large in it now as she realised that it was already past the hour at which she had promised to return.

A. Kenney, *Memories of a Militant*

> The passage from Annie Kenney's autobiography reveals the impact Christabel Pankhurst had upon this working-class girl, which was to make her that leader's faithful lieutenant throughout the campaign. Kenney's continuing commitment to the cause are revealed by the purple, green and white covers of the first edition in 1924.

Christmas, 1904, and the beginning of the New Year, 1905, were weeks of sadness and grave anxiety on account of my mother's health. She was too ill for Christmas festivities, and the New Year had scarcely dawned when she died.

My mother's faith was more the faith of a child. The only thing she desired was a heaven where she could be at peace; release from a world full of struggle to make both ends meet, a world full of anxiety and hard labour.

To my mother I owe all that I have ever been, or ever done that has called upon courage or loyalty for its support.

It was in the same year that I met Miss Christabel Pankhurst.

With my mother's death the cement of love that kept the home life together disappeared. We felt more like individuals in a big world than a family group, and each planned his life according to his or her ideals.

How little I realized the far-reaching effect that such an apparently simple action as joining a choir would have on my life! My object in joining the Oldham Clarion Vocal Union was a desire for companionship among people whose ideas were in harmony with my own. I made good friends with another member of the choir, Miss Jane Ogden, who was also a member of the Oldham Trades Council. The Council had invited Miss Christabel Pankhurst and Miss Theresa Billington to speak on Woman Suffrage, and Miss Ogden asked me to attend the meeting as her guest.

I had never heard about Votes for Women. Politics did not interest me in the least. I had never read any newspaper but the *Clarion*. I went to the meeting spontaneously, as I have done with most things in my life. I was not particularly excited, the name Pankhurst conveyed nothing to me.

I heard Miss Pankhurst and Miss Billington (now Mrs. Billington Greig) speak. Miss Pankhurst was more hesitating, more nervous than Miss Billington. She impressed me, though. She was most impersonal and full of zeal. Miss Billington used a sledge-hammer of logic and cold reason – she gave me the impression that she was a good debater. I liked Christabel Pankhurst: I was afraid of Theresa Billington.

The questions and the answers on 'Limited Suffrage' were Greek to me. I did not know to what they were referring.

When the meeting was over, those in the audience whose minds responded more to cold logic, drifted towards Theresa Billington; those who responded to the human side, drifted towards Miss Pankhurst. It was amusing. It was like a table where two courses were being served, one hot, the other cold. I found myself, plate in hand, where the hot course was being served. Before I knew what I had done I had promised to work up a meeting for Miss Pankhurst among the factory-women of Oldham and Lees. I walked to the station with her, and before we separated she had asked me to spend the following Saturday afternoon with them at their home in Nelson Street, Manchester.

The following week I lived on air; I simply could not eat; I wanted to be quiet and alone. I did not feel elated or excited. A sense of deep stillness took possession of me. It was as though half of me was present; where the other half was I never asked. For the first time in my life I experienced real loneliness. I instinctively felt that a great change had come. I was losing my old girl-friends of the factory.

E. Robins, *The Convert*

Elizabeth Robins was a prominent actress, playwright, journalist, WSPU activist and member of the Women Writers' Suffrage League. Her novel, which explores the growing feminist consciousness of its heroine Vida Levering, was based upon her highly successful play *Votes for Women!* and retains much of its dramatic qualities. Initially unsympathetic to the cause, Vida's own experiences of sexual injustice and the irritating triviality of her social circle make her increasingly interested, and she summons a working-class campaigner to tell her about the movement.

A few moments after, she was again established in her sofa corner, and the door of her sitting-room opened. 'The lady, miss.' Into the wide, harmonious space was ushered a hot and harassed-looking woman, in a lank alpaca gown and a tam-o'-shanter. Miss Claxton's clothes, like herself, had borne the heat and burden of the day. She frowned as she gave her hand.

'I am late, but it was very difficult to get away at all.'

Miss Levering pushed towards her one of the welcoming great easy-chairs that stood holding out cool arms and a lap of roses. The tired visitor, with her dusty clothes and brusque manner, sat down without relaxing to the luxurious invitation. Her stiffly maintained attitude and direct look said as plain as print, Now what excuse have you to offer for asking me to come here? It may have been recollection of Mrs. Fox-Moore's fear of 'the thin end of the wedge' that made Miss Levering smile as she said –

'Yes, I've been expecting you for the last half hour, but it's very good of you to come at all.'

Miss Claxton looked as if she quite agreed.

'You'll have some tea?' Miss Levering was moving towards the bell.

'No, I've had my tea.'

The queer sound of 'my' tea connoting so much else! The hostess subsided on to the sofa.

'I heard you speak the other day as I told you in my note. But all the same I came away with several unanswered questions – questions that I wanted to put to you quietly. As I wrote you, I am not what *you* would call a convert. I've only got as far as the inquiry stage.'

Miss Claxton waited.

'Still, if I take up your time, I ought not to let you be out of pocket by it.'

The hostess glanced towards the little spindle-legged writing-table, where, on top of a heap of notes, lay the blue oblong of a cheque-book.

'We consider it part of every day's business to answer questions,' said Miss Claxton.

'I suppose I can make some little contribution without – without its committing me to anything?'

'Committing you –'

'Yes; it wouldn't get into the papers,' she said, a little shamefaced, 'or – or anything like that.'

'It wouldn't get into the papers unless you put it in.'

The lady blinked. There was a little pause. She was not easy to talk to – this young woman. Nor was she the ideal collector of contributions.

'That was a remarkable meeting you had in Hyde Park last Sunday.'

'Remarkable? Oh, no, they're all pretty much alike.'

'Do they all end like that?'

'Oh, yes; people come to scoff, and by degrees we get hold of them – even the Hyde Park loafers.'

'I mean, do they often crowd up and try to hustle the speakers?'

'Oh, they are usually quite good-natured.'

'You handled them wonderfully.'

'We're used to dealing with crowds.'

Her look went round the room, as if to say, 'It's this kind of thing I'm not used to, and I don't take to it over-kindly.'

'In the crush at the end,' said Miss Levering, 'I overheard a scrap of conversation between two men. They were talking about you. "Very good for a woman," one said.'

Miss Claxton smiled a scornful little smile.

'And the other one said, "It would have been very good for a man. And personally," he said, "I don't know many men who could have kept that crowd in hand for two hours." That's what two men thought of it.'

She made no answer.

'It doesn't seem to me possible that your speakers average as good as those I heard on Sunday.'

'We have a good many who speak well, but we look upon Ernestine Blunt as our genius.'

'Yes, she seems rather a wonderful little person, but I wrote to you because – partly because you are older. And you give me the impression of being extremely level-headed.'

'Ernestine Blunt is level-headed too,' said Miss Claxton, warily.

She was looking into the lady's face, frowning a little in that way of hers, intent, even somewhat suspicious.

'Oh, I dare say, but she's such a child!'

'We sometimes think Ernestine Blunt has the oldest head among us.'

'Really,' said Miss Levering. 'When a person is as young as that, you don't know how much is her own and how much borrowed.'

'She doesn't need to borrow.'

'But *you*. I said to myself, "That woman, who makes other things so clear, she can clear up one or two things for me."'

'Well, I don't know.' More wary than ever, she suspended judgment.

'I noticed none of you paid any attention when the crowd called out – things about –'

Miss Claxton's frown deepened. It was plain she heard the echo of that insistent, never-answered query of the crowd, 'Got your dog-whip, miss?' She waited.

It looked as though Miss Levering lacked courage to repeat it in all its violent bareness.

'– when they called out things – about the encounters with the police. It's those stories, as I suppose you know, that have set so many against the movement.'

No word out of Miss Claxton. She sat there, not leaning back, nor any longer stiffly upright, but hunched together like a creature ready to spring.

'I believed those stories too; but when I had watched you, and lis-

tened to you on Sunday,' Miss Levering hastened to add, a little
shamefaced at the necessity, 'I said to myself, not' (suddenly she
stopped and smiled with disarming frankness) – 'I didn't say, "That
woman's too well-behaved, or too amiable;" I said, "She's too intelligent. That woman never spat at a policeman."'

'Spit? No,' she said grimly.

'"Nor bit, nor scratched, nor any of those things. And since the
papers have lied about that," I said to myself, "I'll got to headquarters for information."'

'What papers do you read?'

'Oh, practically all. This house is like a club for papers and magazines. My brother-in-law has everything.'

'The *Clarion*?'

'No, I never saw the *Clarion*.'

'The *Labour Leader*?'

'No.'

'The *Labour Record*?'

'No.'

'It is the organ of our party.'

'I – I'm afraid I never heard of any of them.'

Miss Claxton smiled.

'I'll take them in myself in future,' said the lady on the sofa. 'Was
it reading those papers that set you to thinking?'

'Reading papers? Oh, no. It was –' She hesitated, and puckered
up her brows again as she stared round the room.

'Yes, go on. That's one of the things I wanted to know, if you don't
mind – how you came to be identified with the movement.'

A little wearily, without the smallest spark of enthusiasm at the
prospect of imparting her biography, Miss Claxton told slowly, even
dully, and wholly without passion, the story of a hard life met single-
handed from even the tender childhood days – one of those recitals
that change the relation between the one who tells and the one who
listens – makes the last a sharer in the life to the extent that the two
can never be strangers any more. Though they may not meet, nor
write, nor have any tangible communication, there is understanding
between them.

At the close Miss Levering stood up and gave the other her hand.
Neither said anything. They looked at each other.

After the lady had resumed her seat, Miss Claxton, as under some
compulsion born of the other's act of sympathy, went on –

'It is a newspaper lie – as you haven't needed to be told – about the spitting and scratching and biting – but the day I was arrested, the day of the deputation to Effingham, I saw a policeman knocking some of our poorer women about very roughly' (it had its significance, the tone in which she said 'our poorer women'). 'I called out that he was not to do that again. He had one of our women like this, and he was banging her against the railings. I called out if he didn't stop I would make him. He kept on' – a cold glitter came into the eyes – 'and I struck him. I struck the coward in the face.'

The air of the mild luxurious room grew hot and quivered. The lady on the sofa lowered her eyes.

'They must be taught,' the other said sternly, 'the police must be taught, they are not to treat our women like that. On the whole the police behave well. But their power is immense and almost entirely unchecked. It's a marvel they are as decent as they are. How should *they* be expected to know how to treat women? What example do they have? Don't they hear constantly in the courts how little it costs a man to be convicted of beating his own wife?' She fired the questions at the innocent person on the sofa, as if she held her directly responsible for the need to ask them. 'Stealing is far more dangerous; yes, even if a man's starving. That's because bread is often dear and women are always cheap.'

She waited a moment, waited for the other to contradict or at least resent the dictum. The motionless figure among the sofa cushions, whose very look and air seemed to proclaim 'some of us are expensive enough,' hardly opened her lips to say, as if to herself –

'Yes, women are cheap.'

Perhaps Miss Claxton thought the agreement lacked conviction, for she went on with a harsh hostility that seemed almost personal –

'We'd rather any day be handled by the police than by the self-constituted stewards of political meetings.'

Partly the words, even more the look in the darkening face, made Miss Levering say –

'That brings me to something else I wanted to be enlightened about. One reason I wrote to ask for a little talk with *you* specially, was because I couldn't imagine your doing anything so futile as to pit your physical strength – considerable as it may be – but to put your muscle against men's is merely absurd. And I, when I saw how intelligent you were, I saw that you know all that quite as well as I. Why, then, carry a whip?'

The lowered eyelids of the face opposite quivered faintly.

'You couldn't think it would save you from arrest.'

'No, not from arrest.' The woman's mouth hardened.

'I know' – Miss Levering bridged the embarrassment of the pause – 'I know there must be some rational explanation.'

But if there were it was not forthcoming.

'So you see your most indefensible and even futile-appearing action gave the cue for my greatest interest,' said Vida, with a mixture of anxiety and bluntness. 'For just the woman you were, to do so brainless a thing – what was behind? That was what I kept asking myself.'

'It – isn't – only – *rough* treatment one or two of us have met' – she pulled out the words slowly – 'it's sometimes worse.' They both waited in a curious chill embarrassment. 'Not the police, but the stewards at political meetings, and the men who volunteer to "keep the women in order," they' – she raised her fierce eyes and the colour rose in her cheeks – 'as they're turning us out they punish us in ways the public don't know.' She saw the shrinking wonder in the woman opposite, and she did not spare her. 'They punish us by underhand maltreatment – of the kind most intolerable to a decent women.'

'Oh, no, no!' The other face was a flame to match.

'Yes!' She flung it out like a poisoned arrow.

'How *dare* they!' said Vida in a whisper.

'They know we dare not complain.'

'Why not?'

A duller red overspread the face as the woman muttered, 'Nobody, no woman, wants to talk about it. And if we did they'd only say, "See! you're killing chivalry." *Chivalry!*' She laughed. It was not good to hear a laugh like that.

The figure on the sofa winced. 'I assure you people don't know,' said Vida.

'It's known well enough to those who've had to suffer it, and it's known to the brutes of men who –'

'Ah, but you *must* realize' – Miss Levering jumped to her feet – 'you must admit that the great mass of men would be indignant if they knew.'

'You think so?' The question was insulting in its air of forbearance with a fairy-tale view of life.

'Think so? I *know* it. I should be sorry for my own powers of judgment if I believed the majority of men were like the worst specimens – like those you –'

'Oh, well, we don't dwell on that side. It's enough to remember that women without our incentive have to bear worse. It's part of a whole system.'

'I shall never believe that!' exclaimed Vida, thinking what was meant was an organized conspiracy against the Suffragettes.

'Yes, it's all part of the system we are in the world to overturn. Why should we suppose we'd gain anything by complaining? Don't hundreds, thousands of meek creatures who have never defied anybody, don't they have to bear worse ignominies? Every man knows that's true. Who troubles himself? What is the use, we say, of crying about individual pains and penalties? No. The thing is to work day and night to root out the system that makes such things possible.'

'I still don't understand – why you thought it would be a protection to carry –'

'A man's fear of ridicule will restrain him when nothing else will. If one of them is publicly whipped, *and by a woman*, it isn't likely to be forgotten. Even the fear of it – protects us from some things. After an experience some of the women had, the moment our committee decided on another demonstration, little Mary O'Brian went out, without consulting anybody, and bought me the whip. "If you will go," she said, "you shan't go unarmed. If we have that sort of cur to deal with, the only thing is to carry a dog-whip."'

Miss Claxton clenched her hands in their grey cotton gloves. There was silence in the room for several seconds.

'What we do in asking questions publicly – it's only what men do constantly. The greatest statesman in the land stops to answer a man, even if he's a fool naturally, or half drunk. They treat those interrupters with respect, they answer their questions civilly. They are men. They have votes. But women: "Where's the chucker out?"'

'Are you never afraid that all you're going through may be in vain?'

'No. We are quite certain to succeed. We have found the right way at last.'

'You mean what are called your tactics?'

'I mean the spirit of the women. I mean: not to mind the price. When you've got people to feel like that, success is sure.'

'But it comes very hard on those few who pay with the person, as the French say, pay with prison – and with –'

'Prison isn't the worst!'

A kind of shyness came over the woman on the sofa; she dropped her eyes from the other's face.

'Of course,' the ex-prisoner went on, 'if more women did a little it wouldn't be necessary for the few to do so much.'

'I suppose you are in need of funds to carry on the propaganda.'

'Money isn't what is most needed. One of our workers – a little mill girl – came up from the country with only two pounds in her pocket to rouse London. And she did it!' her comrade exulted. 'But there's a class we don't reach. If only' – she hesitated and glanced reflectively at the woman before her.

'Yes?' Miss Levering's eye flew to the cheque-book.

'If only we could get women of influence to understand what's at stake,' said Miss Claxton, a little wistfully.

'They don't?'

'Oh, some. A few. As much as can be expected.'

'Why do you say that?'

'Well, the upper-class women, I don't say all' (she spoke as one exercising an extreme moderation); 'but many of them are such sexless creatures.'

Miss Levering opened wide eyes – a glint of something like amazed laughter crossed her face, as she repeated –

'*They* are sexless, you think?'

'We find them so,' said the other, firmly.

'Why' – Miss Levering smiled outright – 'that's what they say of you.'

'Well, it's nonsense, like the rest of what they say.'

The accusation of sexlessness brought against the curled darlings of society by these hard-working, hard-hitting sisters of theirs was not the least ironic thing in the situation.

'Why do you call them – ?'

'Because we see they have no sex-pride. If they had, they couldn't do the things they do.'

'What sort of things?'

'Oh, I can't go into that.' She stood up and tugged at her wrinkled cotton gloves. 'But it's easy for us to see they're sexless.' She seemed to resent the unbelief in the opposite face. 'Lady Caterham sent for me the other day. You may have heard of Lady Caterham.'

Miss Levering suppressed the fact of how much, by a vague-sounding –

'Y – yes.'

'Well, she sent for me to – Oh, I suppose she was curious!'

'Like me,' said the other, smiling.

'*She's* a very great person in her country, and she *said* she sympathized with the movement – only she didn't approve of our tactics, she said. We are pretty well used by now to people who don't approve of our tactics, so I just sat and waited for the "dog-whip."'

It was obvious that the lady without influence in her county winced at that, almost as though she felt the whip on her own shoulders. She was indeed a hard-hitter, this woman.

'I don't go about talking of why I carry a whip. I *hate* talking about it,' she flung the words out resentfully. 'But I'd been sent to try to get that woman to help, and so I explained. I told her when she asked why it seemed necessary' – again the face flushed – 'I told her! – more than I've told you. And will you believe it, she never turned a hair. Just sat there with a look of cool curiosity on her face. Oh, they have no sex-pride, those upper-class women!'

'Lady Caterham probably didn't understand.'

'Perfectly. She asked questions. No, it just didn't matter much to her that a woman should suffer that sort of thing. She didn't feel the indignity of it. Perhaps if it had come to her, *she* wouldn't have suffered,' said the critic, with a grim contempt.

'There may be another explanation,' said Miss Levering, a little curtly, but wisely she forbore to present it.

If the rough and ready reformer had chilled her new sympathizer by this bitterness against 'the parasite class,' she wiped out the memory of it by the enthusiasm with which she spoke of those other women, her fellow-workers.

'Our woman are wonderful!' she lifted her tired head. 'I knew they'd never had a chance to show what they were, but there are some things – No! I didn't think women had it in them.'

She had got up and was standing now by the door, her limp gown clinging round her, her weather-beaten Tam on one side. But in the confident look with which she spoke of 'our women,' the brow had cleared. You saw that it was beautiful. Miss Levering stood at the door with an anxious eye on the stair, as if fearful of the home-coming of 'her fellow-coward,' or, direr catastrophe – old Mr. Fox-Moore's discovering the damning fact of this outlaw's presence under his roof! Yet, even so, torn thus between dread and desire to pluck out the heart of the new mystery, 'the militant woman,' Miss Levering did not speed the parting guest. As though recognizing fully now that the prophesied use was not going to be made of the 'thin end of the wedge,' she detained her with –

'I wonder when I shall see you again.'

'I don't know,' said the other, absently.

'When is the next meeting?'

'Next Sunday. Every Sunday.'

'I shall be glad to hear you speak again; but – you'll come and see me – here.'

'I can't. I'm going away.'

'Oh! To rest, I hope.'

'Rest?' She laughed at an idea so comic. 'Oh, no. I'm going to work among the women in Wales. We have great hopes of those West-country women. They're splendid! They're learning the secret of co-operation, too. Oh, it's good stuff to work on – the relief of it after London!'

Miss Levering smiled. 'Then I won't be seeing you very soon.'

'No.' She seemed to be thinking. 'It's true what I say of the Welsh women, and yet we oughtn't to be ungrateful to our London women either.' She seemed to have some sense of injustice on her soul. 'We've been seeing just recently what they're made of, too!' She paused on the threshold and began to tell in a low voice of women 'new to the work,' who had been wavering, uncertain if they could risk imprisonment – poor women with husbands and children. 'When they heard *what it might mean* – this battle we're fighting – they were ashamed not to help us!'

'You mean –' Vida began, shrinking.

'Yes!' said the other, fiercely. 'The older women saw they ought to save the younger ones from having to face that sort of thing. That was how we got some of the wives and mothers.'

She went on with a stern emotion that was oddly contagious, telling about a certain scene at the Headquarters of the Union. Against the grey and squalid background of a Poor Women's movement, stood out in those next seconds a picture that the true historian who is to come will not neglect. A call for recruits with this result – a huddled group, all new, unproved, ignorant of the ignorant. The two or three leaders, conscience-driven, feeling it necessary to explain to the untried women that if they shared in the agitation, they were not only facing imprisonment, but unholy handling.

'It was only fair to let them know the worst,' said the women at the door, 'before they were allowed to join us.'

As the abrupt sentences fell, the grim little scene was reconstituted; the shrinking of the women who had offered their services ignorant of this aspect of the battle – their horror and their shame. At the memory of that hour the strongly-controlled voice shook.

'They cried, those women,' she said.

'But they came?' asked the other, trembling, as though for her, too, it was vital that these poor women should not quail.

'Yes,' answered their leader a little hoarsely, 'they came!'

E. Gore-Booth, 'The Street Orator'

Eva Gore-Booth has been described as a mystic as well as a poet. Campaigning as a suffragist in the north of England, she first inspired the young Christabel Pankhurst. This poem from *The Agate Lamp*, one of her many collections, draws upon parallels between her native Ireland and the areas around Manchester in which she spoke with characteristic spirituality.

At Clitheroe from the Market Square,
    I saw rose-lit the mountains gleam,
I stood before the people there
    And spake as in a dream.

At Oldham of the many mills
    The weavers are of gentle mind;
At Haslingden one flouted me,
    At Burnley all the folks were kind.

At Ashton town the rain came down,
    The east wind pierced us through and through,
But over little Clitheroe,
    The sky was bright and blue.

At Clitheroe through the sunset hour

My soul was very far away:
I saw Ben Bulben's rose and fire
   Shining afar o'er Sligo Bay.

At Clitheroe round the Market Square
   The hills go up, the hills go down,
Just as they used to go about
   A mountain-guarded Irish town.

Oh, I have friends in Haslingden,
   And many friends in Hyde,
But 'tis at little Clitheroe
   That I would fain abide.

3

Militancy and militarism

The writings in this section explore some of the debates which arose around the issue of militancy as a tactic but also convey the extent to which a militarism of language and symbol dominated the literature and iconography of the movement. From the outset women campaigning for the vote drew upon the vocabulary of battle and invested the figure of the woman warrior, epitomised in Joan of Arc, with powerful emotional significance. In the poetry especially we can see how such a language informs the images of struggle. The relationship between this discourse and its appropriateness to suffrage deeds was nevertheless debated with some subtlety, as the short story 'The Women at the Gate' demonstrates.

If militarism in rhetoric was generally prevalent, militancy of deed had a much more specific history. Suffrage activity, as seen in dramatic demonstrations, marches on Westminster, and huge rallies organised by the WPSU, grew in strength and efficiency from 1906 onwards, but met with increasing opposition in the form of arrests, imprisonment and escalating police brutality. Frustration at the lack of progress in Parliament led to the start of window-breaking in June 1908. In January 1910 a brief truce brought about a suspension of militant tactics, renewed for a short time in November and then fully resumed a year later with window-breaking, arson and attacks on post boxes. The death of Emily Wilding Davison, killed when she rushed out on to the race track at the 1913 Derby, into the path of the King's horse, gave militancy its first martyr. The slashing of the *Rokeby Venus* in 1914 by Mary Richardson added a further dimension to militant action.

For some, militancy in itself represented the only means of symbolic protest available to women in which the male spheres of activity and male space itself might be disrupted. Others saw it as a response to the brutality and even indecency that had become increasingly evident in male treatment of the suffragettes. To those involved in the constitutional side of reform, such as Helena Swanwick, however, militancy became a danger and a diversion from the cause.

In the pages that follow, various interpretations and assessments of militancy are offered, from seeing it as a necessary sacrifice, suggested in the short story 'A Lost Dog', to compensation for an unfulfilled existence, hinted at in May Sinclair's novel *The Tree of Heaven*. Condemnation of militancy is provided by the suffragist Ada Nield Chew through her cameo of 'Mrs Stubbs', while Cecily Hamilton uses the First World War as a context in which suffragette militancy appears trivial and trivialising. Militancy was, therefore, a contentious and divisive strategy within the campaign.

E. W. Davison, 'L'Envoi'

Emily Wilding Davison, most notable for being the first 'martyr' to the cause, wrote this poem when in Holloway in 1912. From the biography by Gertrude Colmore it would appear that she often thought of herself as a soldier.

Stepping onwards, oh my comrades!
Marching fearless through the darkness,
Marching fearless through the prisons,
With the torch of freedom guiding!

See the face of each is glowing,
Gleaming with the love of freedom;
Gleaming with a selfless triumph,
In the cause of human progress!

Like the pilgrim in the valley,
Enemies may oft assail us,
Enemies may close around us,
Tryants, hunger, horror, brute-force.

But the glorious dawn is breaking,
Freedom's beauty sheds her radiance;
Freedom's clarion call is sounding,
Rousing all the world to wisdom.

E. Smyth, 'The March of the Women'

Devoting herself to the cause for two years, Ethel Smyth used
her energies and talents as a composer to create this march
which became a familiar battle-cry at rallies and processions.

Shout, shout – up with your song,
  Cry with the wind, for the dawn is breaking;
March, march, swing you along,
  Wide blows our banner, and hope is waking.
Song with its story, dreams with their glory,
  Lo! they call, and glad is their word!
Hark, hark, hear how it swells,
  Thunder of freedom, the voice of the Lord!

Long, long – we in the past
  Cowered in dread from the light of heaven,
Strong, strong – stand we at last,
  Fearless in faith and with sight new given.
Strength with its beauty, Life with its duty
  (Hear the call, oh hear and obey!)
These, these – beckon us on!
  Open your eyes to the blaze of day.

Hail, hail – ye who have dared
  First in the battle to strive and sorrow!
Scorned, spurned – naught ye have cared,
  Raising your eyes to a wider morrow.
Ways that are weary, days that are dreary,
  Toil and pain in faith have ye borne;
Hail, hail – victors ye stand
  Wearing the wreath that the brave have worn.

Life, strife – these two are one.
  Naught can ye win but by faith and daring.
On, on – that ye have done
  But for the work of today preparing.
Firm in reliance, laugh a defiance –
  (Laugh in hope, for sure is the end).
March, march, many as one,
  Shoulder to shoulder and friend to friend.

W. A. N., 'The Vote'

This poem was published in *The Vote*, on 1 May 1914, and offers various interpretations of what the vote might mean to women, emphasising the general good that might come from female enfranchisement. *The Vote* was the newspaper of the Women's Freedom League, and was edited by Charlotte Despard.

The vote in itself is just nothing,
'Tis only a means to an end.
Look round you – look under the surface,
And see what we're seeking to mend.

Don't blame us if sometimes it happens,
We do things that you wouldn't do;
But make up your mind for an effort,
To see things from our point of view.

The homeless – the helpless – the outcast;
Ye critics who sit at your ease,
Say what are our militant tactics
When weighed in the balance with these?

The evil that's common you swallow,
With oceans of clap-trap and froth;
But our mildly militant methods
Are swamped in your vials of wrath.

Yet is not the one like the camel,
The other the wee little gnat;
The first you can gulp without effort,
The second you can't swallow that.

Yet ours is the cause of the woman,
'In poverty, hunger and dirt;
Who sews with a second invisible thread
At a shroud as well as a shirt.'

And ours is the cause of the children

Whose right is the freedom from care;
Let all have a place in the sunlight
Where now they are lacking a share.

And ours is the cause of the toiler,
Who dies on the alter of greed;
Who seeks to go armed to his battle,
Regardless of nation or creed.

And ours is the cause of the fallen,
The women who traffic in shame;
Dare you tell me you think that it's just
To give her the whole of the blame?

Environment made her and shaped her;
Its forces are constant and true;
If you'd only been placed in her cradle,
You might have been she – and she *you*.

'Tis this that compels us to struggle,
'Tis owned that our motives are pure;
'Tis justice that beckons us onward,
And gives us the strength to endure.

And though – like the vote – we are nothing,
Our cause is so lofty and just;
We cannot shrink out of the battle,
And dare not abandon our Trust.

E. Sharp, 'The Women at the Gate'

Evelyn Sharp's short story, from her collection *Rebel Women*, published in its second edition of 1915 by the United Suffragists and with an introduction by Elizabeth Robins, not only shows suffrage activism but also sharpens the definition of militancy by the debate between a range of characters over the nature and significance of 'war'. Most of the stories in the collection first appeared as sketches in the *Manchester Guardian*, *Daily Chronicle* and *Votes for Women*.

'Funny, isn't it?' said the young man on the top of the omnibus.

'No,' said the young woman from whom he appeared to expect an answer, 'I don't think it is funny.'

'Take care,' said the young man's friend, nudging him, 'perhaps she's one of them!'

Everybody within hearing laughed, except the woman, who did not seem to be aware that they were talking about her. She was on her feet, steadying herself by grasping the back of the seat in front of her, and her eyes, non-committal in their lack of expression, were bent on the roaring, restless crowd that surged backwards and forwards in the Square below, where progress was gradually becoming an impossibility to the stream of traffic struggling towards Whitehall. The thing she wanted to find was not down there, among the slipping horses, the swaying men and women, the moving lines of policemen; nor did it lurk in those denser blocks of humanity that marked a spot, here and there, where some resolute, battered woman was setting her face towards the gate of St. Stephen's; nor was the thing she sought to be found behind that locked gate of liberty where those in possession, stronger far in the convention of centuries than locks or bars could make them, stood in their well-bred security, immeasurably shocked at the scene before them and most regrettably shaken, as some of them were heard to murmur, in a lifelong devotion to the women's cause.

The searching gaze of the woman on the omnibus wandered for an instant from all this, away to Westminster Bridge and the blue distance of Lambeth, where darting lamps, like will-o'-the-wisps come to town, added a touch of magic relief to the dinginess of night. Then she came back again to the sharp realism of the foreground and found no will-o'-the-wisps there, only the lights of London shining on a picture she should remember to the end of her life. It did not matter, for the thing beyond it all that she wanted to be sure of, shone through rain and mud alike.

'Lookin' for a friend of yours, p'raps?' said a not unfriendly woman with a baby, who was also standing up to obtain a more comprehensive view of what was going on below.

'No,' was the answer again, 'I am looking at something that isn't exactly there; at least –'

'If I was you, miss,' interrupted the facetious youth, with a wink at his companion, 'I should chuck looking for what ain't there, and –'

She turned and smiled at him unexpectedly. 'Perhaps you are right,' she said. 'And yet, if I didn't hope to find what isn't there, I couldn't go through with what I have to do to-night.'

The amazed stare of the young man covered her, as she went swiftly down the steps of the omnibus and disappeared in the crowd.

'Balmy, the whole lot of 'em!' commented the conductor briefly.

The woman with the passionless eyes was threading her way through the straggling clusters of people that fringed the great crowd where it thinned out towards Broad Sanctuary. A girl wearing the militant tricolour in her hat, brushed against her, whispered, 'Ten been taken, they say; they're knocking them about terribly to-night!' and passed noiselessly away. The first woman went on, as though she had not heard.

A roar of voices and a sudden sway of the throng that pinned her against some railings at the bottom of Victoria Street, announced the eleventh arrest. A friendly artisan in working clothes swung her up till she stood beside him on the stone coping, and told her to 'ketch on.' She caught on, and recovered her breath laboriously.

The woman, who had been arrested after being turned back from the doors of the House repeatedly for two successive hours, was swept past in the custody of an inspector, who had at last put a period to the mental and physical torment that a pickpocket would have been spared. A swirling mass of people, at once interested and puzzled, sympathetic and uncomprehending, was swept along with her and round her. In her eyes was the same unemotional, detached look that filled the gaze of the woman clinging to the railings. It was the only remarkable thing about her; otherwise, she was just an ordinary workaday woman, rather drab-looking, undistinguished by charm or attraction, as these things are generally understood.

'Now then, please, every one who wants a vote must keep clear of the traffic. Pass along the footway, ladies, if you please; there's no votes to be had in the middle of the roadway,' said the jocular voice of the mounted constable, who was backing his horse gently and insistently into the pushing, struggling throng.

The jesting tone was an added humiliation; and women in the crowd, trying to see the last of their comrade and to let her know that they were near her then, were beaten back, hot with helpless anger. The mounted officer came relentlessly on, successfully sweeping the pavement clear of the people whom he was exhorting with so much official reasonableness not to invade the roadway. He paused once to salute and to avoid two men, who, having piloted a lady through the backwash of the torrent set in motion by the plunging horse, were now hoisting her into a place of safety just beyond the spot where the artisan and the other woman held on to the railings.

'Isn't it terrible to see women going on like this?' lamented the lady breathlessly. 'And they say some of them are quite nice – like us, I mean.'

The artisan, who, with his neighbour had managed to evade the devastating advance of the mounted policeman, suddenly put his hand to his mouth and emitted a hoarse cheer.

'Bravo, little 'un!' he roared. 'Stick to it! Votes for women, I say! Votes for women!'

The crowd, friendly to the point of admiring a struggle against fearful odds which they yet allowed to proceed without their help, took up the words with enthusiasm; and the mud-bespattered woman went away to the haven of the police station with her war-cry ringing in her ears.

The man who had led the cheer turned to the woman beside him, as though to justify his impulse. 'It's their pluck,' he said. 'If the unemployed had half as much, they'd have knocked sense into this Government long ago!'

A couple of yards away, the lady was still lamenting what she saw in a plaintive and disturbed tone. Unconsciously, she was putting herself on the defensive.

'I shouldn't blame them,' she maintained, 'if they did something really violent, like – like throwing bombs and things. I could understand that. But all this – all this silly business of trying to get into the House of Commons, when they know beforehand that they can't possibly do it – oh, it's so sordid and loathsome! Did you see that woman's hair, and the way her hat was bashed in, and the mud on her nose? Ugh!'

'You can't have all the honour and glory of war, and expect to keep your hair tidy too,' observed one of the men, slightly amused.

'War!' scoffed his wife. 'There's none of the glory of war in this.'

Her glance ranged, as the other woman's had done, over the dull black stream of humanity rolling by at her feet, over the wet and shining pavements, casting back their myriad distorted reflections in which street lamps looked like grinning figures of mockery – over the whole drear picture of London at its worst. She saw only what she saw, and she shuddered with distaste as another mounted officer came sidling through the crowd, pursuing another hunted rebel woman, who gave way only inch by inch, watching her opportunity to face once more towards the locked gate of liberty. Evidently, she had not yet given sufficient proof of her unalterable purpose to have earned the mercy of arrest; and a ring of compassionate men formed round her as a body-guard, to allow her a chance of collecting her forces. A reinforcement of mounted police at once bore down upon the danger spot, and by the time these had worked slowly through the throng, the woman and her supporters had gone, and a new crowd had taken the place of the former one.

'Oh, there's none of the glory of war in that!' cried the woman again, a tremble in her voice.

'There is never any glory in war – at least, not where the war is,' said her second companion, speaking for the first time. His voice travelled to the ear of the other woman, still clinging to the railings with the artisan. She glanced round at him swiftly, and as swiftly let him see that she did not mean to be recognized; and he went on talking as if he had not seen her turn round.

'This is the kind of thing you get on a bigger scale in war,' he said, in a half-jesting tone, as if ashamed of seeming serious. 'Same mud and slush, same grit, same cowardice, same stupidity and beastliness all round. The women here are fighting for something big; that's the only difference. Oh, there's another, of course; they're taking all the kicks themselves and giving none of 'em back. I suppose it has to be that way round when you're fighting for your souls and not for your bodies.'

'I didn't know you felt like that about it,' said the woman, staring at him curiously. 'Oh, but of course you can't mean that real war is anything like this wretched scuffle of women and police!'

'Oh, yes,' returned the other, in the same tone of gentle raillery. 'Don't you remember Monsieur Bergeret? He was perfectly right. There is no separate art of war, because in war you merely practise the arts of peace rather badly, such as baking and washing, and cooking and digging, and travelling about. On the spot it is a wretched scuffle; and the side that wins is the side that succeeds in making the other side believe it to be invincible. When the women can do that, they've won.'

'They don't look like doing it to-night, do they?' said the woman's husband breezily. 'Thirteen women and six thousand police, you know!'

'Exactly. That proves it,' retorted the man, who had fought in real wars. 'They wouldn't bring out six thousand police to arrest thirteen men, even if they all threw bombs, as your wife here would like to see.'

'The police are not there only to arrest the women –'

'That's the whole point,' was the prompt reply. 'You've got to smash an idea as well as an army in every war, still more in every revolution, which is always fought exclusively round an idea. If thirteen women batter at the gates of the House of Commons, you don't smash the idea by arresting the thirteen women, which could be done in five minutes. So you bring out six thousand police to see if that will do it. That is what lies behind the mud and the slush – the idea you can't smash.'

A man reeled along the pavement and lurched up against them.

'Women in trousers! What's the country coming to?' he babbled; and bystanders laughed hysterically.

'Come along; let's get out of this,' said the woman's husband hurriedly; and the trio went off in the direction of the hotel.

The woman with the passionless eyes looked after them. 'He sees what we see,' she murmured.

'Seems he's been in the army, active service, too,' remarked the artisan in a sociable manner. 'I like the way he conversed, myself.'

'He understands, that is all,' explained his companion. 'He sees what it all means – all this, I mean, that the ordinary person calls a failure because we don't succeed in getting into the House. Do you remember, in "Agamemnon" – have you read "Agamemnon"?'

It did not strike her as strange that she should be clasping iron railings in Westminster, late on a wet evening, talking to a workingman about Greek tragedy. The new world she was treading to-night, in which things that mattered were given their true proportions, and important scruples of a lifetime dwindled to nothingness, gave her a fresh and a whimsical insight into everything that happened; and the odd companion that chance had flung her, half an hour ago, became quite easily the friend she wanted at the most friendless moment she had ever known.

The man, without sharing her reasons for a display of unusual perception, seemed equally unaware of any strangeness in the situation.

'No, miss, I haven't read it,' he answered. 'That's Greek mythology, isn't it? I never learnt to speak Greek.'

'Nor I,' she told him; 'but you can get it translated into English prose. It reminds me always of our demonstrations in Parliament Square, because there is a chorus in it of stupid old men, councillors, they are, I think, who never understand what is going on, however plainly it is put to them. When Cassandra prophesies that Agamemnon is going to be murdered – as we warn the Prime Minister when we are coming to see him – they pretend not to see what she is driving at, because if they did, they would have to do something. And then, when her prophecy comes true and he is murdered – of course, the analogy ends here, because we are not out to murder anybody, only to make the Prime Minister hear our demands – they run about wringing their hands and complaining; but nobody does anything to stop it. It really is rather like the evasions of the Home Office when people ask questions in Parliament about the prison treatment of the Suffragettes, isn't it?'

'Seems so,' agreed her new friend, affably.

'And then,' continued the woman, scorn rising in her voice,' when Clytaemnestra comes out of the house and explains why she has murdered her husband, they find plenty to say because there is a woman to be blamed, though they never blamed Agamemnon for doing far worse things to her. That is the way the magistrate and the daily papers will talk to-morrow, when our women are brought up in the police court.'

'That's it! Always put all the blame on the women,' said the artisan, grasping what he could of her strange discourse.

Big Ben tolled out ten strokes, and his companion, catching her breath, looked with sudden apprehension at the moving, throbbing block of people, now grown so immense that the police, giving up the attempt to keep the road clear, were merely concerned in driving back the throng on four sides and preserving an open space round the cluster of buildings known to a liberty-loving nation as the People's House. The gentlemen, who still stood in interested groups behind the barred gates of it, found the prospect less entertaining now that the action had been removed beyond the range of easy vision; and some of the bolder ones ventured out into the hollow square, formed by an unbroken line of constables, who were standing shoulder to shoulder, backed by mounted men who made little raids from time to time on the crowd behind, now fast becoming a very ugly one. Every possible precaution was being taken to avoid the chance of annoyance to any one who might still wish to preserve a decorous faith in the principle of women's liberty.

Meanwhile, somewhere in that shouting, hustling, surging mass of humanity, as the woman onlooker knew full well, was the twelfth member of the women's deputation that had been broken up by the police, two hours ago, before it could reach the doors of the House; and knowing that her turn had come now, she pictured that twelfth woman beating against a barrier that had been set up against them both ever since the world grew civilized. There was not a friend near, when she nodded to the artisan and slipped down from her temporary resting-place. The respectable and sympathetic portion of the crowd was cut off from her, away up towards Whitehall, whither it had followed the twelfth woman. On this side of Parliament Square all the idlers, all the coarse-tongued reprobates of the slums of Westminster, never far distant from any London crowd, were herded together in a stupid, pitiless, ignorant mob. The slough of mud underfoot added the last sickening touch to a scene that for the flash of an instant made her heart fail.

'St. James's Park is the nearest station, miss,' said the man, giving her a helping hand. 'Don't advise you to try the Bridge; might find it a bit rough getting across.'

She smiled back at him from the kerbstone, where she stood hovering a second or two on the fringe of the tumult and confusion. Her moment's hesitation was gone, and the sure look had come back to her eyes.

'I am not going home,' she told him. 'I am the thirteenth woman, you see.'

She left the artisan staring at the spot near the edge of the pavement where the crowd had opened and swallowed her up.

'And she so well-informed too!' he murmured. 'I don't like to think of it – I don't like to think of it!'

Shortly after midnight two men paused, talking, under the shadow of Westminster Abbey, and watched a patrol of mounted police that ambled at a leisurely pace across the deserted Square. The light in the Clock Tower was out. Thirteen women, granted a few hours' freedom in return for a word of honour, had gone to their homes, proudly conscious of having once more vindicated the invincibility of their cause; and some five or six hundred gentlemen had been able to issue in safety from the stronghold of liberty, which they had once more proved to themselves to be impregnable. And on the morrow the prisoners of war would again pay the price of the victory that both sides thought they had won.

'If that is like real war too,' said one of the men to the other, who had just made these observations aloud, 'how does anybody ever know which side has won?'

'By looking to see which side pays the price of victory,' answered the man who had fought in real wars.

E. Smyth, *Female Pipings in Eden*

> In her recollections of Emmeline Pankhurst, Ethel Smyth makes the connection between Joan of Arc and suffrage militancy, and more specifically Mrs Pankhurst's heroism, which was much favoured in militant rhetoric.

In the year 1920 when Joan of Arc was canonised, the present writer was perhaps not alone in wondering how it came to pass that the most markedly patriotic of nations had let centuries elapse before paying this tribute to the woman who had driven the hereditary foe back across the Channel for all time. Only by degrees did the explanation present itself. Joan had defied the greatest power on earth, had not shrunk from telling the Church that behind her was One whose commands had to be obeyed, with or without her Bishop's blessing, and of course the Hierarchy was not disposed to create a dangerous precedent by handing this rebel a halo.

Nor was that all. Whatever dastardly deeds have been done in history, there is only one with which the delivering of Joan into the hands of the English can be classed – the deed that ended on Calvary. And neither individuals nor Governments love those whom they have shamefully entreated. Hence the Maid had to wait more than four hundred years for admission into the Calendar.

To turn to the present day; the axiom 'no taxation without representation' being a fundamental article of our constitution, the men who, in spite of John Stuart Mill, not only made a practice of rifling our pockets, but hounded on the ignorant masses to see nothing but impudence in our demand for the vote, were playing a time-honoured but none the less ugly political game. As for militancy, I think half the nation dimly understands to-day that such an out-break was above all things a black mark against those in power, although, by way of saving their faces, politicians will go on for years to come qualifying militancy as monstrous, ridiculous, or uncalled for, according to the temperament of the speaker. Thus, since many women still let men set the key for them in the judging of public matters, decades may elapse before Mrs. Pankhurst is seen for what she really was – an even more astounding figure than Joan of Arc, in that instead of performing her miracles in an age of romance, religious faith, and mystic exaltation, round about her blared the hard, sceptical light of the twentieth century.

Some day, but not yet awhile, the whole story of her life will be pieced together and told by some one properly equipped for the telling. That person will have to be a born writer, a seer, and I think a woman. Meanwhile the impressions and experiences of one who was closely associated with her during the terrible years between 1911 and the outbreak of the war, and who remained more or less in touch with her to the end, should be fixed in black and white before we of her generation are past telling either lies or the truth about her.

Of late, reliving the past in order to write this monograph, above all going once more through certain letters that travelled from England to Egypt – whither the recipient had fled in order to escape the combined pull of the suffrage and human affection – again and again a sense of the overwhelming character of that whole happen-ing has come sweeping in like the sea, and for a while the pen refused to travel smoothly and objectively its appointed course.

It has often been observed that genius – and no wonder, since genius represents a whole world – is full of contradictions. I think nothing but the hope that this fragmentary record may some day be of use to an ultimate biographer could embolden even an intimate friend to attempt a portrait of one who was as simple as she was complex, as temperate as she was passionate, as loving as she was heartless; who, little as in her bottomless humility she guessed it, was of a breed it is difficult for us ordinary mortals to portray – the breed of heroes and heroines.

It is just five years since she died. She had never set any value on her life, and at the last laid it down for her country as deliberately as any man who had volunteered for the Great War in 1914. And remember – for greatly as she disliked references to her age there is no harm in mentioning it now – remember she was seventy when the supreme sacrifice was made!

But England has not done with her yet. At this very moment (June 1933) a fuss is going on in East Anglia about unjust tithes, and lo! two women farmers, nieces of one of our great politicians – a half-friend of the type Mrs. Pankhurst hated and despised more than an enemy – have been heading a rebellion, rescuing a cow that was about to be distrained and routing the police! I think if those two ringleaders had listened carefully they might have heard a voice whispering in their ear: 'Well done, women!'

Yes! however it was in bygone days with Cranmer, however it may be in Germany in the year 1933, Mrs. Pankhurst, who maintained, and with truth, that she was law-abiding by nature, lit a fire in the souls of English women that will never be extinguished. And though their male relations may not proclaim the fact on the house-top, I believe they are secretly glad that so it is!

E. Zangwill, *The Call*

In this scene from Edith Zangwill's novel, masculine aggression is depicted in the treatment of the Women's Deputation and shown as a justification for suffrage militancy.

Although she had refused to go on the deputation, Ursula naturally attended the Conference the next day at Caxton Hall. It met at noon, simultaneously with the re-assembling of Parliament. Presently a woman hurried into the hall and up on to the platform. She began speaking to the Leader in a low voice. This was the messenger bringing the report of the Prime Minister's speech. The Leader rose. 'As we expected,' she said 'the Prime Minister has omitted all reference to Woman Suffrage. Further, he has announced the dissolution for next Monday.' There was an outburst of hisses and groans. The Leader raised her hand. 'The motto of this Union is deeds not words. The deputation will start at once.'

The total number of volunteers for the deputation was over three hundred. It had, however, been arranged that it should be divided up into detachments of not more than a dozen, starting at a few minutes interval, so as to keep within the legal number. Thus the hall only emptied itself slowly. Ursula sat on for an hour, and then, getting tired of waiting, went off to see what was happening. The crowd, as she went down Victoria Street, was noticeably less dense than at the previous raid, probably because this one had been less advertised. Parliament Square itself had been cleared by the police. Presently, looking across the green, she saw a little group of women standing straightly in front of St. Stephen's entrance. She recognized the Leader and most of the first detachment, all women of a certain age and celebrity. So they had not been admitted. It was extraordinarily stupid, if nothing else, of the Prime Minister, she reflected.

By this time she had worked her way sufficiently near the front of the crowd to see clearly what was going on. Policemen at intervals were keeping back the people; then came a clear space, and then a continuous line of stalwart, dark figures. As on the previous occasion, a woman here and there was trying to press her way through the cordon of police. There was one doing it just in front of her. But it was different from the last time – Ursula felt it instinctively. She saw the policeman raise his fist. The woman thudded on to the ground. He had deliberately knocked her down!

Ursula's heart seemed to stop beating. Even through her recent experiences she had never before seen a woman struck. And this woman had grey hair. For one moment a lamentable heap lay in the road and then she was up, and again rushing forward. This time Ursula could not quite see what the policeman did to her; the result, however, was the same. Again the woman was lying in the road. But now she did not move; she was evidently hurt, perhaps stunned. Ursula vainly tried to press through to her assistance. Then she saw a gentleman, who was standing in the front row, step forward. That was all right, Ursula felt with relief; he looked strong; he would be able to help the woman better than she could herself. The gentleman approached the prostrate figure. He lifted his foot. There was time for a flash of puzzled speculation to dart through Ursula's brain and the boot swung heavily into the woman's back.

'You brute! You brute!' Ursula's exclamation was hardly audible; she was half sobbing. 'Let the woman alone,' a working-man shouted more effectually. 'The perlice can do their own dirty work.' 'Garn – serves 'er right!' This was from yet another source and was followed by some outrageously foul remarks. Meanwhile the kicker had retired back into the crowd, satisfied apparently with his achievement.

All this time the woman on the ground had lain silent and motionless. Now she suddenly sat up. Blood was running from a cut in her forehead; probably in falling she had struck against the kerb. She got to her feet and stood swaying, her hand pressed to her head. Then she staggered – forward.

There was a cheer. The woman's courage had impressed the crowd. 'Let her through.' 'Why can't you arrest her?' came in angry shouts. 'They've had orders not to arrest,' someone near Ursula volunteered. 'That's why they're knocking them about.' 'They'll kill her then before they've done with her!'

The police, too, may have feared this result; the streaming blood probably impressed them. There was a hurried consultation between two constables as the woman weakly pressed up against them. Then followed a merciful arrest.

The scene that Ursula had just witnessed had certainly no bearing on the primal question of Woman Suffrage, nor even on the secondary issue of the desirability of militant tactics. At the most it only showed what one woman was prepared to suffer in order to gain the Vote, and how, under present conditions, she might be treated. And yet, illogically enough, nothing before had ever fired Ursula with such an irresistible passion for Woman Suffrage, with such a burning faith in the value of militancy. The Cause, from being an intellectual desirability, suddenly became a religion. Militancy was no longer tactics; it was martyrdom.

The rest was simple. When the thing was viewed in this new light, how could she remain out of it? Yes, she had been sheltering behind the other women, as the Leader had said, sheltering behind this grey-haired woman, whom she had seen lying there kicked and bleeding. She wanted to rush to Caxton Hall – to volunteer on the spot – the last detachment could hardly yet have left. But the thought of Tony came, and even at this moment withheld her. She owed it to Tony to write to him first. After all, it were not as if this were her last chance. She had already heard it announced that if Parliament dissolved next week without considering their Bill, there would be another deputation. She would go on that deputation, but now she would go home.

A. Mollwo, *A Fair Suffragette*

Mollwo's light romance, published fairly early in the campaign
in 1909, nevertheless suggests that police brutality is in itself a
transgression of ideologies of femininity and a validation of the
women's actions. This section is entitled 'The storming of the
House of Parliament'.

'The Suffragettes are raising "red rebellion" outside the Houses of
Parliament!'
    'What?'
In the act of lighting a cigarette, Mowbray stopped short, letting
the wax vesta burn down to his fingers; he dropped it with a muttered imprecation, and stared at the speaker.
    'My dear fellow I knew you would be interested, smiled the other.
'How is it you are not in "the House"'
    Oh, simply business. Have been detained all the afternoon with a
confounded solicitor over some beastly mortgages. Seeing it was so
late, I decided to dress and dine before going down. But what's this
about the Suffragettes?'
    'Well,' said his friend with an air of keen enjoyment, 'they have
been at it since five o'clock, and it seems there is no stopping
them. They have invaded the outer and inner lobby, and shouted
for votes in their own truly orthodox and peculiar style. They
have been thrown out, and have returned to the charge again and
again. The women have been very determined and the authorities
equally so, for mounted police have actually been called out
against them.'
    'No!'
    'It is quite true. If you go down, you will see for yourself. There
are rumours that some of the women have been handled rather
roughly, and that one or two have been injured, but I cannot vouch
for the accuracy of that statement, it is only what is passing from
mouth to mouth.'
    'Scandalous!' ejaculated Mowbray. He was getting into his coat
hurriedly, and the word came out with a puff of his cigarette.
    'What is scandalous? The behaviour of the women? I quite agree
with you.'
    'No, not the women! The employing of mounted police against
them. Disgraceful! Unheard of! Abominable!'

'You don't mean to say you take the part of these women, Mowbray?'

'I would take the part of anybody against brutality. Using brute force against a crowd of women! What are men coming to?'

'What are women coming to?'

'You forget these women are our mothers, and our wives, and our sisters, and our sweethearts!'

'Then they should behave as such.'

'If we forget that we are men, we cannot expect them to remember that they are women.'

'I beg your pardon, we look to women to teach us to be good, to inculcate in us lofty and noble impulses and aspirations, by the force of their virtuous living and bright example. Destroy this ideal of womanhood, and you destroy all that is best and bravest in man. A man must be brave, and a woman must be gentle. A man may be good, but a woman must be. That's my idea, and I say that all this shouting, and screaming, and playing the fool generally over this rotten suffrage business, this wanting what they have no business to want, tends to lower the dignity of their own sex, and demoralize the two.'

'Oh, you poor women! you poor women!' murmured Mowbray as he went out. 'We expect so much from you, and we give you so little in return.'

He hailed a cab, and was driven rapidly in the direction of Westminster.

Long before he reached the vicinity, he saw signs of a great and extraordinary disturbance. He sprang to the ground, paid the man, and walked quickly towards Parliament Square. As he drew near, it appeared to his amazed eyes as if a veritable battle were taking place. The crowd which had assumed enormous proportions was beyond anything he had imagined. Some hundreds, perhaps thousands strong, eddied and swirled in the semi-darkness round a body of shrieking, shouting, excited women, who were making mad rushes first this way, then that, in the vain, but desperate and determined attempt to break through the impenetrable human wall of police who were drawn across Palace yard two deep.

'Just as the crowd was thickest, while the air was rent with the shouts of the people and the hoarse commands of police officers, on came a rush of mounted police, which caused a stampede that for a moment looked dangerous. The Square was given over for an instant to riot.' (Vide. Daily Mail.)

Mowbray, whose one thought was of Gipsie, whose one anxiety was lest she should be in the midst of that rough, pushing, shouting, seething whirl of humanity – elbowed his way through, using his fists freely. He must find her if she were there, he must take her out of it, away – anywhere to safety.

Heavens! to conceive the possibility of her being there even, was torture! The picture of her fragile, slender little body at the mercy of this yelling, excited crowd, torn first one way, then another, insulted by angry policemen, knocked under the feet of the horses – No, surely her own womanly dignity, her own sense of the fitness of things would have kept her back from being a party to such an insane and impotent demonstration. There was a fine line which must be drawn somewhere. But as these thoughts tumbled over each other in his brain, while he fought and struggled and pushed his way from side to side, gazing eagerly, anxiously into the face of each hot, dishevelled, exhausted female, he came across, counter thoughts succeeded them rapidly, and put the former out of court.

He knew that when one is enthusiastic, excited, wound up, and determined, sense counts as nought. If one always stopped to think of the sense of the thing, one might never act at all. One did the thing, and thought of the advisability afterwards.

'Oh, how easily things go wrong!' Nothing would ever go wrong if we were always sensible. Alas, we are not! No! thank heaven, we are not! It would be a terribly monotonous world if we were.

Mowbray received a blow in the face, and he gave one back in return with interest. He was hot and dishevelled and inflamed himself now. His silk hat had a nasty dent in it, his coat was badly torn. He must find Gipsie, he must find her. He was sure she was there – sure!

'Oo are you a shoven' at?' cried a man's rough voice in his ear.

'Who the devil are you talking to?' retorted Mowbray.

The shouting and shrieking had become almost deafening, the prancing and the backing of the mounted men's horses, was sickening in the way the people were forced back upon each other, the stronger jostling and tumbling over the weaker. There was a sudden, sharp cry from a woman close at hand –

Mowbray fought his way frantically through the surging mass of people. A girl hatless, untidy, with tumbled, black hair, lay in the dust beneath the horses' feet.

He was down beside her in a moment dragging her from the

backing horses, hurling angry defiance at the police who would have kept him back.

'Let me be,' he cried, 'and don't dare to touch me. I know this lady. I will take her to a place of safety.'

'The police station is the best place for the likes of 'er,' said a constable gruffly. 'She had given us more trouble than enough.'

Mowbray did not trouble to answer, he had got Gipsie, and it was enough for him. Her eyes were closed. He could not tell if she were badly hurt or not. He struggled through the crowd, and the people made way when they saw that he bore a fainting woman in his arms.

As he essayed to get free of the mob that pressed round, and hemmed him in on all sides, he strove to collect his thoughts, to consider what he had best do, how he must act, for act he must, and promptly.

His pulses were throbbing wildly, the blood surged in his brain, his whole heart bounded with mad, intoxicating joy at the knowledge that he held the girl whom he loved in his arms for one delicious moment, brief though he knew that moment must be, and the tumult of his emotions, was such that it almost bereft him for the time being of the power for coherent thought. He passed into a side street which was comparatively clear, and halted a moment. A man who had been dodging his footsteps silently for no apparent reason, stopped when he stopped, and glanced at him with sly, furtive eyes.

'Fetch me a cab,' said Mowbray authoritatively, 'a four wheeler, I'll pay you well'.

The man was off like a shot, and Mowbray, with one foot raised on a step, supported Gipsie on his knee, and looked anxiously in her face. He had quite decided that the best thing to do was to take her home immediately to her mother in Cadogan Gardens. It was after ten o'clock; whether she was much or little hurt, the sooner she was under her mother's care the better.

He scanned her features fearfully by the feeble light of the street lamp, to discover any possible wound or bruise from the kick of a horse, lifting the rough, tumbled hair from her brow with tender, delicate fingers. But he could discern nothing of the kind. Perhaps she was only stunned by the fall on the hard pavement. He devoutly hoped that such was the case.

Two minutes barely elapsed before the ruffianly looking touter was back with a cab.

'You've been jolly quick, my man,' said Mowbray, as he stepped with his burden into the cab. 'Here is something for your pains. Tell the driver Cadogan Gardens, and to look sharp.'

The man took the small coin with a muttered, 'thank you, Sir,' he stared at it incredulously – then took it to the lamp post and looked at it again, turning it over and over in his grimy hands. Suddenly he spit upon it with quick vehemence.

Mowbray smiled as he saw the action, and still more at the fervent, 'God bless you, Sir,' that the man sent after the departing cab.

He turned his attention to Gipsie, and began to chafe her cold hands in his own strong, warm ones, calling her softly by her name. The temptation was strong upon him to press her little fingers to his lips, but he refrained. He would take nothing from her that she did not herself give him. He had no business to take anything at all as he knew well.

He presently became aware that her eyes were open, and that she was gazing at him in a strange, bewildered sort of way.

'Is that you, Mr Mowbray?' she asked faintly. 'How is it we are here together, you and I?'

'Thank God, you are better!' he exclaimed fervently. 'I have been so terribly anxious about you!'

'Oh, I remember,' she said with a quick shudder, 'I was knocked down in that awful rush. I suppose I must have hurt my head, it feels so light and stupid. I remember seeing the horses rearing over me, but nothing more.'

'You must not talk,' he said with gentle authority. 'I expect you have got slight concussion. I am taking you home, we shall not be long.'

'How did you come to be there?' she insisted – 'to find me?'

Mowbray looked out of the carriage window, he dared not meet her eyes, lest she should read all that was written in his own.

'I heard you troublesome little women were making a fuss at Westminster. I feared you might be there – I came to see,' he answered lightly.

Gipsie was moved. The tears started to her eyes. She reached out her hand and touched his softly.

'Thank you,' she said simply.

H. G. Wells, *Ann Veronica*

H. G. Wells takes a more ironic stance on the stock image of
the ill-treated old lady in the deputation to Parliament, presenting her here as a comic grotesque. His novel, described on
publication in 1909 as a 'poisonous book', caused more
concern in its depiction of extra-marital relationships than in
its treatment of the suffrage cause.

So Ann Veronica, enterprising and a little dubious as ever, mingled
with the stream of history and wrote her Christian name upon the
police-court records of the land.

But out of a belated regard for her father she wrote the surname
of some one else.

Some day, when the rewards of literature permit the arduous
research required, the Campaign of the Women will find its Carlyle,
and the particulars of that marvellous series of exploits by which
Miss Brett and her colleagues nagged the whole Western world into
the discussion of women's position become the material for the most
delightful and amazing descriptions. At present the world waits for
that writer, and the confused record of the newspapers remains the
only resource of the curious. When he comes he will do that raid of
the pantechnicons the justice it deserves; he will picture the orderly
evening scene about the Imperial Legislature in convincing detail;
the coming and going of cabs and motor-cabs and broughams
through the chill, damp evening into New Palace Yard, the reinforced but untroubled and unsuspecting police about the entries of
those great buildings whose square and panelled Victorian Gothic
streams up from the glare of the lamps into the murkiness of the
night; Big Ben shining overhead, an unassailable beacon, and the
incidental traffic of Westminster, cabs, carts, and glowing
omnibuses going to and from the bridge. About the Abbey and
Abingdon Street stood the outer pickets and detachments of the
police, their attention all directed westward to where the woman in
Caxton Hall, Westminster, hummed like an angry hive. Squads
reached to the very portals of that centre of disturbance. And
through all these defences and into Old Palace Yard, into the very
vitals of the defenders' position, lumbered the unsuspected vans.

They travelled past the few idle sightseers who had braved the
uninviting evening to see what the Suffragettes might be doing; they

pulled up unchallenged within thirty yards of those coveted portals. And then they disgorged.

Were I a painter of subject pictures, I would exhaust all my skill in proportion and perspective and atmosphere upon the august seat of empire, I would present it grey and dignified and immense and respectable beyond any more verbal description, and then in vivid black and very small, I would put in those valiantly impertinent vans, squatting at the base of its altitudes and pouring out a swift straggling rush of ominous little black objects, minute figures of determined women at war with the universe.

Ann Veronica was in their very forefront.

In an instant the expectant calm of Westminster was ended, and the very Speaker in the chair blenched at the sound of the policemen's whistle. The bolder members in the House left their places to go lobbyward, grinning. Others pulled hats over their noses, cowered in their seats, and feigned that all was right with the world. In Old Palace Yard everybody ran. They either ran to see or ran for shelter. Even two Cabinet Ministers took to their heels, grinning insincerely. At the opening of the van doors and the emergence into the fresh air Ann Veronica's doubt and depression gave place to the wildest exhilaration. That same adventurousness that had already buoyed her through crises that would have overwhelmed any normally feminine girl with shame and horror now became uppermost again. Before her was a great Gothic portal. Through that she had to go.

Past her shot the little old lady in the bonnet, running incredibly fast, but otherwise still alertly respectable, and she was making a strange threatening sound as she ran, such as one would use in driving ducks out of a garden – 'B-r-r-r-r-r –!' and pawing with black-gloved hands. The policemen were closing in from the sides to intervene. The little old lady struck like a projectile upon the resounding chest of the foremost of these, and then Ann Veronica had got past and was ascending the steps.

Then most horribly she was clasped about the waist from behind and lifted from the ground.

At that a new element poured into her excitement, an element of wild disgust and terror. She had never experienced anything so disagreeable in her life as the sense of being held helplessly off her feet. She screamed involuntarily – she had never in her life screamed before, and then she began to wriggle and fight like a frightened animal against the men who were holding her.

The affair passed at one leap from a spree to a nightmare of violence and disgust. Her hair got loose, her hat came over one eye, and she had no arm free to replace it. She felt she must suffocate if these men did not put her down, and for a time they would not put her down. Then with an indescribable relief her feet were on the pavement, and she was being urged along by two policemen, who were gripping her wrists in an irresistible expert manner. She was writhing to get her hands loose and found herself gasping with passionate violence, 'It's damnable! – damnable!' to the manifest disgust of the fatherly policeman on her right.

Then they had released her arms and were trying to push her away. 'You be off home, missie,' said the fatherly policeman. 'This ain't no place for you.'

He pushed her a dozen yards along the greasy pavement with flat, well-trained hands that there seemed to be no opposing. Before her stretched blank spaces, dotted with running people coming towards her, and below them railings and a statue. She almost submitted to this ending of her adventure. But at the word 'home' she turned again.

'I won't go home,' she said; 'I won't!' and she evaded the clutch of the fatherly policeman and tried to thrust herself past him in the direction of that big portal. 'Steady on!' he cried.

A diversion was created by the violent struggles of the little old lady. She seemed to be endowed with superhuman strength. A knot of three policemen in conflict with her staggered towards Ann Veronica's attendants and distracted their attention. 'I *will* be arrested! I *won't* go home!' the little old lady was screaming over and over again. They put her down, and she leaped at them; she smote a helmet to the ground.

'You'll have to take her!' shouted an inspector on horseback, and she echoed his cry: 'You'll have to take me!' They seized upon her and lifted her, and she screamed. Ann Veronica became violently excited at the sight. 'You cowards!' said Ann Veronica, 'put her down,' and tore herself from a detaining hand and battered with her fists upon the big red ear and blue shoulder of the policeman who held the little old lady.

So Ann Veronica also was arrested.

And then came the vile experience of being forced and borne along the street to the police-station. Whatever anticipation Ann Veronica had formed of this vanished in the reality. Presently she was going through a swaying, noisy crowd, whose faces grinned and stared pitilessly in the light of the electric standards. 'Go it, miss!' cried one. 'Kick aht at 'em!' though, indeed, she went now with Christian meekness, resenting only the thrusting policemen's hands. Several people in the crowd seemed to be fighting. Insulting cries became frequent and various, but for the most part she could not understand what was said. 'Who'll mind the baby nar?' was one of the night's inspirations, and very frequent. A lean young man in spectacles pursued her for some time, crying 'Courage! Courage!' Somebody threw a dab of mud at her, and some of it got down her neck. Immeasurable disgust possessed her. She felt draggled and insulted beyond redemption. She could not hide her face. She attempted by a sheer act of will to end the scene, to will herself out of it anywhere. She had a horrible glimpse of the once nice little old lady being also borne stationward, still faintly battling and very muddy – one lock of greyish hair straggling over her neck, her face scared, white, but triumphant. Her bonnet dropped off and was trampled into the gutter. A little Cockney recovered it, and made ridiculous attempts to get to her and replace it.

'You must arrest me!' she gasped breathlessly, insisting insanely on a point already carried; 'you shall!'

K. Roberts, *Some Pioneers and a Prison*

> In her second account of suffrage experiences, published in 1913, Kathleen Roberts creates a dialogue in which the Married Woman is made aware of the reasons behind militancy.

'How nice of your landlady to make such delicious sandwiches. Do you know that this is the fourth one that I have eaten?'

'Take some more. We shall not get sandwiches in Holloway. The food there is not appetising. However, thanks to the hunger strike, we are now permitted the following privileges under Rule 243*a*: a visit once a month, a letter once a fortnight, one parcel of food every week can be sent in if not exceeding 11 lb. in weight; we are allowed to wear our own clothes, and to have four books every week.'

'Tell me about the hunger strike. How did it originate?'

'It was started in June last year, as a protest against second division treatment, among ordinary criminals, being given to women who had committed political offences, if what we did could really be called an offence at all, while men like the cattle raiders in Ireland were recognised as political offenders and received first division treatment. The hunger strike was a species of passive resistance. Petitions having proved useless, it was determined to make a protest by politely and quietly declining to wear the prison clothes, or eat the prison food, so long as first division treatment was refused. The authorities, by order of the Government, tried by every means in their power to break down the resistance of the women: solitary confinement, punishment cells, handcuffs, and, finally, forcible feeding, with, in many cases, much unnecessary brutality and violence; but everything failed, as physical force must eventually do if used against spiritual force. If these women had died, others would have been found to take their places. It is impossible even for a Liberal Government to kill an Idea. That battle cost the lives of a few, and the health of most of those who went through it; but it has secured slightly better conditions and a different status for political prisoners in the future. It is a thing which we can always be proud of, that – even after forcible feeding was permitted, or, rather, ordered by the Home Secretary – not one of our women gave in.'

The Married Woman finished drinking her coffee and replaced the cup on the tray.

'I have been thinking,' she said slowly, 'that the mistake which the leaders of the WSPU have made, is that they have not been militant enough. It seems absurd that they should have gone on for years simply asking questions at political meetings, or going in a Deputation to see the Prime Minister, and being imprisoned for months at a time merely because they refused to turn back, while men have always done so much more, and history has proved that they were right in doing so.'

'But you must remember that if, as some maintain, there is one law for the rich, and another for the poor, there is very much more certainly one law for men and another for women. That has been proved over and over again in this Agitation. There is an unwritten, though generally accepted grammar book, in which "hooligan" is the feminine for "hero," and "Raid" the feminine for "Deputation." I have not the smallest doubt that, later on, possibly very soon if it is forced upon us, we shall go a step further – a step nearer to what men would do under similar circumstances. At the same time, I feel equally sure that when that happens, public opinion will again condemn the women. All the years of peaceful and consequently futile agitation will be forgotten, together with the educational and propaganda work all over the country, while the new step only is criticised and blamed.'

'But I feel certain that until more is done, the Government will not take any steps towards remedying the present injustice.'

'I am convinced of that also, and so are many others; but Christabel has always said that we want to be able to look back afterwards and feel that we have hurt no one beside ourselves, and done nothing which was not proved to be absolutely necessary. The leaders have really been marvellous in the way they have advocated patience and restrained the rank and file from going too far. If it had not been for their influence, there is no doubt that real offences would have been committed long ago; but we all love and reverence them too much not to carry out their wishes in the matter. The most wonderful thing to me, in all the wonders of this enormous Movement, is the patience and self-control of our members. Repeatedly, I have heard the men who work with us marvel at it, and yet it is quite common to hear people talk of Suffragettes as if they were hysterical and excitable – liable to do rash things on the spur of the moment. Personally, I have never met any people so extraordinarily devoid of these characteristics, in spite of their enthusiasm for the Cause. One of my strongest reasons now for wishing that the Women's Suffrage Bill should pass soon is so that the militant methods may stop. I realise what the cost is to those who have to do the things, as I think only those who have taken part can realise, and I know that if still more has to be done – women will be found ready to sacrifice themselves.'

'Can *nothing* be done to convince this idiotic Government that there really is a great and widespread demand for Woman's Suffrage in the country?'

'They are perfectly well aware of the demand. It is a recognised fact, that there have been more great meetings and monster petitions and peaceful agitation over this question, during the last forty years, than there has ever been in connection with any other political reform. However, as Zangwill says, "it is necessary to have a vote in order to get a vote," and so long as we are governed by people who are willing to sacrifice principle to party, the prospect of getting the Woman's point of view recognised is small. It is obvious to the meanest intellect that if women had had the driving power of the vote, no Bill, which had such a demand as this behind it, could possibly have been ignored or shelved, or talked out repeatedly for years, as ours has been.'

The Married Woman rose and began to unpack the small bag which represented her 'prison luggage.'

'Well, I hope the leaders will soon advocate at least the breaking of some windows,' she said cheerfully; 'if they do, I shall certainly take part. Considering how often men have broken the windows at perfectly peaceful Suffragist Meetings, and nothing has been done to them at all, not to mention their own political protests, where window breaking has been looked upon as a mild preliminary form of warfare against injustice, it would be impossible for the Government, or the public, not to recognise the fact, that in our case it is absolutely justifiable and only too long delayed.'

'I am not so sure of that. However, we shall see. A great deal of patience is needed in this battle, also, as our colours indicate, much courage and faith.'

'I think it must be easier to cultivate courage, or even faith, than to have patience. I have been interested in this question for one week, and have worked for it during part of one day, but I feel already that, if we do not get a Woman's Suffrage Bill passed almost immediately, I shall do something desperate.'

The Grass Widow laughed merrily. 'We must really go to bed in the meantime. It is dreadfully late, and to-morrow morning you have got that letter to write to your husband, before we pack our bags, and start for Bow Street.'

Anon., 'There was a small woman called G'

> This adaptation of limerick form was published anonymously in *Holloway Jingles* (1912), mocking the responses of authority to militant action.

There was a small woman called G,
Who smashed two big windows at B—

They sent her to jail, her fate to bewail,
For Votes must be kept, must be kept for the male.

They asked that small woman called G,
Why she smashed those big windows at B—
She made a long speech, then made her defence,
But it wasn't no use, their heads were so dense;
They just hummed the refrain, altho' it is stale—
Votes must be kept, must be kept for the male.

They sent her to H for six months and a day,
In the coach Black Maria she went sadly away;
But she sang in this strain, as it jolted and rumbled,
We will have the Vote, we will not be humbled.
We must have the vote by hill and by dale,
Votes shall not alone be kept for the male.

J. Gonne, 'Wails of the Weary'

Josephine Gonne's collection of humorous poetry, presumably published at the height of the campaign, offers variations on the theme of responses to militancy. Included here are the 'wails' of trapped police authorities, and a dialogue revealing unexpected defenders of militancy in 'Backers'.

Wails of the Weary – No. 1.

'It's really jolly awkward'
    Said Swells, 'with due respect,
But unconcerned tranquillity
    No longer I affect.
They've blocked the front, they've block'd the back,
    And now, I've just found out,
They've been and block'd the dust-shoot,
    So how shall we get out?'

'They've block'd the streets, they've block'd the lanes,
    They've block'd the Treasury door,

And all the other bolt-holes
   We've always used before.
They've block'd the way to Humhum Yard,
   And – both of us are stout
   But – they've even block'd the keyholes,
   So how shall we get out?'

'My feet are worn, with walking,
   My clothes are worn, with wear,
My tongue is torn, with talking,
   My corns are cured, with care;
My teeth are tired, with gnashing,
   My mind is dim, with doubt,
My brains are thin, with thinking,
   For – how shall we get out?'

'If I had known, as know I now,
   The perils which beset
The pathways of policemen,
   When they fight the Suffragette,
If I'd foreseen starvation,
   As now, without a doubt,
I'd have "gone and swept a crossing,"
   For how *can* we get out?'

Wails of the Weary – No. 3

'We've dodged you round the "Commons,"
   And oh! it's such a bore,
We've had to go to meetings,
   Behindhand, and before.
We've had to leave our meetings,
   By many a small back door,
So don't say "Votes for Women,"
   We can't bear it any more.'

In blues to duty we shall go,
   So comely to be seen,
But we're faring forth to football,
   Wearing Purple, White, and Green.

Backers!

The Policeman
'Why do you back them, Mr. Bobby
   Peeler?
Why do you back these women from the
   Strand?'
      'In a horrid scene of strife
      A woman saved my life
By taking her own in her hand.'

The Sailor
'Why do you back them, handy Mr. Jack
   Tar?
Who do you back these women from the
   Strand?'
      'I know what it can be
      To face a raging sea,
Taking my life in my hand.'

The Soldier
'Why do you back them, gallent Mr. Atkins?
Why do you back these women from the
   Strand?'
      'I'm very often sent
      To quell some discontent,
Taking my life in my hand.'

The Fireman
'Why do you back them, fearless Mr.
   Firebox?
Why do you back these women from the
   Strand?'
      'On roofs I've had to climb,
      Many and many a time,
Taking my life in my hand.'

The Doctor
'Why do you back them, gentle Mr. Pill-
   box?
Why do you back these women from the
   Strand?'
      'I know what it would mean,
      Down at Winson Green,
To take my life in my hand.'

A. Bennett, *The Lion's Share*

While unsympathetic in its presentation of suffrage leaders, Arnold Bennett's novel uses this lively incident to suggest that excitement and action as much as political principles attracted women to militant behaviour. Bennett supported women's suffrage in general, although in its depiction of activists his novel shows more engagement with the character of Jane Foley, the working-class campaigner, than with her politics. He had difficulties in getting the book published, although he promised the periodical editors that suffragism wouldn't triumph in it. It was finally published by Cassell's in 1916.

In the following month, on a Saturday afternoon, Audrey, Miss Ingate, and Jane Foley were seated at an open-air café in the Blue City.

The Blue City, now no more, was, as may be remembered, Birmingham's reply to the White City of London, and the imitative White City of Manchester. Birmingham, in that year, was not imitative, and, with its chemical knowledge, it had discovered that certain shades of blue would resist the effects of smoke far more successfully than any shade of white. And experience even showed that these shades of blue were improved, made more delicate and romantic, by smoke. The total impression of the show – which it need hardly be said was situated in the polite Edgbaston district – was ethereal, especially when its minarets and towers, all in accordance with the taste of the period, were beheld from a distance. Nor was the exhibition entirely devoted to pleasure. It had a moral object, and that object was to demonstrate the progress of civilisation in our islands. Its official title, indeed, was 'The National Progress Exhibition,' but the citizens of Birmingham and the vicinity never called it anything but the Blue City.

On that Saturday afternoon a Cabinet Minister historically hostile to the idols of Birmingham was about to address a mass meeting in the Imperial Hall of the Exhibition, which held seven thousand people, in order to prove to Birmingham that the Government of which he was a member had done far more for national progress than any other Government had done for national progress in the same length of time. The presence of the Cabinet Minister accounted for the presence of Jane Foley; the presence of

Jane Foley accounted for the presence of Audrey; and the presence of Audrey accounted for the presence of Miss Ingate.

Although she was one of the chief organisers of victory, and perhaps – next to Rosamund and the family trio whose Christian names were three sweet symphonies – the principal asset of the Suffragette Union, Jane Foley had not taken an active part in the Union's arrangements for suitably welcoming the Cabinet Minister; partly because of her lameness, partly because she was writing a book, and partly for secret reasons which it would be unfair to divulge. Nearly at the last moment, however, in consequence of news that all was not well in the Midlands, she had been sent to Birmingham, and, after evading the watch of the police, she had arrived on the previous day in Audrey's motor-car, which at that moment was waiting in the automobile park outside the principal gates of the Blue City.

The motor-car had been chosen as a means of transit for the reason that the railway stations were being watched for notorious suffragettes by members of a police force whose reputations were at stake. Audrey owed her possession of a motor-car to the fact that the Union officials had seemed both startled and grieved when, in response to questions, she admitted that she had no car. It was communicated to her that members of the Union as rich as she reputedly was were expected to own cars for the general good. Audrey thereupon took measures to own a car. Having seen in many newspapers an advertisement in which a firm of middlemen implored the public thus: 'Let us run your car for you. Let us take all the worry and responsibility,' she interviewed the firm, and by writing out a cheque disembarrassed herself at a stroke of every anxiety incident to defective magnetos, bad petrol, bad rubber, punctures, driving licences, bursts, collisions, damages, and human chauffeurs. She had all the satisfactions of owning a car without any of the cares. One of the evidences of progress in the Blue City was an exhibit of this very firm of middlemen.

From the pale blue tripod table at which sat the three women could be plainly seen the vast Imperial Hall, flanked on one side by the great American Dragon Slide, a side-show loudly demonstrating progress, and on the other by the unique Joy Wheel side-show. At the doorway of the latter a man was bawling proofs of progress through a megaphone.

Immense crowds had been gathering in the Imperial Hall, and the lines of political enthusiasts bound thither were now thinning. The Blue City was full of rumours, as that the Cabinet Minister was too afraid to come, as that he had been smuggled to the hall inside a tea-chest, and as that he had walked openly and unchallenged through the whole Exhibition. It was no rumour, but a sure fact, that two women had been caught hiding on the roof of the Imperial Hall, under natural shelters formed by the beams and boarding supporting the pediment of the eastern façade, and that they were ammunitioned with flags and leaflets and a silk ladder, and had made a hole in the roof exactly over the platform. These two women had been seen in charge of policemen at the Exhibition police-station. It was understood by many that they were the last hope of militancy that afternoon; many others, on the contrary, were convinced that they had been simply a feint.

'Well,' said Miss Ingate suddenly, glancing up at the Imperial clock, 'I think I shall move outside and sit in the car. I think that'll be the best place for me. I said that night in Paris that I'd get my arm broken, but I've changed my mind about that.' She rose.

'Winnie,' protested Audrey, 'aren't you going to see it out?'

'No,' said Miss Ingate.

'Are you afraid?'

'I don't know that I'm afraid. I played the barrel-organ all the way down Regent Street, and it was smashed to pieces. But I don't want to go to prison. Really, I don't *want* to. If me going to prison would bring the Vote a single year nearer, I should say: "Let it wait a year." If me not going to prison meant no Vote for ever and ever, I should say: "Well, struggle on without the Vote." I've no objection to other people going to prison, if it suits them, but it wouldn't suit me. I know it wouldn't. So I shall go outside and sit in the car. If you don't come, I shall know what's happened, and you needn't worry about me.'

The dame duly departed, her lips and eyes equally ironic about her own prudence and about the rashness of others.

'Let's have some more lemonade – shall we?' said Jane Foley.

'Oh, let's!' agreed Audrey, with rapture. 'And more sponge-cake, too! You do look lovely like that!'

'Do I?'

Jane Foley had her profuse hair tightly bound round her head and powdered grey. It was very advisable for her to be disguised, and her bright hair was usually the chief symptom of her in those distur-

bances which so harassed the police. She now had the appearance
of a neat old lady kept miraculously young by a pure and cheerful
nature. Audrey, with a plain blue frock and hat which had cost more
than Jane Foley would spend on clothes in twelve months, had a face
dazzling by its ingenuous excitement and expectation. Her little
nose was extraordinarily pert; her forehead superb; and all her gestures had the same vivacious charm as was in her eyes. The white-
aproned, streamered girl who took the order for lemonade and
sponge-cakes to a covered bar ornamented by advertisements of
whisky, determined to adopt a composite of the styles of both the
customers on her next ceremonious Sunday. And a large proportion
of the other sippers and nibblers and of the endless promenading
crowds regarded the pair with pleasure and curiosity, never sus-
pecting that one of them was the most dangerous woman in
England.

The new refreshments, which had been delayed by reason of an
altercation between the waitress and three extreme youths at a
neighbouring table, at last arrived, and were plopped smartly down
between Audrey and Miss Foley. Having received half a sovereign
from Audrey, the girl returned to the bar for change. 'None o' your
sauce!' she threw out, as she passed the youths, who had apparently
discovered new arguments in support of their case. Audrey was fired
by the vigorous independence of the girl against three males.

'I don't care if we are caught!' she murmured low, looking for the
future through the pellucid tumbler. She added, however: 'But if we
are, I shall pay my own fine. You know I promised that to Miss
Ingate.'

'That's all right, so long as you don't pay mine, my dear,' said Jane
Foley with an affectionate smile.

'Jenny!' Audrey protested, full of heroine-worship. 'How could
you think I would ever do such a mean thing!'

There came a dull, vague, voluminous sound from the direction
of the Imperial Hall. It lasted for quite a number of seconds.

'He's beginning,' said Jane Foley. 'I do feel sorry for him.'

'Are we to start now?' Audrey asked deferentially.

'Oh, no!' Jane laughed. 'The great thing is to let them think everything's all right. And then, when they're getting careless, let go at
them full bang with a beautiful surprise. There'll be a chance of
getting away like that. I believe there are a hundred and fifty stewards in the meeting, and they'll every one be quite useless.'

At intervals a muffled roar issued from the Imperial Hall, despite the fact that the windows were closely shut.

In due time Jane Foley quietly rose from the table, and Audrey did likewise. All around them stretched the imposing blue architecture of the Exhibition, forming vistas that ended dimly either in the smoke of Birmingham or the rustic haze of Worcestershire. And, although the Imperial Hall was crammed, every vista was thickly powdered with pleasure-seekers and probably pleasure-finders. Bands played. Flags waved. Brass glinted. Even the sun feebly shone at intervals through the eternal canopy of soot. It was a great day in the annals of the Blue City and of Liberalism.

And Jane Foley and Audrey turned their backs upon all that, and – Jane concealing her limp as much as possible – sauntered with affected nonchalance towards the precincts of the Joy Wheel enclosure. Audrey was inexpressibly uplifted. She felt as if she had stepped straight into romance. And she was right – she had stepped into the most vivid romance of the modern age, into a world of disguises, flights, pursuits, chicane, inconceivable adventures, ideals, martyrs and conquerors, which only the Renaissance or the twenty-first century could appreciate.

'Lend me that, will you?' said Jane persuasively to the man with the megaphone at the entrance to the enclosure.

He was, quite properly, a very loud man, with a loud thick voice, a loud purple face, and a loud grey suit. To Audrey's astonishment, he smiled and winked, and gave up the megaphone at once.

Audrey paid sixpence at the turnstile, admittance for two persons, and they were within the temple, which had a roof like an umbrella over the central, revolving portion of it, but which was somewhat open to the skies around the rim. There were two concentric enclosing walls, the inner one was unscalable, and the outer one about five feet six inches high. A second loud man was calling out: 'Couples please. Ladies *and* gentlemen. Couples if *you* please.' Obediently, numbers of the crowd disposed themselves in pairs in the attitudes of close affection on the circling floor which had just come to rest, while the remainder of the numerous gathering gazed upon them with sarcastic ecstasy. Then the wheel began slowly to turn, and girls to shriek in the plenitude of happiness. And progress was proved geometrically.

Jane, bearing the megaphone, slipped by an aperture into the space between the two walls, and Audrey followed. Nobody gave attention to them except the second loud man, who winked the wink of knowledge. The fact was that both the loud men, being unalterable Tories, had been very willing to connive at Jane Foley's scheme for the affliction of a Radical Minister.

The two girls over the wall had an excellent and appetising view of the upper part of the side of the Imperial Hall, and of its high windows, the nearest of which was scarcely thirty feet away.

'Hold this, will you?' said Jane, handing the megaphone to Audrey.

Jane drew from its concealment in her dress a small piece of iron to which was attached a coloured streamer bearing certain words. She threw, with a strong movement of the left arm, because she was left-handed. She had practised throwing; throwing was one of her several specialities. The bit of iron, trailing its motto like a comet its tail, flew across space and plumped into the window with a pleasing crash and disappeared, having triumphed over uncounted police on the outskirts and a hundred and fifty stewards within. A roar from the interior of the hall supervened, and varied cries.

'Give me the meg,' said Jane gently.

The next instant she was shouting through the megaphone, an instrument which she had seriously studied:

'Votes for women. Why do you torture women? Votes for women. Why do you torture women?'

The uproar increased and subsided. A masterful voice resounded within the interior. Many people rushed out of the hall. And there was a great scurry of important and puzzled feet within a radius of a score of yards.

'I think I'll try the next window,' said Jane, handing over the megaphone. 'You shout while I throw.'

Audrey's heart was violently beating. She took the magaphone and put it to her lips, but no sound would come. Then, as though it were breaking through an obstacle, the sound shot forth, and to Audrey it was a gigantic voice that functioned quite independently of her will. Tremendously excited by the noise, she bawled louder and still louder.

'I've missed,' said Jane calmly in her ear. 'That's enough, I think. Come along.'

'But they can't possibly see us,' said Audrey, breathless, lowering the instrument.

'Come along, dear,' Jane Foley insisted.

People with open mouths were crowding at the aperture of the inner wall, but, Jane going first, both girls pushed safely through the throng. The wheel had stopped. The entire congregation was staring agog, and in two seconds everybody divined, or had been nudged to the effect, that Jane and Audrey were the authoresses of the pother.

Jane still leading, they made for the exit. But the first loud man rushed chivalrously in.

'Perlice!' he cried. 'Two bobbies a-coming.'

'Here!' said the second loud man. 'Here, misses. Get on the wheel. They'll never get ye if ye sit in the middle back to back.' He jumped on to the wheel himself, and indicated the mathematical centre. Jane took the suggestion in a flash; Audrey was obedient. They fixed themselves under directions, dropping the megaphone. The wheel started, and the megaphone rattled across its smooth surface till it was shot off. A policeman ran in, and hesitated; another man, in plain clothes, and wearing a rosette, ran in.

'That's them,' said the rosette. 'I saw her with the grey hair from the gallery.'

The policeman sprang on to the wheel, and after terrific efforts fell sprawling and was thrown off. The rosette met the same destiny. A second policeman appeared, and with the fearless courage of his cloth, undeterred by the spectacle of prostrate forms, made a magnificent dash, and was equally floored.

As Audrey sat very upright, pressing her back against the back of Jane Foley and clutching at Jane Foley's skirts with her hands behind her – the locked pair were obliged thus to hold themselves exactly over the axis of the wheel, for the slightest change of position would have resulted in their being flung to the circumference and into the blue grip of the law – she had visions of all her life just as though she had been drowning. She admitted all her follies and wondered what madness could have prompted her remarkable escapades both in Paris and out of it. She remembered Madame Piriac's prophecy. She was ready to wish the past year annihilated and herself back once more in parental captivity at Moze, the slave of an unalterable routine imposed by her father, without responsibility, without initiative and without joy. And she lived again through the scenes in which she had smiled at the customs official, fibbed to Rosamund, taken the wounded Musa home in the taxi, spoken privily with the ageing yacht-owner, and laughed at the drowned detective in the area of the palace in Paget Gardens.

Everything happened in her mind while the wheel went round once, showing her in turn to the various portions of the audience, and bringing her at length to a second view of the sprawling policemen. Whereupon she thought queerly: 'What do I care about the vote, really?' And finally she thought with anger and resentment: 'What a shame it is that women haven't got the vote!' And then she heard a gay, quiet sound. It was Jane Foley laughing gently behind her.

'Can you see the big one now, darling?' asked Jane roguishly. 'Has he picked himself up again?'

Audrey laughed.

And at last the audience laughed also. It laughed because the big policeman, unconquerable, had made another intrepid dash for the centre of the wheel and fallen upon his stomach as upon a huge india-rubber ball. The audience did more than laugh – it shrieked, yelled, and guffawed. The performance to be witnessed was worth ten times the price of entry. Indeed no such performance had ever before been seen in the whole history of popular amusement. And in describing the affair the next morning as 'unique' the *Birmingham Daily Post* for once used that adjective with absolute correctness. The policemen tried again and yet again. They got within feet, within inches, of their prey, only to be dragged away by the mysterious protector of militant maidens – centrifugal force. Probably never before in the annals of the struggle for political freedom had maidens found such a protection, invisible, sinister and complete. Had the education of policemen in England included a course of mechanics, these particular two policemen would have known that they were seeking the impossible and fighting against that which was stronger than ten thousand policemen. But they would not give up. At each fresh attempt they hoped by guile to overcome their unseen enemy, as the gambler hopes at each fresh throw to outwit chance. The jeers of the audience pricked them to desperation, for in encounters with females like Jane Foley and Audrey they had been accustomed to the active sympathy of the public. But centrifugal force had rendered them ridiculous, and the public never sympathises with those whom ridicule has covered. The strange and side-splitting effects of centrifugal force had transformed about a hundred indifferent young men and women into ardent and convinced supporters of feminism in its most advanced form.

In the course of her slow revolution Audrey saw the rosetted steward arguing with the second loud man, no doubt to persuade him to stop the wheel. Then out of the tail of her eye she saw the steward run violently from the tent. And then while her back was towards the entrance she was deafened by a prodigious roar of delight from the mob. The two policemen had fled also – probably for reinforcements and appliances against centrifugal force. In their pardonable excitement they had, however, committed the imprudence of departing together. An elementary knowledge of strategy should have warned them against such a mistake. The wheel stopped immediately. The second hand man beckoned with laughter to Jane Foley and Audrey, who rose and hopefully skipped towards him. Audrey at any rate was as self-conscious as though she had been on the stage.

'Here's th' back way,' said the second loud man, pointing to a coarse curtain in the obscurity of the nether parts of the enclosure.

They ran, Jane Foley first, and vanished from the regions of the Joy Wheel amid terrific acclamations given in a strong Midland accent.

The next moment they found themselves in a part of the Blue City which nobody had taken the trouble to paint blue. The one blue object was a small patch of sky, amid clouds, overhead. On all sides were wooden flying buttresses, supporting the boundaries of the Joy Wheel enclosure to the south-east, of the Parade Restaurant and Bar to the south-west, and of a third establishment of good cheer to the north. Upon the ground were brick-ends, cinders, bits of wood, bits of corrugated iron, and all the litter and refuse cast out of sight of the eyes of visitors to the Exhibition of Progress.

With the fear of the police behind them they stumbled forward a few yards, and then saw a small ramshackle door swinging slightly to and fro on one hinge. Jane Foley pulled it open. They both went into a narrow passage. On the mildewed wall of the passage was pinned up a notice in red ink: 'Any waitress taking away any apron or cap from the Parade Restaurant and Bar will be fined one shilling.' Farther on was another door, also ajar. Jane Foley pushed against it, and a tiny room of irregular shape was disclosed. In this room a stout woman in grey was counting a pile of newly laundered caps and aprons, and putting them out of one hamper into another. Audrey remembered seeing the woman at the counter of the restaurant and bar.

'The police are after us. They'll be here in a minute,' said Jane Foley simply.

'Oh!' exclaimed the woman in grey, with the carelessness of fatigue. 'Are you them stone-throwing lot? They've just been in to tell me about it. What d'ye do it for?'

'We do it for you – amongst others,' Jane Foley smiled.

'Nay! That ye don't!' said the woman positively. 'I've got a vote for the city council, and I want no more.'

'Well, you don't want us to get caught, do you?'

'No, I don't know as I do. Ye look a couple o' bonny wenches.'

'Let's have two caps and aprons, then,' said Jane Foley smoothly. 'We'll pay the shilling fine.' She laughed lightly. 'And a bit more. If the police get in here we shall have to struggle, you know, and they'll break the place up.'

Audrey produced another half-sovereign.

'But what shall ye do with yer hats and coats?' the woman demanded.

'Give them to you, of course.'

The woman regarded the hats and coats.

'I couldn't get near them coats,' she said. 'And if I put on one o' them there hats my old man 'ud rise from the grave – that he would. Still, I don't wish ye any harm.'

She shut and locked the door.

In about a minute two waitresses in aprons and streamered caps of immaculate purity emerged from the secret places of the Parade Restaurant and Bar, slipped round the end of the counter, and started with easy indifference to saunter away into the grounds after the manner of restaurant girls who have been gifted with half an hour off. The tabled expanse in front of the Parade erection was busy with people, some sitting at the tables and supporting the establishment, but many more merely taking advantage of the pitch to observe all possible exciting developments of the suffragette shindy.

And as the criminals were modestly getting clear, a loud and imperious voice called:

'Hey!'

Audrey, lacking experience, hesitated.

'Hey there!'

They both turned, for the voice would not be denied. It belonged to a man sitting with another man at a table on the outskirts of the

group of tables. It was the voice of the rosetted steward, who beckoned in a not unfriendly style.

'Bring us two liqueur brandies, miss,' he cried. 'And look slippy,
if ye please.'

The sharp tone, so sure of obedience, gave Audrey a queer sensation of being in reality a waitress doomed to tolerate the rough bullying of gentlemen urgently desiring alcohol. And the fierce thought
that women – especially restaurant waitresses – must and should
possess the Vote surged through her mind more powerfully than
ever.

'I'll never have the chance again,' she muttered to herself. And
marched to the counter.

'Two liqueur brandies, please,' she said to the woman in grey, who
had left her apron calculations. 'That's all right,' she murmured, as
the woman stared a question at her. Then the woman smiled to
herself, and poured out the liqueur brandies from a labelled bottle
with startling adroitness, and dashed the full glasses on to a brass
tray.

As Audrey walked across the gravel carefully balancing the tray,
she speculated whether the public eye would notice the shape of her
small handbag, which was attached by a safety pin to her dress
beneath the apron, and whether her streamers were streaming out
far behind her head.

Before she could put the tray down on the table, the rosetted
steward, who looked pale, snatched one of the glasses and gulped
down its entire contents.

'I wanted it!' said he, smacking his lips. 'I wanted it bad. They'll
catch 'em all right. I should know the young 'un again anywhere.
I'll swear to identify her in any court. And I will. Tasty little piece o'
goods, too! . . . But not so good-looking as you,' he added, gazing
suddenly at Audrey.

'None o' your sauce,' snapped Audrey, and walked off, leaving
the tray behind.

The two men exploded into coarse but amiable laughter, and
called to her to return, but she would not. 'You can pay the other
young lady,' she said over her shoulder, pointing vaguely to the
counter where there was now a bevy of other young ladies.

Five minutes later Miss Ingate, and the chauffeur also, received
a very appreciable shock. Half an hour later the car, having called
at the telegraph office, and also at the aghast lodgings of the wait-

resses to enable them to reattire and to pack, had quitted
Birmingham.

That night they reached Northampton. At the post office there
Jane Foley got a telegram. And when the three were seated in the
corner of the curtained and stuffy dining-room of the small hotel,
Jane said, addressing herself especially to Audrey:

'It won't be safe for us to return to Paget Gardens tomorrow. And
perhaps not to any of our places in London.'

'That won't matter,' said Audrey, who was now becoming accustomed to the world of conspiracy and chicane in which Jane Foley
carried on her existence with such a deceiving air of the matter-of-
fact. 'We'll go anywhere, won't we, Winnie?'

And Miss Ingate assented.

'Well,' said Jane Foley. 'I've just had a telegram arranging for us
to go to Frinton.'

'You don't mean Frinton-on-Sea?' exclaimed Miss Ingate, suddenly excited.

'It *is* on the sea,' said Jane. 'We have to go through Colchester.
Do you know it?'

'Do I know it!' repeated Miss Ingate. 'I know everybody in
Frinton, except the Germans. When I'm at home I buy my bacon at
Frinton. Are you going to an hotel there?'

'No,' said Jane. 'To some people named Spatt.'

'There's nobody that is anybody named Spatt living at Frinton,'
said Miss Ingate.

'They haven't been there long.'

'Oh!' murmured Miss Ingate. 'Of course if that's it . . . ! I can't
guarantee what's happened since I began my pilgrimages. But I think
I shall wriggle off home quietly as soon as we get to Colchester. This
afternoon's business has been too feverish for me. When the policeman held up his hand as we came through Blisworth I thought you
were caught. I shall just go home.'

'I don't care much about going to Frinton, Jenny,' said Audrey.

Indeed, Moze lay within not many miles of Frinton-on-Sea.

Then Audrey and Miss Ingate observed a phenomenon that was
both novel and extremely disturbing. Tears came into the eyes of
Jane Foley.

'Don't say it, Audrey, don't say it!' she appealed in a wet voice. 'I
shall have to go myself. And you simply can't imagine how I hate
going all alone into these houses that we're invited to. I'd much

sooner be in lodgings, as we were last night. But these homes in quiet
places here and there are very useful sometimes. They all belong to
members of the Union, you know; and we have to use them. But I
wish we hadn't. I've met Mrs. Spatt once. I didn't think you'd throw
me over just at the worst part. The Spatts will take all of us and be
glad.'

('They won't take me,' said Miss Ingate under her breath.)

'I shall come with you,' said Audrey, caressing the recreant who,
while equal to trifles such as policemen, magistrates, and prisons,
was miserably afraid of a strange home. In fact Audrey now liked
Jane much more than ever, liked her completely – and perhaps
admired her rather less, though her admiration was still intense.
And the thought in Audrey's mind was: 'Never will I desert this girl!
I'm a militant, too, now, and I shall stick by her.' And she was full
of a happiness which she could not understand and which she did
not want to understand.

The next morning all the newspaper posters in Northampton
bore the words: 'Policemen and suffragettes on Joy Wheel,' or some
variation of these words. And they bore nothing else. And in all the
towns and many of the villages through which they passed on the
way to Colchester, the same legend greeted their flying eyes. Audrey
and Miss Ingate, in the motor-car, read with great care all the
papers. Audrey blushed at the descriptions of herself, which were
flattering. It seemed that the Cabinet Minister's political meeting
had been seriously damaged by the episode, for the reason that
rumours of the performance on the Joy Wheel had impaired the spell
of eloquence and partially emptied the hall. And this was the more
disappointing in that the police had been sure that nothing unto-
ward would occur. It seemed also that the police were on the track
of the criminals.

'Are they!' exclaimed Jane Foley with a beautiful smile.

M. Sinclair, *The Tree of Heaven*

This scene from May Sinclair's novel depicts a group of militants meeting for the first time. Sinclair also seems to suggest
here that the need for vicarious excitement is a motivating
factor in militancy. A well-established novelist, a member of

the Women Writers' Suffrage League and a contributor to
Votes for Women, in this novel Sinclair presents the suffrage
cause as only one of the 'revolutions' taking place at the time.

As Anthony came home early one evening in October, he found a
group of six strange women in the lane, waiting outside his garden
door in attitudes of conspiracy.

Four of them, older women, stood together in a close ring. The
two others, young girls, hung about near, but a little apart from the
ring, as if they desired not to identify themselves with any state of
mind outside their own. By their low sibilant voices, the daring side-
long sortie of their bright eyes, their gestures, furtive and irrepress-
ible, you gathered that there was unanimity on one point. All six
considered themselves to have been discovered.

At Anthony's approach they moved away, with slow, casual steps,
passed through the posts at the bottom of the lane and plunged
down the steep path, as if under the impression that the nature of
the ground covered their retreat. They bobbed up again, one after
the other, when the lane was clear.

The first to appear was a tall, handsome, bad-tempered-looking
girl. She spoke first.

'It's a damned shame of them to keep us waiting like this.'

She propped herself up against Anthony's wall and smouldered
there in her dark, sullen beauty.

'We were here at six sharp.'

'When they know we were told not to let on where we meet.'

'We're led into a trap,' said a grey-haired woman.

'I say, who *is* Dorothea Harrison?'

'She's the girl who roped Rosalind in. She's all right.'

'Yes, but are her people all right?'

'Rosalind knows them.'

The grey-haired woman spoke again.

'Well, if you think this lane is a good place for a secret meeting, *I*
don't. Are you aware that the yard of "Jack Straw's Castle" is
behind that wall? What's to prevent them bringing up five or six
coppers and planting them there? Why, they've only got to post one
'tec at the top of the lane, and another at the bottom, and we're
done. Trapped. I call it rotten.'

'It's all right. Here they are.'

Dorothea Harrison and Rosalind Jervis came down the lane at a leisured stride, their long coats buttoned up to their chins and their hands in their pockets. Their gestures were devoid of secrecy or any guile. Each had a joyous air of being in command, of being able to hold up the whole adventure at her will, or let it rip.

Rosalind Jervis was no longer a bouncing, fluffy flapper. In three years she had shot up into the stature of command. She slouched, stooping a little from the shoulders, and carried her pink face thrust forward, as if leaning from a platform to address an audience. From this salience her small chin retreated delicately into her pink throat.

'Is Miss Maud Blackadder here?' she said, marshalling her six.

The handsome girl detached herself slowly from Anthony's wall.

'What's the point,' she said, 'of keeping us hanging about like this –'

'Till *all* our faces are known to the police –'

'There's a johnnie gone in there who can swear to *me*. Why didn't you two turn up before?' said the handsome girl.

'Because,' said Dorothea, 'that johnnie was my father. He was pounding on in front of us all up East Heath Road. If we'd got here sooner I should have had to introduce you.'

She looked at the six benevolently, indulgently. They might have been children whose behaviour amused her. It was as if she had said, 'I avoided that introduction, not because it would have been dangerous and indiscreet, but because it would have spoiled your fun for you.'

She led the way into the garden and the house and through the hall into the schoolroom. There they found eleven young girls who had come much too soon, and, mistaking the arrangements, had rung the bell and allowed themselves to be shown in.

The schoolroom had been transformed into a sort of meeting hall. The big oblong table had been drawn across one end of it. Behind it were chairs for the speakers, before it were three rows of chairs where the eleven young girls sat scattered, expectant.

The six stood in the free space in front of the table and looked at Rosalind with significance.

'This,' said Rosalind, 'is our hostess, Miss Dorothea Harrison. Dorothy, I think you've met Mrs. Eden, our Treasurer. This is our Secretary, Miss Valentina Gilchrist; Miss Ethel Farmer; Miss Winifred Burstall –'

Dorothy greeted in turn Mrs. Eden, a pretty, gentle woman with a face of dreaming tragedy (it was she who had defended Rosalind outside the gate); Miss Valentina Gilchrist, a middle-aged woman who displayed a large, grey pompadour above a rosy face with turned-back features which, when she was not excited, had an incredulous, quizzical expression (Miss Gilchrist was the one who had said they had been led into a trap); Miss Ethel Farmer, fair, attenuated, scholastic, wearing pince-nez with an air of not seeing you; and Miss Winifred Burstall, weather-beaten, young at fifty, wearing pince-nez with an air of seeing straight through you to the other side.

Rosalind went on. 'Miss Maud Blackadder –'

Miss Blackadder's curt bow accused Rosalind of wasting time in meaningless formalities.

'Miss – ' Rosalind was at a loss.

The other girl, the youngest of the eight, came forward, holding out a slender, sallow-white hand. She was the one who had hung with Miss Blackadder in the background.

'Desmond,' she said. 'Phyllis Desmond.'

She shrugged her pretty shoulders and smiled slightly, as much as to say, 'She forgets what she ought to remember, but it doesn't matter.'

Phyllis Desmond was beautiful. But for the moment her beauty was asleep, stilled into hardness. Dorothy saw a long, slender, sallow-white face, between sleek bands of black hair; black eyes, dulled as if by a subtle film, like breath on a black looking-glass; a beautiful slender mouth, pressed tight, holding back the secret of its sensual charm.

Dorothy thought she had seen her before, but she couldn't remember where.

Rosalind Jervis looked at her watch with a business-like air; paper and pencils were produced; coats were thrown on the little school-desks and benches in the corner where Dorothy and her brothers had sat at their lessons with Mr. Parsons some twelve years ago; and the eight gathered about the big table, Rosalind taking the presidential chair (which had once been Mr. Parsons' chair) in the centre between Miss Gilchrist and Miss Blackadder.

Miss Burstall and Miss Farmer looked at each other, and Miss Burstall spoke.

'We understand that this was to be an informal meeting. Before we begin business I should like to ask one question. I should like to know what we are and what we are here for?'

'We, Mrs. Eden, Miss Valentina Gilchrist, Miss Maud Blackadder and myself,' said Rosalind in the tone of one dealing reasonably with an unreasonable person, 'are the Committee of the North Hampstead Branch of the Women's Franchise Union. Miss Gilchrist is our Secretary, I am the President, and Miss Blackadder is – er – the Committee.

'By whom elected? This,' said Miss Burstall, 'is most irregular.'

Rosalind went on: 'We are here to appoint a Vice-President, to elect members of the Committee and enlist subscribers to the Union. These things will take time.'

'*We* were punctual,' said Miss Farmer.

Rosalind did not even look at her. The moment had come to address the meeting.

'I take it that we are all agreed as to the main issue, that we have not come here to convert each other, that we all want Women's Franchise, that we all mean to have it, that we are all prepared to work for it, and, if necessary, to fight for it, to oppose the Government that withholds it by every means in our power –'

'By ever constitutional means,' Miss Burstall amended, and was told by Miss Gilchrist that, if she desired proceedings to be regular, she must not interrupt the Chairwoman.

'– To oppose the Government that refuses us the vote, whatever Government it may be, regardless of party, by *every means in our power.*'

Rosalind's sentences were punctuated by a rhythmic sound of tapping. Miss Maud Blackadder, twisted sideways on the chair she had pushed farther and farther back from the table, so as to bring herself completely out of line with the other seven, from time to time, rhythmically, twitching with impatience, struck her own leg with her own walking-stick.

Rosalind perorated. 'If we differ, we differ, not as to our end, but solely as to the means we, personally and individually, are prepared to employ.' She looked round. 'Agreed?'

'Not agreed,' said Dorothy and Miss Burstall and Miss Farmer all at once.

'I will now call on Miss Maud Blackadder to speak. She will explain to those of you who are strangers' (she glanced comprehensively at the eleven young girls) 'the present programme of the Union.'

'I protest,' said Miss Burstall. 'There has been confusion.'

'There really *has*, Rosalind,' said Dorothy. 'You *must* get it straight. You can't start all at sixes and sevens. I protest too.'

'We all three protest,' said Miss Farmer, frowning and blinking in an agony of protest.

'Silence, if you please, for the Chairwoman,' said Miss Gilchrist. 'May we not say one word?'

'You may,' said Rosalind, 'in your turn. I now call on Miss Blackadder to speak.'

At the sound of her own name Miss Blackadder jumped to her feet. The walking-stick fell to the floor with a light clatter and crash, preluding her storm. She jerked out her words at a headlong pace, as if to make up for the time the others had wasted in futilities.

'I am not going to say much, I am not going to take up your time. Too much time has been lost already. I am not a speaker, I am not a writer, I am not an intellectual woman, and if you ask me what I am and what I am here for, and what I am doing in the Union, and what the Union is doing for me, and what possible use I, an untrained girl, can be to you clever women' (she looked tempestuously at Miss Burstall and Miss Farmer who did not flinch), 'I will tell you. I am a fighter. I am here to enlist volunteers. I am the recruiting sergeant for this district. That is the use my leaders, who should be *your* leaders, are making of *me*.'

Her head was thrown back, her body swayed, rocked from side to side with the violent rhythm of her speech.

'If you ask me why they have chosen *me*, I will tell you. It's because I know what I want and because I know how to get what I want.

'I know what I want. Oh, yes, you think that's nothing; you all think you know what you want. But do you? *Do* you?'

'Of course we do!'

'We want the vote!'

'Nothing but the vote!'

'*Nothing but?* Are you quite sure of that? Can you even say you want it till you know whether there are things you want more?'

'What are you driving at?'

'You'll soon see what I'm driving at. I drive straight. And I ride straight. And I don't funk my fences.

'Well – say you all want the vote. Do you know how much you want it? Do you know how much you want to pay for it? Do you know what you're prepared to give up for it? Because, if you don't know *that*, you don't know how much you want it.'

'We want it as much as you do, I imagine.'

'You want it as much as I do? Good. *Then* you're going to pay the price whatever the price is. *Then* you're ready to give up everything else, your homes and your families and your friends and your incomes. Until you're enfranchised you are not going to own any *man* as father, or brother, or husband' (her voice rang with a deeper and stronger vibration), 'or lover, or friend. And the man who does not agree with you, the man who refuses you the vote, the man who opposes your efforts to get the vote, the man who, whether he agrees with you or not, *will not help you to get it*, you count as your enemy. That is wanting the vote. That is wanting it as much as I do.

'You women – are you prepared to go against your men? To give up your men?'

There were cries of 'Rather!' from two of the eleven young girls who had come too soon.

Miss Burstall shook her head and murmured, 'Hopeless confusion of thought. If *this* is what it's going to be like, heaven help us!'

'You really *are* getting a bit mixed,' said Dorothy.

'We protest –'

'Protest then; protest as much as you like. Then we shall know where we are; then we shall get things straight; then we can begin. You all want the vote. Some of you don't know how much, but at least you know you want it. Nobody's confused about that. Do you know how you're going to get it? Tell me that.'

Lest they should spoil it all by telling her, Miss Blackadder increased her vehement pace. 'You don't because you can't, and *I* will tell you. You won't get it by talking about it or by writing about it, or by sitting down and thinking about it; you'll get it by coming in with me, coming in with the Women's Franchise Union, and fighting for it. Fighting women, not talkers – not writers – not thinkers are what we want!'

She sat down, heaving a little with the ground-swell of her storm, amid applause in which only Miss Burstall and Miss Farmer did not join. She was now looking extraordinarily handsome.

Rosalind bent over and whispered something in her ear. She rose to her feet again, flushed, smiling at them, triumphant.

'Our Chairwoman has reminded me that I came here to tell you what the programme of our Union is. And I can tell you in six words. It's Hell-for-leather, and it's Neck-or-nothing!'

'Now,' said Rosalind sweetly, bowing towards Miss Burstall, 'it's your turn. We should like to know what you have to say.'

Miss Burstall did not rise. And in the end Dorothy spoke.

'My friend, Miss Rosalind Jervis, assumed that we were all agreed, not only as to our aims, but as to our policy. She has not yet discriminated between constitutional and unconstitutional means. When we protested she quashed our protest. We took exception to the phrase "every means in our power," because that would commit us to all sorts of unconstitutional things. It is in my power to squirt water into the back of the Prime Minister's neck, or to land a bomb in the small of his back, or in the centre of the platform at his next public meeting. We were left to conclude that the only differences between us would concern our choice of the squirt or the bomb. As some of us here might equally object to using the bomb or the squirt, I submit that either our protest should have been allowed or our agreement should not have been taken for granted at the start.

'Again, Miss Maud Blackadder, in her sporting speech, her heroic speech, has not cleared the question. She has appealed to us to come in, without counting the cost; but she has said nothing to convince us that when our account at our bank is overdrawn, and we have declared war on all our male friends and relations, and have left our comfortable homes, and are all camping out on the open Heath – I repeat, she has said nothing to convince us that the price we shall have paid is going to get us the thing we want.

'She says that fighters are wanted, and not talkers and writers and thinkers. Are we not then to fight with our tongues and with our brains? Is she leaving us anything but our bare fists? She has told us that she rides straight and that she doesn't funk her fences; but she has not told us what sort of country she is going to ride over, nor where the fences are, nor what Hell-for-leather and Neck-or-nothing means.

'We want meaning; we want clearness and precision. We have not been given it yet.

'I would let all this pass if Miss Blackadder were not your colour-sergeant. Is it fair to call for volunteers, for raw recruits, and not tell them precisely and clearly what services will be required of them? How many' (Dorothy glanced at the eleven) 'realise that the leaders of your Union, Mrs. Palmerston-Swete, and Mrs. Blathwaite, and Miss Angela Blathwaite, demand from its members blind, unquestioning obedience?'

Maud Blackadder jumped up.

'I protest. I, too, have the right to protest. Miss Harrison calls me to order. She tells me to be clear and precise. Will she be good enough to be clear and precise herself? Will she say whether she is with us or against us? If she is not with us she *is* against us. Let her explain her position.'

She sat down; and Rosalind rose.

'Miss Harrison,' she said, 'will explain her position to the Committee later. This is an open meeting till seven. It is now five minutes to. Will any of you here' – she held the eleven with her eyes – 'who were not present at the meeting in the Town Hall last Monday, hold up your hands? No hands. Then you must all be aware of the object and the policy and the rules of the Women's Franchise Union. Its members pledge themselve to help, as far as they can, the object of the Union; to support the decisions of their leaders; to abstain from public and private criticism of those decisions and of any words or actions of their leaders; and to obey orders – not blindly or unquestioningly, but within the terms of their undertakings.

'Those of you who wish to join us will please write your names and addresses on the slips of white paper, stating what kind of work you are willing to do, and the amount of your subscription, if you subscribe, and hand your slips to the Secretary at the door, as you go out.'

Miss Burstall and Miss Farmer went out. Miss Blackadder counted – 'One – two –'

Eight of the eleven young girls signed and handed in the white slips at the door, and went out.

'Three – four –'

Miss Blackadder reckoned that Dorothea Harrison's speech had cost her five recruits. Her own fighting speech had carried the eleven in a compact body to her side: Dorothea's speech had divided and scattered them again.

Miss Blackadder hurled her personality at the heads of audiences in the certainty that it would hit them hard. That was what she was there for. She knew that the Women's Franchise Union relied on her to wring from herself the utmost spectacular effect. And she did it every time. She never once missed fire. And Dorothea Harrison had come down on the top of her triumph and destroyed the effect of all her fire. She had corrupted five recruits. And supposing there *was* a secret programme she had betrayed the women of the Union to four-teen outsiders, by giving it away. Treachery or no treachery, Dorothea Harrison would have to pay for it.

Everybody had gone except the members of the Committee and Phyllis Desmond, who waited for her friend, Maud Blackadder.

Dorothy remembered Phyllis Desmond now; she was that art-student girl that Vera knew. She had seen her at Vera's house.

They had drawn round the table again. Miss Blackadder and Miss Gilchrist conferred in whispers.

'Before we go,' said Rosalind, 'I propose that we ask Miss Dorothea Harrison to be our Vice-President.'

Miss Gilchrist nodded to Miss Blackadder, who rose. It was her moment.

'And *I* propose,' she said, 'that before we invite Miss Harrison to be anything, we ask her to define her position – clearly and precisely.'

She made a sign, and the Secretary was on her feet.

'And first we must ask Miss Harrison to explain *how* she became possessed of the secret policy of the Union which has never been discussed of the General Committee.'

'Then,' said Dorothy, 'there *is* a secret policy?'

'You seem to know it. We have the right to ask *how* you know. Unless you invented it.'

Dorothy faced them. It was inconceivable that it should have happened, that she should be standing there, in the old schoolroom of her father's house, while two strange women worried her. She knew that her back was to the wall and that the Blackadder girl had been on the watch for the last half-hour to get her knife into her. (Odd, for she had admired the Blackadder girl and her fighting gestures.) It was inconceivable that she should have to answer to that absurd committee for her honour. It was inconceivable that Rosalind, her friend, should not help her.

Yet it had happened. With all her platform eloquence Rosalind couldn't, for the life of her, get out one heroic, defending word. From the moment when the Gilchrist woman had pounced, Rosalind had simply sat and stared, like a rabbit, like a fish, her mouth open for the word that would not come. Rosalind was afraid to stand up for her. It was dreadful, and it was funny to see Rosalind looking like that, and to realise the extent of her weakness and her obstinacy.

Yet Rosalind had not changed. She was still the school-girl slacker who could never do a stroke of work until somebody had pushed her into it, who could never leave off working until stopped by the same hand that had set her going. Her power to go, and to let herself rip, and the weakness that made her depend on Dorothy to start her were the qualities that attracted Dorothy to Rosalind from the beginning. But now she was the tool of the fighting Suffrage Women. Or if she wasn't a tool, she was a machine; her brain was a rapid, docile, mechanical apparatus for turning out bad imitations of Mrs. Palmerston-Swete and the two Blathwaites. Her air of casual command, half-swagger, half-slouch, her stoop and the thrusting forward of her face, were copied sedulously from an admired model.

Dorothy found her pitiable. She was hypnotised by the Blathwaites, who worked her and would throw her away when she was of no more use. She hadn't the strength to resist the pull and the grip and the drive of other people. She couldn't even hold out against Valentina Gilchrist and Maud Blackadder. Rosalind would always be caught and spun round by any movement that was strong enough. She was foredoomed to the Vortex.

That was Dorothy's fault. It was she who had pushed and pulled the slacker, in spite of her almost whining protest, to the edge of the Vortex; and it was Rosalind, not Dorothy, who had been caught and sucked down into the swirl. She whirled in it now, and would go on whirling, under the impression that her movements made it move.

The Vortex fascinated Dorothy even while she resisted it. She liked the feeling of her own power to resist, to keep her head, to beat up against the rush of the whirlwind, to wheel round and round outside it, and swerve away before the thing got her.

For Dorothy was afraid of the Feminist Vortex, as her brother Michael had been afraid of the little vortex of school. She was afraid of the herded women. She disliked the excited faces, and the high voices skirling their battle-cries, and the silly business of committees, and the platform slang. She was sick and shy before the tremor and the surge of collective feeling; she loathed the gestures and the movements of the collective soul, the swaying and heaving and rushing forward of the many as one. She would not be carried away by it; she would keep the clearness and hardness of her soul. It was her soul they wanted, these women of the Union, the Blathwaites and the Palmerston-Swetes, and Rosalind, and the Blackadder girl and the Gilchrist woman; they ran out after her like a hungry pack yelping for her soul; and she was not going to throw it to them. She would fight for freedom, but not in their way and not at their bidding.

A. N. Chew, 'Mrs Stubbs on Militancy'

Ada Nield Chew, an extremely active suffragist and trade unionist, published many pieces of journalism which included a series based around the opinions of Mrs Stubbs, a fictional farmer's wife. This deceptively 'commonsensical' description of militancy first appeared in *The Common Cause*, the paper of the NUWSS.

A bright spring day was drawing to its close. The sun went down behind gathering clouds, and the westernly wind, which at noon-day had tempered the sun's rays, had now a keen edge and conveyed more than a hint of a coming midnight storm. It was nearing the 12th of May, and by that time Mr. Stubbs, like all good farmers, liked to have his year's potato crop underground, well planted and manured. To-day, every available person had been pressed into service, and even the small hands of the children had placed many potatoes at the requisite point of distribution in the even rows of ploughed earth, receiving a reward of a penny per row for their labours. Now the last seedling had been put in and covered, and the coming storm was viewed with complacency. Potato planting is back-aching work, however, and the settle beside the fire had an even more than ordinarily inviting look.

The milk had been duly despatched on its evening rounds, and Mrs. Stubbs' batch of golden loaves decorated the dresser, bearing testimony to the busy use of her hands during the day which some of us had spent in the fields. Those same hands were now clicking the knitting needles – putting new feet on Mr. Stubbs' stockings. In that big kitchen, even when the lamp is lit, it is too dim in the late evening to sew or to read, except near the lamp, and that is sacred to Mr. Stubbs, who looks upon the evening paper and the lamp as his special prerogative. To-night there was as yet only the fire-light, for Mr. Stubbs was out 'bedding' such of the livestock as was as yet housed indoors. Some of us were glad of an excuse to be idle; and

Mrs. Stubbs can knit just as well in the dark as in the daylight, which is lucky, seeing that she says she could never get through her week's work if she wasted a minute of time.

A lifelong friend of Mrs. Stubbs and of my own, who once lived in the village, but who is now earning her living in a big city, was on holiday and had come in for a chat. She is a dear gentle creature to whom it would give pain to hurt a fly. That she is also a militant Suffragist is one of those queer anomalies to which time accustoms us. I long ago ceased arguing with her about militancy, and am content to enjoy and to count myself blessed in her friendship, but I rather anticipated hearing Mrs. Stubbs' views of militant tactics – which I knew would come before long.

It was the village cobbler, who called to bring home some shoes which he had had for mending, who started the theme.

'So tha't none i' prison, wench,' he said to my friend, with the familiarity of one who has known one in long clothes. 'Eaw's that? Owd Jinkins towd me as tha belunged to the winder-smashin' lot; and sin' then A've leawked every mornin' i' th'paper to seigh if tha'd done owt. It gives yer an interest in it, when someb'dy as yer know's gooin' to be copped.'

'Ay,' said Mrs Stubbs. 'Eau is it, Mary wench, as tha'rt loose yet?'

'Because I'm a coward,' was the reply. 'I haven't courage enough to do what so many brave women are doing. Some day, perhaps.'

Mrs. Stubbs gave her a look of which the kindliness could be felt as well as seen. 'Nay, nay, Mary,' said she. 'Dunna be tragic. Sey tha's too much sense to get ta'en up. What good is it goin' to dow thee to goo to prison? What good does it ever do anybody t'goo to prison, for that matter? Tha rowins thi own 'ealth, an'tha owds wimmin up for a spectikkle – as kneauin' noo better thin men. Prisons an bin made bi men, an' loike most things as they'n tried to make beaut wimmin, they're noo good to nobody!'

'But don't you see,' said Mary, 'that's not it. We can't get attended to unless we damage property; and property's so sacred that doing that soon gets us into their man-made prisons. We are not responsible for their prisons, or for getting into them.'

'Neaw, that strikes mae as bein' soft,' said Mrs Stubbs. 'To sey you anna responsible for your own acts is to put yersels on a level wi' childer an' lunatics; an' to say yo canna get attention beaut gooin' to prison is just as soft. Yo dunna get attended to if yo dun break winders . . .'

'But look what a furore we've created,' said Mary, eagerly. 'We're the talk of the country.'

'Ay, of course!' said Mrs. Stubbs, drily. 'If that's what yo caw'n gettin' attended to, yo've got what yo' waanted. Anybody as waants to get to prison con get theer if they tri'en. Thur's noo special distinction i' that. What are yo' meightherin' abeaut then if yo'n got what yo' waanted? A thought it was votes yo wan after.'

'You know it is,' was the reproachful reply. 'Whoever heard of our agitation until we begin to go to prison?'

'Moost on us arna deaf an' bleent, and as tek'n any interest in what's gooin' on,' said Mrs. Stubbs. 'But it strikes mae as rather a 'opeless task yo'n taken on, if yo'n got to keep dowin' mooar an' mooar damidge just for keep fooaks talkin' abeaut it. What's the good on 'em talkin' abeaut settin' fire to 'eauses – that doesna bring votes no nearer. Men lik'n that sooart o' stuff, bless yer, an' dunna care eaw lung yo' keep'n it up. They'd any time sooner talk abeaut damidge an' destruction than abeaut dowin' summat sensible. Men an' lads an allis leave work to watch a feight. A'm surprised at wimmin playin' up to 'em like they are dowin', an' givin' 'em an excuse for dowin' what any wimmin ought to put deawn as much as we can. It's hard enuf for an ordinary woman to keep that soide of a man bottom-soide up i' ordinary everyday loife. Give 'em an excuse to feight an' to punish an' they'n keep on for ever, but that's aw yo'n get eaut on 'em.'

'But they did nothing before!' said Mary. 'We have at least made ourselves an annoyance to them.'

'Aye,' said Mrs. Stubbs, 'if aw yo' waant'n is to plague 'em, yo' con done that, o' coorse. Any woman as waants to raise the devil in a mon con dow it. Bur th' devil's noo good if yo' waant things mended. Ea's on'y good at destruction. If Mestur Stubbs is bent on dowin' summat as A know will do us noo good, A mak' up me mind theer an' then as it shanner be done. Bur A dunna begin bi werritin' un an' makin' 'is loife a misery to 'im. An' if eawr Joe, as is gettin' a big 'un neaw, an' thinks 'e knows mooar thin 'is feyther an' mother put together, talks abeaut doin' summat soft loike gooin' for a sojer or a sailor, A dunna start cawin' 'im a bad lad, an' makin' im 'ate the sight o' me; nor A dunna dow as 'is feyther is a bit too ready at – lickin' 'im into shape wi' the strap – thur's better ways thin them, lass!'

'But they're degrading ways!' was the passionate reply. 'We don't believe in wheedling. Women should be ashamed of getting what they want by coaxing.'

''Ere, 'ere!' said Mrs. Stubbs, as her husband came in, and took up his place in the armchair by the lamp. 'Noobody seighs mae wheedlin' an' coaxin', neether John 'Ennery nor the lads.'

'Neaw!' broke in Mr. Stubbs. 'Th' only toime tha wheedled an' coaxed was when tha was persuadin' mae t' 'ave thee. Bur tha's none done so much of it sin', by gow! Bur they're all loike that, arna they, Mestur Smith?' to the cobbler. The cobbler looked at Mrs. Stubbs with a laugh.

'Nay,' said she to him. 'Tha darsna say that's true. Ever'body as' as lived lung enuf i' this village knows as John Ennery Stubbs was the soft un, when wea were courtin'. It was 'im as did the wheedlin' an' coaxin'! Bur tha'll never get what tha waant, wench,' to Mary, 'bu feightin' men wi' their own weapons. A dunna feight my lot, but they'n any of 'em confess in their sensible minutes as A know what's best for us as well as they dun, an' it's just as well to know what A think abeaut it before they dun anything fresh!'

'Aye,' said Mr. Smith. 'Wea aw know aa Mrs. Stubbs' husband an' lads are generally glad enuf to dow what 'er waants. Eauw does 'er manage it, Mestur Stubbs?'

Mr. Stubbs scratched his head.

'Nay, A dunna know,' he said, after a short pause. 'But if A goo me oown way it allis turns eawt wrong; an' if 'er says "dow it" it turns eawt right. Soo A should be a foo' to tek no notice on 'er, shouldna A?'

'Ah,' Mary said, 'that's all right. But we have such awful tyrants to deal with.'

Mrs. Stubbs looked at her with an understanding kindliness, as she said gently, 'Nay, that's where tha makes a mistake, Mary. What's the good o' uz wimmin treatin' men as if they wan eaur enemies? They arna. They're eaur children, an' we're responsible for 'em. If my lads an noo respect for wimmin, it'll be becos A avna respected wimmin myself. Wea'n got to bring men to that frame o' mind when they'n be ashamed o' keepin' us eaut o' votin'. Bur your methods puts their minds off votin' awtogether, an' on'y stops 'em from seighing what's right. 'Ere am A, tellin' my lads as feightin' is on'y fur savidges, an' as 'uman beins ought to know better than to feight; an' then wimmin must start the same game! You're behind the toimes, Mary wench; feightin's eaut o' date on'y fur young lads an' for men as dunna know no better.'

T. Billington-Greig, *The Militant Suffrage Movement: emancipation in a hurry*

Withdrawing from the WSPU at an early stage, Teresa Billington-Greig published this critique of militant suffragism in 1911, attacking militancy as a strategy and accusing the Pankhursts of establishing an emotional tyranny.

I do not believe in the modern militant suffrage movement. I have believed in it, worked in it, suffered in it, and rejoiced in it, and I have been disillusioned. I do not believe in votes for women as a panacea of all evils. I do not believe that any and every interest and consideration and principle should be sacrificed to the immediate getting of any measure of suffrage legislation. Votes for women we must have, and many other things for women; but votes for women over-hurried and at any price may cost us too dear. I do not believe that woman is the superior of man any more than I believe that she is his inferior. Pretensions of sex-superiority are like bad coins; they are just as bad whichever face is turned up. I do not believe that the best avenue for the emancipation of women is through emotionalism, personal tyranny, and fanaticism. To none of these things do I subscribe.

I am setting out to condemn the militant suffrage movement, but not to condemn militancy, for I shall be a militant rebel to the end of my days. I am setting out to expose the tone and tactics of the Women's Social and Political Union and the suicidal weakness of the Women's Freedom League. I have served in both these societies, have shared the burdens of the early days in both, have had my part in their successes and in their failures, and now I find both inadequate, fallen from a high estate full of promise to narrowness and incapacity. I do not condemn the present day militancy because it has gone too far. I fear that it has not gone far enough, and that it will never rise to the heights to which it originally showed potential claim. What I condemn in militant tactics is the small pettiness, the crooked course, the double shuffle between revolution and injured innocence, the playing for effects and not for results – in short, the exploitation of revolutionary forces and enthusiastic women for the purposes of advertisement. These are the things by which militancy has been degraded from revolution into political chicane; these are the means by which it has been led to perjure its soul: it is against these evils that I mean to use the whole strength of my power of protest. I am not at all concerned that the militant movement has outraged convention, that it has shocked self-satisfied and blind benevolence, that it has made the exquisite and dainty suffer pangs of revulsion against sordid realities; it is not for convention that I plead. The crime of the militant suffrage movement in my eyes is that it is not real, that it is itself dangerously and determinedly conventional, that its militancy claims to be but is not revolution, that it has given itself over to the demon of hurry and has abused the great cleansing forces by means of which the world is carried into purgatorial fires and brought out purified. Other movements have failed in rebellion, but it has been left to this woman's movement to ape rebellion while belittling and abusing it. Other rebellions have failed; this movement has failed rebellion.

. . .

The sudden rehabilitation of October changed this outlook at once. It began to appear as though women and the world were riper for advance than we had dreamed. We held out our hands to the acknowledgment we had never counted upon, and felt the sudden promise of the dawn. And almost before we had uttered our thanks for the unexpected lifting of our burden we knew that it was a false promise, a mistaken acceptance, not a dawn but a mirage. We had won a new position indeed, but one full of dangers.

We were now met with unhealthy hero-worship and exaggerated devotion. New members tended to worship us rather than to understand and co-operate with us. The Press found sudden explanations for, and extenuations of, our unruly conduct. The pose of propriety was made almost inevitable by the obvious shock of surprise which showed itself when we were beheld in the social circles that had been barred against us. 'These militant suffragettes are actually ladies!' was the gasping cry; and straightway most of us became ladies again, and the rebel woman was veneered over or given hasty burial.

The chorus of approval and excuse brought out another weakness: it confirmed in us the pose of martyrdom of which we had been rather ashamed until then, and it strengthened that curious mental and moral duplicity which allowed us to engineer an outbreak and then lay the burden of its results upon the authorities. The final responsibility of the Government for women continuing unenfranchised is quite another thing from that special and detailed responsibility which had been placed upon the shoulders of the Ministry after the first protest and which had come to follow each successive one. The Government holds the key of legislation; but it is expected also to administer the laws, and those who deliberately set out to break laws, even for the good reason that they are urgent to share in making them, cannot expect immunity. Women who are out to fight organised authority are rebels, and they should never forget the fact; they should stand frankly forth as rebels; they should confine their attacks upon the enemy to the primary cause of revolt and should not belittle their final object and descend to prevarication by making a grievance of every response to their disorder. This is a particularly pernicious course when at the same time it is frankly admitted that the movement lives and grows by its outbreaks. Under these circumstances the only course consonant with self-respect is for the rebels to admit their own responsibility for the disorder and to take the consequences.

The feeling within the Union against this double shuffle, this game of quick change from the garments of the rebel to those of the innocent martyr, was swamped by the public approval and extenuation of our protests. We were too speedily rehabilitated; we were exonerated before we had declared ourselves. We were accepted into respectable circles not as rebels but as innocent victims, and as innocent victims we were led to pose. If we had frankly and strongly stated that we had set out to make the Government imprison us, that we had deliberately chosen just those lines of protest and disorder that would irritate those in authority into foolish retaliation, if we had told the truth, the very proper persons who became our champions would have spent many weary months and years in condemning us before they had finally realised the value and intention of our efforts.

Under these influences of rehabilitation the movement became conventionalised and narrowed and hypocritical. We were accepted for what we were not, and immediately began to live up – or down – to the standard expected of us. There came to be one speech for the council chamber and another for the platform; the propaganda of the society suffered a sudden loss of breadth; the industrial evils which had formed the basis of much of our appeal were gradually pushed aside for the consideration of technical, legal, and political grievances; the advocacy of reformed sex-relations was reduced to the vaguest generalities, and even these were discouraged; the working-class women were dropped without hesitation and the propaganda of the organisation confined to the middle and upper classes; the 'advanced' women, an eminently undesirable class in a socially superior society, were even more speedily driven out or silenced.

. . .

The Women's Social and Political Union now depends upon personal dominance for its existence. The leaders impose a yoke of emotional control by which the very virtues of the members are exploited; they produce a system of mental and spiritual slavery. The women who succumb to it exhibit a type of self-subjection, not less objectionable than the more ordinary self-subjection of women to men, to which it bears a close relation. The yoke is imposed by a mingling of elements of deliberately worked up emotion, by the exercise of affectional and personal charm, by an all-pervading system of mutual glorification in which each of the three leaders by turn sounds the praises of the others, by the deliberate exclusion of other women from all positions of prominence, by a policy of shameless boasting and booming, by an ingenious system of clever special pleading through which everything the Political Union does is chronicled and magnified, and everything that other suffragists do is belittled or ignored, and by that undoubted financial and political stage management which caters for all the elements of snobbery and narrowness and intolerance, while employing the language of outlaws in revolt. This obsession is one of the most remarkable manifestations to be seen in the political life of to-day. As with all emotional degradations, its victims glory in it. Every woman snared ensnares her fellow and adds the weight of her obsession to the burden upon the minds of the rest. Under this direction the militant movement is a movement of political revivalism – that, and nothing more.

The individual members of this society are not the only suffragists affected. The bad influence is strong enough to affect all. Though the Political Union at the worst is insolently and brutally indifferent to the rights of other societies, and at the best scornfully tolerant of them, these other societies yield to its pretensions at the cost of their own progress. The National Union of Suffrage Societies at first made a practice of repudiation after every militant demonstration, but this has died down. To quote a well-known suffragist politician, it has been found that it does not pay. The amazing protest of November last, prior to the Dissolution – which appeared to have nothing to recommend it, and seriously hampered progress along the only avenue of advance open at that time – was merely commented upon adversely in the editorial notes of *The Common Cause*. The necessary public exposure of the folly of militant action at that juncture was not forthcoming. The Freedom League officials dared to defend their abstention – and the most assertive section of their members rose in arms.

In this particular society the obsession has acted in three ways: It has limited and restricted militant action to the lines approved in practice by the WSPU – every deviation from the political lines of protest employed by Mrs. Pankhurst having been criticised or boycotted to death; it has applied the same rule of weak imitation to the general election policy; and it has insisted upon the suppression of any murmur of dissent from the decrees of Clement's Inn. The attitude of its members towards the Police Court protests, the Bermondsey protest, and the Tax-Resistance movement, as well as the inconsistency in the policies applied by the League in the January and December elections, can all be quoted in support of the statement that the Freedom League has neglected the first law of self-preservation, and has destroyed its own potentialities by a policy of weak imitation and weaker adulation.

In part the suffrage societies that have suffered from this disease have been impressed by the smart methods and the noise and rush and the poses of omnipotence and revolution; in part they have yielded because they have found that protest not only failed to secure redress of grievances, but rather intensified the loss to be endured; and in part they have submitted because of the fear of harming the suffrage cause in the public eye by exposing the disunion that existed. A show of peace has thus been preserved in the suffrage world, but it has been the sort of peace preserved in many households where one member of the family is a bully and the rest for the sake of name and blood are constrained to hide their injuries, and to put a fair face upon an unhappy condition.

The cultivation of personal dominance by the leaders of the Political Union is not an unconscious or accidental happening. It is deliberate. It finds its origin in a determination to win early results, in egotism, and in an experience that has bred distrust in the majority of other women. Before the militant movement began Mrs. Pankhurst laboured long among women who could be, and had been, deceived by party leaders or cajoled by husband, brother, or son; and she has come to believe that the only honest and independent feminism is the feminism that agrees with her, accepts her leadership, and is prepared to submit conscience and principles to her dictation. Only those women are to be trusted who can be dominated and controlled. She and her co-adjutors are convinced that they are capable of carrying the suffrage movement to victory; they believe that other women admitted to the inner councils will only interfere with the carrying out of their plans; they believe that the spirit of unquestioning submission in the mass of members is preferable to voting rights and free discussion because it is the only condition which will give them complete and continuous control of the machine by which their desires can be realised. They do not believe that any other women in the world are to be trusted with a share of the power and direction of the movement, and they are determined to take no risks with colleagues, with constitutions, or with loyalty. They believe in themselves – a most commendable thing to do in reason – but they believe in themselves in a way which destroys their belief in other women, and this is neither admirable nor wise. I do not want to magnify the evil of this distrust. I have not a great deal of trust in either men or women in the mass myself, but I have less trust in the leaders of the mass. There is far more danger of corruption and one-sidedness, of narrowness and final shipwreck in absolutely unlimited autocracy than in the stupidest forms of democracy. And the choice in this movement was not between the one and the other; there were middle ways open for use, which would have provided a wide discretion for the leaders and the right of some share of control for the members; but these were rejected. The clean sweep of machinery was the only thing which would give the trinitarian group unlimited power, and the clean sweep of machinery it had to be.

H. Swanwick, *I Have Been Young*

Although a committed suffragist Helena Swanwick disap-
proved of what she saw as the disruptiveness and divisiveness
of militant tactics. Resigning as editor of *The Common Cause*
because she was unable to express her strong opinions on militancy, she uses her autobiography to re-state her case.

My impressions of the 'Militants,' as they were called, deepened and
widened, but more and more I realized that their ways were not for
me. I attended many of their meetings and reported a good many. A
considerable number of my friends were among them. So that, right
or wrong, my opinion was founded upon knowledge. Though I had
not personally known any of the Pankhurst family, I had lived in
Manchester long enough to know a good deal about them;
Christabel had been at the University. I had a great admiration for
Mrs. Pankhurst, whose eloquence came from the deep heart of
womanhood and put into burning words what millions of women
must have inarticulately felt for centuries. For – let there be no
mistake about it – this movement was not primarily political; it was
social, moral, psychological and profoundly religious.

This little woman, not young, with tragic smouldering eyes, a
deep voice and a Lancashire burr (I can still hear her cry 'Join uzz!')
could play upon her audience with untaught art that comes from
passionate sincerity and passionate courage. I heard her often, and
I never found her dull, until a melancholy night in 1915, when the
ghost of the woman she had been talked unbelievable nonsense
about Germans at a Queen's Hall meeting. There was a man there,
I remember, who maintained that the stewards at Liberal meetings
between 1906 and 1914 had been 'Huns.' 'You will remember,' he
roared, 'with what brutality these stewards treated the women?'
Then, after a dramatic pause, he leant forward and snarled, 'It was
not for nothing that they spoke with a foreign accent and in a guttural tongue.' Mrs. Pankhurst nodded approval. I was so startled by
this absurdity that I let out a shout of laughter. But the audience
turned on me with a shocked 'Hush!' I had brawled in church.
Nothing was, at that time, too fantastic to be believed against
Germans.

I felt some admiration for Christabel's impudence and quick wit.
She was particularly agile at question time, but her accounts of

things had little relation to facts. She seemed to me a lonely person; with all her capacity for winning adorers (women and men) with all the brightness of her lips and cheeks and eyes, she was, unlike her sisters, cynical and cold at heart. She gave me the impression of fitful and impulsive ambition and of quite ruthless love of domination. I used to find many of her speeches silly: heaven was to come down on earth, sweating to be abandoned, venereal diseases to disappear, eternal peace to reign. Meanwhile, she created the atmosphere of a dog-fight. There grew up by degrees, the insolence of dictatorship.

Sylvia was more interesting. She was essentially an artist, drawn into the unsuitable and unsympathetic political machine. Martyrdom, in itself, attracted her, and she would go great lengths in inviting it. She was a very provoking colleague, owing to her habit of going her own separate way, even after she had joined others in hammering out an agreed way. There might have been give and take, and they would, perhaps, loyally carry out the agreed compromise, only to find that, like one of the hoops in 'Alice's' game of croquet, Sylvia had wandered off to another part of the field. She was, however, more lovable than Christabel and her devotion to the people with whom she was later to make her home in the East-end of London was beautiful.

Certain of the militants were *Frondeuses*, and they made a policy of martyrdom. This was deeply repugnant to me. If derision, persecution, martyrdom come to one by reason of what conscience compels one to do, or say, one must take them in one's stride. But to say: 'the world is vulgar and must have sensation before it will take notice, therefore we must have martyrs, and if authority refuses to make martyrs of us, we will provoke martyrdom' – this strikes me as dishonest and cynical. Dishonest because it is 'faked' martyrdom, cynical because it attempts to base a reform not upon right reason but upon ballyhoo. It has often been said that, anyhow, it was the militant suffragettes and not the constitutional suffragists who won the vote. There are many more comments to be made on that than I have room for here. But I would claim for Mrs. Fawcett's great Union, not only her devoted record of over half a century's persistent toil, but its fruits in a national membership far exceeding in numbers that of the militant societies and an income from gifts, in the year 1912, of £42,000. Without that long, steady controlled pressure, there would have been no deep cultivation of public opinion.

. . .

Whatever admiration and cordiality there might be between individuals, the attitude of the militant leaders towards us was one of uncivil contempt. Like all moderate parties, we were kicked on both sides and, while we had to endure the stones and offal which were frequently hurled at us on their account, we were constantly told by wobbly politicians that they could no longer support us unless we somehow stopped the militants. Another favourite imbecility was the declaration that they could do nothing 'until you women all unite' (as if men had ever 'all united' about anything!) To this Mrs. Fawcett's answer was 'Yes? Shall we all break windows or shall we all not break windows?'

C. Hamilton, *William – an Englishman*

> Published in 1919, the author Cicely Hamilton herself described this as 'really a "suffrage novel"', dating its inspiration from 'a gathering where I heard certain members of the militant section hold forth on the subject of their "war". Most politicians indulge in exaggerated speech and the suffragettes are no exception to the rule' (*Life Errant*, p. 84). On their honeymoon in Belgium and unaware of the outbreak of the First World War, the supposedly radical activists Griselda and William are confronted with the realities of militarism.

A man stepped suddenly out from behind the shifting horses – so suddenly that they both started. He had been standing by the gate with the bridles gathered in his hand, hidden by his charges from William and Griselda as they had been hidden from him. When, hearing their voices, he stepped into sight, he stood with his heels together, very erect and staring at them – a young man squarely and sturdily built, with under his helmet a reddish face and a budding black moustache. He was clad in a tight-fitting greyish uniform, and a sword hung by his side. He stared and the pair stared back at him – curiously but not quite so openly.

'It's a soldier,' Griselda commented – adding, like William, 'I wonder –' They both wondered so much that they hesitated and slackened their pace; the presence of a military man but complicated the problem of the farm. Coupled with the absence of the Peys family, it revived their suspicions of the night before, their suspicions of crime and a hasty flight from justice . . . and involuntarily their eyes turned to the garden, and sought the outline of the grave beyond the gooseberry bushes.

'It really does look,' Griselda whispered, 'as if there was something – not right.'

As she whispered the soldier rapped out a loud monosyllable; it was enunciated so curtly and sharply that they started for the second time and came to an involuntary halt. For the space of a second or two they stood open-mouthed and flustered – and then Griselda, recovering from the shock, expressed her indignant opinion.

'How rude!' she said. 'What does he shout at us like that for?'

'I suppose,' her husband conjectured, 'he wants us to stop.'

'Well,' said Griselda, 'we have stopped.' Her tone was nettled and embittered. It annoyed her to realize that, involuntarily and instinctively, she had obeyed an official order; it was not, she felt, what her Leaders would expect from a woman of her training and calibre. It was that and not fear that disconcerted her – for, after the first shock of surprise at the man's rough manner, neither she nor her husband were in the least overawed; on the contrary, as they stood side by side with their baggage in their hands, gazing into the sunburnt face of the soldier, something of the contempt they felt for his species was reflected in their light-blue eyes. Of the two pairs of light-blue eyes William's perhaps were the more contemptuous: his anti-militarism was more habitual and ingrained than Griselda's.

What William looked at was a creature (the soldier) of whom he knew little and talked much; his experience of the man of war was purely insular, and his attitude towards him would have been impossible in any but a native of Britain. He came of a class – the English lower middle – which the rules of caste and tradition of centuries debarred from the bearing of arms; a class which might, in this connection, have adapted to its own needs the motto of the House of Rohan. 'Roi ne puis; prince ne daigne; Rohan je suis,' might have been suitably englished in the mouths of William's fellows as, 'Officer I cannot be; private I will not be; tradesman or clerk I am.' Further, he had lived in surroundings where the soldier was robbed of his terrors; to him the wearer of the king's uniform was not only a person to whom you alluded at Labour meetings with the certainty of raising a jeer, but a target at whom strikers threw brickbats and bottles with energy and practical impunity. Should the target grow

restive under these attentions and proceed to return them in kind, it
was denounced in Parliament, foamed at by the Press, and possibly
court-martialled as a sop to indignant Labour. Thus handicapped
it could hardly be looked on as a formidable adversary . . . and
William, without a thought of fear, stared the field-grey horseman
in the eyes.

The field-grey horseman, on his side, stared the pair of civilians
up and down – with a glance that matched the courtesy of his recent
manner of address – until, having surveyed them sufficiently, he
called over his shoulder to some one unseen within the house. There
was something in his face and the tone of his loud-voiced hail that
made the temper of Griselda stir within her; and for the second time
that morning she wished for a command of the language of the
country – this time for the purposes of sharp and scathing rebuke.
As a substitute she assumed the air of cold dignity with which she
had entered the taxi on the night of her protest at the meeting.

'Come on, William,' she said. 'Don't take any notice of him, dear.'

The advice, though well meant, was unfortunate. As William
attempted to follow both it and his wife, the soldier moved forward
and struck him a cuff on the side of the head that deposited him
neatly on the grass. Griselda, who – in order to convey her contempt
for official authority and disgust at official insolence – had been
pointedly surveying the meeting of hill and horizon, heard a whack
and scuffle, a guttural grunt and a gasp; and turned to see William,
with a hand to his cheek, lying prone at the feet of his assailant. She
rounded on the man like a lion, and perhaps, with her suffragette
training behind her, would have landed him a cuff in his turn; but
as she raised her arm it was caught from behind and she found
herself suddenly helpless in the grasp of a second grey-clad soldier
– who, when he heard his comrade's hail, had come running out of
the house.

'Let me go,' she cried, wriggling in his grasp as she had wriggled
aforetime in the hands of a London policeman, and kicking him
deftly on the shins as she had been wont to kick Robert on his. For
answer he shook her to the accompaniment of what sounded like
curses – shook her vehemently, till her hat came off and her hair fell
down, till her teeth rattled and the landscape danced about her.
When he released her, with the final indignity of a butt with the knee
in the rear, she collapsed on the grass by her husband's side in a
crumpled, disreputable heap. There for a minute or two she lay

gasping and inarticulate – until, as her breath came back and the landscape ceased to gyrate, she dragged herself up into a sitting position and thrust back the hair from her eyes. William, a yard or two away, was also in a sitting position with his hand pressed against his cheekbone; while over him stood the assailants in field-grey, apparently snapping out questions.

'I don't understand,' she heard him protest feebly, 'I tell you I don't understand. Griselda, can't you explain to them that I don't speak French!'

'Comprends pas,' said Griselda, swallowing back tears of rage. 'Comprends pas – so it's not a bit of good your talking to us. Parlez pas français – but that won't prevent me from reporting you for this disgraceful assault. You cowards – you abominable cowards! You're worse than the police at home, which is saying a good deal. I wonder you're not ashamed of yourselves. I've been arrested three times and I've never been treated like this.'

At this juncture one of the men in field-grey seized William by the collar and proceeded to turn out his pockets – extracting from their recesses a purse, a pipe, a handkerchief, a fountain pen, and a green-covered Cook's ticket. He snapped back the elastic on the Cook's ticket, and turned the leaves that remained for the journey home.

'London,' he ejaculated suddenly, pronouncing the vowels in un-English fashion as O's.

'London!' his companion echoed him – and then, as if moved by a common impulse, they called on the name of Heinz.

There was an answering hail from the farmhouse kitchen, whence issued promptly a fattish young man with a mug in his hand, and a helmet tilted on his nose. With him the assailants of William and Griselda entered into rapid and throaty explanations; whereat Heinz nodded assentingly as he advanced down the garden path to the gate, surveying the captives with interest and a pair of little pigs'-eyes. Having reached the gate he leaned over it, mug in hand, and looked down at William and Griselda.

'English,' he said in a voice that was thicker than it should have been at so early an hour of the morning; 'English – you come from London? . . . I have been two years in London; that is why I speak English. I was with a hairdresser in the Harrow Road two years; and I know also the Strand and the Angel and Buckingham Palace and the Elephant.' (He was plainly proud of his acquaintance with London topography.) 'All of them I know, and when we arrive in

London I shall show them all to my friends.' He waved his hand vaguely and amiably to indicate his grey-clad companions. 'You come from London, but you shall not go back there, because you are now our prisoners. I drink your damn bad health and the damn bad health of your country and the damn bad health of your king.'

He suited the action to the word and drained his mug; and having drained it till it stood upright upon his nose, proceeded to throw it over his shoulder to shatter on the brick path. Whether from natural good temper or the cheering effect of potations his face was wreathed in an amiable smile as he crossed his arms on the bar of the gate and continued to address his audience –

'We shall take you to our officer and you will be prisoners, and if you are spies you will be shot.'

There was something so impossible about the announcement that William and Griselda felt their courage return with a rush. Moreover, though the words of Heinz were threatening the aspect of Heinz was not; his fat young face with its expansive and slightly inebriated smile was ridiculous rather than terrifying, even under the brim of a helmet. William, thankful for the English acquired during the two years' hairdressing in the Harrow Road, admonished him with a firmness intended to sober and dismay.

'This is not a time for silly jokes. I am afraid that you do not realize the seriousness of the situation. I shall feel it my duty to make a full report to your superiors – when you will find it is no laughing matter. My wife and I, proceeding quietly to the station, have been grossly and violently assaulted by your two companions. We gave them no provocation, and the attack was entirely uncalled for. I repeat, I shall feel it my duty to report their conduct in the very strongest terms.'

He felt as he spoke that the reproof would have carried more weight had it been delivered in a standing position; but his head still reeled from the stinging cuff it had received and he felt safer where he was – on the ground. It annoyed him that the only apparent effect of his words upon Heinz was a widening of his already wide and owlish smile.

'Oh, you'll report their conduct, will you?' he repeated pleasantly and thickly. 'And who will you report it to, old son?'

William stiffened at the familiarity, and the tone of his reply was even colder and more dignified than that of the original rebuke.

'To the nearest police authority; I shall not leave Belgium until my complaint has been attended to. If necessary I shall apply for redress to the British Consul in Brussels.'

The expansive smile on the face of Heinz was suddenly ousted by an expression of infinite astonishment. His fat chin dropped, his little eyes widened, and he pushed back his helmet, that he might stare the better at William.

'Say it again,' he demanded – slowly and as if doubtful of his ears. 'You shall apply to the British Consul – the British Consul at Brussels?'

'Certainly,' William assured him firmly; and Griselda echoed 'Certainly.' The threat they judged had made the desired impression, for so blank and disturbed was the countenance of Heinz that his two companions broke into guttural questioning. The former hair-dresser checked them with a gesture and addressed himself once more to William.

'I think,' he announced, 'you are balmy on the crumpet, both of you. Balmy,' he repeated, staring from one to the other and apparently sobered by the shock of his own astonishment. Suddenly a gleam of intelligence lit up his little pig's-eyes – he leaned yet further over the gate, pointed a finger and queried –

'You do not read the newspapers?'

'As a rule I do,' William informed him, 'but we have not seen any lately – not since we left England.'

'And how long is it since you left England?'

William told him it was over three weeks.

'Three weeks,' the other repeated, 'three weeks without news-papers . . . and I think you do not speak French, eh?'

'My wife,' William answered, 'understands it – a little. But we neither of us speak it.' His manner was pardonably irritated, and if he had not judged it imprudent he would have refused point-blank to answer this purposeless catechism. Nor was his pardon-able irritation lessened when amusement once more gained the upper hand in Heinz. Suddenly and unaccountably he burst into hearty laughter – rocked and trembled with it, holding to the gate and wiping the tears from his cheeks. Whatever the joke it appealed also to his comrades, who, once it was imparted between Heinz's paroxysms, joined their exquisite mirth to his own. The three stood swaying in noisy merriment, while Griselda, white-faced and tight-lipped, and William with a fast disappearing left eye awaited in acute and indignant discomfort some explanation of a jest that struck them as untimely. It came only when Heinz had laughed himself out. Wiping the tears once more from his eyes, and with a voice still weakened by pleasurable emotion, he gave them in simple and unpolished language the news of the European cataclysm.

'I tell you something, you damn little ignorant silly fools. There is a war since you came to Belgium.'

Probably they thought it was a drunken jest, for they made no answer beyond a stare, and Heinz proceeded with enjoyment.

'A War. The Greatest that ever was. Germany and Austria – and Russia and France and Belgium and England and Servia.'

He spoke slowly, dropping out his words that none might fail of their effect and ticked off on a finger the name of each belligerent.

'Our brave German troops have conquered Belgium and that is why we are here. We shall also take Paris and we shall also take Petersburg and we shall also take London. We shall march through Regent Street and Leicester Square and over Waterloo Bridge. Our Kaiser Wilhelm shall make peace in Westminster Abbey, and we shall take away all your colonies. What do you think of that, you damn little fools?'

There are statements too large as there are statements too wild for any but the unusually imaginative to grasp at a first hearing. Neither William nor Griselda had ever entertained the idea of a European War; it was not entertained by any of their friends or their pamphlets. Rumours of war they had always regarded as foolish and malicious inventions set afloat in the interest of Capitalism and Conservatism with the object of diverting attention from Social Reform or the settlement of the Woman Question; and to their ears, still filled with the hum of other days, the announcement of Heinz was even such a foolish invention. Nor, even had they given him credence, would they in these first inexperienced moments have been greatly perturbed or alarmed; their historical ignorance was so profound, they had talked so long and so often in terms of war, that they had come to look on the strife of nations as a glorified scuffle on the lines of a Pankhurst demonstration.

W. B. Baldry, *From Hampstead to Holloway*

In 'A Suffragette is born – not made', the opening chapter of
Burton Baldry's crude anti-suffrage satire, complete with
cartoon illustrations, its heroine Kate Denver is presented as a
strident woman from the moment of her birth. Published in
1909, the book may have been directed at readers who sub-
scribed to the 'masculine' periodicals that its author edited.

Kate Denver came into this sinful but comfortable world on 5th
November 1880, and the house inhabited by her parents was known
as 29 Argyle Road, Hampstead.

If this was to be a novel, it would be superfluous to chronicle the
above fact, as it would not merely be useless, but might, as the chapters went on, lead to somewhat serious complications. I mention the
date of her birth, not because, in the light of after events, it is appropriate, but merely for the sake of accuracy; and I mention the house,
and the road, because many misguided people have a mania for
staring at houses that happen to be mentioned in their daily papers,
or in a book they chance to alight on.

If you should be tempted to motor down to Hampstead (on a
Vanguard) to get a glimpse of this historic residence, you will discover, probably much to your annoyance, that it is exactly the same
as every other house in that road. It has nothing whatever to distinguish it from its neighbours.

But, withal, the house wherein a celebrity is born is always disappointing – it is seldom different from an ordinary house. It would
be far more gratifying to our sense of what 'ought to be' if a window
were broken, the bay slightly out of the square – or even if the letter
box happened to be where the knocker should ordinarily find a
resting place.

But no, there is nothing out of the ordinary. It is merely commonplace. A law should be passed, by which a celebrity should be
compelled to be born in a house totally different from that of the
ordinary person.

Like the house in which she was born the new baby was quite
ordinary looking. Perhaps to look ordinary in these bustling days of
originality is somewhat of a blessing – though a plain face will often
act as an effective disguise.

Yet, for that matter, if we could but have seen many of the present-day eminent people in their cradles, we should not, I am sure, hold them in such awe and wonder, or treat them with such respect.

Fancy being shown a fat bouncing baby of fourteen months, and it being pointed out to you that there you beheld the future Prime Minister. Why, if ever he did rise to that height you would never think of him as the leader of the country's fortunes. You could never think of him as a great man. You would always remember him as the kiddie that said, 'Yah, yah' at you, with a strong Scotch accent, from the depths of a pretty cradle.

First impressions may not be right but they are generally lasting.

At the age of eight weeks the baby was taken to be christened, and it was at this ceremony – her first appearance in public, as it were – that she showed signs, which, when her future actions are taken into account, can only be regarded as significant.

The ceremony proceeded without a hitch until the particular part was reached when the minister takes the baby into his rms.

She submitted to this quite passively – I might say eagerly. She was as quiet as a baby of eight weeks knows how to be. But when the minister came to pronounce the words, 'Kate Elizabeth' (of course, she was not old enough to choose her own name, or she would not have chosen those two appellatives), 'I baptise thee –' there was a terrible screech, and the beautiful silver shell which was being used in the ceremony found a resting place with more haste than dignity in the centre of the aisle. The minister tried to look unconcerned, but failed lamentably, and the ceremony was proceeded with under great difficulties.

Eventually the infant was taken back to Argyle Road after having created a disturbance upon her first appearance in public – branded for life.

Perhaps you may think that I am giving undue prominence to what is, after all, only a commonplace incident; but I contend, after a close study of Kate Denver's life, that it is worthy of note.

You will realise that it was precisely at the moment when she was being dictated to by a 'mere' (why 'mere' I cannot say, but I have an idea that it is the correct term) man, that she so violently protested. Admittedly she was in the wrong, and she lost her case, but the fact remains that it was under protest.

Mrs H. Ward, *Delia Blanchflower*

A prolific novelist, Mrs Humphry Ward sustained her opposition to women's suffrage over several decades. Here she shows
her eponymous heroine falling under the dangerous influence
of the militant Gertrude Marvell.

What was she before she knew Gertrude? She thought of that earlier
Delia as of a creature almost too contemptible to blame. From the
maturity of her twenty-one years she looked back upon herself at
seventeen or eighteen with wonder. That Delia had read nothing –
knew nothing – had neither thoughts nor principles. She was her
father's spoilt child and darling; delighting in the luxury that surrounded his West Indian Governorship; courted and flattered by the
few English of the colonial capital, and by the members of her
father's staff; with servants for every possible need or whim; living
her life mostly in the open air, riding at her father's side through the
sub-tropical forests of the colony; teasing and tyrannising over the
dear old German governess who had brought her up, and whose
only contribution to her education – as Delia now counted education – had been the German tongue. Worth something! – but not all
those years, 'when I might have been learning so much else, things
I shall never have time to learn now! – things that Gertrude has at
her fingers' ends. Why wasn't I taught properly – decently – like any
Board-school child! As Gertrude says, we women want everything
we can get! We *must* know the things that men know – that we may
beat them at their own game. Why should every Balliol boy – years
younger than me – have been taught his classics and mathematics,
– and have everything brought to him – made easy for him – history,
political economy, logic, philosophy, laid at his lordship's feet, if he
will just please to learn! – while I, who have just as good a brain as
he, have had to pick up a few scraps by the way, just because nobody
who had charge of me ever thought it worth while to teach a girl?
But I have a mind! – an intelligence! – even if I am a woman; and
there is all the world to know. Marriage? Yes! – but not at the sacrifice of everything else – of the rational, civilised self.'

   On the whole, though, her youth had been happy enough, with
recurrent intervals of ennui and discontent; intervals too of poetic
enthusiasm, or ascetic religion. At eighteen she had been practically
a Catholic, influenced by the charming wife of one of her father's

aides-de-camp. And then – a few stray books or magazine articles had made a Darwinian and an agnostic of her; the one phase as futile as the other.

'I knew nothing – I had no mind!' – she repeated with energy – 'till Gertrude came.'

And she thought with ardour of that intellectual awakening, under the strange influence of the apparently reserved and impassive woman, who had come to read history with her for six months, at the suggestion of a friend of her father's, a certain cultivated and clever Lady Tonbridge, 'who saw how starved I was.'

So, after enquiry, a lady who was a BA of a west-country university, where she had taken every possible high honour in history and economics – Delia's ambition would accept nothing less – had been found, who wanted for health's sake a winter in a warm climate, and was willing to read history with Governor Blanchflower's half-fledged daughter.

The friendship had begun, as often, with a little aversion. Delia was made to work, and having always resented being made to do anything, for about a month she disliked her tutor, and would have persuaded Sir Robert to send her away, had not England been so far off, and the agreement with Miss Marvell, whose terms were high, unusually stringent. But by the end of the month the girl of eighteen was conquered. She had recognised in Gertrude Marvell accomplishments that filled her with envy, together with an intensity of will, a bitter and fiery purpose, that astounded and subdued a young creature in whom inherited germs of Southern energy and passion were only waiting the touch that starts the ferment. Gertrude Marvell had read an amazing amount of history, and all from one point of view: that of the woman stirred to a kind of madness by what she held to be the wrongs of her sex. The age-long monopoly of all the higher forces of civilisation by men; the cruel and insulting insistence upon the sexual and maternal functions of women, as covering the whole of her destiny; the hideous depreciation of her as an inferior and unclean creature to which Christianity, poisoned by the story of Eve, and a score of barbarous beliefs and superstitions more primitive still, had largely contributed, while hypocritically professing to enfranchise and exalt her; the unfailing doom to 'obey,' and to bring forth, that has crushed her; the labours and shames heaped upon her by men in the pursuit of their own selfish devices; and the denial to her, also by men, of all the higher and spiritual activities, except those allowed by a man-made religion: – this feminist gospel, in some respects so bitterly true, in others so vindictively false, was gradually and unsparingly pressed upon Delia's quick intelligence. She caught its fire; she rose to its call; and there came a day when Gertrude Marvell, breaking through the cold reserve she had hitherto interposed between herself and the pupil who had come to adore her, threw her arms round the girl, accepting from her what were practically the vows of a neophyte in a secret and revolutionary service.

Joyous, self-dedicating moment! But it had been followed by a tragedy: the tragedy of Delia's estrangement from her father. It was not long before Sir Robert Blanchflower, a proud self-indulgent man, with a keen critical sense, a wide acquaintance with men and affairs, and a number of miscellaneous acquirements of which he never made the smallest parade, had divined the spirit of irreconcilable revolt which animated the slight and generally taciturn woman, who had obtained such a hold upon his daughter. He, the god of his small world, was made to feel himself humiliated in her presence. She was, in fact, his intellectual superior, and the truth was conveyed to him in a score of subtle ways. She was in his house simply because she was poor, and wanted rest from excessive overwork, at someone else's expense. Otherwise her manner suggested – often quite unconsciously – that she would not have put up with his household and its regulations for a single day.

Then, suddenly, he perceived that he had lost his daughter, and the reason of it.

4

The prison experience

Imprisonment was an important part of suffrage protest, offering opportunities for publicity and sacrifice, but, like militancy, it also provided a significant symbolism and discourse. At various stages of the campaign imprisonment demanded different kinds of sacrifice and was interpreted accordingly.

The first suffrage campaigners to go to prison for the cause were Christabel Pankhurst and Annie Kenney in 1905, arrested for their interruption of a Liberal Rally at the Free Trade Hall in Manchester. As more and more upper- and middle-class women became involved in the WSPU the publicity created by their imprisonment was of great value to the cause. In October 1906 various prominent women were arrested and treated as common criminals; in 1907 confrontations following the first Women's Parliament at Caxton Hall led to over fifty arrests; and in February 1908 Mrs Pankhurst herself was arrested. From then on the number of prison sentences escalated. By the Coronation Procession of 1911 seven hundred 'ex-prisoners' were given a place of honour at the head of the marching women. Setting a precedent for others, Marian Wallace Dunlop went on hunger strike in 1909, but in September of that year the authorities struck back with forcible feeding of hunger strikers. This soon offered a new and shocking form of martyrdom for other women. In 1913 the notorious 'Cat and Mouse Act' – The Prisoners Temporary Discharge Act – was introduced. Aimed at preventing the unconditional release of ill hunger strikers, it allowed them release from prison on licence for several days, with re-arrest imminent as soon as they were recovered.

If imprisonment meant some hardship, the horrors of hunger striking and forcible feeding were much more extreme. Vividly detailed in fictional and autobiographical writings, this resistance to food and drink acquired deep symbolic significance in the battle over women's bodies and rights. It also raised further questions about the suffragettes' status as non-political prisoners, imposed upon them by the authorities. Government inconsistency in the handling of suffrage prisoners was memorably exposed by Lady Constance Lytton, who received preferential treatment when her title was known, being released because of a 'weak heart', but received far harsher treatment and was pronounced fit and healthy when incarcerated in Walton Gaol in the disguise of 'Jane Warton', a working-class woman.

As the writing in this section shows, prison offered a physical and metaphorical space in which women could contest the impositions of male authority. Not only are we given detailed accounts of existence in prison, which reveal the extent of suffrage sacrifice, but the imagery and incidents of daily life become the means of representing the wider legal, social and ideological constraints women faced. Within this dramatic arena, the suffragettes discovered a powerful language and symbolism through which to articulate their oppression.

T. Gough, 'Foreword to *Holloway Jingles*'

This small publication, containing sixteen poems by women in prison during a period of hunger striking in April 1912, was published by the Glasgow Branch of the WSPU. In her introduction Teresa Gough moves from her memories of specific individuals in that context to a mystificatory and forward-looking celebration of the experience.

Comrades, it is the eve of our parting. Those of us who have had the longest sentences to serve have seen many a farewell waved up towards our cell windows from the great prison gate as time after time it opened for release. The jail yard, too, where we exercise, now seems spacious, though at first it was thronged with our fellow-prisoners. Yet not one of them has really left us. Whenever in thought we re-enter that yard, within its high, grim walls we see each as we knew her there: our revered Leader, Mrs. Pankhurst, courageous, serene, smiling; Dr. Ethel Smyth, joyous and terrific, whirling through a game of rounders with as much intentness as if she were conducting a symphony; Dr. L. Garrett Anderson, in whose eyes gaiety and gravity are never far apart – but we cannot name them all, for there are scores whose brave faces made that yard a pleasant place.

The passing of the weeks was punctuated by the flowers that blossomed in those grim surroundings; sturdy crocuses, then daffodils and tulips, and now the lilacs are in bloom. Always, too, we had the sunshine, for the skies were kind.

And within the walls? Ah! there, too, the love that shines through the sun and the skies and can illuminate even the prison cell, was round us, and worked through us and miracles were wrought. We have each been witness of some wonder worked by that omniscient love which is the very basis of our movement.

At these words other faces will rise up before the mind's eye, bruised, perhaps degraded, crushed, sullen, sorrowful, sometimes beautiful, but always endeared to us by the thought that it is for their sakes we get the strength to carry on this struggle.

In service to you, O sad sisters, in your hideous prison garb, we gain the supremacy of our souls. And 'we need not fear that we can lose anything by the progress of the soul.'

K. Emerson, 'The Women in Prison'

Kathleen Emerson was active in the Irish Women's Franchise League, and had been arrested for window-breaking. In her contribution to *Holloway Jingles*, the stones of the prison are transformed into an image of freedom.

Oh, Holloway, grim Holloway,
With grey, forbidding towers!
Stern are thy walls, but sterner still
Is women's free, unconquered will.
And though to-day and yesterday
Brought long and lonely hours,
Those hours spent in captivity
Are stepping-stones to liberty.

L. Grey, 'To D. R. in Holloway'

Laura Grey is described in other accounts of prison life as running round the prison yard, taking part in drama productions and, at one point, looking 'bad, nails and fingers bluish'. This short poem is one of the most interesting and enigmatic in *Holloway Jingles*. I have been unable to discover the identity of 'D. R.'.

Beyond the bars I see her move,
　　A mystery of blue and green,
As though across the prison yard
　　The spirit of the spring had been.
And as she lifts her hands to press
　　The happy sunshine of her hair,
From the grey ground the pigeons rise,
　　And rustle upwards in the air,
As though her two hands held a key
　　To set imprisoned spirits free.

E. A. Wingrove, 'There's a strange sort of college'

From *Holloway Jingles* (1912). This poem demonstrates the skill with which suffrage writers drew upon established discourses, in this case those of scholarship and fellowship traditionally associated with a masculine sphere, and reworked them in the context of the cause. I have as yet been unable to trace any information about the writer, Edith Aubrey Wingrove.

There's a strange sort of college,
　　And the scholars are unique,
Yet the lessons are important which they learn;
　　They fit them for the fight,
　　For all that's true and right,
And for liberty and justice make them burn.

There the scholars are the teachers,
　　And the staff they are the taught,
Though they sometimes try to get the upper hand;
　　But their rules they are too grim,
　　So they find they must give in
To that gallant, honour-loving little band.

It is there you grow quite knowing,
   If you ever have been dull,
For the things you see and hear they make you wise;
   There we take our F. H. G.,
   A very high degree,
And the hand-grip of true friendship – that's the prize.

There the terms they often vary,
   Some are long and some are short,
But the rules they never alter in the least;
   They go on from day to day,
   In the same old prosy way,
And the food you get there isn't quite a feast.

Just watch those scholars' faces,
   It's truth on them you'll find,
Hear their laughter ringing out so clear and bright;
   'Unto others you must do
   As you'd have them do to you,'
Is their motto, and you know that they are right.

When you're singing 'Rule, Britannia,'
   Britons never shall be slaves,
Remember it's not words which tell but deeds;
   'Tis actions brave and strong
   Which always right the wrong.
For justice unto freedom always leads.

Hark to the trumpet calling!
   Come out and take your place
'Neath the standard of the purple, white, and green;
   True courage must prevail,
   For the tyrants we assail,
It's the grandest fight the world has ever seen.

The students and the college
   Are known throughout the world,
Of God's truth the light upon them never sets;
   'Tis the prison, cold and grey,
   Of noted Holloway,
And the scholars are my colleague Suffragettes.

M. M'P., 'To a Fellow Prisoner (Miss Janie Allan)'

From *Holloway Jingles*: Miss Janie Allan was a prominent sup-
porter of the militant suffrage cause in Scotland, both finan-
cially and in active campaigning. At the time this poem was
written, she was imprisoned in Holloway for four months for
window-smashing. The author of the poem, 'M. M'P.', seems
likely to be another Scottish suffragette, Margaret McPhun,
who also served two months' hard labour in Holloway in
1912, after smashing a window of the Local Government
Office in Westminster. The poem itself offers an interesting
example of the range of images used to emphasise the nobility
and sacrifice of women within the movement.

Upon thy pure and stedfast brow there lies
A tender sorrow – and in thine eyes
(Serene and passionless as dawn's deep grey,
E'er yet the golden sandalled day
Trips joyously o'er hill and wood,)
A melancholy, calm and sweet, doth brood.

No darkling shadow of the prison cell
Dare cast o'er thee its grim, benumbing spell.
Floats then some music, sad and soft to thee,
By angels borne to thine attuned ears?
Dull echoes of the moaning, human sea
Whose waves are blood and tears,
Faint sob and murmur of despairing strife,
Low cry of yearning agonising life?

Or is thy sorrow's food
Vision of outraged womanhood?
Throbs thy heart with stinging pain
To the misery and shame
Of these thy sisters – cast away
Like frail, sweet flowers of one brief day?

Or like the butterfly that dies
In dust from which it cannot rise;
Or wounded bird, beating with bleeding wings

The cold, hard earth – while rings
The merry laughter of its murderer's song?
How long shall these things be, oh God, how long?

'For these things our eyes are dim.' – Lamentations v. 17

M. C. R., 'Before I came to Holloway'

The 'M. C. R.' of this poem from *Holloway Jingles* would
appear to be Madeleine Caron Rock, a published poet in her
own right and an active suffragette. In its reversal of the expectations and terminology of prison life, her poem is characteristic of suffrage writing on imprisonment. 'Dx' as referred to in
the poem was the block in Holloway Prison to which suffragettes were usually assigned.

Before I came to Holloway,
    It was not cold nor illness,
Nor harshness that I feared, oh stay!
    It was the deathly stillness.

Inside, it's bang with supper, or
    It's dinner or 'your apple;'
Or 'pass out, please, to exercise,'
    Or 'pass along to chapel.'

'Tis 'close your door there,' 'pass out, please,'
    It's clattering with the rations,
'Baths,' turning locks, and clinking keys,
    And 'any applications?'

All day it's 'have you got those?' Oh,
    Bells, bangings, people larking;
'You cleaners there,' 'Miss So-and-so,'
    Or 'are you there, Miss Sharky?'

And if you think you're safely in,
    They must have done their caperin',

Then 'governor,' 'visiting magistrates,'
   'The chaplain,' 'doctor,' 'matron.'

At night, quite late, at nearly six,
   'Haven't they finished speaking?'
Your mattress like the whole Dx
   Is simmering and creaking.

You hear them chopping, stoking too,
   And really all their clamour
Breaks up the peace far more than you
   Or I, with stone and hammer.

Before I came to Holloway
   It was not cold nor illness.
Nor harshness that I feared, oh stay!
   It was the deathly stillness.

E. Crosby, 'Prologue to *Pages from the Diary of a Militant Suffragette*'

Kathleen Roberts uses the word of the American social reformer Ernest Crosby as a prologue, entitled 'The prison', to her semi-fictional account, *Pages from the Diary of a Militant Suffragette*. The archaic and elevated language indicates the symbolic significance attached to imprisonment and links the women's cause to a universal struggle for justice.

And I saw a gaol lifting its grimy walls to heaven. And they that passed by looked at it askance, for they said: 'It is the abode of Sin.'

And to them the broad sky and all the earth was fair to look upon, for they saw the early buds opening, and heard the birds that had come back from the south, and they felt the sun which was new warming the hearts of beast and plant.

But within the prison, and behind its cold, thick buttresses, and its small, round, triple-barred windows, that looked like tunnels, they heard faint groanings and sighings and much lamentation, and they said: 'It is most just, for it is the abode of Sin.'

And I heard a voice saying: 'Woe to the cause that hath not passed through a prison!'

And I looked again, and I saw in the gaol those deliverers who in each age have saved the world from itself, and set it free, and gyves were on their wrists and ankles.

And I saw Israel in the house of bondage before it came forth to preserve Duty for mankind.

Woe to the cause that hath not passed through a prison!

And I saw the Praetorian Hall and One that was bound therein, and the soldiers bowed the knee before Him and mocked Him, and then led Him away to proclaim Love to the world.

Woe to the cause that hath not passed through a prison!

And I saw within the gaol them that gave liberty to the slave, and them that unbound the mind of man, and them that strove to free his conscience, and them that led onward to Freedom, and Justice, and Love.

Woe to the cause that hath not passed through a prison!

And I saw also those in our own time who have counted themselves as nothing if they could but point out God's way unto their brethren; and there were many, too, of the prophets who are still to come, and these were also in bonds.

Woe to the cause that hath not passed through a prison!

And lo! the sky became clouded, and night fell, and there were no birds nor blossoms, but a chill came upon the earth, and they that passed by shivered and trembled; and I beheld, and saw that they were not men, but that they were really wolves, and apes, and swine.

And within the gaol was a great light, and a pleasant warmth came from the barred windows; and I heard a burst of triumphant song.

And the gyres fell from the limbs of the prisoners, and there was great joy.

And they that passed by would come in, but they could not; and now within was freedom, and without was captivity.

And the hosts within held up their arms, and the marks of their shackles were upon them.

But I hid my hands behind me, for there was no mark on my wrists.

Woe to the cause that hath not passed through a prison!

C. Despard, *Outlawed*

Charlotte Despard's novel, written with Mabel Collins, uses a melodramatic and romantic plot to explore injustices meted out to women, but it is only at the beginning of the novel that suffrage is explicitly addressed. Here in the 'foreword' the heroine uses her experience of wrongful imprisonment to speak out at a meeting in the Albert Hall, interrogating existing legislation through the argument that women at present are already treated as 'outlaws'.

What a scene! One of the fierce, vivid, passionate scenes of the nineteenth century. All its bordom, its dullness, its monotony, forgotten, swept aside by a fierce outburst of strong human feeling, by a great revolution in the very heart of the people, springing from the hearths and homes, bursting forth amid families. No mere party struggle this, but a demand from the women of the nation to stand beside the men. A revolution, a great uprising in the very central life of England. What a scene! The Albert Hall packed from floor to ceiling, and all the corridors thronged with those who could not find room within, yet would stay to form part of this vast demonstration; outside, the street thronged in every direction.

Women alone could enter the hall; women filled every available space within it; women crowded the corridors and stood at the gates and submitted to be marshalled and ordered by the police rather than leave the scene.

The platform was banked with superb flowers and masses of bouquets lay before the president of the meeting, who stood, simple, quiet, calm, worn with long years of labour, wearing her doctor's robes, and controlled this dense crowd of revolutionists. Every class was represented in the throng; brilliant and beautiful women, perfectly dressed, and in some instances wearing historical jewels as for a Court function; crowds of graduates of all kinds, wearing their robes and mortar-boards, business women, working women, single women, girls, married women whose husbands resented their presence here and denied their right to be free, and married women whose husbands saw that right, and who waited without to applaud and cheer them. The crowd was listening in a tense silence to a clear, strong, young voice, vibrating with feeling. A tall, beautiful woman was speaking from the platform; young and eager, yet with the ineffaceable marks of suffering and sorrow, and strong emotion, on her face. She was heard with the keenest interest, for it was the agony she had endured and witnessed in her own life which had made her a passionate advocate of woman suffrage as the first step towards the freedom of women. She was Lady Eversley, a bride, whose husband, one of the famous painters of the day, had brought her to the door and encouraged her to the last moment, and who waited without to receive her with love and pride when her great ordeal was over. For it was an ordeal. This was her first speech to a large audience, and she had spent many sad years in solitary confinement and enforced silence within the walls of a prison. In the ignorance and innocence of girlhood she had married blindly, and had escaped from the bondage at the price of suffering punishment for a crime she had not committed. In her perfect, unspotted youth, when her beauty was like that of an opening rose, she had entered into the darkest places of our civilisation, where woman is trodden under foot and dragged in the dirt, simply because she is woman, and as helpless as any slave. Her tragic experience, and the superb manner in which she had emerged from it, ready to devote the remainder of her life to the cause of the freedom of women, had awakened the strongest interest.

'We women,' she was saying, 'are more than disfranchised; we are outlawed. We are not protected by the law. It is in a woman's own personal life, that which concerns all that is best and noblest and most spiritual in her, that she is truly an outlaw, unprotected. Unless fortune favours a woman, unless she is happily married, she is compelled to realise always that she is unprotected, that the law is against her. If, as so many are, thank God, she is happily married and to a good man, then her husband protects her. But all the same she herself is an outlaw, sheltered by him. Let her oppose him – let her imagine herself to be an independent being – and she discovers at once that she is indeed his chattel, safe only while she remains so. If she rebels, the law crushes her, and she can be at any moment thrust forth among the outcasts, though she be perfectly innocent. The law crushes her, and society crushes her, unless she submit absolutely to the unequal treatment meted out to men and women.'

The words rang out, and when the speaker paused for a moment the audience burst forth into deafening applause. It was some time before she could continue her speech. She bowed her head before the enthusiasm and some hot tears fell upon her pale cheeks.

'There are women in prison now,' she said, when at last she could be again heard, 'who were sent there by men – judged, condemned by men – whom no women would have condemned. I long to unlock the gates of that prison I have but lately left and bring them here among you – among other women – but I cannot – they are outlaws, crushed by the law – and we who are here, apparently free, are outlaws as much as they are. I suffered for a crime I did not commit, but the woman who did commit it was driven into desperation by being born an outcast from the class to which she belonged. Her mother dared not own her; had she done so she herself would have become an outcast. To own her would have made no trouble for her father; but he followed the heartless custom of many men, a custom only possible under this system of man-made laws, and never even thought about her existence. This woman sought her own death at last sooner than suffer the punishment of the law. She was a criminal, but she might have been very different had she not been born an outcast and an outlaw.'

Every woman who listened knew the strange story to which she referred, the newspapers having been full of it. But in its full details it could only be told under the cloak of fiction, as it appears in the following pages. In this history the conflict is shown which exists in the centre of our social system and which arises from the one sex being the ruler and the other the ruled.

M. E. and M. D. Thompson, *They Couldn't Stop Us! Experiences of two (usually law-abiding) women in the years 1909–1913*

Margaret and Mary Thompson were imprisoned in 1909, 1911 and, as this account describes, 1912. Margaret wrote up her experiences soon after she came out of prison, but some details here are copied from a diary she scribbled on the back of a calendar while in Holloway. The full text of their suffrage experiences, with its lively title, was published much later, in 1957.

June 2nd. Mrs. Lawrence said to me in the morning that my verses had done good: there had been greater quietness.

Again in the afternoon Mrs. Lawrence said in answer to my question, that she had read my speech (on the slip of pink paper) and that it was very, very good. She was sorry it was not in 'Votes for Women.' She specially liked the last paragraph.

We were sitting on the laundry slab. Miss Potbury was passing us when Mrs. Lawrence caught her and talked about the learning of Italian. Miss Potbury and Miss Allan had been having half an hour or so at the Italian every afternoon. Miss Allan was pretty well ahead with the language and Miss Potbury, by 'nearly cracking her head,' had got up to her.

June 3rd. Miss Roberts and Miss Crocker invited all to come to their cells to take something they were leaving. I got two nails and some paper.

June 4th. Good-byes from Miss Crocker, Miss Roberts and Miss Palethorpe.

I went to see Mr. Hankinson for the first time. He had just been speaking to Mr. Pethick Lawrence. He read aloud a little piece and said he would see Harriet and Mary.

June 5th. Coolish day. Mrs. Boyd thumped me on the back for rheumatism. In the afternoon I saw Mrs. Pankhurst walking alone in the yard. I joined her and we had an interesting talk as we marched round and round. I told her how Miss Cheffin had been brought into the movement; first by seeing the WSPU shop in Folkestone, and how at last she had come up to London to do her bit of protest. I told Mrs. Pankhurst how she (Miss Cheffins) had paid the extra expenses at a Suffrage Meeting. She listened sympathetically.

At 5 o'clock that afternoon Mrs. Pethick Lawrence came buoyantly into my cell and gave me a letter to read written by my sister Elizabeth (Ilkley).

June 6th. At sewing time Miss Collier remarked that she was reading Mazzini's Life, and that he had been in prison. Mrs. Lawrence responded that she had always advised suffragists to read Trevelyan's Garibaldi Books.

June 8th. A wet morning. Found cake, strawberries and cherries from Miss J. Allan on my plate. I went round distributing shortbread much praised (from Rachel, Ilkley).

June 9th. Thunderstorm whilst in church. In the afternoon in the yard Mrs. Pethick Lawrence explained to some of us how she expected that she and Mrs. Pankhurst would be transformed to the first division on Monday or Tuesday and they would at once agitate for the rest of us. If first division refused to us, then they and we would begin the hunger strike on Wednesday, 19th June.

Mrs. Lawrence left us and went to the young people. We found Vera and others squatting round her on the gravel near the laundry. Miss Collier, Miss Hewitt and I also sat round, then others came until we were all round except Mrs. Pankhurst and one other. As Mrs. Pankhurst came towards the group, carrying her chair, Mrs. Lawrence called out, 'Don't you come; you've heard it before.' Mrs. Pankhurst clapped down her chair on the edge of the circle and remarked 'I stand upon my rights.' We all laughed. Mrs. Lawrence then went on to tell her Arabic story. She told it very well. When she and her sister were in Egypt an Arab told this story night after night until they got to know many Arabic words; in fact, got to know the language enough to understand. We all much enjoyed it. Then Mrs. Pankhurst began reminiscences about meetings in early days.

June 10th. In the afternoon in the yard, we felt we ought to have something of an entertainment for the last before *the two* left us. The three grandmothers, Mrs. Heward, Mrs. Boyd and Mrs. Aldham sang together very prettily – songs and catches. Mrs. Pankhurst remarked to Miss Haig that Mrs. Boyd was very pretty. She was pleased as they are cousins. Then Mrs. Lawrence told stories again, Doreen Allen squatting at her feet with an arm on her knee. Very entertaining they were. Vera made a speech as Lord Cromer, with button in eye – very amusing, but not quite so good as at the May day sports. Miss McCrae sang 'Justice Lawrie.' One of the prison visitors, a commissioner or something of the sort, came and spoke to us as we were all sitting together. It amused me to see his attitude; wavering between amusement, kindness *and* the necessity to be stern over sinners, and patronising over women. Mrs. Pankhurst's and Mrs. Lawrence's expressions of face were also interesting.

While at sewing from 4.15, a telegram came from Mr. Marshall, telling of the decision in the House for the transference, but no official notice had yet been received by the two.

June 11th. The two still with us. At sewing Mrs. Lawrence suggested reading Iphigenia and other plays aloud in the yard to all who cared to hear. I warmly seconded the proposal. It was evident she expected us all to be transferred to the first division and thus we would serve out our sentences. She was very cordial when I gave her

Elizabeth's message, and we talked about the Albert Hall Meetings, etc. I noticed Mrs. Lawrence speaking first to one and then another of those she had not yet spoken to.

I had a talk with Miss Cheffins; she explained how she dreaded the forcible feeding. She made caustic comments on Mrs. Lawrence's hopefulness – she had no belief in the Home Secretary's giving in.

June 12th. Dampish morning, but went out. Mrs. Pankhurst and Mrs. Lawrence did not come. We found when we came in from exercise yard that they had been at last transferred to First Division.

Afternoon wet. Talked and played on ground floor, then worked. Did not feel well – accepted Mrs. Terrero's invitation to have tea in her cell. Got parcel as usual from Ilkley – pressed beef, also a large veal roll from Miss Beck. Went round with both. Warmly received by Mrs. Hewitt and Miss Potbury.

June 13th. Plan of campaign begins:–

When, in the morning, an officer opened the door of my cell and shouted 'Any applications today' I answered 'Yes! I want to see the Governor.'

Later, we were all out in the exercise yard, when an officer appeared to take in those who wished to see the Governor. Some were very nervous about having to speak to him, others were spoiling for the fray. I marched in and up the stairs along the corridor, first of a long line of applicants. The Matron and the Governor were standing ready to receive us, one by one, in the passage leading from DX to C.

I began 'Things have changed – have changed since yesterday. Our leaders are no longer with us. Why are we not also transferred to the First Division?'

The Governor replied that he had no power to transfer us, and the only thing for us to do was to petition the Home Secretary. I said 'Petitions do no good.' The Governor was smiling and amiable.

June 14th. All again marched along the corridor to see the Governor.

June 15th. Again we spoke to the Governor.

June 16th. Sunday. When out in the yard, word went round through the wardresses that Mrs. Pankhurst and Mrs Lawrence were coming to church and hoped they would see us all there. Most of us went. Mrs. Lawrence told one of us about the eight Irish suffragists and also about the signature of 140 M.P.s to a petition for our transference.

June 18th. All see the Governor. In answer to the negative reply as to our being put in the First Division, I remarked 'Then, in twenty-four hours' time from now, we shall begin the hunger strike.' The Governor uttered two monosyllables; the second in a higher tone than the first . . Mm . . Mhm – a truly Northumbrian reply. The thought of it amused me at times during those dull, apprehensive hours.

H. Mitchell, *The Hard Way Up*

Detailing her arrest and imprisonment in Manchester's Strangeways Prison in 'Prison for a night', Hannah Mitchell makes the point that for a married, working-class woman, prison was hardly a liberating or uplifting experience.

The basement of the Manchester Police Court was then, and still is, a horrible place to wait in, like a cattle stall with bars in front. One other woman went with us in the van to Strangeways. She was being sent to prison for fighting with her neighbours.

'I only called her a cow,' she told us, 'and so she is.'

She gave us her opinion of the police in language which coincided with my own thoughts on the subject. We all felt that we had not had even half-a-crown's worth of defiance out of the affair, as we had no intention of clashing with the police at Belle Vue, but we mentally vowed that next time the law should have something to complain of.

At Strangeways, we were not badly treated, being excused the bath which our fellow prisoner was compelled to take. We heard her loudly complaining that the water was cold and dirty and there was no soap. The wardress kindly allowed us to change in her own room, giving us a sheet to use as a screen. The prison dress was horrible, coarse and unshapely. It consisted of a wide skirt, thickly gathered at the waist, a sort of short jacket or bed gown, such as was worn a hundred years ago, in a horrible drab stuff stamped with a black arrow, one flannel singlet, a coarse calico chemise, no knickers or corsets, short thick stockings without garters and heavy shoes which would have fitted a navvy; mine were different sizes. There was a blue check apron with a sort of check duster for a handkerchief. Even our hairpins were taken away, and we were compelled to push our hair into the prison cap. This cap was the only decent thing given to us. Adela whispered to me that I looked like a queen in mine. I did not feel very queenly; ugly dress makes one feel ugly. Besides, it was very uncomfortable. It was all too big, and the absence of garters and knickers made one feel almost naked.

We all had a sort of numbered badge; mine was H.10, the number of my cell. The cell itself was not too unpleasant, and quite clean. There were two blankets and a straw mattress which would have been comfortable enough, but it was too short, being only long enough for a child's cot. However, I was so tired that I slept fairly well until the bell rang at 6 a.m., when the door was unlocked; and we were ordered out to the lavatories where we washed and emptied our slops. We were then taken out for exercise, so called, which meant just walking round and round in a circle, without being allowed to speak to each other. I found this very hard, as my shoes kept slipping off, and the stockings, also much too big, fell down over my ankles. When I returned to the cell, I remedied this by tearing up the rags given me to polish my 'tins' with, and using them for garters. I think I was then expected to 'make my bed' by rolling up the bedding and stacking it along with the bed against the wall. Instead I just sat on the bed, not caring very much what happened next. I was feeling very ill, having had no food since lunch on the previous day. A tin mug of gruel and a small brown loaf were handed in. The gruel was not too bad, but the bread was quite uneatable. If it had been of sawdust flavoured with road sweepings it could not have tasted worse. My head ached terribly, and I would have given anything for a cup of tea.

But when the door was opened by the Deputy Governor, a woman, and I was told to get ready to go out, as my fine had been paid, I was very angry, and refused to go. She urged me to go, saying kindly that prison was no place for women like us. When I agreed, and my clothes were given to me, I found my one decent suit rolled up in a bundle as if it were the rags of some drunken tramp.

I was not pleased to find my husband outside. He knew that we did not wish our fines to be paid, and was quite in sympathy with the militant campaign, but men are not so singleminded as women are; they are too much given to *talking* about their ideals, rather than *working* for them. Even as Socialists they seldom translate their faith into works, being still conservatives at heart, especially where women are concerned. Most of us who were married found that 'Votes for Women' were of less interest to our husbands than their own dinners. They simply could not understand why we made such a fuss about it.

C. Lytton, *Prisons and Prisoners*

Committed to fighting for political status before suffrage prisoners even before she herself became involved in militancy, Constance Lytton's book is the best-known account of the women's treatment in prison. Her most famous exploit was to disguise herself as the working-class woman, Jane Warton, to reveal how her earlier gentle handling by the prison authorities had been because of her aristocratic status. In this selection of three excerpts from her autobiography she first recounts her attempts to befriend the wardress in an early stretch in prison, then describes her arrest and imprisonment as Jane Warton, and finally depicts her experience of forcible feeding.

Since I had left the general ward there were more opportunities for the officers to show kindness without being detected in 'favouritism,' and I had come to be on very good terms with several of them. Even the ward superintendent, who made a special hobby of outward severity, had relaxed on several occasions. For instance, she stood in the doorway one morning watching me make my bed. She remarked, with the same outward air of contempt that was habitual to her, but with a kindly look in her eyes: 'You're not much used to that, I expect?' I answered: 'Do you think I do it so badly?' She smiled and seemed distressed that I had interpreted her that way. Her anxiety that I should put on flesh while under her charge made her almost motherly at times. I accounted for my small appetite by explaining that I did not spend myself in prison life. 'Don't know about spending yourself, but how about your sensitiveness? Doesn't that "spend" you?' This taunt was because when she renewed the plasters on my cut, which she did very skilfully, I winced a good deal. The sticky plaster adhered closely and the process of removing it generally made me feel faint. I didn't know till she said this that she had even noticed it, but her contempt was softened by a kind smile. I had determined to begin my strike in real earnest the following week if I failed by reasonable pleadings to get sent to the cells. I was anxious that the responsibility of my bad behaviour should not fall on her, and I wished to make very clear that I had no malicious intentions towards her, or anyone else, beyond giving proof to the doctors that I should be better the 'other side.' She was extremely busy and her visits to me never lasted more than a few seconds. I took the first opportunity to say unconcernedly and not looking at her, but with the hope of arousing her curiosity sufficiently for her consent: 'If you should have a spare minute before Sunday, come in to me when I am in my cell, I want to ask you something.' She looked surprised, but said nothing and avoided me for the rest of the day. The following afternoon she looked in hurriedly, saying in her most official voice: 'What is it you want?' I resented the scolding tone and answered without humility, as one would to a fellow-being outside, 'Come near to me, I want to speak to you, but only if you can spare the time.' I was lying on my bed, a privilege I was allowed in the separate cell. She came in, pushed the door to, stood close to my bed-side and said again gruffly, 'What is it?' I reached out my hand to take hers, but meeting with no response I drew it in again. I did not want to get angry with the rebuffs of her officialdom, so I kept my eyes down as I said: 'I like you because you have always treated me the same as the others, yet you have never really been unkind to me. I want to ask you something now, because by Sunday either I shall have had leave to go to the other side or I shall have begun my strike in real earnest and you will be getting more and more angry with me.' She stooped down and said in a low voice of extreme tenderness as if I had been a child: 'Why, I have never been angry with you yet.' I looked up into her eyes. They were lit with kindliness and her whole face beamed on me with genial goodwill. It was a surprising change. The personality was the same, but the mask was off and I realised something of the sacrifice it must be to this woman continually to conceal her good nature under so forbidding a manner. I felt more than ever how wasteful and unreasonable is a system which represses the natural powers of good influence in such a woman and exacts of her, in their stead, an attitude towards the prisoners of so much less worth. Her kindness made my determination to carry out my strike at all costs a much harder job than any amount of her official hardness and reproof would have done. If it had been for any less object than a matter of principle I could not have done it. 'No,' I answered, 'but I haven't yet begun my strike seriously.' I added: 'I don't wish to discuss that now. I want you to tell me when you could come and see us after I am out. Mother will wish to thank you for being kind to me, and to hear about my wicked ways from you. You must come down to us in the country. We are on this line and quite near London.' Her face grew serious again, but remained without the official mask. She shook her head. 'That's impossible,' she said with decision, 'it would be against the rules.' 'There are no prison rules for me once I am free again, and you surely have some holidays when you can do as you like.' 'No, that would be quite against the rules.' I pleaded afresh and with determination. She then tried another tack, said that she had friends of her own to visit in the little time at her disposal. I answered she must bring one of these with her and they would spend the day together with us. But she would have none of it. I said she, of course, felt obliged to rub in the rules and regulations while I was prisoner under her charge and that I respected her for that. It was obvious, however, that such rules would have nothing to do with me once I was free again, that I should write to her after my release, as an ordinary outsider, and make fresh suggestions. I had in mind several instances in which prisoners and warders had continued friendly after release. I asked her to give me her home address or, at least, to tell me her Christian name, for, as several of her sisters were also prison officers in Holloway, I did not want my letter to go to them. She, however, would not tell me any of these things. I asked why it would be against the rules. She answered, 'We are not allowed to hold communication with ex-prisoners,' and vouchsafed no further explanation. I said I thought we Suffragettes might be looked upon as different from the ordinary ex-prisoners. She remained adamant. I felt fresh enmity for the system which continually admitted variation from its rules on the side of less kindness or for reasons of snobbish privilege, but which showed itself rigid and unelastic when it was a case of reasonable, unharmful good-will. But, of course, I immensely respected this woman's loyalty to the system she served and her punctilious adherence to its rules. She had, nevertheless, let go her own voice and her own smile just once upon me. They remained among the joy experiences of Holloway. I wondered if she had ever shown them to the poor woman who screamed and groaned in the cell below mine, or to the yellow-faced patient in the lower ward.

. . .

The police were exceptionally friendly to us, although they were punctilious as to the regulations. For instance, Miss Howey and I were suffering from bad colds and had eucalyptus inhalers in our pockets. We were not allowed to keep these; they were removed with other things, such as a purse, stylo pen, brooches, watch, etc. We were all three allowed to be together and away from other prisoners, locked into a cell of the usual police-station description – that is, unfurnished but for the bare plank, serving as seat or bed, along the wall, and about one and a-half feet from the ground, terminating in a lavatory accommodation under a high-barred window, but now lighted by an electric light in the wall above the door. This cell was scrupulously clean and blankets were supplied to us. Our friends sent us some sandwiches and fruit, and the police themselves provided us with an evening newspaper.

We had been arrested at about 8 o'clock; the police station was some distance from Walton, so it was getting on for 9 o'clock when we were at last shut up after the charges were reported and entered, and we had been stripped by a wardress of our small belongings.

The quick walk from the scene of our arrest, hurried along between two policemen, had been a warming process, after which the cold in the cell seemed intense. The bench being wider than most in police-station cells, Mrs. Nugent lay down at one end, while Elsie Howey and I lay side by side under the same blanket and warmed each other. Mrs. Nugent and Elsie kept up an animated conversation. Elsie told anecdotes of her former imprisonments and those of the fellow-prisoners. I was short of breath and fearfully tired, so I rolled round and kept quite quiet.

At about 12 o'clock the husband of Mrs Nugent had heard of her arrest, and came off to the police station to see her. He came to the door of our cell and was greatly distressed. It was ever so nice to see him. His visit had caused a great deal of concern amongst the police, who recognised him as one of the magistrates. He put himself out to do what he could, and we offered him the comforting news that we were almost sure that his wife would get off, as she had done nothing at all. With that, as his wife was kept standing at the little window so long as he was there, he felt obliged to leave us.

Towards about 3 a.m. we were taken out of the cell and ranged along a seat by the wall of a large room; at the other end was a desk with a policeman sitting at it. We went up in turn to give our names, ages, etc., that is, about seven or eight other prisoners, all females, and our three selves. It was the turn of Jane Warton. She walked across to the policeman, one shoulder hitched slightly above the other, her hair sticking out straight behind and worn in slick bandeaus on either side of her face, her hat trailing in a melancholy way on her head. The large, grey woollen gloves were drawn up over the too short sleeves of her coat; on the collar of it were worn portraits of Mrs. Pankhurst, Mrs. Lawrence and Christabel, in small china brooches; her hat had a bit of tape with 'Votes for Women' written on it, interlaced with the cloth plait that went round it, and eye-glasses were fixed on her nose. Her standing out in the room was the signal for a convulsed titter from the other prisoners. 'It's a shame to laugh at one of your fellow-prisoners,' said the policeman behind the desk, and the tittering was hushed. It was all I could do not to laugh, and I thought to myself 'Is the *Punch* version of a Suffragette overdone?' As I got back to my companions they too were laughing, but I thought it wonderfully kind of the policeman to have spoken on my behalf.

When this process was finished, we three Suffragettes were taken to the policemen's room, where there was a good fire, to wait for our Black Maria. The other prisoners had disappeared. The police sat round and spoke quite pleasantly; there were two or three of them at times. We discussed the chances of women getting the vote, they seemed quite in favour. Elsie Howey and Mrs. Nugent did most of the talking. I warmed myself and saw the police looking at me from time to time, wondering why I did not talk too.

At about 3.30 a.m. or 4 o'clock, Black Maria came and we were put in. This was different from the prison vans I had hitherto seen; it was not broken up into separate cell-like compartments, but was in the form of a double omnibus, one side for men and the other for women, divided by a thin wooden partition, each side having two seats facing each other and extending the length of the carriage. There were no windows; the light filtered in only through the grated ventilators. When we got into this Black Maria there was no one but us three, but we were told to sit near the door, so Mrs. Nugent sat first, then Elsie Howey, and then myself. The jolting of the van is excessive and suggests a complete absence of springs, the noise of its passage through the streets is terrific, to the point of excluding all other sounds – a noise of thundering wheels, of jolts and jars and bumps. I have not yet made out the reason why 3.30 a.m. was selected, none was given at the time to the prisoners.

Our destination was the Bridewell Police Station, but we called on our way at the other police stations in the town, picking up whatever unfortunates they had netted during the night. We called at four different stations, if I remember right. The drive in all took about an hour, and seemed a very long one.

We had not gone far before the rumbling and jolting ceased, the door was thrown open with a sound of keys and great rattling, a shaft of light fell along the 'bus, and lit up momentarily ourselves and those who were thrown in to add to our number. These were the only moments when the occupants had a chance of seeing each other. The door then hastily closed again, darkness, jolting and noise reasserted their grim influence. Drunken voices, the smell of the gin palace, an occasional query and reply shouted through the thin wall to the men on the other side, that was all. Knee to knee, and breath to breath we sat, companions of this world of darkness, fellow-sisters of the order of the outcasts. Before we had finished, we had taken up six women in all.

At the first stop, two Irish girls were let in; some men were put into the other side. The girls were only sufficiently drunk to make them intensely cheerful; they laughed and talked gaily at first and shouted lustily to their companions on the other side. But the effect of the pitch darkness was depressing, and after a time their communications ceased. They sat opposite to us near the door, and whenever there was a gleam of light I watched them, for they gave me immense pleasure. They were quite young, with beautiful arms, which one could see as their sleeves were rolled up; they had shawls on, and their faces were fresh and strong, and pretty, too, had it not been for the effect of the drink; they were as far removed as possible from the degraded town type, in every way they were healthy specimens, fresh from an Irish fishing village. They spoke to us several times, and there was a delightful feeling that disguise or no disguise did not matter with them, but it was difficult to hear what they said in the fearful noise of the Black Maria, and we felt that our answers were mostly lost on them. They put the question in a friendly way: 'What did you get taken up for?' 'We're Suffragettes,' was the all-sufficient reply. This was very interesting, and they had to try to tell the men on the other side, with many a laugh, as a tremendous bit of news.

At another stop, a little woman got in with fair hair, a fluttering white boa, and in a white dress. She was dead drunk, but whereas the others smelt of cheap drink, her breath was of good brandy. She laughed, and now and then gave vent to a half sentence or two that rolled in and out of her sleep.

At the next stop, two were shot in who seemed really deformed with poverty, their complexions yellow, their hands gnarled and worn, their faces of utmost sadness. They said something to each other as they got in – something to give comfort, but their sentences were full of oaths of a senseless kind, and their speech, too, was broken with drink.

Finally, it was another type altogether who was let in. A woman who looked any age, her face of utmost melancholy had yet the appearance of having drunk heavily; she had all the hang of an 'habitual,' her clothes were the dregs of clothes and tumbling off her. When the door was opened for her to be put in, she murmured a few broken words to the effect that her salvation didn't lie in prison.

The Irish girls and the little woman with the white boa were young, the others looked old and worn out.

I think I shall never forget the self-reproach that stung through my whole being when I had thought my intervention necessary between one prisoner and another. On passing some unusual light in the street, which momentarily lit up our van, not enough to see our faces but only to distinguish the outlines of forms, I noticed that the prisoner opposite to Elsie Howey, my neighbour, was leaning forward and bent towards her. The momentary flash of light was too short-lived to judge whether this was a rapid movement perhaps, as I thought, of assault or drunken affection, or whether it was that the position of physical weariness could find no rest from leaning back on the walls of the jolting van. I was unable to see Elsie, but I imagined that she too might be scared by the attention of the prisoner opposite. As the darkness closed in upon us, I thrust my hand into hers; it was welcomed, but quite unnecessary. Before the end of our drive two things were clear – the prisoners might be evil-minded towards all the rest of the world, they might be blind drunk or raging with misery at their own plight, but the one thing impossible to them would have been to hurt a fellow-prisoner. Every one of those pathetic human wrecks, deformed by drink, so that one could not tell if they were guilty of crime besides, overtaken at a moment when their self-respect was lowest, and captured by a punitive system which would do its utmost to dissolve what remained of it, as they were thrust into the black cavity of the van, made a vigorous appeal to their own courage and met with instant response from their unknown companions. It might be only some drunken joke, it was almost invariably accompanied by a laugh, but for each one it had a call on their inmost strength, and it made its appeal to those in the van. Issuing from different spheres of existence, each one representing lives the most remote from one another, scarcely any two alike in a single respect as to detail, their one point of similarity being poverty and that they had given way to drink, the instinct of our first contact, doubtless to each one of us, was repulsion, mistrust, fear of one another. But it lasted for less than the flash of a moment, less than the inhaling of one breath. Our differences were there, but for the time unimportant, whereas the all-embracing fact was our similarity of fate. No need for social laws to bind that company, no rules of the club were necessary, the code of instinct, expediency and honour were all one and spontaneous to us. 'We are all of one blood,' may be a great tie, but 'We are all of one fate' is, while it lasts, a better; the bond of the outcast needs no seal.

We arrived for the fifth time in a courtyard, with a deal of jolting and din; it was the Bridewell Police Station, and we all got out. The little woman in the white dress and fur boa tumbled from the van into the arms of a policeman – she assured us that she loved him on finding herself thus closely against him; he remained stalwart as a piece of wood.

We Suffragettes were put into a cell by ourselves, it was perfectly clean. We had not been there very long before the door was opened with a clang and another woman was thrust in. She was reassuring to look at, smartly dressed with fashionably-shaped brown furs draped round her neck. She had come from Ireland that night and was terribly cold. We gave her the blankets that had been given to us; nothing, however, did much good. She had come over with another woman, who on landing had been taken as 'wanted by the police.' This woman had been arrested, too, as 'her friend,' but she said she was quite sure of getting off, as she had only known the other woman quite a short time, and had no idea that she was in any way 'suspected.' The concern of this woman to get free was natural enough, but she seemed to care not at all for the other one, for whom my heart welled over with sympathy. I thought of her with a more or less deceitful face, but I loved her because she was 'wanted by the police,' and this woman who was with us I wanted to get off, of course, but that was all; I could not feel any sympathy towards her.

We waited in this cell until it was dawning light. It was not a place for sleep, and the cold was terrible. As it was getting towards morning, we were taken out of the cell and led off to wash our hands and faces in another part of the prison. It was fearfully dark in one part, with only a light occasionally here and there, so that one could not see where one was going. On a bench, some ten or twelve little boys were sitting.

It was the first time I thought of children as prisoners. At Newcastle, it was true, I had seen one little boy in the police court, but he was enjoying himself over a cup of soup in the central room with the police, and he was much too small to be convicted, whatever his offences; possibly, if his parents were hopeless, he would have been sent to a reformatory school. That, of course, was bad enough; one knew that for half of the money that would have to be expended there was many a woman in the country who would have cared for him with motherly tenderness. But with these boys, who looked about nine years to fifteen or sixteen years old, it was another matter. The place where they sat, though public, for it was a gangway, was terrible, it was just where the passages seemed to go underground; they were extremely dark, on one side they abutted into a regular network of cells, with small communicating alleys in between. There the boys sat and gazed at the grown-up criminals who appeared from time to time; they looked at us with the greatest curiosity. It was horrible to see them in a place so profoundly ill-suited to children.

The Liverpool organiser, Miss Flatman, and Miss Maude Joachim came to us with the daylight of Saturday, January 15. It was a most unexpected joy to see them – not alone, for that was not allowed, but in one of the many passages near a window with a policeman standing by. I was able to write a little scrap of a letter to Mrs. Pethick Lawrence in the name of 'Jane Warton.' This made me very happy. I believe we were offered breakfast, or should have been able to get it had we asked for it, but, in any case, those surroundings were so wretched that we almost as soon went without, and I was eager to begin the hunger-strike.

As the time of the assembling of the court, 10 o'clock, drew near we waited in different parts of a large and rambling building. At last we were conveyed, through what seemed an underground court, to the foot of a staircase that led right up into the prisoner's dock.

I was the first of the Suffragettes to be taken up. Mr. Shepherd

Little was the magistrate; he seemed to be thoroughly out of temper. They took only two or three minutes convicting me. When the policeman had done his work of charging me with urging the crowd to follow me to the Governor's house, with refusing to desist when called upon by the police, and with throwing a 'missile' (small stone wrapped in paper), I put in, 'I had three stones upon me which I let fall in the Governor's garden. A man in the crowd ran past me just as I was letting go the third – it fell on his shoulder; I apologised to him.'

On the strength of its being my first imprisonment, I was sentenced to a fortnight, 3rd Division, with option of a fine. Just when I had left the court I was called back. The magistrate thought I ought to have a longer sentence, thanks to my having thrown stones, but the clerk thought not, and in the little altercation he got the best of it.

The women of last night were waiting on the stairs. 'How long have you got?' they all said to me. 'Ah! well, buck up,' they added on hearing of fourteen days. Miss Elsie Howey, with the admission of her former imprisonments, got six weeks, and Mrs. Nugent was, to our great joy, released. The policemen downstairs told me that hard labour always accompanied the 3rd Division sentences, unless stated to the contrary.

. . .

The wardress who came most often to my cell was kind to me. I said to her, 'Oh! if you only knew what a nightmare it is, the feeding. I have never been any good at bearing pain, and each time it comes I feel as if I simply couldn't endure it.' 'Oh! well,' she answered, 'it gets better, you'll see.' She said this in a comforting voice, but the vistas of experience it gave of other prisoners who had gone through the process made it anything but a comfort to me. Most of them had been let out half dead before the end of their time, and I had but very little faith in the assurance that it would 'get better.' I asked her after the other Suffrage prisoners, but she could tell me nothing of them. This wardress came back to my cell rather late one day and said to me hurriedly: 'I am going away to the other side of the prison. Will you write to me when you get out?' I told her that I was afraid my letters might get her into trouble, for I felt sure it would not be allowed. She said she was quite sure it would be all right, if I sent it to her name, Miss —. I said, 'Very well, then, I will.'

I was filled with terror in the morning when the gas-jet was put out and in the evening when it was lighted again; within about half an hour of these changes in the light came the doctor and wardresses, the gag and all the fiendish consequences. I walked up and down my cell in a fever of fear, stopping now and then and looking up at the window, from which all good things had seemed to come. I said, 'Oh, God, help me! Oh, God, help me!'

After, I think, the sixth meal, I complained to the doctor that the processes of digestion were absolutely stagnant. I suggested to him that he should leave out one meal, with a view to allowing the natural forces of the body to readjust themselves, unhampered by the kind of paralysing cramp and arresting of the natural functions which resulted from fear. I also suggested that instead of brandy – he had given me another meal of bovril and brandy – fruit juice or the water in which a pear or apple had been stewed should be added to my food. He did not answer me, but turned to the head assistant, whom he had already assured me was a fully-trained nurse, and in a half-insolent, half-contemptuous tone of voice, said: 'Do you understand her? I don't. Does she mean that she is constipated? If so, you see about it.' Very likely I had spoken unintelligibly. I seldom had interviewed a doctor on my own behalf, and am not versed in their technical language. Whenever I spoke to this doctor it was either immediately before or after the feeding, so that my nerves were unstrung. Moreover, prisoners are made to feel in the presence of nearly every prison official that they are the scum of the earth, suspected of deceit, prejudged and found wanting; this has a paralysing effect on a prisoner's powers of expression. The chief assistant was the woman who took me daily to the weighing machine. She was kind and refined in her ways. I explained to her what I wanted, I reminded her several times about this; once I spoke again to the doctor of it, but I was never given either a drug, or, so far as I know, the fruit juice in my food.

I asked the doctor if a smaller tube could not be used for the feeding. He answered, 'If I fed you through the nose it would be with a smaller tube.' I suggested that the smaller tube should be used through the mouth, if he thought that process the easiest. He said, 'Well, that might be,' but the tube was never changed to a smaller one. As to my suggestion about omitting a meal, he also seemed to think it plausible, but he promised nothing, and fed me in the evening, saying that I had again lost weight, so that he could not leave me without food. Of course, this quite ignored my argument that until I began to keep down the food I could not profit by it or gain in weight.

G. Colmore, *The Life of Emily Davison*

Colmore's biography, published soon after Davison's death and magnificent funeral, links her martyrdom to earlier acts of sacrifice. Here she details an incident in which the suffragette barricaded herself in her cell, forcing the authorities into extreme measures to get her out. Her actions gained publicity outside Strangeways; a question was asked in Parliament, and the Governor of the prison received an admonition for the mishandling of the situation.

Emily, when she left Strangeways Gaol in September, had a foreboding that she had not seen the last of it. The foreboding was soon to be fulfilled; on October 21st she was once more shut up in one of its solitary cells. She, together with her fellow-prisoners, had begun the hunger-strike in Bury Police Court, and the day after she entered the Manchester Prison she was subjected to forcible feeding. It was in the evening that the matron, two doctors, and five or six wardresses entered her cell. The senior doctor sounded her; then –

'I am going to feed you by force,' he said.

Emily protested that such an operation performed against her will was illegal. The doctor's only reply was that it was no concern of his.

Grasped by the wardresses, she was forced down on the bed, while the senior doctor, seizing her by the hair – the fair, abundant hair that was her chief beauty – pulled her head by it violently on to the pillow.

'The scene which followed,' said Emily, when speaking of it afterwards, 'will haunt me with its horror all my life, and is almost indescribable. While they held me flat, the elder doctor tried all round my mouth with a steel gag to find an opening. On the right side of my mouth two teeth are missing; this gap he found, pushed in the horrid instrument, and prised open my mouth to its widest extent. Then a wardress poured liquid down my throat out of a tin enamelled cup. What it was I could not say, but there was some medicament which was foul to the last degree. As I would not swallow the stuff and jerked it out with my tongue, the doctor pinched my nose and somehow gripped my tongue with the gag. The torture was barbaric.'

That first ordeal took place on Friday evening; on Monday Emily was put into an adjoining cell, while the window she had broken in the one to which she was first consigned was mended. Entering, she saw that this cell contained two plank beds, the bed belonging to it and the one they had taken from her that morning. Instantly she perceived that here was the means to barricade the door, and as soon as the wardress was gone, quick as thought and very quietly, she put the two beds lengthways one beyond the other across the floor of the cell. A space of about two feet remained between the second bed and the wall; the stool, legs upwards, filled it, and the wedge not being quite firm, her two slippers and a hairbrush were jammed in to make it quite secure. On the only doubtful spot, the place where the two beds joined, she sat down, and, having piled up the table and mattress to add to the weight, quietly waited.

Presently the wardress returned, unlocked the door, and found it would not move. The spy-hole revealed the reason, and Emily was implored to open. She smiled and said, 'No.'

All the afternoon she sat on her barricade. People came again and again alternately begging and threatening, people who did not know Emily Davison. An attempt was made to prise open the door, and then came a man in authority.

'Get off the planks!'

No answer, no movement.

'Davison, if you don't get off those planks and open the door we shall turn the hose-pipe on you.'

Years ago a little child had stood with her back to the wall, hands behind her, feet firmly planted. 'Do come and be good!' authority had pleaded, and the answer had gone back: 'I don't want to be good.' The woman's back was against the wall now, very firm were her feet, she was determined that in the prison sense of the words she would not 'be good.' She sat motionless and calm and silent.

There was a ladder at the window, a crash of glass, and through the breach made, the nozzle of a hose-pipe. It took some time to fix the pipe; when it was fixed they gave her one more chance, those people who did not know Emily Davison nor the spirit of the Union.

Then came the punishment. At first the stream went over her head; she took hold of the bed boards and sat firm. The course of the stream was altered and came upon her full force, with power that seemed terrific, cold as ice. 'I had to hold on,' she said, 'like grim death.' It seemed as if it lasted for an age, that icy flow; it actually did last for something like a quarter of an hour, full and strong upon her; and still the back of her spirit was against the wall, and the feet of her will were immovable.

At last the operator paused, and a voice called. 'Stop!' it said. 'No more, no more.'

Authority had done its worst and failed. After all the door must be burst open. But, if it fell, it would fall on the prisoner; the men outside knew it, so did the woman within. Even at that time Emily and many others had conceived the idea that life would have to be sacrificed before the cause was won; and as she waited, watching the door, fascinated but not afraid, the thought in her mind was that the moment for the sacrifice had come. But the time was not yet.

They called to her to move off the plank, and she did not move; the door gave, and she did not move. But hands caught it before it fell, and as the gap widened a male warder rushed in, saying, as he seized the prisoner: 'You ought to be horsewhipped for this.'

The water – six inches deep it was – rushed out into the corridor. Emily was hurried into her former cell, where her clothes were torn off her; she was wrapped in blankets, and then carried off in an invalid chair to the hospital. A hot bath, bed between blankets with a hot bottle, and wondering wardresses commenting on her iron determination.

And after that she was forcibly fed again, and it was the nasal tube that was used now; up one nostril it goes and down into the throat; if it does not go down properly the doctor pushes it down with his hand. No wonder, when they made the prisoner get up the next morning, that they had to put her back to bed again. There she stayed till Thursday, when she was made to get up and go out for exercise. But the limit of bodily endurance had been reached: she must not die on the authorities' hands – on Thursday afternoon she was released.

Coming out of prison she found that the story of the hose-pipe was known all over England, and had been brought up in Parliament – to her surprise, as she had feared all news of her and her fellow-prisoners had been suppressed. 'Is Right beginning to prevail over Might at last?' she wondered. No, not yet; and now that she is dead, still not yet.

G. Colmore, *Suffragette Sally*

In her novel, published in 1911, two years after the Strangeways incident, Colmore creates a rather similar scenario in which Sally resists the prison authorities and gains spiritual strength in the struggle.

On remand

'With bars they blur the gracious moon,
    And blind the goodly sun:
And they do well to hide their Hell,
    For in it things are done
That Son of God nor son of Man
    Ever should look upon!'

Ballad of Reading Gaol

Sally had been obliged to leave Mrs. Blake, greatly to her regret, for she and the little dressmaker got on well together; and yet Sally was very proud. For now she was one of the regular workers for the Union, and all her labour, all her mind, all her energy, could be given to the cause to which she had already given so much. She was not always in London now; she was sent hither and thither, to work under the direction of one or other of the organisers; to do, in this place or that, work that by her could be done. In October, at the time of Lady Henry's short imprisonment, she was in Bristol; in November she was back in London; in December she found herself in Brummage.

Sally worked cheerfully, loyally, her pride in her work and her position making her humble. She was proud in that she had been accorded honours which to her were of the highest; she had been entertained at a breakfast on her release from prison, had been cheered, applauded, welcomed, had been received with as much enthusiasm as if she had been Lady 'Ill herself. If only Mr. Bilkes could have seen her! Bilkes had never been cheered in all his life; of that she felt sure; whereas she, the 'general,' whom he had kissed in private and tyrannised over in public, had been driven in procession through London, never more to do the bidding of Bilkes and his kind.

But she was humble, in that, or so it seemed to her, she had done so little. She had been to prison once, but there were others who had passed through the ordeal twice, thrice, many times; and just because Sally had hated prison, she admired those who had endured more of it than she had. She had undergone the hunger strike; but that, to her, seemed a little thing, since, at the time she had gone through it, the terror of the forcible feeding had not been added to its pains. Lady 'Ill had braved that terror, and though she had not actually experienced it – 'an' the only decent thing them bosses ever done was to say as she wasn't fit for it' – she had faced it nevertheless. Sally's imagination was not of the strongest kind, but she shrank from the forcible feeding.

There were many enduring it now, in this very town of Brummage, in Wenlock Gaol. Mrs. Law, the working woman, on whose behalf Lady Henry Hill had had herself arrested, to see if there were any difference made in the treatment of women of known position and women of none, had been released at last and taken to a nursing home; but there were others in her place; and still honourable members in the House of Commons treated the woman's movement as a joke; and still women, who worked prominently in the political field on behalf of men, held meetings to protest against other women working politically on behalf of themselves and their fellow women.

In Christmas week Sally found herself at Belton Head. It was a sorrowful time for Sally, for every year since she and Joe had kept company they had spent Christmas together, and now there was to be no more Joe. But a day or two before leaving Brummage she had had a letter from him, in which he told her that he had followed her advice and taken up with Mary Ann Dobbs. It was the best thing he could do; it was the thing she had told him to do; and yet when Sally heard the news she knew that she had had a secret hope that he would find it impossible to take up with anybody but herself. She, like Edith Carstairs, had had visions of golden days ahead, when the vote would be won, and there would be no suffrage question to stand between a girl and her lover.

Well, it was a good thing there was work to be done; it was a good thing, if the bosses, when safe in the House of Commons, refused to listen to women, that one of them was coming to Belton Head, where it might be possible to get speech of him. Possible, it perhaps might be, but not easy; for the suffragettes, lightly spoken of as futile demonstrators, were, in fact, recognised as a formidable force; and wherever a Cabinet Minister went, he was surrounded by number-less precautions and protected by large bodies of police. The strange thing was that, in spite of police and precautions, the suffragettes generally managed to reach the place where they meant to be; and outside the Reform Club, on the 21st of December, a dozen of them were waiting when the Minister's motor-car drew up.

Sally had thought much about the bosses, had wondered often what they looked like, but she had never seen one till now. He did not look very different from anybody else, not more imposing, not more formidable. But she must not stand staring there; she had her part to play. That part was not to address the Minister, but to dis-tract attention while her companions surrounded him. She was glad she had not to speak to him; she did not want to speak; she could not, she told herself, talk grand enough. A street crowd she did not mind, nor one of her own degree; but a boss needed a lady to address him.

Her own part, however, she could do, and she did it deftly. She had an empty ginger-beer bottle in her hand, and she threw it into the car from which the Minister had alighted; she threw it, without hurting anybody, exactly where she meant it to go. The act called attention to the car; it also called attention to Sally, who was arrested for disorderly conduct, and taken before a magistrate. She could not be tried then, so was remanded for a week. That was good; whatever her sentence, she would not, at any rate, have to spend Christmas in prison; she knew that she would be bailed out, and, later in the afternoon, applied for bail.

'So that I can have my Christmas dinner at home,' said Sally. Joe was gone for ever, but she had still the mother who was 'put upon.'

But no, even though she promised to be of good behaviour till after the time of remand, bail was not allowed; Christmas must be spent in prison after all.

Sally's heart sank; it was a dreary prospect; more than dreary, for the spectre of forcible feeding stood waiting in the foreground; and in her mind was the knowledge of what had been done, in divers ways, to the prisoners at Wenlock Gaol, besides the recollection of her own imprisonment in Holloway. Then comfort sprang up within her; she was not convicted, had not been tried yet, was on remand; she could meet with no very bad treatment.

The treatment, she found, was just the same as if she had been convicted, except that she was allowed to wear her own clothing; and she had no choice, therefore, in her loyalty to the plan of campaign, but to protest against it. She remembered the dark, damp cell of her previous imprisonment, and her body was less strong than it had been at that time; but she remembered too that other women had gone through worse sufferings than her own, and made up her mind to put up with whatever might be in store for her.

She refused the prison food, and had, at any rate, the satisfaction of knowing that for that night, whatever might come later, she would breathe fresh air. Before lying down to sleep, Sally broke her windows. The air smelt doubly sweet coming through those broken panes, perhaps because the air inside was so close and stale; but whatever the reason, the fact remained, and she made the most of it.

But now, she knew, she must expect the worst; the refractory cell would be her lot, cold and airless and damp; and solitude and feeding by force. But her spirit rose to the call upon it; and even while her dread became more definite, her courage grew. 'In for a penny, in for a pound,' she thought; and in the morning, half in fear and half in defiance, she barricaded her cell.

There was not a great deal wherewith to construct a barricade, but Sally made the most of what there was, and for a good little while kept the officials out. It was exciting, the most exciting experience she had ever had; the joy of battle awoke in her, and coolness developed as the contest lengthened; there was satisfaction in circumventing the enemy, and for a time, in spite of her empty stomach, in spite of her scanty clothing, for her clothes were still wet with the snow of the previous day, and she was clad only in her under-garments; in spite of all this, Sally almost enjoyed herself.

But the battle was an unequal one, and she was bound to lose it. The barricade was broken down, her cell was entered, and then there was no more enjoyment and no more triumph for Sally. It was natural, perhaps, that the head wardress and her subordinates should be angry; natural, perhaps, too, since human nature has its ugly side, that they should vent their anger by an unmerciful pommelling of the refractory prisoner. Sally, when defeat was certain, had retreated to the bed, but she was pulled from off it and left, when her summary punishment was over, lying on the floor.

She lay there for some time, pain-stricken, exhausted, unable to move; and, as she lay, the thought of Joe Whittle came to her, and of Mary Ann Dobbs. She seemed to see them walking together along Camden Road, where she and Joe had often walked; free in the open street, all London theirs to walk in, the whole world theirs. They were happy, and she did not grudge them their happiness, not she; they seemed too far away for her to have a thought of envy. She hardly envied them even their freedom, for freedom was not much use if you could not move, if it hurt you every time you stirred; and it did hurt – oh yes; it was best to lie still. It was cold, though, horribly cold on the floor; better to try and crawl slowly – it doesn't matter how slowly; there is plenty of time in prison – back to the bed. Never mind though it hurts; it will be better when she is once in bed; never mind the getting there! Ah, that's it; at last! Yes, it is better; she can rest now more comfortably; it is good to rest.

Rest truly is good; but, just because it is good, there is none for the wicked; Sally, at any rate, did not have much of it. She had not lain long upon the bed when the doctor came in; a man dapper, young, with a poor opinion of women at best, and none at all for the genus suffragette.

'You have refused your food,' he said.

'Yes.'

'Do you mean to go on refusing?'

'Yes.'

'Then I shall feed you at once.'

Sally made no answer; there seemed to be no answer with any point in it; nor did the doctor seem to expect one. He went away almost immediately; Sally, shivering with cold and dread, asked herself for how long.

It was but a few minutes later that the cell door opened again. So he was back! No, he wasn't; it was women who entered now.

'Get up and put your clothes on!'

'They're wet, 'orrid wet.'

'Put them on, I say!'

'I dunno as I can. I'm bruised an' sore.'

'We'll soon see.'

Sally was dragged off the bed and forced into her clothes, and then came – well, she had foreseen it, of course, had known that it was bound to come – the punishment cell.

Very cold that cell was on this December day; but it must be always cold, in June as well as in December, for no sun could ever reach it, no warm outside air could ever penetrate to its gloomy depths. So Sally thought as she was led into it; so she thought while her hands were handcuffed behind her back; so she felt, more and more certainly, as she lay and shivered on the damp floor, unable to raise herself. She did not see Joe any more now, nor Mary Ann; she was too cold to see anything, and too tired; had it not been for the utter discomfort of the position in which she had been left, she must have slept from exhaustion.

She lay there for some hours, conscious only of pain and cold and stiffness. If she could free her arms! or even just turn over! It was very quiet; it was almost like being dead and buried to lie there, hearing nothing, seeing almost nothing; only that dead people did not feel; at least she hoped not, oh, she hoped not; for it would be awful to be left – left as she was left – left – for ever, in cold and pain.

A wardress came in at last and lifted her on to the board that served for bed. It was better than the floor, and her clothes were getting drier now; but oh, the pain in those arms, dragged backwards, that she could not move! So the day passed.

In the evening the doctor came again, and Sally was removed to another cell, which, he said, would be warmer. The mere prospect of warmth was a boon, but alas for Sally's hopes, the warmth was only prospective; the second cell proved to be as cold as the first. Yet the night was better than the day, in that the handcuffs were removed for a minute or two, and her arms brought to the front of her body before they were put on again. At least she could lie on her back now; that was something; at least and at last, she was able to fall asleep. And while they are asleep all prisoners are free.

The long night

'Our chain on silence clanks.
Time leers between, above his twiddling thumbs.'

George Meredith

The next morning Sally was taken before the visiting magistrates. It was true that she had broken windows; but Sally, on her side, had charges to bring against the prison officials. They had no right to treat her as she had been treated while she was on remand.

Yes, said the magistrates, the wardresses were justified in what they had done.

Sally tried again. They had no right to threaten her with forcible feeding while she was on remand.

She found that a suffragette on remand could be threatened or treated as the prison officials thought fit.

Then back to the cell; and the second day was as long and as lonely as the first; but a worse day, taking it as a whole, because of the evening.

In the evening several wardresses came to Sally in her cell.

'You are to come to the doctor's room.'

'I ain't coming; not of my own will.'

'You had best come quietly. You'll have to come.'

'I ain't comin'.'

Foolish Sally to resist the irresistible! What is the good of it? None, in a sense; in another sense, it was sticking to the protest against being treated other than as a political prisoner. To give in would mean to sanction the treatment awarded to suffragette prisoners, would mean to fail in carrying out the plan of campaign; 'them ladies' would never submit; no more would Sally.

'I ain't comin',' she said.

The wardresses had been upheld by the visiting magistrates, the wardresses could do as they would. They dragged her to the foot of the stairs, with her hands handcuffed behind her; then, face downwards, they carried her by the arms and legs to the doctor's room. After all, they had to do as they were bid, these wardresses; their task was to bring Sally from her cell hither; they had accomplished their task. Or part of their task, for there was more to do yet. The prisoner had to be placed in a chair, the handcuffs removed and her arms held firmly, so that she could not move, while the doctor and his assistant forced down the stomach-tube into the prisoner's stomach, and then poured in the food.

It is well to feed the hungry, and so, and thus, in His Majesty's prisons, in the years of grace 1909 and 1910, prisoners, who adopted the hunger strike, were fed.

The feeding over, Sally was handcuffed once more and walked to the head of the stairs. Strange that she, who had looked with shrinking dread from the attic window in Brunton Street, across roofs and chimney-pots to Holloway Gaol, and had told herself then that prison was a thing she could not face, strange that now, after the worst that prison could bring her, she still had some spirit left.

'I ain't goin' back to that there cell,' said Sally.

There were three wardresses with her: two seized her by the shoulders, the third kicked her from behind. So she went down the stairs, till she reached the bottom step, and at the bottom step the wardresses relaxed their hold. Then, with her hands secured behind her and no means of resisting the impetus of her descent, she fell forward, on her head.

That was the end of the trouble, so far, at any rate, as the wardresses were concerned. Sally made no further resistance; indeed, she lay quite still. The wardress picked her up and carried her to her cell.

. . .

Sally lay in her cell; awake, because the hunger pangs would not let her sleep. The feeding had made her sick and had added pain to faintness; her throat was swollen and sore; her mouth was dry. If only she had somebody to give her a drink as she, in past days, had given drinks to thirsty little Bilkeses!

The night was very long, as nights are in December, and the day, when it came, always lagged in forcing its way into that dark place. Sally lay and thought of those who were thinking of her: of Miss Carstairs with her delicate face, of Lady 'Ill. Those two together always led to Littlehampton. What a time she had had there! a rippin' time. Perhaps, when she came out of prison, she might be able to go to Littlehampton again. She would need what she had gone there for before; a thorough change. To walk along the sands with Lady 'Ill and watch the tide come in! That would make up for all the loneliness, all the suffering. The tide; that was what Lady 'Ill had said about the Cause. 'Nobody can hold the waves back, Sally. In the end the tide must come in.'

'We can't hold it back,' she had said, 'but we can help it on by clearing away the rocks.'

She, Sally, was helping it now, perhaps. Perhaps; but the night was very long.

W. B. Baldry, *From Hampstead to Holloway*

In contrast to the other pieces in this section, Burton Baldry's
anti-suffrage novel shows the prison experience as a turning
point for Kate Denver, revealing the error of her ways and convincing her she is unsuited to the suffrage cause.

After the first three days, however, a change came over her. She
began to realise that the pent-up excitement that had kept her spirit
unflaggingly active during the beginning had almost deserted her.

Cold, white walls are not conducive to excitement of any sort,
and she found in those walls – walls that stared at her incessantly –
a symbol of her future life. They were an echo of what was to be.
She could see nothing ahead but dull drab, and dreariness. And now
her spirit was almost broken. The cause of Woman's Suffrage
seemed to lag a very long way behind. Thoughts of it gave her no
satisfaction. During those long mirthless hours – through the days
that seemed interminable – she was torn by conflicting emotions.

'What is the use of it all?' her heart would cry from within her.

And her spirit, still faintly active – unwilling to give up the struggle without a fight – would reply: 'The good of it all? Why, have not
you given your whole life to this cause? Did you not say, some
months ago, 'I shall never give it up'? Did you not –'

But her heart would make reply – 'All is changed now. Life is a
series of changes, and if one does not keep up with the changes it is
apt to leave one stranded by the roadside. Do you want to be left
stranded by the roadside? Do you want to be left to an uninterest-
ing old age?'

Sometimes she would think of her parents. She would think of her
early days at home – how they had scraped the money together for
her education. 'Poor old mater! I am awfully sorry to have caused
you any pain. You always had such a dread of the police station. I
must go and see you directly I am free.' What a pity it all was –

Yet, at the end of a very short time – an incredibly short time –
her thoughts would always revert to one subject, and her heart
would always be asking the same question: 'What does he think?'

It is a question that has troubled women of all grades since the
time of Adam. It has been responsible for hours of heart-searching
anguish – and when that question has been answered? But that
depends on the woman.

M. Sinclair, *The Tree of Heaven*

Writing in 1917, May Sinclair suggests in her acclaimed novel that the suffrage campaign must be placed in the context of a greater cause. Although a supporter of suffrage, the author herself did not go to prison.

'The fight was only the first part of the adventure. The wonderful thing was what happened afterwards. In prison.

'I didn't think I'd really *like* prison. That was another thing I funked. I'd heard such awful things about it, about the dirt, you know. And there wasn't any dirt in my cell, anyhow. And after the crowds of women, after the meetings and speeches, the endless talking and the boredom, that cell was like heaven.

'Thank God, it's always solitary confinement. The Government doesn't know that if they want to make prison a deterrent they'll shut us up together. You won't give the Home Secretary the tip, will you?

'But that isn't what I wanted to tell you about.

'It was something bigger, something tremendous. You'll not believe this part of it, but I was absolutely happy in that cell. It was a sort of deep-down, unexcited happiness. I'm not a bit religious, but I *know* how the nuns feel in *their* cells when they've given up everything and shut themselves up with God. The cell was like a convent cell, you know, as narrow as that bit of shadow there is, and it had nice whitewashed walls, and a plank bed in the corner, and a window high, high up. There ought to have been a crucifix on the wall above the plank-bed, but there wasn't a crucifix. There was only a shiny black Bible on the chair.

'Really, Frank, if you're to be shut up for a month with just one book, it had better be the Bible. Isaiah's ripping. I can remember heaps of it: "In the habitation of jackals, where they lay, shall be grass with reeds and rushes. And an highway shall be there. . . . The redeemed shall walk there: and the ransomed of the Lord shall return with singing unto Zion" . . . . "They that wait upon the Lord shall renew their strength; they shall mount up with wings as eagles; they shall run, and not be weary; they shall walk, and not faint." I used to read like anything; and I thought of things. They sort of came to me.

'That's what I wanted to tell you about. The things that came to me were so much bigger than the thing I went in for. I could see all along we weren't going to get it that way. And I knew we *were* going to get it some other way. I don't in the least know how, but it'll be some big, tremendous way that'll make all this fighting and fussing seem the rottenest game. That was one of the things I used to think about.'

'Then,' he said, 'you've given it up? You're coming out of it?'

She looked at him keenly. 'Are those still your conditions?'

He hesitated one second before he answered firmly. 'Yes, those are still my conditions. You still won't agree to them?'

'I still won't agree. It's no use talking about it. You don't believe in freedom. We're incompatible. We don't stand for the same ideals.'

'Oh, Lord, what *does* that matter?'

'It matters most awfully.'

'I should have thought,' said Drayton, 'It would have mattered more if I'd had revolting manners, or an impediment in my speech, or something.'

'It wouldn't, *really*.'

'Well, you seem to have thought about a lot of things. Did you ever once think about me, Dorothy?'

'Yes, I did. Have you ever read the Psalms? There's a jolly one that begins: "Blessed be the Lord my strength, which teacheth my hands to war, and my fingers to fight.' I used to think of you when I read that. I thought of you a lot.

'That's what I was coming to. It was the queerest thing of all. Everything seemed ended when I went to prison. I knew you wouldn't care for me after what I'd done – you must really listen to this, Frank – I knew you couldn't and wouldn't marry me; and it somehow didn't matter. What I'd got hold of was bigger than that. I knew that all this Women's Suffrage business was only a part of it, a small, ridiculous part.

'I sort of saw the redeemed of the Lord. They were men, as well as women, Frank. And they were all free. They were all free because they were redeemed. And the funny thing was that you were part of it. You were mixed up in the whole queer, tremendous business. Everything was ended. And everything was begun; so that I knew you understood even when you didn't understand. It was really as if I'd got you tight, somehow; and I knew you couldn't go, even when you'd gone.'

5

Questions of identity

For the woman involved, the campaign offered a new sense of their personal and political identities. As the battle raged over what it should and could mean to be a woman in the early twentieth century, existing concepts of female identity were dramatically challenged. In this final section the effect of the suffrage movement upon individual subjectivities is explored but the writing here also demonstrates the conflicting representations of womanhood that were at stake.

Most obviously, the suffrage movement led women to a new understanding of their positions as political subjects. Evelyn Sharp described Christabel Pankhurst's greatest asset as her ability to make women demand rights rather than beg favours. For the women involved in the movement, however, it offered more than the promise of a vote. As Helena Swanwick robustly points out in her autobiography: 'let there be no mistake about it – this movement was not primarily political; it was social, moral, psychological and profoundly religious'. Her sense of its far-reaching and transformational power is to be found in most writers in this section.

For someone like Margaret Haig the explanation offered is a practical one: the movement gave a chance of activity. The thrill of action, the chance to escape from the boredom of middle-class female lives, was also a theme favoured by male novelists, such as Arnold Bennett and H. G. Wells, who used it to play down the political agenda of feminism. In their novels the desire for activity and liberation in their heroines also finds an outlet in marriage to an exciting suitor.

The campaign, as the excerpt from *The Judge* suggests, could exert a powerful influence upon young minds. But the struggle provided social as well as spiritual benefits, offering an educative experience and a point of entry into the public sphere. Women encountered fresh ideas, were introduced to new books and discovered a different intellectual and political community. Several accounts in this section indicate how heady that mix could be. Some demonstrate the terrors and satisfactions of speaking in public for the first time.

While many welcome the freedoms offered by the cause, others, however, express anxieties about the pressure toward conformity and the dangers of ideological constraint. Cicely Hamilton articulates a concern about the roles it imposed upon women and May Sinclair's novel reveals a fear about the overwhelming effects of collectivity. Anti-suffrage campaigners used similar arguments in their writing, as *The Home-Breakers* and *Delia Blanchflower* show, but in those instances it is the threat to traditional concepts of femininity that is feared.

In the following excerpts the writers engage with competing images of 'the suffragette' but underpinning these texts is a much more complex debate about women's role in the public sphere, female subjectivity and the boundaries of gendered identity.

E. Gibson, 'Woman'

Elizabeth Gibson, published this collection of poetry, *From the Wilderness* herself in 1910. In it she explores such abstract subjects as 'Poverty', 'Sex', 'Man' and 'Luxury'. Although the poems do not explicitly address women's suffrage, women's rights were a central concern to the writer.

I met a woman walking through the world,
And I stopped to bid her good-day.
She was walking with a will;
So I asked her where she was going.
'Everywhere,' she replied.
I asked her whence she came,
And she answered: 'From the ends of the earth.'
'Of what land are you an inhabitant?'
'Of every land I have heard of.'
'Of what city are you a citizen?'
'Of every city I can imagine.'
'Where are your children?'
'All over the earth. Every child that is born is mine. I suckle every living baby.'

'Who is your husband?'

'Every man is my husband.'

'Why have you left him?'

'That he may know the bitterness of life without me.'

'When will you return to him?'

'When he has learnt that I am his equal.'

Then she bade me good-day; and I watched her ascend the summit of the world to see how man was faring.

And as she turned I heard God cry: 'Thou hast done well.'

A. Mollwo, *A Fair Suffragette*

A characteristic theme of suffrage fiction is that of mis/recognition of the suffragette. This rather conventional example, Chapter 1 of Adrienne Mollwo's novel, published in 1909, adopts a male perspective on the 'mystery of woman' in the person of Gipsie Grey.

'Hansom, Sir?'

'No, I'll walk, just see that my bag is sent round to my rooms at once, porter. Here!' and handing the man a fee, Vernon Mowbray walked briskly down the platform. He turned a corner sharply, colliding as he did so with a passenger hurrying in the opposite direction. He fell back a step, and lifted his hat with a murmured word of apology. The girl raised her eyes with a smile of pardon and passed on, but the man stood staring after her.

'What eyes!' he ejaculated, 'large and full and soft – soft as velvet!' He watched her dainty form as she threaded her way among the busy throng until she was lost to sight, and then turned on his heel slowly and walked away. As he passed out into the street and moved in the direction of Piccadilly, he found his mind dwelling on the slight incident.

'I wonder who she is?' he thought. 'I would give much to know.'

It was a warm morning about a week later. Mowbray felt lazy – he often felt lazy, and eyed his pile of letters on the breakfast table with anything but pleasure. He took up one idly and glanced through it. It was from his friend Sir Charles Dalny and ran as follows:–

My dear fellow,

If you've nothing better to do, can you put in a few days with us on the river, and sample our new Bungalow? We have a saucy little Suffragette staying with us, perfectly rabid, – crams politics down our throats all day. Kittsie's in despair, – wants you to take her in tow, – the other fellows all fight shy of her. 'Phone me that you'll come, there's a good chap!
Yours ever,
Charlie.

Mowbray smiled involuntarily. He caught up the receiver and rang up No. 100.

'Hulloa! Is that you old chap – Oh Thanks awfully, but I can't take on the job, I can't indeed! – What do you say? – all rot! – I tell you I haven't the courage of a chicken this hot weather – What's that? – "A jolly little girl, just my style?" I daresay, anything else? How the deuce do you know what my style is? Well, I'll be a martyr for once – To-morrow – Paddington – 3.30? All right! Au revoir.'

The two men travelled down together the following afternoon. It was a brilliant day in early June, the sky cloudless, the vegetation luxurious, the heat tempered by a soft breeze. They were old friends and had much in common, and many topics to discuss of mutual interest. It was only as they neared their journey's end that Dalny suddenly laughed, and tossed away his cigar.

'By Jove, old fellow, you've got your work cut out for you for the next few days!'

His companion smiled calmly.

'That's as it may be, how if I don't take the lady on?'

Dalny roared.

'You can't help yourself. Kittsie says you're the only man she knows who could tackle Gipsie Grey, but 'pon my soul, I don't believe a whole army of men could. She's as obstinate as a little pig, and as illogical, and never knows when she is beaten. She always argues round in a circle, and commences again at the same point, after it has been threshed out a dozen times. I won't argue with her now, she's too exasperating, and as Kittsie says, I have quite enough politics in "the House" without having them thrust down my throat perpetually at home. But here we are!'

The Bungalow was but a few minutes' walk from the station, so Mowbray, leaving his baggage in charge of his man, followed Sir Charles down some rough steps on to a narrow thickly wooded path which, winding in and out by the river, led them directly into his pretty grounds.

A small group of men and women were collected on the sunlit lawn under the shade of drooping trees. It was a charming, picturesque scene, full of colour and life and repose. The cool river, the bright green grass, the brilliant flower beds, the fair women and the lazy men.

The two pedestrians were greeted with a shout, and Lady Dalny arose from a small rustic tea table where she was presiding, and came forward.

'How delightful!' she cried, 'You dear men, you are just in time for a cup of tea! How do you do, Mr. Mowbray? So glad to see you, what have you been doing with yourself all this time? Let me present you to these ladies. Mr. Mowbray, – Miss Brown, Miss Howard, Lady Blanch Seacombe, Miss Grey.'

Mowbray bowed mechanically, then started as a pair of soft brown eyes met his own, eyes like brown velvet. Where had he seen that piquant little face before? He searched at the back of his brain, and memory came with a rush. He smiled involuntarily, and the girl coloured slightly, as she drew back and let her pretty lashes fall.

'You two are going to be great friends,' said Sir Charles wickedly, coming up behind. 'This is our little suffragette, Mowbray; you who are so great on politics, and such an ardent advocate of women's rights are sure to sympathise with Miss Grey.'

Mowbray smiled again.

'I will do my best,' he said, and then Lady Dalny called them for tea.

At dinner that night Gipsie Grey was apportioned to Vernon Mowbray! He was nothing loth. She was dainty to look upon, and pleased his fastidious taste, she also interested him. He was glad to meet her, to know her; he felt he should like to study her, to find if a soul lay behind those great velvet eyes, the eyes he had seen but once before in a flash, in a single moment of time, yet which had haunted his dreams since. He smiled at the idea that she was a suffragette, 'a baby playing at politics,' it was too incongruous. He had expected to meet a blue stocking, a thin, angular, spectacled person, with whom he was to do penance for the next few days, and lo, there appeared a little brown fairy, a little warm, sympathetic woman, made to love and be loved.

He noted with approval her gown as he gave her his arm, an

amber crepe de chine, fashioned with fine old lace, almost too handsome a dress for the occasion, but it suited her well, the soft colour
but enhancing her rare dark beauty. It was quite a tableful of pretty
women and handsome men, but somehow the other girls seemed
insipid beside Gipsie. 'Gipsie, what an appropriate name,' thought
Mowbray, as he took his seat. He was almost startled when she said
calmly, in her low, contralto voice:–

'Is it true you are fond of politics, Mr. Mowbray?'

He looked at her indulgently, so she had begun on her pet subject.
After all, what did it matter what they talked about so long as he
caught an occasional glance from her pretty eyes.

'Fond of politics is hardly the word, Miss Grey, I am naturally
interested in the affairs of my country, as indeed all men ought to
be.'

'And women too,' she interrupted, eagerly. 'Don't you think so?'

Mowbray smiled.

'Well, I don't know that I've ever given the subject a thought.
Now that you ask me, I really don't think it is necessary for women
to bother themselves about politics, indeed I should imagine it were
infinitely better for them to leave the subject severely alone.'

'A man's eternal answer, one sided and childish to a degree.'

'Why, may I ask?'

'It is childish because it is no answer to the question at all –
and one sided because it is only dealing with the male point of
view, and ignoring the fact that women have also a point of view,
and as mothers of the human race should be encouraged rather
than discouraged, to interest themselves in the affairs of their
country.

'Maybe,' he assented somewhat dubiously.

'How can a woman be interested in her country and government
if she knows nothing of the working of the Government? She may
read the result in history of the actions of former governments, but
she may not read and criticise the actions of her own particular
Government.'

'No one prevents her reading the Parliamentary report as much
as she likes,' observed Mowbray.

'I thought you said she were better advised to leave it alone.'

'Well, I do think so,' he admitted, 'a woman has plenty of things
to do without politics, which are absolutely of no use to her. She had
her household to superintend, her children – if she be married – to

care for, her wardrobe to interest her,' here he glanced smilingly at Gipsie, but she actually sniffed.

'Oh, you men!' she cried, 'you are all alike. You forget the many women who have no husbands, no children, no wardrobes – the many single women of the middle class who work; who must work because their fathers and brothers can't or won't work for them and yet are hated and taunted by the men for so working. It is not necessary for these women to know, to understand, to be interested in the domestic policy of the government – these women who are employed in many cases by the Government – who have rights to be protected, wrongs to be adjusted, injuries for which to be compensated. But no, women, are classed with lunatics and children, criminals and paupers. You men are so selfish, that you want to keep everything for yourselves, and in your own hands; so short sighted that you do not perceive that it is for the future good of the race that women should be given a voice in the conduct of affairs. And when women protest, they are told to go home and "nurse the baby" – We haven't all got babies to nurse,' added Gipsie with unconscious naïveté. 'According to men however, women are nobodies, they always have been, and you want to keep them so, but you won't – you won't.!'

Mowbray smiled in spite of himself.

'Come, Miss Grey,' he interposed mildly, 'you are letting your chicken get quite cold, and you haven't tasted your champagne!'

He noticed Sir Charles gazing amusedly in their direction with an 'I told you so' look on his face.

'Women are not nobodies,' he added softly, 'they never have been, and never will be.'

Gipsie relapsed into silence, and Mowbray studied her quietly. Presently when the dessert was on the table, she said suddenly –

'If you were a married man – I beg your pardon, perhaps you are married?'

'No, I am not married,' he answered with another smile.

'Well, if you were a married man and a member of Parliament – you are a member of Parliament I believe?'

'Yes.'

'And you were intensely interested in political affairs, as you ought to be, and are, I suppose, and you came home evening after evening when something great and momentous was on, when perhaps you were making big speeches, and helping to make history, when you felt you wanted some one intimate to sympathise in your lofty ideals, some one dear to you to be interested in your grand schemes, your great enterprises, some one closer than those outside, nearer than your men friends, whom it would rest you to confide in, some one who would say, "I know, I comprehend, I sympathise with all your undertakings, I understand all that is in your heart." In that day when you came to your home and found your wife too busy to listen to you, busy with Martha-like cares about her household, or taken up with visiting, or ordering new gowns or a thousand and one things, I ask you in that day would you not give everything for a wife who knew and loved politics?'

Mowbray was surprised and somewhat amused. He began to see there was a depth and pertinacity of purpose about Gipsie that he had not given her credit for, but he merely remarked:

'It is quite possible for a political woman to be hard and unsympathetic, and for a woman unlearned and ignorant of politics to be sweet and tender and loving.'

'Oh, but you miss my point,' cried the girl impatiently, 'Is it not natural that a wife interested in affairs of the day should take more pride in her husband's career than a wife not similarly interested? The one would be patient and tolerant of her husband's late nights and many engagements, the other petulant, impatient, annoyed.'

'You talk like a book,' said the man. 'I–' but here Lady Dalny rose, so he only whispered with a smile as she passed out, 'To be continued in our next.'

'By Jove, you've had a doing, Mowbray!' cried Sir Charles, 'I've been watching you two, and I don't believe the little chatterbox ate a morsel of dinner. Gad, she's a caution!'

Mowbray laughted and yawned. 'She's a charming little woman,' he declared. 'I find her most interesting.'

'Phew!' whistled Sir Charles.

'You'll soon get sick of it, my dear fellow,' observed Captain Pilcher, one of the men, languidly, 'One innings was enough for me, I couldn't stick another, 'pon my word!'

Mowbray moved impatiently, somehow the conversation jarred, he changed it abruptly, and shortly after the men flocked to the drawing-room.

G. Colmore, 'Pluck'

Gertrude Colmore's short story mocks the stereotypes with which the suffragettes are caricatured, and demonstrates that supposedly masculine qualities are to be found within the campaigners.

She came into the ABC tea-room almost timidly, yet with complete self-possession.

The room was nearly filled, chiefly with very young men, and it was not easy to find a seat. She paused at the door, looking to right and left; then her eyes lighted on a free table, and she made her way to it.

She was daintier than most of the women who came to that particular shop; she had what the youth at a neighbouring table called a genteel air. She was dainty, too, in her ways. When her cup of coffee, her boiled egg and roll and butter were brought her, she ate and drank in a leisurely, somewhat fastidious fashion, opening the egg carefully so that the yolk did not overflow and stain the plate with a yellow stain, as was the fate of so many plates in that close room, where haste or habit or hunger trampled on the graces of life.

The youth at the neighbouring table watched her with admiring and curious eyes. He had finished his meat pie and tea, and had nothing to do but read the racing news or look about him while he smoked a cigarette. This girl was more attractive even than the tips given by his favourite racing expert, and he looked at her more than at the paper in his hand.

She was a cut above the girls he was used to, so he told himself; more stylish, more of the lady; too modest-looking, he thought, for an actress, yet as cool in her ways as if she were used to being looked at by all the world. Wasn't she perhaps an actress after all? Surely – in the shop window – or was it the papers – ? Somewhere – he became more and more sure – somewhere – he had seen the face – certainly – with other faces. In a row of portraits was it? – or a row of photos? – or – or –

Suddenly he knew. Like their cheek to give herself such airs! They had plenty of that. But he knew; he wasn't to be taken in. Of course, of course; that was it; he remembered now. She was a well-known suffragette.

The youth's face had changed; the naive admiration had gone; in its place was a smirk of contempt. The girl, as unconscious of the one as she had been of the other, continued slowly to eat her meal, pausing now and again to make notes in the margin of a book which she had taken from her bag and which lay open on the table beside her plate.

She did not notice that a youth had left a neighbouring table and taken a seat at her own; she was certainly startled when a voice said close to her: 'I know who you are.'

Startled she was for a moment, but her eyes were calm as she returned his gaze: 'Indeed!'

'Yes, and I could – 'He looked round the room. 'I know most of the fellows here, and they're dead set, I can tell you, against you and your lot. You might have a rough time of it if I was to give you away.'

Her look would have been pathetic but for its fearlessness. 'I'm used to rough times.'

'Rough times are for rough women. I wonder you aren't ashamed of yourself.'

'I suppose you are the kind that would wonder.' She looked at him scrutinisingly. 'And yet – you might be amongst our admirers, if you could only manage to understand.'

'Understand? Understand, indeed! 'Tain't my understanding that's wrong.'

'You're quite sure of that?' She half smiled as she spoke.

'It don't take any particular understanding to know what's decent behaviour.'

'Decency is a difficult question.' She was still quite good-humoured. 'You must admit, though, that we have some good qualities – pluck, for instance.'

'Not my idea of pluck – to go –'

'What is your idea?'

'Well, I heard of a plucky thing the other day – a woman, too, it was. There was a child by the canal, Regent's Park way – you know how these little beggars will play close down by the water – fell in, and a woman fished him out.'

'Went in after him, do you mean?'

'Yes, that's what I mean; deep water. There's pluck for you, the real article.'

'Could she swim?'

''Pears she could. She was off with her coat and shoes in no time, the fellow said who told me, and into the water like a knife. What do you think of that?'

The girl shrugged her shoulders. 'It doesn't take half the pluck to do a thing like that it does to go on a deputation.'

'You mean to tell me –?'

'Well, she could swim, you see. And besides a flood of water isn't a quarter as cruel as a flood of brutal men.'

'All very well to say that, but –'

'Say! I know it. You haven't been in a mob of savages; I have.'

'And you haven't been in the water and risked your life to save a child. And to sneer at a woman who'd do a thing like that, well, it's – it's all of a piece –'

'I'm not sneering. I only say it doesn't take half so much courage to do the one as to do the other. And I know what I'm talking about.'

'Oh you do, do you? And pray how do you know what sort of pluck it take to jump into the water like that woman?'

Again she shrugged her shoulders. 'Because, as it happens, I was the woman.'

'You? You?'

At the sight of his face she laughed.

'You're kidding me,' he said, making fun. By Jove –'

'Oh no. You ask your friend. I had a purple coat and skirt on and a green felt hat and a white blouse; and in pulling me out – for I had been in some time and was rather done – my arm got hurt.' She turned back her sleeve and showed a bandage. 'You ask your friend.'

'That's right. I remember,' he said. 'And you did that – you?'

'Yes, I, and I tell you it wasn't half as bad to do as many of the things I've done. Now I must go. Good morning!'

As she rose, he rose too. He could not take off his hat to her since it hung upon a peg close by; but he moved a chair aside for her to pass, and stood with bent head as she made her way between the tables to the door.

E. Sharp, 'Patrolling the Gutter'

In her collection of short stores *Rebel Women* Evelyn Sharp frequently returns to the theme of identity, exploring it through the daily activities of the suffragettes. Here, with characteristic humour and self-awareness, she demonstrates the conflicting constructions of femininity imposed upon women when they enter public space.

'I suppose we had better start,' faltered the tall woman in purple.

'I can't think of a reasonable excuse for delaying any longer,' sighed the girl in green.

'Come along!' said a third, making a great show of the courage she did not feel.

Nobody came along. Under some pretext or another we still lingered, though there were ten of us and the space in our Suffragette shop was uncomfortably limited. Most people, the even tenor of whose lives had not been ruffled by the call of a great cause, might have thought the day an unpropitious one to choose for patrolling the gutter, even for the sake of advertising a meeting of rebel women in the Albert Hall. A strong south-west wind, a real London drizzle overhead and thick mud underfoot, could hardly be held to offer striking attractions to a band of naturally timorous ladies, girt about with sandwich-boards, preparing to issue forth in procession into the conventional streets of Kensington. If we had been less timorous we should probably have postponed the expedition; but the last fear that rebel women ever learn to overcome is the fear of being thought afraid, so this was an alternative that did not suggest itself to anybody.

'I never realized before what it meant to be a belted knight, but I do now,' remarked our literary member, trying in vain to free her hands from their cardboard bonds in order to straighten a crooked hat. 'If anything or anybody were to unhorse us and make us bite the dust – isn't that what belted knights were always doing to one another in the Middle Ages? – we should have to lie on our backs, as they did, till some one came and picked us up.'

'I feel like a pantomime super, myself,' observed somebody else, twirling round in order to get a full-length back view of herself in the glass. 'I shall never get accustomed to the make-up,' she added ruefully, as she once more swept the greater part of our stock of pamphlets from the counter to the floor, and had to stand helpless and repentant while the shop secretary picked them up, not for the first time in the course of these trial manoeuvres.

'If you don't start soon, there will be nothing saleable left in the place,' said the shop secretary pointedly.

'Well, what are you waiting for?' demanded the girl in green, trying to infuse a little real impatience into her tone.

'Courage,' confessed the woman in purple, gloomily.

'Oh, nonsense!' said our literary member, without, however, moving any nearer to the door. 'Think of George Herbert:

God gave thy soul brave wings; put not those feathers
Into a bed to sleep out all ill weathers.'

We all tried to think of George Herbert, but without marked success.

'I can't think of anything but the ill weather waiting for us outside and all the people I know in Kensington,' said the tall woman, voicing bluntly and concisely what the rest of us were feeling.

'Do you think the people we know would ever recognize us in these things?' asked some one in a moment of real inspiration; and under the influence of this new and cheering suggestion we formed up hastily in single file and really made a start.

The secretary of another local branch, who had dropped in to seek recruits for a similar poster parade in her district, observed significantly as we filed past her that it was most important to be as well dressed as possible in her neighbourhood. Neither this, nor the first comment that reached our ears as we plunged into the street, added particularly to our good opinion of ourselves.

'Well, I must say you ladies don't think of appearances, that you don't!' was the comment of the street. At a less sensitive moment we might have derived comfort from the tone of admiration in which this was uttered. As it was, an outrageous remark that followed did far more to raise our drooping spirits. This one was made by a girl, wearing a flaming hat and blouse that not one of us would have had the courage to put on before going for a walk, even if supported by so magnificent a youth as the one on whose arm she leaned as she criticized.

'Brazen, ain't they?' she said.

After that, it was easy to laugh and go ahead in a world that could always be counted upon to feed the most unsatisfied sense of humour. Otherwise, for the first half-hour or so, I doubt if we should have felt acutely conscious of anything but the traffic. Glorious as it may seem to the imaginative to suffer for a cause, one finds it difficult, when carrying sandwich-boards in its service, to detach from this distant and problematic reward the more immediate prospect of being run down from behind by a skidding motor-omnibus. In time, no doubt, it would be possible to acquire the easy swagger of the real sandwich man, though the real sandwich man would under no circumstances be submitted, as we were, to a definite onslaught from every impudent tradesman's boy who whizzed past us on a tricycle. As it was, no one could have said that our pace bore the slightest resemblance to the leisurely saunter of the professional patroller of the gutter. In spite of conscientious efforts on our part to maintain the regulation distance from one another, none of us could resist the impulse to catch up the next woman in front; and as our leader, the tall woman in purple, desired nothing more than to cover the prescribed route and return to the shelter of home as quickly as possible, only he who ran could have read the announcement printed on our boards, as we raced breathlessly along the edge of the pavement. At the same time, we found, nobody had the slightest difficulty in reading the identity of those who carried the boards.

'Suffer-a-gettes! Look at 'em!' roared an omnibus driver.

'Well, why not?' responded a gallant cabman from the shelter we were approaching. 'Why shouldn't Mrs. Pank'urst 'ave a vote, same as you an' me? Ain't she got as much sense in her 'ead as what *I* 'ave?' He modulated his belligerent shout to a dulcet undertone as we came alongside. 'The whole of the four-wheel trade is with you, ladies,' he told us confidentially.

A block in the traffic caused us all to close up for a moment, and we compared notes hurriedly.

'Not so bad as we expected, is it?' said our literary comrade, who was one of those to overhear the friendly remark made by the representative of the four-wheel trade.

The girl in green reserved her opinion. 'It makes one feel desperately sorry for the poor men who have to do this sort of thing, not for a cause, but for a living,' she said feelingly.

The girl in green was by nature sentimental. Having once sold a suffrage paper in the street for half a day, she found herself incapable ever afterwards of resisting the appeal of the street hawker, with the result that her flat became a depôt for patent toasting-forks, bone collar-studs, and quivering, iridescent beetles. Her latest conviction that a human link existed between her and all sandwich-men received, however, a slight shock as soon as we encountered one of these. Melting with compassion, she tried in a single look to express all she felt for his hard lot, but was met by a still more eloquent expression of pity from his eye – the one that did not wink – and became henceforth a little dubious about that particular human link. We tried, but without much success, to rekindle her faith in human links generally, by pointing out that his scorn was probably aroused by the unprofessional appearance of her sandwich boards, one of which was slipping its ribbon moorings as she went by.

Perhaps the most startling conversion we made in the course of our parade was that of the baby. Up to that moment it has been a plain and placid, contented baby, banging its Teddy bear happily against the side of the perambulator. When it saw our procession coming along, with flying colours and flapping boards, it dropped the Teddy bear on the pavement and emitted an amazing remark that sounded to all of us, except our literary member, like 'Ga-ga-ga—ga-*ga!*' Our literary member, being imaginative, declared that what the baby really said was – 'Hooray! Votes for Women!' – and the baby's nurse, who had to soil her white cotton gloves by picking the Teddy bear out of the mud, seemed inclined to agree with her.

'Them 'orrible Suffragettes!' she said crossly; and remembering the militant countenance of the baby we had converted, we felt bound to forgive her for feeling uneasy about the baby's future. Our triumph was short-lived, however, for we were scarcely out of hearing of the baby's gurgles when a gentleman outside a public-house informed us, with some difficulty of utterance, that we were a disgrace to our sex.

'What do they mean, blocking up the King's 'Ighway, undreds and undreds of 'em?' he grumbled fiercely. As the girl in green observed, he was not in a condition when it would be fair to challenge his ability to count.

On the whole, the triumphs won as usual, and the insults were too funny and pathetic, both at once, to hurt much. There was the lady who told us very distinctly what she thought of us, and then dropped her skirts in the mud, a real feminine sacrifice, to take one of our handbills, because her hard heart was melted by the absent-minded smile of our literary member, who mistook her for a sup-porter. There was the clergyman who stood with his hat in his hand the whole time our procession was going by; there was the senti-mentalist who, after telling each one of us in turn to go home and mind the baby, said in a tone of concentrated despair to the last of us – 'What would you do if you had twins?' And, of course, there was the messenger-boy who stood just out of reach and yelled –

'Want yer rights? Then you won't git 'em! Sooner give 'em to tomcats, I would!'

By the time we arrived in sight of home, even the woman in purple had become hardened to the perils and vicissitudes of the road and smiled quite easily at the postman who stood at the corner of the street. But when we found ourselves inside the shop, in full view of the shop looking-glass, it required all our newly won insensibility to stifle an inward consciousness that the glories of a militant campaign still remained rather spiritual than actual. Our hair was damp and straight, our cardboard armour limp and bent; our skirts were caked with mud, and our boots strongly resembled those that one sometimes sees sticking out of river sand at low tide. For once, our literary comrade refrained from asking us to turn to George Herbert or anybody else for poetic consolation.

On the other hand, the postman's criticism became wildly, disproportionately cheering.

'Votes for women!' he shouted after us with a sneer, as we slowly passed indoors out of his sight. 'Votes for a few rich women, that's all you're after!'

Under the circumstances, it was very pleasant to be mistaken for representatives of the rich and cultured classes.

R. West, *The Judge*

Rebecca West's novel, published in 1922, draws to an extent upon her own suffrage experiences and adolescence in Edinburgh, but her ability to view the cause with a critical detachment is also revealed in this passage. It offers two views of a suffrage meeting: one from the young, passionate and naive Ellen Melville and another from the novel's romantic lead, the experienced and much-travelled Richard Yaverland. The dual perspective allows for an empathy with Ellen's emotional involvement but contrasts this with a critical masculine reading of the occasion. The reader is left to evaluate their different responses.

'Is my frock hooked up all the way down?' wondered Ellen, as she stood with her back to a pillar in the Synod Hall. 'Not that I care a

button about it myself, but for the sake of the Cause . . .' But that
small worry was just one dark leaf floating on the quick sunlit river
of her mind, for she was very happy and excited at these Suffrage
meetings. She had taken seven shillings and sixpence for pamphlets,
the hall was filling up nicely, and Miss Traquair and Dr. Katherine
Kennedy and Miss Mackenzie and several members of the local militant suffrage society had spoken to her as they went to their places
just as if they counted her grown-up and one of themselves. And she
was flushed with the sense of love and power that comes of comradeship. She looked back into the hideous square hall, with its rows
of chattering anticipant people, and up to the gallery packed with
faces dyed yellowish drab by the near unmitigated gas sunburst, and
she smiled brilliantly. All these people were directing their attention
and enthusiasm to the same end as herself: would feel no doubt the
same tightness of throat as the heroic women came on the platform,
and would sanctify the emotion as sane by sharing it; and by their
willingness to co-operate in rebellion were making her individual
rebellious will seem less like a schoolgirl's penknife and more like a
soldier's sword. 'I'm being a politikon Zoon!' she boasted to herself.
She had always liked the expression when she read it in *The
Scotsman* leaders.

And here they were! The audience made a tumult that was half
applause and half exclamation at a prodigy, and the three women
who made their way on the platform seemed to be moving through
the noise as through a viscid element. The woman doctor, who was
to be the chairman, lowered her curly grey head against it buttingly;
Mrs Ormiston, the mother of the famous rebels Brynhild, Melissa,
and Guendolen, and herself a heroine, lifted a pale face where defiance dwelt among the remains of dark loveliness like a beacon lit on
a grey castle keep; and Mrs. Mark Lyle, a white and golden wonder
in a beautiful bright dress, moved swimmingly about and placed
herself on a chair like a fastidious lily choosing its vase. Oh! it was
going to be lovely! Wasn't it ridiculous of that man Yaverland to
have stayed away and missed all this glory, to say nothing of wasting
a good half-crown and a ticket which someone might have been glad
of? It just showed that men were hopeless and there was no doing
anything for them.

But then suddenly she saw him. He was standing at one of the
entrances on the other side of the hall, looking tremendous and
strange in a peaked cap and raindashed oilskins, as though he had

recently stood on a heeling deck and shouted orders to cutlassed seamen, and he was staring at the tumult as if he regarded noise as a mutiny of inferiors against his preference for calm. By his side a short-sighted steward bent interminably over his ticket. 'The silly gowk!' fumed Ellen. 'Can the woman not read? It looks so ineffi-cient, and I want him to think well of the movement.' Presently, with a suave and unimpatient gesture, he took his ticket away from the peering woman and read her the number. 'I like him!' said Ellen. 'There's many would have snapped at her for that.'

She liked, too, the way he got to his seat without disturbing his neighbours, and the neathandedness with which he took off his cap and oilskins and fell to wiping a pair of motor-goggles while his eyes maintained a dark glance, too intense to flash, on the women on the platform. 'How long he is looking at them!' she said to herself presently. 'No doubt he is taken up by Mrs. Mark Lyle. I believe such men are very susceptible to beautiful women. I hope,' she con-tinued with sudden bitterness, 'he is as susceptible to spiritual beauty and will take heed of Mrs. Ormiston!' With that, she tried herself to look at Mrs. Ormiston, but found she could not help watching the clever way he went on cleaning the goggles while his eyes and attention were fixed otherwise. There was something ill-tempered about his movements which made her want to go danc-ingly across and say teasing things to him. Yet when a smile at some private thought suggested by the speech broke his attention, and he began to look round the hall, she was filled with panic at the prospect of meeting his eyes. She did not permit herself irrational emotions, so she pretended that what she was feeling was not terror of this man, but the anger of a feminist against all men, and stared fiercely at the platform, crying out silently: 'What have I to do with this man? I will have nothing to do with any man until I am great. Then I suppose I will have to use them as pawns in my political and financial intrigues.'

Through this gaping at the client from Rio she had missed the chairman's speech. Dr. Munro had just sat down. Her sensible square face looked red and stern, as though she had just been obliged to smack someone, and from the tart brevity of the applause it was evident that that was what she had been doing. This rupture of the bright occasion struck Ellen, who found herself suddenly given over to irritations, as characteristic of the harshness of Edinburgh life. Here was a cause so beautiful in its affirmation of

freedom that it should have been served only by the bravery of dignified women and speeches lucent with reason and untremulously
spoken, by things that would require no change of quality but only
rearrangement to be instantly commemorable by art; and yet this
Scotch woman, moving with that stiffness of the mental joints which
nations which suffer from it call conscientiousness, had managed to
turn a sacramental gathering of the faithful into a steamy short-
tempered activity, like washing-day. 'Think shame on yourself, Ellen
Melville!' she rebuked herself. 'She's a better woman than ever
you'll be, with the grand work she's done at the Miller's Wynd
Dispensary.' But that the doctor was a really fine woman made the
horsehair texture of her manner all the more unpleasing, for it
showed her sinisterly illustrative of a community which had reached
an intellectual standard that could hardly be bettered and which
possessed certain moral energy, and yet was content to be rude.
Amongst these people Ellen felt herself, with her perpetual tearful
desire that everybody should be nice, to be a tenuous and transpar-
ent thing. She doubted if she would ever be able to contend with
such as they. 'Maybe I shall not get on after all!' she thought, and
her heart turned over with fear.

But Mrs. Ormiston was speaking now. Oh, it was treason to complain against the world when it held anything so fine as this! She
stood very far forward on the platform, and it seemed as though she
had no friends in the world but did not care. Beauty was hers, and
her white face, with its delicate square jaw and rounded temples,
recalled the pansy by its shape. She wore a dress of deep purple, that
colour which is almost a sound, an emotion, which is seen by the
mind's eye when one hears great music. Her hoarse, sweet North-
country voice rushed forth like a wind bearing the sounds of a bat-
tlefield, the clash of arms, the curses hurled at an implacable and
brutish enemy, the sights of the dying – for already some had died;
and with a passion that preserved her words from the common swift
mortality of spoken things she told stories of her followers' brave
deeds which seemed to remain in the air and deck the hall like war-
tattered standards. She spoke of the women who were imprisoned
at Birmingham for interrupting Mr. Asquith's meeting, and how
they lay now day and night in the black subterranean prison cells,
huddled on the tree-stumps that were the only seats, clad in nothing
but coarse vests because they would not wear the convict clothes,
breathing the foul sewage-tainted air for all but that hour when they

were carried up to the cell where the doctor and the wardresses waited to bind and gag them and ram the long feeding-tube down into their bodies. This they had endured for six weeks, and would for six weeks more. She spoke with a proud reticence as to her sufferings, about her recent sojourn in Holloway, from which she had gained release by hunger-striking a fortnight before.

'Ah, I could die for her!' cried Ellen to herself, wet-eyed with loyalty. 'If only it weren't for mother I'd go to prison to-morrow.' Her love could hardly bear it when Mrs. Ormiston went on, restrained rage freezing her words, to indict the conspiracy of men that had driven her and her followers to revolt: the refusal to women of a generous education, of a living wage, of opportunities for professional distinction; the social habit of amused contempt at women's doings; the meanness that used a woman's capacity for mating and motherhood to bind her a slave either of the kitchen or of the streets. All these things Ellen knew to be true, because she was poor and had had to drink life with the chill on, but it did not sadden her to have her reluctant views confirmed by the woman she thought the wisest in the world, for she felt an exaltation that she was afraid must make her eyes look wild. It had always appeared to her that certain things which in the main were sombre, such as deep symphonies of an orchestra, the black range and white scaurs of the Pentland Hills against the south horizon, the idea that at death one dies utterly and is buried in the earth, were patterns cut from the stuff of reality. They were relevant to fate, typical of life, in a way that gayer things, like the song of girls or the field-checked pleasantness of plains or the dream of a soul's holiday in eternity, were not. And in the bitter eloquence of this pale woman she rapturously recognised that same authentic quality.

But what good was it if one woman had something of the dignity of nature and art? Everybody knew that the world was beautiful. She sent her mind out from the hall to walk in the night, which was not wet, yet had a bloom of rain in the air, so that the lights shone with a plumy beam and all roads seemed to run to a soft white cliff. Above, the Castle Rock was invisible, but certainly cut strange beautiful shapes out of the mist; beneath it lay the Gardens, a moat of darkness, raising to the lighted street beyond terraces planted with rough autumn flowers that would now be close-curled balls curiously trimmed with dew, and grass that would make placid squelching noises under the feet; and at the end of the Gardens were the two

Greek temples that held the town's pictures – the Tiepolo, which shows Pharaoh's daughter walking in a fardingale of gold with the negro page to find a bambino Moses kicking in Venetian sunlight; the Raeburns, coarse and wholesome as a home-made loaf; the lent Whistler collection like a hive of butterflies. And at the Music Hall Frederick Lamond was playing Beethoven. How his strong hands would beat out the music! Oh, as to the beauty of the world there was no question!

But people weren't as nice as things. Humanity was no more than an ugly parasite infesting the earth. The vile quality of men and women could hardly be exaggerated. There was Miss Coates, the secretary of the Anti-Suffrage Society, who had come to this meeting from some obscure motive of self-torture and sat quite close by, jerking her pale face about in the shadow of a wide, expensive hat (it was always women like that, Ellen acidly remarked, who could afford good clothes) as she was seized by convulsions of contempt for the speaker and the audience. Ellen knew her very well, for every Saturday morning she used to stride up in an emerald green sports skirt, holding out a penny in a hand that shook with rage, and saying something indistinct about women biting policemen. On these occasions Ellen was physically afraid, for she could not overcome a fancy that the anklebones which projected in geological-looking knobs on each side of Miss Coates's large flat brogues were a natural offensive weapon like the spurs of a cock; and she was afraid also in her soul. Miss Coates was plainly, from her yellow but animated pallor, from her habit of wearing her blouse open at the neck to show a triangle of chest over which the horizontal bones lay like the bars of a gridiron, a mature specimen of a type that Ellen had met in her schooldays. There had been several girls at John Thompson's, usually bleached and ill-favoured victims of anæmia or spinal curvature, who had seemed to be compelled by something within themselves to spend their whole energies in trying, by extravagances of hair-ribbon and sidecombs and patent leather belts, the collection of actresses' postcards, and the completest abstention from study, to assert the femininity which their ill-health had obscured. Their efforts were never rewarded by the companionship of any but the most shambling kind of man or boy; but they proceeded through life with a greater earnestness than other children of their age, intent on the business of establishing their sex. Miss Coates was plainly the adult of the type, who had found in Anti-

Suffragism, that extreme gesture of political abasement before the
male, a new way of calling attention to what otherwise only the
person who was naturally noticing about clothes would detect. It
was a fact of immense and dangerous significance that the
Government and the majority of respectable citizens were on the
side of this pale, sickly, mad young woman against the brave, beautiful Mrs. Ormiston. People were horrible.

. . .

There was a roar of applause, and she found that Mrs. Ormiston
had finished her speech. This was another iniquity to be charged
against Mr. Philip. The thought of him had robbed her of heaven
knows how much of the wisdom of her idol, and it might be a year
or more before Mrs. Ormiston came to Edinburgh again. She could
have cried as she clapped, but fortunately there was Mrs. Mark Lyle
yet to speak. She watched the advance to the edge of the platform
of that tall, beautiful figure in the shining dress which it would have
been an understatement to call sky-blue, unless one predicated that
the sky was Italian, and rejoiced that nature had so appropriately
given such a saint a halo of gold hair. Then came the slow, clear voice
building a crystal bridge of argument between the platform and the
audience, and formulating with an indignation that was fierce, yet
left her marmoreal, an indictment against the double standard of
morality and the treatment of unmarried mothers.

Ellen clapped loudly, not because she had any great opinion of
unmarried mothers, whom she suspected of belonging to the same
type of woman who would start on a day's steamer excursion and
then find that she had forgotten the sandwiches, but because she was
a neat-minded girl and could not abide the State's pretence that an
illegitimate baby had only one parent when everybody knew that
every baby had really two. And she fell to wondering what this thing
was that men did to women. There was certainly some definite
thing. Children, she was sure, came into the world because of some
kind of embrace; and she had learned lately, too, that women who
were very poor sometimes let men do this thing to them for money:
such were the women whom she saw in John Square, when she came
back late from a meeting or a concert, leaning against the garden-
railings, their backs to the lovely nocturnal mystery of groves and
moonlit lawns, and their faces turned to the line of rich men's houses
which mounted out of the night like a tall, impregnable fortress.
Some were grey-haired. Such traffic was perilous as it was ugly, for

somehow there were babies who were born blind because of it. That was the sum of her knowledge. What followed the grave kisses shown in pictures, what secret Romeo shared with Juliet, she did not know, she would not know.

Twice she had refused to learn the truth. Once a schoolfellow named Anna McLellan, a minister's daughter, a pale girl with straight, yellow hair and full, whitish lips, had tried to tell her something queer about married people as they were walking along Princes Street, and Ellen had broken away from her and run into the Gardens. The trees and grass and daffodils had seemed not only beautiful but pleasantly unsmirched by the human story. And in the garret at home, in a pile of her father's books, she had once found a medical volume which she knew from the words on its cover would tell her all the things about which she was wondering. She had laid her fingers between its leaves, but a shivering had come upon her, and she ran downstairs very quickly and washed her hands. These memories made her feel restless and unhappy, and she drove her attention back to the platform and beautiful Mrs. Mark Lyle. But there came upon her a fantasy that she was standing again in the garret with that book in her hands, and that Mr. Philip was leaning against the wall in that dark place beyond the window laughing at her, partly because she was such a wee ninny not to know, and partly because when she did know the truth there would be something about it which would humiliate her. She cast down her eyes and stared at the floor so that none might see how close she was to tears. She was a silly weak thing that would always feel like a bairn on its first day at school; she was being tormented by Mr. Philip. Even the very facts of life had been planned to hurt her.

Oh, to be like that man from Rio! It was his splendid fate to be made tall and royal, to be the natural commander of all men from the moment that he ceased to be a child. He could captain his ship through the steepest seas and fight the pirate frigate till there was nothing between him and the sunset but a few men clinging to planks and a shot-torn black flag floating on the waves like a rag of seaweed. For rest he would steer to small islands, where singing birds would fly out of woods and perch on the rigging, and brown men would come and run aloft and wreathe the masts with flowers, and shy women with long, loose, black hair would steal out and offer palm-wine in conches, while he smiled aloofly and was gracious. It would not matter where he sailed; at no port in the world would sorrow wait for him, and everywhere there would be pride and honour and stars pinned to his rough coat by grateful kings. And if he fell in love with a beautiful woman he would go away from her at once and do splendid things for her sake. And when he died there would be a lying-in-state in a great cathedral, where emperors and princes would file past and shiver as they looked on the white, stern face and the stiff hands clasped on the hilt of his sword, because now they had lost their chief defender. Oh, he was too grand to be known, of course, but it was a joy to think of him.

She looked across the hall at him. Their eyes met.

There had mounted in him, as he rode through the damp night on his motor-cycle, such an inexplicable and intense exhilaration, that this ugly hall which was at the end of his journey, with its stone corridors in which a stream of people wearing mackintoshes and carrying umbrellas made sad noises with their feet, seemed an anti-climax. It was absurd that he should feel like that, for he had known quite well why he was coming into Edinburgh and what a Suffrage meeting would be like. But he was angry and discontented, and impatient that no deflecting adventure had crossed his path, until he arrived at the door which led to the half-crown seats and saw across the hall that girl called Ellen Melville. The coarse light deadened the brilliance of her hair, so that it might have been but a brightly coloured tam-o'-shanter she was wearing; and now that that obvious beauty was not there to hypnotise the eye the subtler beauty of her face and body got its chance. 'I had remembered her all wrong,' he said to himself. 'I was thinking of her as a little girl, but she's a beautiful and dignified woman.' And yet her profile, which showed against the dark pillar at which she stood, was very round and young and surprised, and altogether much more infantile than the proud full face which she turned on the world. There was something about her, too, which he could not identify, which made him feel the sharp yet almost anguished delight that is caused by the spectacle of a sunset or a foam-patterned breaking wave, or any other beauty that is intense but on the point of dissolution.

The defile of some women on to the platform and a clamour of clapping reminded him that he had better be getting to his seat, and he found that the steward to whom he had given his ticket, a sallow young woman with projecting teeth, was holding it close to her eyes with one hand and using the other to fumble in a leather bag for some glasses which manifestly were not there. He felt sorry for her because she was not beautiful like Ellen Melville. Did she grieve at it, he wondered; or had she, like most plain women, some scrap of comeliness, slender ankles or small hands, which she pathetically invested with a magic quality and believed to be more subtly and authentically beautiful than the specious pictorial quality of other women? In any case she must often have been stung by the exasperation of those at whom she gawked. He took the ticket back from her and told her the number of his seat. It was far forward, and as he sat down and looked up at the platform he saw how vulgarly mistaken he had been in thinking – as just for the moment that the sallow woman with the teeth had stopped and fumbled beside him he certainly had thought – that the Suffrage movement was a fusion of the discontents of the unfit. These people on the platform were real women. The speaker who had risen to open the meeting was a jolly woman like a cook, with short grey curly hair; and her red face was like the Scotch face – the face that he had looked on many a time in all parts of the world and had always been glad to see, since where it was there was sense and courage. She was the image of old Captain Guthrie of the *Gondomer*, and Dr. Macalister at the Port Said hospital, and that medical missionary who had come home on the *Celebes* on sick leave from Mukden. Harsh things she was saying – harsh things about the decent Scotch folks who were shocked by the arrest of Suffragettes in London for brawling, harsh suggestions that they would be better employed being shocked at the number of women who were arrested in Edinburgh for solicitation.

He chuckled to think that the Presbyterian woman had found out the Presbyterian man, for he did not believe, from his knowledge of the world, that any man was ever really as respectable as the Presbyterian man pretended to be. The woman who sat beside her, who was evidently the celebrated Mrs. Ormiston, was also a personage. She had not the same stamp of personal worth, but she had the indefinable historic quality. For no reason to be formulated by the mind, her face might become a flag to many thousands, a thing to die for, and, like a flag, she would be at their death a mere martial mark of the occasion, with no meaning of pity.

The third woman he detested. Presumably she was at this meeting because she was a loyal Suffragist and wanted to bring an end to the subjection of woman, yet all the time that the other woman was speaking her beautiful body practised fluid poses as if she were trying to draw the audience's attention to herself and give them facile romantic dreams in which the traditional relations of the sexes were rejoiced in rather than disturbed. And she wore a preposterous dress. There were two ways that women could dress. If they had work to do they could dress curtly and sensibly like men and let their looks stand or fall on their intrinsic merits; or if they were among the women who are kept to fortify the will to live in men who are spent or exasperated by conflict with the world, the wives and daughters and courtesans of the rich, then they should wear soft lustrous dresses that were good to look at and touch and as carefully beautiful as pictures. But this blue thing was neither sturdy covering nor the brilliant fantasy it meant to be. It had the spurious glitter of an imitation jewel. He knew he felt this irritation about her partly because there was something base in him, half innate and half the abrasion his present circumstances had rubbed on his soul, which was willing to go on this stupid sexual journey suggested by such vain, passive women, and the saner part of him was vexed at this compliance; he thought he had a real case against her. She was one of those beautiful women who are not only conscious of their beauty but have accepted it as their vocation. She was ensphered from the world of creative effort in the establishment of her own perfection. She was an end in herself as no human, save some old saint who has made a garden of his soul, had any right to be.

That little girl Ellen Melville was lovelier stuff because she was at grips with the world. This woman had magnificent smooth wolds of shoulders and a large blonde dignity; but life was striking sparks of the flint of Ellen's being. There came before him the picture of her as she had been that day in Princes Street, with the hairs straggling under her hat and her fierce eyes holding back the tears, telling him haughtily that a great cause made one indifferent to discomfort; and he nearly laughed aloud. He looked across the hall at her and just caught her switching her gaze from him to the platform. He felt a curious swaggering triumph at the flight of her eyes.

But Mrs. Ormiston had begun to speak, and he, too, turned his attention to the platform. He liked this old woman's invincible quality, the way she had turned to and made a battering-ram of her own meagre middle-aged body to level the walls of authority; and she reminded him of his mother. There was no physical likeness, but plainly this woman also was one of those tragically serious mothers in whose souls perpetual concern for their children dwelt like a cloud. He thought of her as he had often thought of his mother, that it was impossible to imagine her visited by those morally blank moods of purely sensuous perception which were the chief joy he had found in life. Such women never stood upright, lifting their faces to the sunlight, smiling at the way of the wind in the tree-tops; they seemed to be crouched down with ear to earth, listening to the footsteps of the events which were marching upon their beloved.

The resemblance went no further than this spiritual attitude, for this woman was second-rate stuff. Her beauty was somehow shoddy, her purple gown the kind of garment that a clairvoyant might have worn, her movements had the used quality of photographers' poses. Publicity had not been able to change the substance of the precious metal of her soul, but it had tarnished it beyond all remedy. She alluded presently to her preposterously-named daughters, Brynhild, Melissa and Guendolen, and he was reminded of a French family of musicians with whom he had travelled on the steamer between Rio and Sao Paulo, a double-chinned swarthy Madame and her three daughters, Céline, Rosane and Juliette, who sat about on deck nursing musical instruments tied with grubby scarlet ribbons, silent and dispirited, as though they were so addicted to public appearance that they found their private hours an embarrassment. But he remembered with a prick of compunction that they had made excellent music; and that, after all, was their business in life. So with the Ormistons. In the pursuit of liberty they had inadvertently become a troupe, but they had fought like lions. And they were giving the young that guarantee that life is really as fine as story-books say, which can only be given by contemporary heroism. Little Ellen Melville, on the other side of the hall, was lifting the most wonderful face all fierce and glowing with hero-worship. 'That's how I used to feel about Old Man Guthrie of the *Gondomar* when I was seventeen,' he thought. 'It's a good age. . . .'
. . .

The detestable blonde was now holding the platform in attitudes such as are ascribed to goddesses by British sculptors, and speaking with a slow, pure gusto of the horrors of immorality. For a moment her allusions to the wrongs of unmarried mothers made him think of the proud but defeated poise of his mother's head, and then the peculiar calm, gross qualities of her phrases came home to him. He wondered how long she had been going on like this, and he stared round to see how these people, who looked so very decent, whom it was impossible to imagine other than fully dressed, were taking it. Without anticipation his eyes fell on Ellen and found her looking very Scotch and clapping sturdily. Of course it must be all right, since everything about her was all right, but he searched this surprising gesture as though he were trying to read a signal, till with a quick delight he realised that this was just the final proof of how very much all right she was. Only a girl so innocent that these allusions to sex had called to her mind no physical presentations whatsoever could have stood there with perked head and made cymbals of her hands. Evidently she did nothing by halves; her mind was white as her hair was red.

He felt less appalled by this speech now that he saw that it was powerless to wound simplicity, but he still hated it. It was doing no good, because it was a part of the evil it attacked; for the spirit that makes people talk coarsely about sex is the same spirit that makes men act coarsely to women. It was not Puritanism at all that would put an end to this squalor and cruelty, but sensuality. If you taught that these encounters were degrading, then inevitably men treated the women whom they encountered as degraded; but if you claimed that even the most casual love-making was beautiful, and that a woman who yields to a man's entreaty gave him some space of heaven, then you could insist that he was under an obligation of gratitude to her and must treat her honourably. That would not only change the character of immorality, but would also diminish it, for men have no taste for multiplying their responsibilities.

Oh, women were the devil! All except his mother. They were the clumsiest of biological devices, and as they handed on life they spoiled it. They stood at the edge of the primeval swamps and called the men down from the highlands of civilisation and certain cells determined upon immortality betrayed their victims to them. They served the seed of life, but to all the divine accretions that had gathered round it, the courage that adventures, the intellect that creates, the soul that questions how it came, they were hostile. They hated the complicated brains that men wear in their heads as men hated the complicated hats that women wear on their heads; they hated men to look at the stars because they are sexless; they hated men who loved them passionately because such love was tainted with the romantic and imaginative quality that spurs them to the folly of science and art and exploration. And yet surely there were other women. Surely there was a woman somewhere who, if one loved her, would prove not a mere possession who would either bore one or go and get lost just when one had grown accustomed to it, but would be an endless research. A woman who would not be a mere film of graceful submissiveness but real as a chemical substance, so that one could observe her reactions and find out her properties; and like a chemical substance, irreducible to final terms, so that one never came to an end. A woman who would get excited about life as men do and could laugh and cheer. A woman whose beauty would be forever significant with speculation. He perceived with a shock that he was thinking of this woman not as one thinks of a hypothetical person, but with the glowing satisfaction which one feels in recounting the charms of a new friend. He was thinking of some real person. It was someone he had met quite lately, someone with red hair. He was thinking of that little Ellen Melville.

He looked across the hall at her. Their eyes met.

G. Colmore, *Suffragette Sally*

This scene, 'A protest', from Colmore's novel depicts Edith, the least radical of the three central female characters, taking a bold step in entering the public sphere and making her voice heard.

'While we are coldly discussing a man's career, sneering at his mistakes, blaming his rashness, and labelling his opinions, . . . that man, in his solitude, is perhaps shedding hot tears because his sacrifice is a hard one, because strength and patience are failing him to speak the difficult word, and do the difficult deed.'

George Eliot

Edith was back in the beloved solitude of the lane. The peace of it, the healing, the exquisite tender voices of silent, natural things which had neither language nor speech! She needed those voices to still the rough, harsh sounds that rang in her inward ears; she needed the peace and the silence, to wash away the stains which lay dark on memory's latest pages.

The hall with the bazaar stalls round the walls made a clear picture on those pages; clear and clean compared with the pages

which followed. Parts of those pages were blurred, parts were
vividly black; on one was a little white space of wondrous peace.

She had stood in the chattering, careless crowd waiting for the
opening of the bazaar. She had presented the ticket of admittance
provided for her, and who should know her for a forbidden, disturbing suffragette? She looked as gentle as she was, more than
usually timid, far less aggressive than most of those about her.

Edith was in a dream, and a dream that had the tense, terror-laden
atmosphere of nightmare. Longing intensely to flee from her surroundings, she yet was constrained to remain; the paralysing spell
of nightmare was upon her, and the curious dream influence which
makes strange unexpected things seem hardly strange. Otherwise,
to raise her eyes to the platform and see, beside the minister who
was to open the bazaar, the man whom of all men she most at that
moment desired not to see, would surely have been bewilderingly
startling, instead of seeming the cruel climax that she had waited for.
Not that it made any real difference; all that there had been or might
have been between Cyril Race and herself had ended when she
entered the hall that afternoon; and yet his presence intensified, if
anything could intensify, the horror of the ordeal through which she
had to pass.

That was another of the things that people did not seem to realise
when they spoke of cheap martyrdom; the pain of forfeiting the
approval of those whose good opinion was amongst one's most precious possessions. It was hard enough to go against the outside
world, but a hundred, a thousand times harder to thwart the ideas,
brave the affection, of one's nearest and dearest; relations, friends,
a lover that was or might have been. The opinion of the outside
world was nothing compared with that.

Edith was glad she was smaller than the average woman; Race
would not notice her in the crowd; till the inevitable moment she
was likely to remain unseen.

The Minister had begun his speech now; all chattering was
hushed; attention was concentrated upon his words. For two
minutes he spoke, and then, from the back of the hall, the cry rang
out: 'Votes for women!'

What followed was ugly: a rush of stewards, shouts of 'Out with
her!' mingled with cries of 'Fair play!'; a scuffle; a woman dragged
and hustled through the people and out of the door.

Quiet again; the stewards cast searching glances here, there, everywhere; were there any more of those accursed suffragettes about? None, at any rate, whose looks betrayed them. The speech went on; Edith knew that it would continue uninterrupted for five minutes; her eyes sought the clock.

'Sir, will you give justice to wom –'

Before the words were out of the second interrupter's mouth she was set upon, seized, dragged out by many pairs of hands. How strong these suffragettes were supposed to be! So many men combined to throw them out; yet having made their protest, they offered no resistance to ejection.

Edith caught sight of the face of interrupter number two as she was borne past her; it was white, and there was blood upon it. She herself was number three. Four more minutes and then – What was it she had to say? 'Women tax-payers demand the vote.' Was that it? 'Women tax-payers demand the vote. Women tax-payers demand the vote. Women –' 'To give the vote to those women who pay rates and taxes –' Where was she? In the market-place at Charters Ambo, begging rough men for signatures? Hateful it was. Then Cyril Race had come along, and Cyril Race – certainly she had seen him just now, while she was still able to see. Now she could see nothing; it was all half dark and blurred about her; nothing – and yet – there was something she must – she *must* see. The clock, yes, and the moving hand.

She is not at Charters Ambo, not in the market-place. No, she is indoors – of course – in the hall, and when the hand touches the next figure – she can see it now, the hand, and how near to the figure it is. To call out before all these people, and be set upon and hurt! Can she? Yes, for she must – if – if her voice will come.

The hand moves; moves; there, it has touched the figure. Now; she must speak now; but – but –

The hand has touched the figure and passed it and the speech goes on. Edith had not spoken. She has failed; utterly and miserably failed. Her throat was dry and hard; her voice would not come; because, as she tells herself in an agony, she is a coward, has failed for very fear. It seemed to her then that the suffering of the shrinking and the dread was nothing, nothing at all compared with the agony of self-reproach which overwhelmed her now. If she could only have her chance again, she would brave it all, the pain, the humiliation, everything. But the chance is over; she has failed utterly.

Five minutes more had passed; it was the turn of number four. She was braver than Edith, and promptly the words came: 'The women of England –'

She got no further. A hand was over her mouth; hands dragged her head back and grasped her throat. She was not far from Edith, and Edith could see.

How dry her throat was! Her tongue seemed fast to the roof of her mouth. Could she ever manage to get out the sentence that her comrade had not been able to finish? Yes, for the power that had forced her here was paramount now, and her voice came to her and rang out clear: 'The women of England demand the vote.'

And then a miracle happened. All at once, or so it seemed to her, she was caught up out of the turmoil and the dread, and set in a place of peace. The angry shoutings were very far away; the hustling crowd and those advancing hands had surely no power to hurt; in any case, the dread has gone from her, and she has no more fear.

They have found her now, the little slender figure amidst the taller ones; very easy is this suffragette to drag across the hall and send flying from the door. In truth, she hardly knows what is happening to her; she is hurt, but feels no pain; is roughly handled, cuffed, bruised, but, in her self-consciousness, is alive only to a sense of movement and confusion. Stewards and policemen convey her out of the hall; she stumbles on the step outside, puts out a blindly groping arm, strikes something, clutches, and is clutched. When sight and sense come back to her she is in custody; she has assaulted a policeman.

Is it really all over, and she back in the haunts she loves? Oh, blessed, beautiful sights and sounds of the kind familiar country! Stand very still, Edith, and fairies may flit there from tree to hedge; for it is twilight, when fairies are most prone to show themselves.

She hardly knew whether she had been grateful or not to Cyril Race for bailing her out; yet she was grateful when she found herself with Rachel Cullen in the little green quiet room, and felt that but for Race she would not have been there. He came the next morning and took her to the police-court; and afterwards to the station. His evidence was sufficient to rebut the charge of assault, and Edith was free to go home.

On the platform she thanked him for what he had done. Hitherto she had hardly spoken; on the previous evening she had felt too dazed and too ill, had been in too much pain to speak; and this morning, so grave and quiet and withal so peremptory was he, that she hardly knew whether she was in the company of a friend or in the custody of a gaoler.

'I thank you very much for what you have done for me,' she said. 'I am grateful, though I cannot say it properly, and all the more so that I know very well that you entirely disapprove of me and my doings.'

'You poor little girl,' he answered, 'do you think I don't know that you have been pushed into this, that you have been led on and carried away by a mistaken impulse of loyalty?'

Edith shook her head. 'Not much impulse about it. It was a long-drawn-out deliberate resolve that went before – before yesterday.'

'You are not meant for that sort of thing. It's not your rôle.'

'Is any woman meant for it?'

'Most certainly I think not.'

'Then why are we driven to do these hateful things?'

'Heaven only knows. I don't.'

'The Government does.'

Race shrugged his shoulders. 'Don't let us get into argument,' he said after a moment's pause, 'because I might get angry with you. As we are parting, we may as well part with as little bitterness as may be.'

The train was alongside the platform now, and Edith held out her hand. 'Good-bye and thank you. If there is any bitterness, it is all on your side,' she said.

'Good-bye. You should rest altogether when you reach home.'

'Is there any bitterness?' she asked. She was in the train now, seated, looking out at him. He looked straight back at her.

'I wanted you,' he said, 'for my very own. You must have known that. And now –'

'You don't want a suffragette.'

His eyes, that were hard, softened a little as he looked at her. 'I haven't only myself to think of. If I had – But it would be incongruous and absurd, as things are, for a member of the Government to think of – as you say – a suffragette.'

The train was moving; away from love, from hope; though Edith had told herself that hope was dead, it had an extraordinary vitality and seemed to be standing now beside Cyril Race on the platform. Yet she had plucked up spirit enough to give him an answer.

'And quite impossible for a suffragette to think of a member of the Government.'

'And that was quite true,' she told herself, as she paused in the peace of the lane, recalling her words.

At that moment, indeed, she wanted nothing more than peace.

E. Robins, *The Convert*

Typical of Robins's novel in its articulation of a range of con-flicting opinions, this passage again addresses the difficulty of finding a public voice. By viewing Vida Levering's speech from the perspective of her ex-lover Stonor this scene, like that in *The Judge*, also explores the interrelationship of public and private constructions of femininity.

Stonor made a sharp move forward, and took her by the arm.

'We're going now,' he said.

'Not yet – oh, *please* not just yet,' she pleaded as he drew her round. 'Geoffrey, I do believe –'

She looked back, with an air almost bewildered, over her shoul-der, like one struggling to wake from a dream.

Stonor was saying with decision to Lady John, 'I'm going to take Jean out of this mob. Will you come?'

'What? Oh, yes, if you think' – she had disengaged the chain of her eyeglass at last. 'But isn't that, surely it's –'.

'Geoffrey –!' Jean began.

'Lady John's tired,' he interrupted. 'We've had enough of this idiotic –'

'But you don't see who it is, Geoffrey. That last one is –' Suddenly Jean bent forward as he was trying to extricate her from the crowd, and she looked in his face. Something that she found there made her tighten her hold on his arm.

'We can't run away and leave Aunt Ellen,' was all she said; but her voice sounded scared. Stonor repressed a gesture of anger, and came to a standstill just behind two big policemen.

The last-comer to that strange platform, after standing for some seconds with her back to the people and talking to Ernestine Blunt, the tall figure in a long sage-green dust coat and familiar hat, had turned and glanced apprehensively at the crowd.

It was Vida Levering.

The girl down in the crowd locked her hands together and stood motionless.

The Socialist had left the platform with the threat that he was 'coming down now to attend to that microbe that's vitiating the air on my right, while a lady will say a few words to you – if she can myke 'erself 'eard.'

He retired to a chorus of cheers and booing, while the chairman, more harassed than ever, it would seem, but determined to create a diversion, was saying that some one had suggested – and it's such a good idea I'd like you to listen to it – that a clause shall be inserted in the next Suffrage Bill that shall expressly give to each Cabinet Minister, and to any respectable man, the power to prevent a vote being given to the female members of his family, on his public declaration of their lack of sufficient intelligence to entitle them to one.'

'Oh! oh!'

'Now, I ask you to listen as quietly as you can to a lady who is not accustomed to speaking – a – in Trafalgar Square, or – a – as a matter of act, at all.'

'A dumb lady!'

'Hooray!'

'Three cheers for the dumb lady!'

The chairman was dreadfully flustered at the unfortunate turn his speech had taken.

'A lady who, as I've said, will tell you, if you'll behave yourselves –'

'Oh! oh!'

'Will tell you something of her impression of police-court justice in this country.'

Jean stole a wondering look at Stonor's sphinx-like face as Vida Levering came forward.

There she stood, obviously very much frightened, with the unaccustomed colour coming and going in her white face – farther back than any of the practised speakers – there she stood like one who too much values the space between her and the mob voluntarily to lessen it by half an inch. The voice was steady enough, though low, as she began.

'Mr. Chairman, men, and women –'

'Speak up.'

She flushed, came nearer to the edge of the platform, and raised the key a little.

'I just wanted to tell you that I was – I was present in the police court when the women were charged for creating a disturbance.'

'You oughtn't to get mix'd up in wot didn't concern you!'

'I – I –' She stumbled and stopped.

'Give the lady a hearing,' said a shabby art-student, magisterially. He seemed not ill-pleased when he had drawn a certain number of eyes to his long hair, picturesque hat, and flowing Byronic tie.

'Wot's the lydy's nyme?'

'I ain't seen this one before.'

'Is she Mrs. or Miss?'

'She's dumb, anyway, like 'e said.'

'Haw! haw!'

The anxious chairman was fidgeting in an agony of apprehension. He whispered some kind prompting word after he had flung out –

'Now, see here, men; fair play, you know.'

'I think I ought –' Vida began.

'No wonder she can't find a word to say for 'em. They're a disgryce, miss – them women behind you. It's the w'y they goes on as mykes the Governmint keep ye from gettin' yer rights.'

The chairman had lost his temper. 'It's the way *you* go on,' he screamed; but the din was now so great, not even he could be heard. He stood there waving his arms and moving his lips while his dark eyes glittered.

Miss Levering turned and pantomimed to Ernestine, 'You see it's no use!'

Thus appealed to, the girl came forward, and said something in the ear of the frantic chairman. When he stopped gyrating, and nodded, Miss Blunt came to the edge of the platform, and held up her hand as if determined to stem this tide of unfavourable comment upon the dreadful women who were complicating the Election difficulties of both parties.

'Listen,' says Ernestine; 'I've got something to propose.' They waited an instant to hear what this precious proposal might be. 'If the Government withholds the vote because they don't like the way some of us ask for it, let them give it to the quiet ones. Do they want to punish all women because they don't like the manners of a handful? Perhaps that's men's notion of justice. It isn't ours.'

'Haw! haw!'

'Yes' – Miss Levering plucked up courage, seeing her friend sailing along so safely. 'This is the first time I've ever "gone on," as you call it, but they never gave me a vote.'

'No,' says Miss Ernestine, with energy – 'and there are' – she turned briskly, with forefinger uplifted punctuating her count – 'there are two, three, four women on this platform. Now, we all want the vote, as you know.'

'Lord, yes, we know *that*.'

'Well, we'd agree to be disfranchised all our lives if they'd give the vote to all the other women.'

'Look here! You made one speech – give the lady a chance.'

Miss Blunt made a smiling little bob of triumph. 'That's just what I wanted you to say!' And she retired.

Miss Levering came forward again. But the call to 'go on' had come a little suddenly.

'Perhaps you – you don't know – you don't know –'

'*How're* we going to know if you can't tell us?' demanded a sarcastic voice.

It steadied her. 'Thank you for that,' she said, smiling. 'We couldn't have a better motto. How *are* you to know if we can't somehow manage to tell you?' With a visible effort she went on, 'Well, *I* certainly didn't know before that the sergeants and policemen are instructed to deceive the people as to the time such cases are heard.'

'It's just as hard,' said a bystander to his companion, '*just* as hard for learned counsel in the august quiet of the Chancery Division to find out when their cases are really coming on.'

'You ask, and you're sent to Marlborough Police Court,' said Miss Levering, 'instead of to Marylebone.'

'They oughter send yer to 'Olloway – do y' good.'

'You go on, miss. Nobody minds'im.'

'Wot can you expect from a pig but a grunt?'

'You are told the case will be at two o'clock, and it's really called for eleven. Well, I took a great deal of trouble, and I didn't believe what I was told.' She was warming a little to her task. 'Yes, that's almost the first thing we have to learn – to get over our touching faith that because a man tells us something, it's true. I got to the right court, and I was so anxious not to be late, I was too early.'

'Like a woman!'

'The case before the Suffragists' was just coming on. I heard a noise. I saw the helmets of two policemen.'

'No, you didn't. They don't wear their helmets in court.'

'They were coming in from the corridor. As I saw them, I said to myself, "What sort of crime shall I have to sit and hear about? Is this a burglar being brought along between the two big policemen, or will it be a murderer? What sort of felon is to stand in the dock before the people, whose crime is, they ask for the vote?' But try as I would, I couldn't see the prisoner. My heart misgave me. Is it some poor woman, I wondered?'

A tipsy tramp, with his battered bowler over one eye, wheezed out, 'Drunk again!' with an accent of weary philosophy. 'Syme old tyle.'

'Then the policeman got nearer, and I saw' – she waited an instant – 'a little thin, half-starved boy. What do you think he was charged with?'

'Travellin' first with a third-class ticket.' A boy offered a page out of personal history.

'Stealing. What had he been stealing, that small criminal? *Milk*. It seemed to me, as I sat there looking on, that the men who had had the affairs of the world in their hands from the beginning, and who've made so poor a business of it –'

'Oh, pore devils! give 'em a rest!'

'Who've made so bad a business of it as to have the poor and the unemployed in the condition they're in to-day, whose only remedy for a starving child is to hale him off to the police court, because he had managed to get a little milk, well, I did wonder that the men refuse to be helped with a problem they've so notoriously failed at. I began to say to myself, "Isn't it time the women lent a hand?"'

'Doin' pretty well fur a dumb lady!'

'Would you have women magistrates?'

She was stumped by the suddenness of the query.

'Haw! haw! Magistrates and judges! *Women!*'

'Let 'em prove first they're able to –'

It was more than the shabby art-student could stand.

'The schools are full of them!' he shouted. 'Where's their Michael Angelo? They study music by thousands: where's their Beethoven? Where's their Plato? Where's the woman Shakespeare?'

'Where's their Harry Lauder?'

At last a name that stirred the general enthusiasm.

'Who is Harry Lauder?' Jean asked her aunt.

Lady John shook her head.

'Yes, wot 'ave women ever *done?*'

The speaker had clenched her hands, but she was not going to lose her presence of mind again. By the time the chairman could make himself heard with, 'Now, men, it's one of our British characteristics that we're always ready to give the people we differ from a hearing,' Miss Levering, making the slightest of gestures, waved him aside with a low –

'It's all right.'

'These questions are quite proper,' she said, raising her voice. 'They are often asked elsewhere; and I would like to ask in return: Since when was human society held to exist for its handful of geniuses? How many Platos are there here in this crowd?'

'Divil a wan!' And a roar of laughter followed that free confession.

'Not one,' she repeated. 'Yet that doesn't keep you men off the register. How many Shakespeares are there in all England to-day? Not one. Yet the State doesn't tumble to pieces. Railroads and ships are built, homes are kept going, and babies are born. The world goes on' – she bent over the crowd with lit eyes – 'the world goes on *by virtue of its common people.*'

There was a subdued 'Hear! hear!'

'I am not concerned that you should think we women could paint great pictures, or compose immortal music, or write good books. I am content' – and it was strange to see the pride with which she said it, a pride that might have humbled Vere de Vere – 'I am content that we should be classed with the common people, who keep the world going. But' – her face grew softer, there was even a kind of camaraderie where before there had been shrinking – 'I'd like the world to go a great deal better. We were talking about justice. I have been inquiring into the kind of lodging the poorest class of homeless women can get in this town of London. I find that only the men of that class are provided for. Some measure to establish Rowton Houses for Women has been before the London County Council. They looked into the question very carefully – so their apologists say. And what did they decide? They decided that they could do nothing.

'Why could that great, all-powerful body do nothing? Because, they said, if these cheap and decent houses were opened, the homeless women in the streets would make use of them. You'll think I'm not in earnest, but that was actually the decision, and the reason given for it. Women that the bitter struggle for existence had forced into a life of horror might take advantage of the shelter these decent, cheap places offered. But the *men*, I said! Are the men who avail themselves of Lord Rowton's hostels, are *they* all angels? Or does wrong-doing in a man not matter? Yet women are recommended to depend on the chivalry of men!'

The two tall policemen who had been standing for some minutes in front of Mr. Stonor in readiness to serve him, seeming to feel there was no further need of them in this quarter, shouldered their way to the left, leaving exposed the hitherto masked figure of the tall gentleman in the motor cap. He moved uneasily, and, looking round, he met Jean's eyes fixed on him. As each looked away again, each saw that for the first time Vida Levering had become aware of his presence. A change passed over her face, and her figure swayed as if some species of mountain-sickness had assailed her, looking down from that perilous high perch of hers upon the things of the plain. While the people were asking one another, 'What is it? Is she going to faint?' she lifted one hand to her eyes, and her fingers trembled an instant against the lowered lids. But as suddenly as she had faltered, she was forging on again, repeating like an echo of a thing heard in a dream –

'Justice and chivalry! Justice and chivalry remind me of the story that those of you who read the police-court news – I have begun only lately to do that – but *you*'ve seen the accounts of the girl who's been tried in Manchester lately for the murder of her child.'

People here and there in the crowd regaled one another with choice details of the horror.

'Not pleasant reading. Even if we'd noticed it, we wouldn't speak of it in my world. A few months ago I should have turned away my eyes and forgotten even the headline as quickly as I could.'

'My opinion,' said a shrewd-looking young man, 'is that she's forgot what she meant to say, and just clutched at this to keep her from drying up.'

'Since that morning in the police-court I read these things. This, as you know, was the story of a working girl – an orphan of seventeen – who crawled with the dead body of her new-born child to her master's back door and left the baby there. She dragged herself a little way off and fainted. A few days later she found herself in court being tried for the murder of her child. Her master, a married man, had of course reported the "find" at his back door to the police, and he had been summoned to give evidence. The girl cried out to him in the open court, "You are the father!" He couldn't deny it. The coroner, at the jury's request, censured the man, and regretted that the law didn't make him responsible. But' – she leaned down from the plinth with eyes blazing – 'he went scot free. And that girl is at this moment serving her sentence in Strangeways Gaol.'

Through the moved and murmuring crowd, Jean forced her way, coming in between Lady John and Stonor, who stood there immovable. The girl strained to bring her lips near his ear.

'Why do you dislike her so?'

'I?' he said. 'Why should you think –'

'I never saw you look as you did;' with a vaguely frightened air she added, 'as you do.'

'Men make boast' – the voice came clear from the monument – 'that an English citizen is tried by his peers. What woman is tried by hers?'

'She mistakes the sense in which the word was employed,' said a man who looked like an Oxford Don.

But there was evidently a sense, larger than that one purely academic, in which her use of the word could claim its pertinence. The strong feeling that had seized her as she put the question was sweeping the crowd along with her.

'A woman is arrested by a man, brought before a man judge, tried by a jury of men, condemned by men, taken to prison by a man, and by a man she's hanged! Where in all this were *her* "peers"? Why did men, when British justice was born – why did they so long ago insist on trial by "a jury of their peers"? So that justice shouldn't miscarry – wasn't it? A man's peers would best understand his circumstances, his temptation, the degree of his guilt. Yet there's no such unlikeness between different classes of men as exists between man and woman. What man has the knowledge that makes him a fit judge of woman's deeds at that time of anguish – that hour that some woman struggled through to put each man here into the world. I noticed when a previous speaker quoted the Labour Party, you applauded. Some of you here, I gather, call yourselves Labour men. Every woman who has borne a child is a Labour woman. No man among you can judge what she goes through in her hour of darkness.'

Jean's eyes had dropped from her lover's set white face early in the recital. But she whispered his name.

He seemed not to hear.

The speaker up there had caught her fluttering breath, and went on so low that people strained to follow.

'In that great agony, even under the best conditions that money and devotion can buy, many a woman falls into temporary mania, and not a few go down to death. In the case of this poor little abandoned working girl, what man can be the fit judge of her deeds in that awful moment of half-crazed temptation? Women know of these things as those know burning who have walked through fire.'

Stonor looked down at the girl at his side. He saw her hands go up to her throat as though she were suffocating. The young face, where some harsh knowledge was struggling for birth, was in pity turned away from the man she loved.

The woman leaned down from the platform, and spoke her last words with a low and thrilling earnestness.

'I would say in conclusion to the women here, it's not enough to be sorry for these, our unfortunate sisters. We must get the conditions of life made fairer. We women must organize. We must learn to work together. We have all (rich and poor, happy and unhappy) worked so long and so exclusively for men, we hardly know how to work for one another. But we must learn. Those who can, may give money. Those who haven't pennies to give, even those people are not so poor but what they can give some part of their labour – some share of their sympathy and support. I know of a woman – she isn't of our country – but a woman who, to help the women strikers of an oppressed industry to hold out, gave a thousand pounds a week for thirteen weeks to get them and their children bread, and help them to stand firm. The masters were amazed. Week after week went by, and still the people weren't starved into submission. Where did this mysterious stream of help come from? The employers couldn't discover, and they gave in. The women got back their old wages, and I am glad to say many of them began to put by pennies to help a little to pay back the great sum that had been advanced to them.'

'She took their pennies – a rich woman like that?'

'Yes – to use again, as well as to let the working women feel they were helping others. I hope you'll all join the Union. Come up after the meeting is over and give us your names.'

As she turned away, 'You won't get any men!' a taunting voice called after her.

The truth in the gibe seemed to sting. Forestalling the chairman, quickly she confronted the people again, a new fire in her eyes.

'Then,' she said, holding out her hands – 'then *it is to the woman I appeal!*' She stood so an instant, stilling the murmur, and holding the people by that sudden concentration of passion in her face. 'I don't mean to say it wouldn't be better if men and women did this work together, shoulder to shoulder. But the mass of men won't have it so. I only hope they'll realize in time the good they've renounced and the spirit they've aroused. For I know as well as any man could tell me, it would be a bad day for England if all women felt about all men *as I do.*'

She retired in a tumult. The others on the platform closed about her. The chairman tried in vain to get a hearing from the swaying and dissolving crowd.

Jean made a blind forward movement towards the monument. Stonor called out, in a toneless voice –

'Here! follow me!'

'No – no – I –' The girl pressed on.

'You're going the wrong way.'

'*This* is the way –'

'We can get out quicker on this side.'

'I don't *want* to get out.'

'What?'

He had left Lady John, and was following Jean through the press.

'Where are you going?' he asked sharply.

'To ask that woman to let me have the honour of working with her.'

The crowd surged round the girl.

'Jean!' he called upon so stern a note that people stared and stopped.

Others – not Jean.

M. Haig. *This was My World*

Margaret Haig, a founder of *Time and Tide*, a successful busi-nesswoman and, later, Viscountess Rhondda, stresses in her autobiography the benefits she gained from the educative expe-rience of the suffrage movement.

The militant suffrage movement was a thrilling discovery. It supplied the answer to a thousand puzzling problems. And it gave a chance of activity. A cousin, Florence Haig, a contemporary of my mother's, an artist who lived in Chelsea, had been caught up into it, and when she came out of prison we, much interested all three of us to hear all about it, asked her down to Llanwern. That was in the early days of the suffrage movement, when the whole idea of prison was still very much of a novelty. The result of her visit, so far as I was concerned, was the determination to walk in a Suffrage Procession to Hyde Park. I was within a month of getting married at the time, and had a certain difficulty – though really not so very much – in persuading my future husband that there was no harm in the plan. My mother accompanied me, (a) because she did not think that an unmarried girl should walk unchaperoned through the gutter, (b) because she believed in votes for women. In the event I thoroughly enjoyed the procession, which she did not. She came of a generation which took the gutter and casual street insults hard.

I do not remember that at that time I had thought the thing out at all. I had been brought up, it is true, in a home which believed in votes for women, but up till that visit of Cousin Florence's the fact had meant, so far as I was aware, very little to me. And when she came I went into the militant movement instinctively, thrilled with this chance for action, this release for energy, but unaware that this at last was what I had, all unconsciously, been seeking for, and, at first, totally ignorant of, and unconcerned with, the arguments for our cause. It was a temperamental, not in any sense an intellectual, conversion.

Having made up my mind, however, I had to discover why I believed what I did. Through the following year I got and read every book and every pamphlet for and against suffrage. I had drawers and drawers full of pamphlets; the house was thick with them. . . . My intellectual assent was complete, but it came second, not first.

It must have been about that time that I had a chance conversation with a country neighbour – a girl I knew well, a kindly, pleasant, capable, very average girl, of twenty-eight or nine – in the course of which, in one unconscious phrase, she summed up all that was by then trying to become articulate in my revolt against the life the average well-to-do woman was expected to lead. She was setting off to play bridge. It was a lovely afternoon in late April and the country was looking perfect. It seemed great waste to spend the day indoors unless one need. 'Why,' said I, 'do you play bridge in the afternoon?' A shadow crossed her face and a queer, discontented inflection came into her voice. 'One must do something,' she said; 'I'd sooner wear out than rust out.' And playing bridge was 'wearing out' . . . that is a definition which I shall never forget.

One sometimes hears people who took part in the suffrage campaign pitied. And indeed one knows that there were those to whom it was a martyrdom, who gave everything they had – health, and even life – for it. Such names as Lady Constance Lytton's come to one's mind; the story of the imprisonment which ruined her health and shortened her life – among the most dramatic epics that I know – will some day be better known than it is yet. Or one remembers those years under the Cat and Mouse Act, when month after month Mrs. Pankhurst, coming near to death in prison, would be let loose to recover, and then hunted down again. That was a ghastly happening; it is difficult to believe that life to her just then can have been anything but pure nightmare. But for me, and for many other young women like me, militant suffrage was the very salt of life. The knowledge of it had come like a draught of fresh air into our padded, stifled lives. It gave us release of energy, it gave us that sense of being of some use in the scheme of things, without which no human being can live at peace. It made us feel that we were part of life, not just outside watching it. It made us feel that we had a real purpose and use apart from having children. (Greatly though I wanted children, the idea that having them was in itself a sufficient justification for existence had never satisfied me. I had found a sentence somewhere to the effect that if the sole purpose of man is reproduction he is of no more use than would be a hammer whose sole function was to make other hammers. It was a sentence which had stuck firmly in my mind, for it expressed what I had always felt, yet found no words for.) It gave us hope of freedom and power and opportunity. It gave us scope at last, and it gave us what normal healthy youth craves – adventure and excitement. Prison itself, its loneliness (I only tasted it once), its sense of being padlocked in, was indeed sheer taut misery – and there was a lot of dull drudgery too, as there is in all work; but the things people expected one to mind, speaking at rowdy street-corner meetings, selling papers in the gutter, walking clad in sandwich boards in processions, I for my part thoroughly enjoyed, and I suspect that most of my contemporaries did the same. We were young, after all, and we enjoyed experience. These things might frighten us a little in project, but they satisfied the natural appetite of youth for colour and incident.

. . .

One of the first effects that joining the militant movement had on me, as perhaps on the majority of those of my generation who went into it, was that it forced me to educate myself. I had joined this cause that my cousin thought worth going to prison for in complete conviction of the obvious rightness of its ideals, and working against the majority opinion of the country in association with a like-minded group soon roused in me a strong emotional response. But once joined I had to rationalise my emotions. Why did I know I was right? In anything that has mattered to me I have never argued from premises to conclusions. I have always found myself at the conclusion and had to go back and unearth the subconscious premises that led me there. So I started to read – or rather I started to read on new lines.

I read to begin with, of course, the whole literature of feminism: leaflets, pamphlets, books in favour and books against. Of books that mattered dealing directly with feminism there were curiously few. Only three now stay in my mind: John Stuart Mill's 'Subjection of Women,' Olive Schreiner's 'Woman and Labour,' Cicely Hamilton's 'Marriage as a Trade'; and perhaps one should add a fourth, Shaw's 'Quintessence of Ibsenism.' Of course, there were stray passages in others; one or two of Israel Zangwill's Essays, for example, I find unforgettable to this day. Of books which indirectly reinforced the suffrage position the number was, however, legion. One of those which had the most effect on me personally was 'Mrs. Warren's Profession' (a play which sent many a woman to prison), together with the preface to 'Plays Unpleasant.' But from feminist literature proper a dozen paths led out into other subjects, each of which bore on feminism in one way or another, and each of which needed exploring. One wanted to read up political science and economics. One wanted to have some general idea of psychology, of sociology, and even of anthropology. And one wanted to get at the theories and the reasons behind the facts. That was what was interesting; and as I read on, politics and the theory of politics fascinated me. Different systems of government, why they succeeded, why they failed. Different races, how far they needed different treatment.

International reactions, what caused them. These things interested me more and more. These things interested me most of all.
. . .
Certainly it was during those years of fused enthusiasm rather than during the ordinary years of school and college that, reading, studying, thinking, puzzling, I got the best of what education I have had. And, as I have said, I suspect that that is true of many another militant of my generation.

G. Colmore, ''Ope'

Perhaps the most memorable of Colmore's short stories, this tale of misrecognition makes a powerful case for the transformational power of the suffrage cause.

Her real name was Margaret Clarkson, but in the neighbourhood which she frequented she was generally known as Maggs, and at the Pig and Whistle she went by the name of the Suffragette. For Maggs, a poor thing when sober, a creature depressed, sullen, and dull to the verge of stupidity, became, when treated by her public-house patrons, of quite different disposition.

As she scraped through the drab hours of the day, earning her bread by an odd job here, a penny begged there, a cup of tea given by those generous housewives of the poor who are more compassionate than critical, her eyes had no light, her features no play, and her hair, in its untidy knot, seemed to lack both life and abundance. But when the evening came, and the little woman – for she was small of stature and meagre of frame – stood amongst the customers of the Pig and Whistle; when, her own small store of coppers exhausted, she was plied with a glass from one and a glass from another; then her sullenness turned to gaiety, her dulness disappeared, a strain of abandonment replaced her depression.

And then, when her eyes were alight and her tongue had grown saucy, one of the men would say, with adjectives and adjurations more comfortably omitted: 'Now, my gal, give us the Suffragette!'

She was willing, always willing, to accede to the request, and it did not take her long to dress for the part. All that was needed was to loosen her hair – and it did not require much loosening; to run her hands through it – and it was wonderful how the wispy locks flew out in vigorous disorder; to give her skirt a hitch and her bodice a pull; and there she was, a typical Suffragette; the Suffragette of the newspapers, of convention, of the House of Commons.

And then the fun began. She screamed, she kicked, she proclaimed her need of a husband, she swore that if one of the men did not marry her she would bite them all round, and that if they would not kiss her – and this always brought down the house – she wouldn't touch her dinner, not she, not a morsel of it. It was rich, it was fine, it was exquisitely funny; her audience never tired of her representation; especially as Maggs was imaginative in her cups, and would constantly add fresh touches, thus heightening expectation and quickening an interest which might have flagged.

And then, in the heyday of her popularity, she disappeared.

Weeks went by, and the figure that was so listless as Maggs, so sprightly as the Suffragette, was looked for in vain by the customers of the Pig and Whistle.

In the early summer it was, when the evenings had grown long, that she reappeared. The door was pushed open, and, with the same old dragging step, the same old silent, sullen Maggs came in amongst her patrons; the same, yet with a difference. Dragging her step still was, yet firmer than of old; silent she was as ever, yet the expression of her face, though somewhat sullen in its sobriety, was next door to being alert. Moreover her hat, shabby as always, was no longer battered – or as little battered as a hat that has passed through battering experiences can ever hope to be – and was set straight on her head; and the well-known rent on the left shoulder of her gown had been patched.

She was met by a rush of questions, by offers of drinks, by a welcome as genuine as it was vociferous; for she was amusing when she was half drunk, and her would-be hosts had missed her antics.

She shook her head at the offers of drinks and stood silent till the questioning died down. The silence was like her; the refusal of drink was unprecedented. When at last she spoke, it was in answer to a request to 'give us the Suffragette.'

'Yes,' she said, 'it's wot I come for; an' I can show yer better'n ever I could. I bin studyin' they Suffragettes an' their goin's on; I bin at their meetin's – never mind 'ow I come ter go – an' I knows wot they're after.'

She looked round at her audience.

'You're a ignorant lot, you 'ere; same as me when I used ter come an' carry on. I didn't know nuffin – no more'n you do now, an' that there Suffragette bus'ness o' mine was rotten. You tyke an' look at me now, as I stan' 'ere, with me 'air tidy an' me 'at straight, an' if yer wants ter know wot a suffragette's reely like, yer'll begin ter 'ave a notion.'

She paused, and the pause was filled with jokes that were half jeers, with laughter that was half puzzled. Was she serious, this buffoon who had mocked so often and so aptly? Or were these words of hers an introduction to some new 'turn' acquired in her absence and to be made more spicy by contrast?

'Are you 'ired out to speak for 'em?' asked a man when the jokes slackened.

'Wot 'ave they give yer?' said another.

'Give me?' Maggs answered; 'I'll tell yer wot they've give me.' Her eyes brightened as they had been used to brighten when drink was doing its work, save that the light in them was steadier, more serene; her figure straightened itself. 'They've give me 'OPE.'

Capitals but faintly convey what the little wastrel woman put into the word; it was as though the spirit of Hope itself spoke through the lips that want and wickedness had twisted long ago out of the lines in which Nature had set them.

''Ope,' she repeated. 'Parsons in prisons ain't never give me none; lydies with trackses nor yet soup tickets never give me none; a mis-er'ble sinner, that was all I was – till I come across the Suffragettes. There wasn't no more talk of sinners; wot *they* says was as I was a woman; wot *they* says was wot a woman ought ter be – yes, blime me, an' wot a woman *can* be an' *as* ter be. I tell yer, you as is snig-gerin' an' starin' there, the knowin' of it an' the feelin' of it 'as made a woman of me. An' that's why I come to-night – for the last time, swelp me Gawd – ter tell yer somethin' of wot a Suffragette's reely like. 'Alf afraid I was – yes, more'n 'alf – ter come, afraid of 'ow yer'd larf; only Suffragettes ain't never afraid, not of larfin,' nor prisons, nor laws, nor nuffin', an' so I come. It makes yer brave, it do, ter be a Suffragette. 'Cos why? It gives yer 'ope.'

She looked round and smiled – a smile that no one there had ever seen on her face before; and then she went out.

For perhaps a minute and a half no one spoke in the bar of the Pig and Whistle.

H. Johnston, *Mrs Warren's Daughter*

As the title indicates, this novel by Sir Harry Johnston, published in 1920, is a parodic continuation of the play *Mrs
Warren's Profession* by George Bernard Shaw. The daughter of
the infamous Mrs Warren, Vivie, has trained as a lawyer, after
disguising herself as a man, and is now supporting the suffrage
cause in both her male and female personae. Johnston spe-
cialised in continuations of the 'classics' but his subject here
may also have been related to his wife's support for the cause.

On Vivie's return to London, after her Easter holiday, she threw
herself with added zest into the Suffrage struggle. The fortnight of
good feeding, of quiet nights and lazy days under her mother's roof
had done her much good. She was not quite so thin, the dark circles
under her grey eyes had vanished, and she found not only in herself
but even in the most middle-aged of her associates a delightful spirit
of tomboyishness in their swelling revolt against the Liberal leaders.
It was specially during the remainder of 1912 that Vivie noted the
enormous good which the Suffrage movement had done and was
doing to British women. It was producing a splendid camaraderie
between high and low. Heroines like Lady Constance Lytton
mingled as sister with equally heroic charwoman, factory girls, type-
writeresses, waitresses and hospital nurses. Women doctors of
Science, Music, and Medicine came down into the streets and did
the bravest actions to present their rights before a public that now
began to take them seriously. Débutantes, no longer quivering with
fright at entering the Royal Presence, modestly but audibly called
their Sovereign's attention to the injustice of Mr. Asquith's attitude
towards women, while princesses of the Blood Royal had difficulty
in not applauding. Many a tame cat had left the fireside and the
skirts of an inane old mother (who had plenty of people to look after
her selfish wants) and emerged, dazed at first into a world that was
unknown to her. Such had thrown away their crochet hooks, their
tatting-shuttles and fashion articles, their Church almanacs, and
Girl's Own Library books, and read and talked of social, sexual, and
industrial problems that have got to be faced and solved. Colour
came into their cheeks, assurance into their faded manners, sense
and sensibility into their talk; and whatever happened afterwards
they were never crammed back again into the prison of Victorian

spinsterhood. They learnt rough cooking, skilled confectionery, typewriting, bicycling, jiu-jitsu perhaps. 'The maidens came, they talked, they sang, they read; till she not fair began to gather light, and she that was became her former beauty treble,' sang in prophecy sixty years before, the greatest of poets and the poet-prophet of Woman's Emancipation. Many a woman has directly owed the lengthened, happier, usefuller life that became hers from 1910–1911–1912 onwards to the Suffrage movement for the Liberation of Women.

The crises of 1912, moreover, were not so acute as bitterly to envenom the struggle in the way that happened during the two following years. There was always some hope that the Ministry might permit the passing of an amendment to the Franchise Bill which would in some degree affirm the principle of Female Suffrage. It is true that a certain liveliness was maintained by the Suffragettes. The WSPU dared not relax in its militancy lest Ministers should think the struggle waning and Woman already tiring of her claims. The vaunted Manhood Suffrage Bill had been introduced by an anti-woman-suffrage Quaker Minister and its Second reading been proposed by an equally anti-feminist Secretary of State – this was in June–July, 1912; and no member of the Cabinet had risen to say a word in favour of the Women's claims. Still, something might be done in Committee, in the autumn Session – if there were one – or in the following year. There was a simmering in the Suffragist ranks rather than any alarming explosion. In March, before Vivie went to Brussels, Mrs. Pankhurst had carried out a window-smashing raid on Bond Street and Regent Street and the clubs of Piccadilly, during which among the two hundred and nineteen arrests there were brought to light as 'revolutionaries' two elderly women surgeons of great distinction and one female Doctor of Music. In revenge the police had raided the WSPU offices at Clifford's Inn, an event long foreseen and provided against in the neighbouring Chancery Lane.

The Irish Nationalist Party had shown its marked hostility to the enfranchisement of women in any Irish Parliament and so a few impulsive Irish women had thrown things at Nationalist MPs without hurting them. Mr. Lansbury had spoken the plain truth to the Prime Minister in the House of Commons and had been denied access to that Chamber where Truth is so seldom welcome.

In July the slumbering movement towards resisting the payment of taxes by vote-less women woke up into real activity, and there

were many ludicrous and pathetic scenes organized often by Vivie
and Bertie Adams at which household effects were sold and bought
in by friends to satisfy the claims of a tax-collector. In the autumn
Vivie and others of the WSPU organized great pilgrimages – the
marches of the Brown Women – from Scotland, Wales, Devon and
Norfolk to London, to some goal in Downing Street or Whitehall,
some doorstep which already had every inch of its space covered by
policemen's boots. These were among the pleasantest of the manifestations and excited great good humour in the populace of town
and country. They were extended picnics of ten days or a fortnight.
The steady tramp of sixteen to twenty miles a day did the women
good; the food *en route* was abundant and eaten with tremendous
appetite. The pilgrims on arrival on London were a justification in
physical fitness of Women's claim to equal privileges with Man.

Vivie after her Easter holiday took an increasingly active part in
these manifestations of usually good-humoured insurrection. As
Vivien Warren she was not much known to the authorities or to the
populace, but she soon became so owing to her striking appearance,
telling voice and gift of oratory. All the arts she had learnt as David
Williams she displayed now in pleading the woman's cause at the
Albert Hall, at Manchester, in Edinburgh and Glasgow. Countess
Feenix took her up, invited her to dinner parties where she found
herself placed next to statesmen in office, who at first morose and
nervous – expecting every moment a personal assault – gradually
thawed when they found her a good conversationalist, a clever
woman of the world, becomingly dressed. After all, she had been a
third wrangler at Cambridge, almost a guarantee that her subsequent life could not be irregular, according to a man's standard in
England of what an unmarried woman's life should be. She depre-
cated the violence of the militants in this phase.

But she was Protean. Much of her work, the lawless part of it was
organized in the shape and dress of Mr. Michaelis. Some of her
letters to the Press were signed Edgar McKenna, Albert Birrell,
Andrew Asquith, Egmont Harcourt, Felicia Ward, Millicent
Curzon, Judith Pease, Edith Spenser-Churchill, Marianne
Chamberlain, or Emily Burns; and affected to be pleas for the grant-
ing of the Suffrage emanating from the revolting sons or daughters,
aunts, sisters or wives of great statesmen, prominent for their opposition to the Women's Cause. The WSPU had plenty of funds and it
did not cost much getting visiting cards engraved with such names

and supplied with the home address of the great personage whom it was intended to annoy. One such card as an evidence of good faith would be attached to the plausibly-worded letter. The *Times* was seldom taken in, but great success often attended these audacious deceptions, especially in the important organs of the provincial Press. Editors and sub-editors seldom took the trouble and the time to hunt through *Who's Who*, or a Peerage to identify the writer of the letter claiming the Vote for Women. No real combination of names was given, thus forgery was avoided; but the public and the unsuspecting Editor were left with the impression that the Premier's, Colonial Secretary's, Home Secretary's, Board of Trade President's, or prominent anti-suffragist woman's son, daughter, brother, sister, wife or mother-in-law did not at all agree with the anti-feminist opinions of its father, mother, brother or husband. If the politician were foolish enough to answer and protest, he was generally at a disadvantage; the public thought it a good joke and no one (in the provinces) believed his disclaimers.

Vivie generally heckled ministers on the stump and parliamentary candidates dressed as a woman of the lower middle class. It would have been unwise to do so in man's guise, in case there should be a rough-and-tumble afterwards and her sex be discovered. Although in order to avoid premature arrest she did not herself take part in those most ingenious – and from the view of endurance, heroic – stowaways of women interrupters in the roofs, attics, inaccessible organ lofts or music galleries of public baths, she organized many of these surprises beforehand. It was Vivie to whom the brilliant idea came of once baffling the police in the re-arrest of either Mrs. Pankhurst or Annie Kenney. Knowing when the police would come to the building where one or other of these ladies was to make her sensational re-appearance, she had previously secreted there forty other women who were dressed and veiled precisely similarly to the fugitive from justice. Thus, when the force of constables claimed admittance, forty-one women, virtually indistinguishable one from the other, ran out into the street, and the bewildered minions of the law were left lifting their helmets to scratch puzzled heads and admitting 'the wimmen were a bit too much for us, this time, they were.'

In her bedroom at 88–90 she kept an equipment of theatrical dis-guises; very natural-looking moustaches which could be easily applied and which remained firmly adhering save under the appli-

cation of the right solvent; pairs of tinted spectacles; wigs of cred-
ible appearance; different styles of suiting, different types of
women's dress. She sometimes sat in trains as a handsome, impressive matron of fifty-five, with a Pompadour confection and a tor-
toiseshell *face-à-main*, conversing with ministers of state or
permanent officials on their way to their country seats, and saying
'*Horrid* creatures!' if any one referred to the activities of the
Suffragettes. Thus disguised she elicited considerable information
sometimes, though she might really be on her way to organize the
break-up of the statesman's public meeting, the enquiry into dis-
creditable circumstances which might compel his withdrawal from
public life, or merely the burning down of his shooting box.

This life had its risks and perils, but it agreed with her health. It
was exciting and took her mind off Rossiter.

E. Smyth, *Female Pipings in Eden*

A large part of Ethel Smyth's collection of autobiographical
writings contained in this volume is dedicated to a description
of Mrs. Pankhurst. In this incident the identification of a mystical power uniting the women in their commitment to the
cause is both political and personal.

It was in the year 1910 that Mrs. Pankhurst came into my life,
changing, as contact with her was apt to do, its whole tenor. At first
she was indignant, but later on amused, that the full significance of
the suffrage movement and more particularly of militancy should
have been brought home to an English woman by an Austrian novelist, who, together with the presently to be enlightened one, was
extended, wet but rapidly drying, on an Italian beach.

Hermann Bahr, Anna Mildenburg his wife – the most superb of
Isoldes as all who saw her agree – and the present writer had for-
gathered in Venice, and seizing our letters had embarked for the
Lido at what passes in Venice for cock-crow. The two Austrians
swam like fishes, and at the moment I began examining my courier
were engaged in the following aquatic *tour de force*. Bahr, followed
by his wife, would swim out into deep water and spread-eagle
himself on the surface; whereupon Anna, taking a few powerful

strokes, dived through the invisible archway (evidently of the Pointed Order of Gothic) supplied by her lord, the game being to reappear on the other side without having grazed the architecture; as it were a barge shooting London Bridge. This exercise had been invented by Anna, in whose great soul lodges every kind of dramatic genius, from the sublime to the grotesque, and who to-day, as Professor of Dramatic Singing at the Munich Academy of Music, in the intervals of revealing Wagner to her pupils, gives them hair-raising sketches of how the witch in *Hänsel and Gretel* should be played.

The degree of honorary Doctor of Music had recently been conferred on me by the University of Durham, and one of my letters was from an old acquaintance, Lady Constance Lytton, member of the Women's Social and Political Union (the militant society founded by the Pankhursts), enquiring, as was their habit when any woman received a distinction, what my views were on the suffrage in general and militancy in particular.

Presently Bahr, fresh from England, was listening with astonishment to a confession of indifference tinged with distaste and, Heaven forgive me, ridicule. 'Why!' he said, 'the militant movement is the one really alive issue in England . . . perhaps in Europe, and your Mrs. Pankhurst is in my opinion the most astounding personality that even England – a country that is for ever turning out new types of genius – has yet produced.' He told me that he had lately listened to political talk of every description, from debates in the Houses of Parliament to meetings in Trafalgar Square, and had never once heard a poor speech from these so-called wild women . . . 'the only people,' he repeated, 'who are dealing with realities.'

I was deeply impressed, and at once cancelled a projected reply to Lady Constance Lytton which it still makes me hot to think of.

A fortnight later I went to a meeting at Lady Brassey's to hear Mrs. Pankhurst and be introduced to her. A graceful woman rather under middle height; one would have said a delicate-looking woman, but the well-knit figure, the quick deft movements, the clear complexion, the soft bright eyes that on occasion could emit lambent flame, betokened excellent health. She knew I was an artist of sorts and connected with no Suffrage society, hence my reception was, if anything, chilly. But a very short time afterwards, at the fiery inception of what was to become the deepest and closest of friendships, she was told how, at that first confrontation, the words

addressed by the disguised Duke of Kent to Lear instantly came into
my head:

Kent. You have that in your countenance which I would fain call master.
Lear. What's that?
Kent Authority.

Before a fortnight had passed it became evident to me that to keep
out of the movement, to withhold any modicum it was possible to
contribute to that cause, was as unthinkable as to drive art and politics in double harness. At the moment I was deep in certain musical
undertakings. These liquidated, I decided that two years should be
given to the WSPU after which, reversing engines, I would go back
to my job.

Of those years no record exists. I kept no diary, and between
people who meet constantly and are engaged in that particular sort
of activity there can be no correspondence worth the name. She was
a woman who had by nature certain instincts characteristic of royal
personages, and which, if they have them not, it is necessary for
them to cultivate in self-defence. From intimate friendship she had
hitherto held aloof, her boundless love and admiration for her eldest
daughter satisfying all the needs of her heart. I imagine it is unnecessary to dwell on the devotion a magical personality like hers was
able to kindle when she chose; but apart from that it was possible
during these two years to gain insight into parts of her nature of
which few, I think, except myself were aware.

For instance she was immensely responsive to poetry, to scenery,
and when time and opportunity offered, to music. And though once,
on some strange occasion – it must have been a wedding or a funeral
– when we were in church together, she began joining loudly, fervently, even gloatingly in the hymns, and sang flatter than I should
have thought it possible to sing, this did not affect my conviction
that had she not been irrevocably committed to a life of action ('I
am simply an agitator,' she would say), her *flair* for the first rate
would have manifested itself on almost any field. Not that the writer
lays claim to superiority of judgment all round the compass; it is
merely an impression, stated for what it is worth. When in America
or Canada she would often cut out of a periodical or newspaper
some little poem that had caught her fancy, and the quality of these
extracts always made me realise afresh how untrammelled was her
spirit, how original the cast of her mind. During her early life, what

with child-bearing, child-rearing, politics, and a perpetual struggle against poverty, there can have been no leisure for direct culture, yet the fact that she had spent much of her youth in Paris (I cannot recall how or why, but Henri Rochefort comes into it somewhere) and spoke French fluently, saved her from the middle-class greyness of outlook that might otherwise have been hers.

Yet there can have been nothing grey or middle-class minded about her husband – a barrister, friend of J. S. Mill – whom she described as a delightful heroic personality, an idealist, a fighter for lost causes who occasionally told her extremely funny stories, which, when the mood brought such reminiscences uppermost, were passed on to me with apologies, almost with blushes, and carried off by remarks as to how 'angry' she had been with him for relating such anecdotes. Truth to tell they were of the tallest, but invariably so pointful that it was evidently impossible to resist the temptation of sharing them with an appreciative friend. Only once or twice perhaps in the course of our friendship did I benefit by this most passing of moods in one who, in spite of France and Rochefort, had a touch of puritanism in her make-up. This touch would, I imagine, stimulate the anecdote *verve* of a husband, and it certainly made an occasional deviation from the high and dry road very amusing to the friend.

She had no home and at that time was living at the Lincoln's Inn Hotel, close to the WSPU offices, and sometimes I would occupy the second bed in her room. She was not a religious woman in the ordinary sense of the word, nor addicted to metaphysical speculation. But there was in her a deep sense of what in my Carlyle-ridden youth people used to call the Immensities; the things that lie beyond life and death, effort and fruition, success and failure, love and the dying away of love.

I remember one night – 'Census night' it was – when she and I, standing in our dressing gowns at the window, watched the dawn rise beyond the river and fight its way through the mist. She was on the eve of some terrible venture that would end in rough usage and prolonged imprisonment, thinking perhaps of the inevitable hunger-strike, while I, for my part, was tasting the bitter anguish of one fated to look on powerless. Our foreheads pressed against the window pane staring silently into the dawn, gradually we realised that her love for down-trodden women . . . her hope of better things for them . . . my music . . . our friendship . . . that all this was part of the mystery that was holding our eyes. And suddenly it came to us that all was well; for a second we were standing on the spot in a madly spinning world where nothing stirs, where there is eternal stillness. It was a curious experience. Not a word passed between us, but we looked at each other, wondering why we had been so troubled . . . Neither of us ever forgot that dawn.

M. Sinclair, *The Tree of Heaven*

> May Sinclair's novel places the collectivism of the suffrage movement in the context of other 'mass' identifications that threaten to draw the characters into a 'vortex', destroying their individuality in an ostensible fight for freedom. The reference at the end to Schubert should be to Schumann.

Three hundred and thirty women and twenty men waited in the Banquet Hall to receive the prisoners.

The high galleries were festooned with the red, white and blue of the Women's Franchise Union, and hung with flags and blazoned banners. The silk standards and the emblems of the Women's Suffrage Leagues and Societies, supported by their tall poles, stood ranged along three walls. They covered the sham porphyry with gorgeous and heroic colours, purple and blue, sky-blue, and sapphire blue and royal blue, black, white and gold, vivid green, pure gold, pure white, dead-black, orange and scarlet and magenta.

From the high table under the windows streamed seven dependent tables decorated with nosegays of red, white and blue flowers. In the centre of the high table three arm-chairs, draped with the tricolour, were set like three thrones for the three leaders. They were flanked by nine other chairs on the right and nine on the left for the eighteen other prisoners.

There was a slight rustling sound at the side door leading to the high table. It was followed by a thicker and more prolonged sound of rustling as the three hundred and fifty turned in their places.

The twenty-one prisoners came in.

A great surge of white, spotted with red and blue, heaved itself up in the hall to meet them as the three hundred and fifty rose to their feet.

And from the three hundred and fifty there went up a strange, a savage and a piercing collective sound, where a clear tinkling as of glass or thin metal, and a tearing as of silk, and a crying as of children and of small, slender-throated animals were held together by ringing, vibrating, overtopping tones as of violins playing in the treble. And now a woman's voice started off on its own note and tore the delicate tissue of this sound with a solitary scream; and now a man's voice filled up a pause in the shrill hurrahing with a solitary boom.

To Dorothea, in her triumphal seat at Angela Blathwaite's right hand, to Michael and Nicholas and Veronica in their places among the crowd, that collective sound was frightful.

From her high place Dorothea could see Michael and Nicholas, one on each side of Veronica, just below her. At the same table, facing them, she saw her three aunts, Louie, Emmeline, and Edith.

It was from Emmeline that those lacerating screams arose.

The breakfast and the speeches of the prisoners were over. The crowd was on its feet again, and the prisoners had risen in their high places.

Out of the three hundred and seventy-one, two hundred and seventy-nine women and seven men were singing the Marching Song of the Militant Women:

Shoulder to shoulder, breast to breast,
Our army moves from east to west.
   Follow on! Follow on!

With flag and sword from south and north,
The sounding, shining hosts go forth.
   Follow on! Follow on!

Do you not hear our marching feet,
From door to door, from street to street?
   Follow on! Follow on!

Dorothea was fascinated and horrified by the singing, swaying, excited crowd.

Her three aunts fascinated her. They were all singing at the top of their voices. Aunt Louie stood up straight and rigid. She sang from the back of her throat, through a mouth not quite sufficiently open;

she sang with a grim, heroic determination to sing, whatever it might cost her and other people.

Aunt Edie sang inaudibly; her thin shallow voice, doing its utmost, was overpowered by the collective song. Aunt Emmeline sang shrill and loud; her body rocked slightly to the rhythm of a fantastic march. With one large, long hand raised she beat the measure of the music. Her head was thrown back; and on her face there was a look of ecstasy, of a holy rapture, exalted, half savage, not quite sane.

Dorothea was fascinated and horrified by Aunt Emmeline.

The singing had threatened her when it began; so that she felt again her old terror of the collective soul. Its massed emotion threatened her. She longed for her whitewashed prison-cell, for its hardness, its nakedness, its quiet, its visionary peace. She tried to remember. Her soul, in its danger, tried to get back there. But the soul of the crowd in the hall below her swelled and heaved itself towards her, drawn by the Vortex. She felt the rushing of the whirlwind; it sucked at her breath: the Vortex was drawing her too; the powerful, abominable thing almost got her. The sight of Emmeline saved her.

She might have been singing and swaying too, carried away in the same awful ecstasy, if she had not seen Emmeline. By looking at Emmeline she saved her soul; it stood firm again; she was clear and hard and sane.

She could look away from Emmeline now. She saw her brothers, Michael and Nicholas. Michael's soul was the prey of its terror of the herd-soul. The shrill voices, fine as whipcord and sharp as needles, tortured him. Michael looked beautiful in his martyrdom. His fair, handsome face was set clear and hard. His yellow hair, with its hard edges, fitted his head like a cap of solid, polished metal. Weariness and disgust made a sort of cloud over his light green eyes. When Nicky looked at him, Nicky's face twitched and twinkled. But he hated it almost as much as Michael hated it.

She thought of Michael and Nicholas. They hated it, and yet they stuck it out. They wouldn't go back on her. She and Lady Victoria Threlfall were to march on foot before the Car of Victory from Blackfriars Bridge along the Embankment, through Trafalgar Square and Pall Mall and Piccadilly to Hyde Park Corner. And Michael and Nicholas would march beside them to hold up the poles of the standard which, after all, they were not strong enough to carry.

She thought of Drayton, who had not stuck it out. And at the same time she thought of the things that had come to her in her prison cell. She had told him the most real thing that had ever happened to her, and he had not listened. He had not cared. Michael would have listened. Michael would have cared intensely.

She thought, 'I am not come to bring peace, but a sword.' The sword was between her and her lover.

She had given him up. She had chosen, not between him and the Vortex, but between him and her vision which was more than either of them, or than all this.

She looked at Rosalind and Maud Blackadder who sang violently in the hall below her. She had chosen freedom. She had given up her lover. She wondered whether Rosalind or the Blackadder girl could have done as much, supposing they had had a choice?

Then she looked at Veronica.

Veronica was standing between Michael and Nicholas. She was slender and beautiful and pure, like some sacrificial virgin. Presently she would be marching in the procession. She would carry a thin, tall pole, with a round olive wreath on the top of it, and a white dove sitting in the ring of the olive wreath. And she would look as if she was not in the procession, but in another place.

When Dorothea looked at her she was lifted up above the insane ecstasy and the tumult of the herd-soul. Her soul and the soul of Veronica went alone in utter freedom.

> Follow on! Follow on!
> For Faith's our spear and Hope's our sword,
> And Love's our mighty battle lord.
> Follow on! Follow on!

> And Justice is our flag unfurled,
> The flaming flag that sweeps the world.
> Follow on! Follow on!

> And 'Freedom!' is our battle-cry;
> For Freedom we will fight and die,
> Follow on! Follow on!

The procession was over a mile long.

It stretched all along the Embankment from Blackfriars Bridge to Westminster. The Car of Victory, covered with the tricolour, and the bodyguard on thirteen white horses were drawn up beside Cleopatra's Needle and the Sphinxes.

Before the Car of Victory, from the western Sphinx to Northumberland Avenue, were the long regiments of the Unions and Societies and Leagues, of the trades and the professions and the arts, carrying their banners, the purple and the blue, the black, white and gold, the green, the orange and scarlet and magenta.

Behind the Car of Victory came the eighteen prisoners, with Lady Victoria Threlfall and Dorothea at their head, under the immense tricolour standard that Michael and Nicholas carried for them. Behind the prisoners, closing the procession, was a double line of young girls dressed in white with tricolour ribbons, each carrying a pole with the olive wreath and dove, symbolising, with the obviousness of extreme innocence, the peace that follows victory. They were led by Veronica.

She did not know that she had been chosen to lead them because of her youth and her processional, hieratic beauty; she thought that the Union had bestowed this honour on her because she belonged to Dorothea.

From her place at the head of the procession she could see the big red, white and blue standard held high above Dorothea and Lady Victoria Threlfall. She knew how they would look; Lady Victoria, white and tense, would go like a saint and a martyr, in exaltation, hardly knowing where she was, or what she did; and Dorothea would go in pride, and in disdain for the proceedings in which her honour forced her to take part; she would have an awful knowledge of what she was doing and of where she was; she would drink every drop of the dreadful cup she had poured out for herself, hating it.

Last night Veronica had thought that she too would hate it; she thought that she would rather die than march in the procession. But she did not hate it, or her part in it. The thing was too beautiful and too big to hate, and her part in it was too little.

She was not afraid of the procession, or of the soul of the procession. She was not afraid of the thick crowd on the pavements, pressing closer and closer, pushed back continually by the police. Her soul was by itself. Like Dorothea's soul it went apart from the soul of the crowd and the soul of the procession; only it was not proud; it was simply happy.

The band had not yet begun to play; but already she heard the music sounding in her brain; her feet felt the rhythm of the march.

Somewhere on in front the policemen made gestures of release, and the whole procession began to move. It marched to an unheard music, to the rhythm that was in Veronica's brain.

They went through what were once streets between walls of houses, and were now broad lanes between thick walls of people. The visible aspect of things was slightly changed, slightly distorted. The houses stood farther back behind the walls of people; they were hung with people; a swarm of people clung like bees to the house walls.

All these people were fixed where they stood or hung. In a still and stationary world the procession was the only thing that moved.

She had a vague, far-off perception that the crowd was friendly.

A mounted policeman rode at her side. When they halted at the cross streets he looked down at Veronica with an amused and benign expression. She had a vague, far-off perception that the policeman was friendly. Everything seemed to her vague and far off.

Only now and then it struck her as odd that a revolutionary procession should be allowed to fill the streets of a great capital, and that a body of the same police that arrested the insurgents should go with it to protect them, to clear their triumphal way before them, holding up the entire traffic of great thoroughfares that their bands and their banners and their regiments should go through.

She said to herself: 'What a country! It couldn't happen in Germany; it couldn't happen in France, or anywhere in Europe or America. It could only happen in England.'

Now they were going up St. James's Street towards Piccadilly. The band was playing the Marseillaise.

And with the first beat of the drum Veronica's soul came down from its place, and took part in the procession. As long as they played the Marseillaise she felt that she could march with the procession to the ends of the world; she could march into battle to the Marseillaise; she could fight to that music and die.

The women behind her were singing under their breath. They sang the words of the Women's Marseillaise.

And Veronica, marching in front of them by herself, sang another song. She sang the Marseillaise of Heine and of Schubert.

'Dann reitet mein Kaiser wohl über mein Grab,
    Viel' Schwerter klirren und blitzen;
Dann steig' ich gewaffnet hervor aus mein Grab, –
    Den Kaiser, den Kaiser zu schützen!'

The front of the procession lifted as it went up Tyburn Hill.

Veronica could not see Michael and Nicholas, but she knew that they were there. She knew it by the unusual steadiness of the standard that they carried. Far away westwards, in the middle and front of the procession, the purple and the blue, the gold and white, the green, the scarlet and orange and magenta standards rocked and staggered; they bent forwards; they were flung backwards as the west wind took them. But the red, white and blue standard that Michael and Nicholas carried went before her, steady and straight and high.

And Veronica followed, carrying her thin, tall pole with the olive wreath on the top of it, and the white dove sitting in the ring of the wreath. She went with the music of Schubert and Heine sounding in her soul.

Mrs H. Ward, *Delia Blanchflower*

Although anti-suffragette, Mrs Humphry Ward was not unsympathetic to the lack of opportunities for women. This attempt to 'psychologise' the character of militant activist Gertrude Marvell, by depicting her home circumstances, is presented with an odd mixture of disapproval and sympathy.

'Pack the papers as quickly as you can – I am going to town this afternoon. Whatever can't be packed before then, you can bring up to me to-morrow.'

A tired girl lifted her head from the packing-case before which she was kneeling.

'I'll do my best, Miss Marvell – but I'm afraid it will be impossible to finish to-day.' And she looked wearily round the room laden with papers – letters, pamphlets, press-cuttings – on every available table and shelf.

Gertrude gave a rather curt assent. Her reason told her the thing was impossible; but her will chafed against the delay, which her secretary threatened, of even a few hours in the resumption of her work in London, and the re-housing of all its tools and materials. She was a hard mistress; though no harder on her subordinates than she was on herself.

She began to turn her own hand to the packing, and missing a book she had left in the drawing-room the night before, she went to fetch it. It was again a morning of frosty sunshine, and the garden outside lay in dazzling light. The drawing-room windows were open, and through one of them Gertrude perceived Delia moving about outside on the whitened grass. She was looking for the earliest snowdrops which were just beginning to bulge from the green stems, pushing up through the dead leaves under the beech trees. She wore a blue soft shawl round her head and shoulders, and she was singing to herself. As she raised herself from the ground, and paused a moment looking towards the house, but evidently quite unconscious of any spectators, Gertrude could not take her eyes from the vision she made. If radiant beauty, if grace, and flawless youth can 'lift a mortal to the skies,' Delia stood like a young goddess under the winter sun. But there was much more than beauty in her face. There was a fluttering and dreamy joy which belongs only to the children of earth. The low singing came unconsciously from her lips, as though it were the natural expression of the heart within. Gertrude caught the old lilting tune –

'For oh, Greensleeves was all my joy –
For oh, Greensleeves was my heart's delight –
And who but my lady Greensleeves? –'

The woman observing her did so with a strange mixture of softness and repulsion. If Gertrude Marvell loved anybody, she loved Delia – the captive of her own bow and spear, and until now the most loyal, the most single-minded of disciples. But as she saw Delia walk away to a further reach of the garden, the mind of the elder woman bitterly accused the younger. Delia's refusal to join the militant forces in London, at this most critical and desperate time, on what seemed to Gertrude the trumpery excuse of Weston's illness, had made an indelible impression on a fanatical temper. If she had cared – if she had *really* cared – she could not have done any such thing. 'What have I been wasting my time here for?' she asked herself; and reviewing the motives which had induced her to accept Delia's proposal that they should live together, she accused herself sharply of a contemptible lack of judgment and foresight.

For no mere affection for Delia Blanchflower would have influenced her, at the time when Delia, writing to tell her of the approaching death of Sir Robert, implored her to come and share her life.

'You know I shall have money, dearest Gertrude,' – wrote Delia – 'Come and help me to spend it – for the Cause.' And for the sake of the Cause, – which was then sorely in want of money – and only for its sake, Gertrude had consented. She was at that time rapidly becoming one of the leading spirits in the London office of the 'Daughters,' so that to bury herself, even for a time in a country village, some eighty miles from London was a sacrifice. But to secure what seemed likely to be some thousands a year from a willing giver, such a temporary and modified exile had appeared to her worth while; and she had at once planned a campaign of 'militant' meetings in the towns along the South Coast, by way of keeping in touch with 'active work.'

But, in the first place, the extraordinary terms of Sir Robert's will had proved far more baffling than she and Delia had ever been willing to believe. And in the next place, the personality of Mark Winnington had almost immediately presented itself to Gertrude as something she had never reckoned with. A blustering and tyrannical guardian would have been comparatively easy to fight. Winnington was formidable, not because he was hostile, resolutely hostile, to their whole propaganda of violence; that might only have spurred a strong-willed girl to more passionate extremes. He was dangerous, – in spite of his forty years – because he was delightful; because, in his leisurely, old-fashioned way, he was so lovable, so handsome, so inevitably attractive. Gertrude, looking back, realised that she had soon perceived – vaguely at least – what might happen, what had now – as she dismally guessed – actually happened.

The young, impressionable creature, brought into close contact with this charming fellow – this agreeable reactionary – had fallen in love! That was all. But it was more than enough. Delia might be still unconscious of it herself. But this new shrinking from the most characteristic features of the violent policy – this new softness and fluidity in a personality that when they first reached Maumsey had begun already to stiffen in the fierce mould of militancy: – to what could any observer with eyes in their head attribute them but the influence of Mark Winnington – the daily unseen presence of other judgments and other ideals, embodied in a man to whom the girl's feelings had capitulated?

'If I could have kept her to myself for another year, he could have done nothing. But he has intervened before her opinions were anything more than the echoes of mine; – and for the future I shall have less and less chance against him. What shall we ever get out of her as a married woman? What would Mark Winnington – to whom she will give herself, body and soul, – allow us to get out of her? Better break with her now, and disentangle my own life!'

With such thoughts, a pale and brooding woman pursued the now distant figure of Delia. At the same time Gertrude Marvell had no intention whatever of provoking a premature breach which might deprive either the Cause or herself of any help they might still obtain from Delia in the desperate fight immediately ahead. She, personally, would have infinitely preferred freedom and a garret to Delia's flat, and any kind of dependence on Delia's money. 'I was not born to be a parasite!' she angrily thought. But she had no right to prefer them. All that could be extracted from Delia should be extracted. She was now no more to Gertrude than a pawn in the game. Let her be used – if she could not be trusted!

But if this had fallen differently, if she had remained the true sister-in-arms, given wholly to the joy of the fight, Gertrude's stern soul would have clapsed her to itself, just as passionately as it now dismissed her.

'No matter!' The hard brown eyes looked steadily into the future. 'That's done with. I am alone – I shall be alone. What does it signify? – a little sooner or later?'

The vagueness of the words matched the vagueness of certain haunting premonitions in the background of the mind. Her own future always shaped itself in tragic terms. It was impossible – she knew it – that it should bring her any kind of happiness. It was no less impossible that she should pause and submit. That active defiance of the existing order, on which she had entered, possessed her, gripped her, irrevocably. She was like the launched stone which describes its appointed curve – till it drops.

As for any interference from the side of her own personal ties and affections, – she had none.

In her pocket she carried a letter she had received that morning, from her mother. It was plaintive, as usual.

'Winnie's third child arrived last week. It was an awful confinement. The first doctor had to get another, and they only just pulled her through. The child's a misery. It would be much better if it had died. I can't think what she'll do. Her husband's a wretched creature – just manages to keep in work – but he neglects her shamefully – and if there ever is anything to spend, *he* spends it – on his own amusement. She cried the other day, when we were talking of you. She thinks you're living with a rich lady, and have everything you want – and she and her children are often half-starved. 'She might forgive me now, I do think' – she'll say sometimes – 'And as for Henry, if I did take him away from her, she may thank her stars she didn't marry him. She'd have killed him by now. She never could stand men like Henry. Only, when he was a young fellow, he took her in – her first, and then me. It was a bad job we ever saw him.'

'Why are you so set against us, Gertrude? – your own flesh and blood. I'm sure if I ever was unkind to you I'm sorry for it. You used to say I favoured Albert at your expense – Well, he's as good as dead to me now, and I've got no good out of all the spoiling I gave him. I sit at home by myself, and I'm a pretty miserable woman. I read everything I can in the papers about what you're doing – you, who were my only child, seven years before Albert came. It doesn't matter to you what I think – at least, it oughtn't. I'm an old woman, and whatever I thought I'd never quarrel with you. But it would matter to me a good deal, if you'd sometimes come in, and sit by the fire a bit, and chat. It's three years since I've seen you. Winnie says you've forgotten us – you only care about the vote. But I don't believe it. Other people may think the vote can make up for everything – but not you. You're too clever. Hoping to see you,

'Your lonely old mother,

'Janet Marvell.'

To that letter, Gertrude had already written her reply. Some time – in the summer, perhaps, she had said to her mother. And she had added the mental proviso – 'if I am alive.' For the matters in which she was engaged were no child's play, and the excitements of prison and hunger-striking might tell even on the strongest physique.

No – her family were nothing to her. Her mother's appeal, though it should not be altogether ignored, was an insincere one. She had always stood by the men of the family; and for the men of the family, Gertrude, its eldest daughter, felt nothing but loathing and contempt. Her father, a local government official in a western town, a small-minded domestic tyrant, ruined by long years of whisky-nipping between meals; her only brother, profligate and spendthrift, of whose present modes of life the less said the better; her brother-in-law, Henry Lewison, the man whom, in her callow, ignorant youth, she was once to have married, before her younger sister supplanted her – a canting hypocrite, who would spend his day in devising petty torments for his wife, and begin and end it with family prayers: – these types, in a brooding and self-centred mind, had gradually come to stand for the whole male race.

Nor had her lonely struggle for a livelihood, after she had fled from home, done anything to loosen the hold of these images upon her. She looked back upon a dismal type-writing office, run by a grasping employer; a struggle for health, warring with the struggle for bread; sick headache, sleeplessness, anæmia, yet always, within, the same iron will driving on the weary body; and always the same grim perception on the dark horizon of an outer gulf into which some women fell, with no hope of resurrection. She burnt again with the old bitter sense of injustice, on the economic side; remembering fiercely her own stinted earnings, and the higher wages and larger opportunities of men, whom, intellectually, she despised. Remembering too the development of that new and ugly temper in men – men hard-pressed themselves – who must now see in women no longer playthings or sweethearts, but rivals and supplanters.

So that gradually, year by year, there had strengthened in her that strange, modern thing, a woman's hatred of men – the normal instincts of sex distorted and embittered. And when suddenly, owing to the slow working of many causes, economic and moral, a section of the Woman Suffrage movement had broken into flame and violence, she had flung her very soul to it as fuel, with the passion of one to whom life at last 'gives room.' In that outbreak were gathered up for her all the rancours and all the ideals of life, all its hopes and all its despairs. Not much hope! – and few ideals. Her passion for the Cause had been a grim force, hardly mixed with illusion; but it had held and shaped her.

Meanwhile among women she had found a few kindred souls. One of them, a fellow-student, came into money, died, and left Gertrude Marvell a thousand pounds. On that sum she had educated herself, had taken her degree at a west-country university, had moved to London and begun work as a teacher and journalist. Then, again, a breakdown in health, followed by a casual acquaintance with Lady Tonbridge – Sir Robert's offer – its acceptance – Delia!

How much had opened to her with Delia! *Pleasure*, for the first time; the sheer pleasure of travel, society, tropical beauty; the strangeness also of finding herself adored, of feeling that young loveliness, that young intelligence, all yielding softness in her own strong hands –

Well, that was done – practically done. She cheated herself with no vain hopes. The process which had begun in Delia would go forward. One more defeat to admit and forget. One more disaster to turn one's back upon.

And no disabling lamentations! Her eyes cleared, her mouth stiffened. She went quietly back to her packing.

C. Hamilton, *William – an Englishman*

> Cicely Hamilton also offers an account of the psychology and political development of the militant, by tracing the coming together of perfect partners Griselda and William, whose happiness in the common 'struggle' is rudely interrupted by the First World War.

Chapter I

. . .

Within a year, he had found his feet and was a busy and full-blown speaker – of the species that can be relied on to turn on, at any moment, a glib, excited stream of partisan fact and sentiment. His services were in constant demand, since he spoke for anything and everything – provided only the promoters of the meeting were sufficiently violent in their efforts to upset the prevailing order. He had developed and was pleased with himself; Faraday, though still a great man in his eyes, was more of an equal than an idol. He was wonderfully happy in his new, unrestful existence; it was not only that he knew he was doing great good and that applause uplifted him and went to his head like wine; as a member of an organization and swayed by its collective passion, he attained to, and was conscious of, an emotional (and, as he thought, intellectual) activity of which as an individual he would have been entirely incapable. As a deceased statesman was intoxicated with the exuberance of his own verbosity, so William was intoxicated with the exuberance of his own emotions. There were moments when he looked back on his old life and could hardly believe he was the same William Tully who

once, without thought of the Social Revolution, went daily from
Camberwell to the City and back from the City to Camberwell. . . .
As time went on, he was entrusted with 'campaigns' and the stirring
up of revolt; and it was a proud day for him when a Conservative
evening paper, in connection with his share in a mining agitation,
referred to him as a dangerous man. He wondered, with pity for her
blindness, what his mother would have thought if any one had told
her in her lifetime that her son would turn out dangerous.

As a matter of course he was a supporter of votes for women; an
adherent (equally as a matter of course) of the movement in its nois-
iest and most intolerant form. He signed petitions denouncing
forcible feeding and attended meetings advocating civil war, where
the civil warriors complained with bitterness that the other side had
hit them back; and his contempt for the less virulent form of suffragist was as great as his contempt for the Home Secretary and the
orthodox members of the Labour Party. It was at one of these meetings, in December 1913, that he met Griselda Watkins.

Griselda Watkins, then a little under twenty-five, was his exact
counterpart in petticoats; a piece of blank-minded, suburban young-
womanhood caught into the militant suffrage movement and enjoying herself therein. She was inclined to plumpness, had a fresh
complexion, a mouth slightly ajar and suggestive of adenoids, and
the satisfied expression which comes from a spirit at rest. Like
William, she had found peace of mind and perennial interest in the
hearty denunciation of those who did not agree with her.

On the night when William first saw her she wore, as a steward,
a white dress, a sash with the colours of her association and a badge
denoting that she had suffered for the Cause in Holloway. Her
manner was eminently self-conscious and assured, but at the same
time almost ostentatiously gracious and womanly; it was the policy
of her particular branch of the suffrage movement to repress manifestations of the masculine type in its members and encourage fluffi-
ness of garb and appeal of manner. Griselda, who had a natural
weakness for cheap finery, was a warm adherent of the policy, went
out window-smashing in a picture-hat and cultivated ladylike
charm.

She introduced herself to William after the meeting with a compliment on his speech, which had been fiery enough even for her;
they both considered the compliment graceful and for a few minutes
exchanged sympathetic platitudes on martyrdom, civil war and the

scoundrelly behaviour of the Government. Even in those first few minutes they were conscious of attraction for each other and pleased to discover, in the course of their talk, that they should meet again next week on another militant platform.

They met and re-met – at first only on platforms, afterwards more privately and pleasantly. William, when his own meetings did not claim him, took to following Griselda about to hers, that he might listen entranced to the words of enthusiastic abuse that flowed from her confident lips; he had heard them all before and from speakers as confident, but never before had they seemed so inspired and inspiring, never before had he desired with trembling to kiss the lips that uttered them. Griselda, touched as a woman and flattered as an orator by his persistent presence in her audience, invited him to tea at her aunt's house in Balham; the visit was a success, and from that evening (in early March) the end was a foregone conclusion. Their friendship ripened so fast that one night at the beginning of April (1914) William, escorting her home from a meeting, proposed to her on the top of an otherwise empty 'bus, and was duly and sweetly accepted.

There were none of the customary obstacles in the way of the happy pair – on the contrary, all was plain sailing. William's original income had for some years been augmented by his earnings as a speaker, and Griselda's parents had left her modestly provided for. Her aunt, long since converted to the Movement (to the extent of being unable to talk of anything but forcible feeding), smiled blessings on so suitable a match and proceeded to consider the trousseau; and after a little persuasion on William's part the wedding was fixed for July.

Chapter II

The mating of William and Griselda might be called an ideal mating; theirs were indeed two hearts that beat as one. With each day they were happier in each other's company; their minds as it were flowed together and intermingled joyously – minds so alike and akin that it would have been difficult, without hearing the voice that spoke it, to distinguish an utterance of Griselda from an idea formulated by William. Their prominent blue eyes – they both had prominent blue eyes – looked out upon the world from exactly the same point of view; and as they had been trained by the same influences and were incapable of forming an independent judgment, it would not have been easy to find cause of disagreement between them. There are men and women not a few who find their complement in their contrast; but of such were not William and Griselda. Their standard of conduct was rigid and their views were pronounced; those who did not share their views and act in conformity with their standards were outside the pale of their liking. And this not because they were abnormally or essentially uncharitable, but because they had lived for so long less as individuals than as members of organizations – a form of existence which will end by sucking charity out of the sweetest heart alive.

It was well for them, therefore, that their creed, like their code of manners and morals, was identical or practically identical. It was a simple creed and they held to it loyally and faithfully. They believed in a large, vague and beautifully undefined identity, called by William the People, and by Griselda, Woman; who in the time to come was to accomplish much beautiful and undefined Good; and in whose service they were prepared meanwhile to suffer any amount of obloquy and talk any amount of nonsense. They believed that Society could be straightened and set right by the well-meaning efforts of well-meaning souls like themselves – aided by the Ballot, the Voice of the People, and Woman. They believed, in defiance of the teachings of history, that Democracy is another word for peace and goodwill towards men. They believed (quite rightly) in the purity of their own intentions; and concluded (quite wrongly) that the intentions of all persons who did not agree with them must therefore be evil and impure. . . . They were, in short, very honest and devout sectarians – cocksure, contemptuous, intolerant, self-sacrificing after the manner of their kind.

They held, as I have said, to their own opinions strongly and would have died rather than renounce, or seem to renounce, them – which did not restrain them from resenting the same attitude of mind and heart in others. What in themselves they admired as loyalty, they denounced in others as interested and malignant stubbornness. More – it did not prevent them from disliking and despising many excellent persons whose opinions, if analysed, would have proved nearly akin to their own. William, for instance, would all but foam at the mouth when compulsory service in the army was the subject of conversation, and 'militarism,' to him, was the blackest of all the works of the devil; but he was bitter, and violently bitter, against the blackleg who objected to compulsory service in a Trade Union, and had spoken, times without number, in hearty encouragement of that form of siege warfare which is commonly known as a Strike. He was a pacifist of the type which seeks peace and ensues it by insisting firmly, and even to blood, that it is the other side's duty to give way.

Griselda also was a pacifist – when it suited her and when she had got her way. She believed in a future World-Amity, brought about chiefly by Woman; meanwhile, she exulted loudly and frequently in the fighting qualities of her sex. Like William, she had no quarrel with Continental nations; on the contrary, what she had seen of Continental nations during a fortnight's stay at Interlaken had inclined her to look on them with favour. Like William, her combatant instincts were concentrated on antagonists nearer home; she knew them better and therefore disliked them more. It is a mistake to suppose that either nations or individuals will necessarily like the people they see most of; if you must know a man in order to love him, you seldom hate a man with whom you have not acquaintance. Nothing could have been more ideally peaceful than the relations of China and England during the Middle Ages – for the simple reason that China and England knew absolutely nothing of each other. In the same way, if in a lesser degree, Griselda and William had a friendly feeling for Germany and the German people. They had never been to Germany and knew nothing of her history or politics; but they had heard of the Germans as intelligent people addicted to spectacles, beer and sonatas, and established on the banks of the Rhine. And – the Rhine being some way off – they liked them.

As internationalists they had no words too strong for standing armies and their methods; but upon military operations against domestic tyrants they looked with less disapproval. There existed, I believe, in the back of their minds some ill-defined distinction between bloodshed perpetrated by persons clad in uniform and by persons not so clad – between fighting with bayonets and fighting with bombs and brickbats. The one was militarism and unjustifiable; the other heroism and holy. Had you been unkind enough to pen them into a corner and force them to acknowledge that there are many born warriors out of khaki, they would have ended probably by declaring that one should take arms only against tyranny and in a righteous cause – and so have found themselves in entire agreement not only with their adversary but with the Tory Party, the

German Emperor, the professional soldier and poor humanity in general. The elect, when one comes to examine them, are not always so very elect. The difficulty would have been to persuade them that there could be two opinions concerning a cause they espoused; their little vision was as narrow as it was pure, and their little minds were so seldom exhausted by thinking. Apostles of the reign of Woman and of International Amity, they might have been summed up as the perfect type of aggressor.

With regard to what used to be called culture (before August 1914), the attainments of William and Griselda were very much on a level. They read newspapers written by persons who wholly agreed with their views; they read pamphlets issued, and books recommended, by societies of which they were members. From these they quoted, in public and imposingly, with absolute faith in their statements. Of history and science, of literature and art, they knew nothing, or next to nothing; and, their ignorance being mutual, neither bored the other by straying away from the subjects in which both were interested. . . . As I have said, their mating was an ideal mating.

The period of their engagement was not without its beauty; an ever-present consciousness of their mission to mankind did not prevent them from being blissful as loving young couples are blissful – it merely coloured their relations and spiritualized them. One evening, not long before their wedding, they sat together in Battersea Park on a bench and dedicated their mutual lives to the service of Progress and Humanity. They had invented a suitable formula for the occasion and repeated it softly, one after the other, holding each other's hands. Griselda's voice trembled, as she vowed, in semi-ecclesiastical phraseology, that not even her great love for William should wean her from her life's work; and William's voice shook back as he vowed in his turn that not even Griselda, the woman of his dreams, should make him neglectful of the call of Mankind and his duty to the holiest of causes. It was a very solemn little moment; man and woman, affianced lovers, they dedicated themselves to their mission, the uplifting of the human race. They were spared the doubts which would have assailed wiser heads as to the manner of accomplishing their mission; and as they sat side by side on the bench, with their hands clasped, they knew themselves for acceptable types and forerunners of the world they were helping to create. . . . Man and Woman, side by side, vowed to service.

'We shall never forget this evening,' Griselda whispered as the sun dipped down in glory. 'In all our lives there can be nothing more beautiful than this.'

She was right; the two best gifts of life are love and an approving conscience. These twain, William and Griselda, loved each other sincerely – if not with the tempestuous passion of a Romeo and a Juliet, with an honest and healthy affection; they had for each other an attraction which could set their pulses beating and start them dreaming dreams. That evening, on the bench in Battersea Park, they had dreamed their dreams – while their consciences looked on and smiled. They foreshadowed their home not only as a nest where they two and their children should dwell, but as a centre of light and duty – as they understood duty and light; a meeting-place for the like-minded, where fresh courage could be gathered for the strife with prejudice and evil. They pictured themselves (this was in June 1914) as what they would have called Powers – as a man and a woman working for progress and destined to leave their mark. The sense of their destiny awed and elated them – and they walked away from Battersea Park with their hearts too full for speech.

On the way home a flaring headline distracted Griselda temporarily from her dreams. 'Who's this Archduke that's been assassinated?' she asked. (Her morning's reading had been confined to *The Suffragette*.)

'Austrian,' William informed her. (He had read the *Daily Herald*.) 'Franz Joseph – no, Franz Ferdinand – the heir to the Austrian throne.'

'Who assassinated him?' his betrothed inquired, not very much interested.

'I can't remember their names,' William admitted, 'but there seem to have been several in it. Anyhow, he's been assassinated. Somewhere in the Balkans. With bombs.'

'Oh!' said Griselda, ceasing to be interested at all. Her mind had turned from traffic in strange archdukes and was running on a high resolve; the solemn vow of service was translating itself into action.

'I shall go to the meeting to-morrow,' she announced, 'and make my protest.'

William knew what was passing in her mind and made no effort to dissuade her. No more than she dared he let their mutual happiness enervate them – it must urge them to high endeavour, to struggle and sacrifice for the Cause.

'I'll go too,' he said simply, 'if I can manage to get a ticket.'

'Oh, I'll get you a ticket,' Griselda told him; 'they're sure to have some at the office' – and thanked him with a squeeze of the fingers that set his pulses beating.

She was as good as her word, and the next night saw him in a Cabinet Minister's audience. From his seat in the arena (their seats were not together and the pair had entered separately) his eye sought for Griselda and found her easily in the first row of the balcony – most obviously composed and with her gloved hands folded on the rail. She was dressed in pale blue, with a flowered toque perched on her head; her blue silk blouse, in view of possibilities, was firmly connected by safety-pins with the belt of her blue cloth skirt, and her hair secured more tightly than usual by an extra allowance of combs. Previous experience had taught her the wisdom of these measures. As usual, in accordance with the tradition of her party, she had insisted in her costume on the ultra-feminine note; her blouse savoured of Liberty and there was a cluster of rosebuds at her breast. She was breathing quickly, so her mouth was more open than usual; otherwise she gave no sign of mental or physical trepidation – save a studied indifference which might have betrayed her to an eye sufficiently acute. To William she looked adorable and his heart swelled with admiration of her courage and determination to sustain her in her protest to the uttermost; he vowed to himself to be worthy of such a mate.

He did his best to prove himself worthy when the critical moment came. He waited for that moment during more than three-quarters of an hour – for Griselda was not without confederates, and three ladies in picture hats and a gentleman in the garb of a Nonconformist minister had arisen at intervals to make the running before her voice rang out. All were suppressed, though not without excitement; two of the ladies parted with their hats and the clergyman broke a chair. The chair and the clergyman having been alike removed, the audience buzzed down into silence, and for full five minutes there was peace – until the speaker permitted himself a jesting allusion to the recently exported objectors. A man with a steward's rosette in his coat was stationed in the gangway close to William; and as the laughter the jest had provoked died away, he swore under his breath, 'By God, there's another in the balcony!' William swung round, saw Griselda on her feet and heard her voice shrill out – to him an inspiration and a clarion, to the steward a source of profanity.

'Mr. Chairman, I rise to protest against the speaker's gross insult to the noble women who –'

A man in the seat behind clapped his hands on her shoulders and rammed her back into her chair – where she writhed vigorously, calling him coward and demanding how he dared! His grip, sufficiently hard to be unpleasant, roused her fighting instincts and gave a fillip to her conscientious protest; in contact with actual, if not painful, personal violence, she found it easier to scream, hit out and struggle. Two stewards, starting from either end of the row of chairs, were wedging themselves towards her; she clung to her seat with fingers and toes, and shrieked a regulation formula which the meeting drowned in opprobrium. Conscious of rectitude, the jeers and hoots but encouraged her and fired her blood; and when her hands were wrenched from their hold on the chair she clung and clawed to the shoulder of her next-door neighbour – a stout and orthodox Liberal who thrust her from him, snorting indignation. One steward had her gripped under the armpits, the other with difficulty mastered her active ankles; and, wriggling like a blue silk eel and crowing her indefatigable protest, she was bundled in rapid and business-like fashion to a side entrance of the building.

'Cowards!' she ejaculated as she found her feet on the pavement.

'Damned little cat!' was the ungentlemanly rejoinder. 'If you come here again I'll pare your nasty little nails for you.'

And, dabbing a scored left hand with his handkerchief, the steward returned to his duties – leaving Griselda in the centre of a jocular crowd attracted to the spot by several previous ejections. She was minus her rosebuds, her toque and quite half of her hairpins; on the other hand, she held tightly grasped in her fingers a crumpled silk necktie which had once been the property of a stout and orthodox Liberal. She was conscious that she had acted with perfect dignity as well as with unusual courage – and that consciousness, combined with her experience of similar situations, enabled her to sustain with calm contempt the attentions of the jocular crowd.

'You'd like a taxi, I suppose, miss?' the constable on duty suggested – having also considerable experience of similar situations. Griselda assented and the taxi was duly hailed. Before it arrived at the kerb she was joined on the pavement by her lover, who had left the meeting by the same door as his betrothed and in much the same manner and condition; he had parted with a shoe as well as a hat, and one of his braces was broken. A hearty shove assisted him down the steps to the pavement where, to the applause of the unthinking multitude, he fell on his knees in an attitude of adoration before Griselda's friend the constable. Recovering his equilibrium, he would have turned again to the assault; but his game attempt to re-enter the building was frustrated not only by a solidly extended arm of the law but by the intervention of Griselda herself.

'You have done enough for to-night, dear,' she whispered, taking his arm. 'My instructions are not to insist on arrest. We have made our protest – we can afford to withdraw.'

She led the retreat to the taxi with a dignity born of practice; William, now conscious of his snapped brace, following with less deportment. The vehicle once clear of the jeering crowd, Griselda put her arms round her lover and kissed his forehead solemnly.

'My dear one,' she said, 'I am proud of you.'

'Oh, Griselda, I'm proud of you,' he murmured between their kisses. 'How brave you are – how wonderful! – how dared they! . . . I went nearly mad when I saw them handling you – I hit out, and the cowards knocked me down. . . . A woman raising her voice on the side of justice – and they silence her with brutal violence –'

'It's only what we must expect, dear,' she whispered back, stroking his rumpled hair. 'Remember this is War – God knows it's horrible, but we must not shrink from it.'

She spoke from her heart, from the profound ignorance of the unread and unimaginative . . . and once more in the darkness of the taxi the warriors clasped and kissed.

A. Bennett, *The Lion's Share*

> Arnold Bennett too analyses the appeal of the cause. In the dia-
> logue between an exiled leader and the novel's light-hearted
> heroine, he suggests that the former's dedication is also a form
> of self-indulgence. In the character of Rosamund he appears to
> unite features of both Emmeline and Christabel Pankhurst.

Audrey was extremely depressed in the interval after the Beethoven Concerto and before the Lalo. But she was not depressed by the news of the accident to the Zacatecas Oil Corporation in which was the major part of her wealth. The tidings had stunned rather than injured that part of her which was capable of being affected by finance. She had not felt the blow. Moreover she was protected by the knowledge that she had thousands of pounds in hand and also the Moze property intact, and further she was already reconsidering her newly-acquired respect for money. No! What depressed her was a doubt as to the genius of Musa. In the long dreadful pause it seemed impossible that he should have genius. The entire concert presented itself as a grotesque farce, of which she as its creator ought to be ashamed. She was ready to kill Xavier or his responsible representative.

Then she saw the tall and calm Rosamund, with her grey hair and black attire and her subduing self complacency, making a way between the rows of stalls towards her.

'I wanted to see you,' said Rosamund, after the formal greetings. 'Very much.' Her voice was as kind and as unrelenting as the grave.

At this point Miss Ingate ought to have yielded her seat to the terrific Rosamund, but she failed to do so, doubtless by inadvertence.

'Will you come into the foyer for a moment?' Rosamund inflexibly suggested.

'Isn't the interval nearly over?' said Audrey.

'Oh, no!'

And as a fact there was not the slightest sign of the interval being nearly over. Audrey obediently rose. But the invitation had been so conspicuously addressed to herself that Miss Ingate, gathering her wits, remained in her chair.

The foyer – decorated in the Cracovian taste – was dotted with cigarette smokers and with those who had fled from the interval. Rosamund did not sit down; she did not try for seclusion in a corner. She stepped well into the foyer, and then stood still, and absently lighted a cigarette, omitting to offer a cigarette to Audrey. Rosamund's air of a deaconess made the cigarette extremely remarkable.

'I wanted to tell you about Jane Foley,' began Rosamund quietly. 'Have you heard?'

'No! What?'

'Of course you haven't. I alone knew. She has run away to England.'

'Run away! But she'll be caught!'

'She may be. But that is not all. She has run away to get married. She dared not tell me. She wrote me. She put the letter in the manuscript of the last chapter but one of her book, which I am revising for her. She will almost certainly be caught if she tries to get married in her own name. Therefore she will get married in a false name. All this, however, is not what I wanted to tell you about.'

'Then you shouldn't have begun to talk about it,' said Audrey suddenly. 'Did you expect me to let you leave it in the middle! Jane getting married! I do think she might have told me. . . . What next, I wonder! I suppose you've – er – lost her now?'

'Not entirely, I believe,' said Rosamund. 'Certainly not entirely. But of course I could never trust her again. This is the worst blow I have ever had. She says – but why go into that? Well, she does say she will work as hard as ever, nearly; and that her future husband strongly supports us – and so on.' Rosamund smiled with complete detachment.

'And who's he?' Audrey demanded.

'His name is Aguilar,' said Rosamund. 'So she says.'

'Aguilar?'

'Yes. I gather – I say I gather – that he belongs to the industrial class. But of course that is precisely the class that Jane springs from. Odd! Is it not? Heredity, I presume.' She raised her shoulders.

Audrey said nothing. She was too shocked to speak – not pained or outraged, but simply shaken. What in the name of Juno could Jane see in Aguilar? Jane, to whom every man was the hereditary enemy! Aguilar, who had no use for either man or woman! Aguilar, a man without a Christian name, one of those men in connection with whom a Christian name is impossibly ridiculous. How should she, Audrey, address Aguilar in future? Would he have to be asked to tea? These vital questions naturally transcended all others in Audrey's mind. . . . Still (she veered round), it was perhaps after all just the union that might have been expected.

'And now,' said Rosamund at length, 'I have a question to put to you.'

'Well?'

'I don't want a definite answer here and now.' She looked round disdainfully at the foyer. 'But I do want to set your mind on the right track at the earliest possible moment – before any accidents occur.' She smiled satirically. 'You see how frank I am with you. I'll be more frank still, and tell you that I came to this concert to-night specially to see you.'

'Did you?' Audrey murmured. 'Well!'

The older woman looked down upon her from a superior height. Her eyes were those of an autocrat. It was quite possible to see in them the born leader who had dominated thousands of women and played a drawn game with the British Government itself. But Audrey, at the very moment when she was feeling the overbearing magic of that gaze, happened to remember the scene in Madame Piriac's automobile on the night of her first arrival in Paris, when she herself was asleep and Rosamund, not knowing that she was asleep, had been solemnly addressing her. Miss Ingate's often repeated account of the scene always made her laugh, and the memory of it now caused her to smile faintly.

'I want to suggest to you,' Rosamund proceeded, 'that you begin to work for me.'

'For the suffrage – or for you?'

'It is the same thing,' said Rosamund coldly. 'I am the suffrage. Without me the cause would not have existed to-day.'

'Well,' said Audrey, 'of course I will. I have done a bit already, you know.'

'Yes, I know,' Rosamund admitted. 'You did very well at the Blue City. That's why I'm approaching you. That's why I've chosen you.'

'Chosen me for what?'

'You know that a new great campaign will soon begin. It is all arranged. It will necessitate my returning to England and challenging the police. You know also that Jane Foley was to have been my lieutenant-in-chief – for the active part of the operation. You will admit that I can no longer count on her completely. Will you take her place?'

'I'll help,' said Audrey. 'I'll do what I can. I dare say I shan't have much money, because one of those "accidents" you mentioned has happened to me already.'

'That need not trouble you,' replied Rosamund imperturbably. 'I have always been able to get all the money that was needed.'

'Well, I'll help all I can.'

'That's not what I ask,' said Rosamund inflexibly. 'Will you take Jane Foley's place? Will you give yourself utterly?'

Audrey answered with sudden vehemence:

'No. I won't. You didn't want a definite answer, but there it is.'

'But surely you believe in the cause?'

'Yes.'

'It's the greatest of all causes.'

'I'm rather inclined to think it is.'

'Why not give yourself, then? You are free. I have given myself, my child.'

'Yes,' said Audrey, who resented the appellation of 'child.' 'But, you see, it's your hobby.'

'My hobby, Mrs. Moncrieff!' exclaimed Rosamund.

'Certainly, your hobby,' Audrey persisted.

'I have sacrificed everything to it,' said Rosamund.

'Pardon me,' said Audrey. 'I don't think you've sacrificed anything to it. You just enjoy bossing other people above everything, and it gives you every chance to boss. And you enjoy plots too, and look at the chances you get for that! Mind you, I like you for it. I think you're splendid. Only *I* don't want to be a monomaniac, and I won't be.' Her convictions seemed to have become suddenly clear and absolutely decided.

'Do you mean to infer that I am a monomaniac?' asked Rosamund, raising her eyebrows – but only a little.

'Well,' said Audrey, 'as you mentioned frankness – what else would you call yourself but a monomaniac? You only live for one thing – don't you, now?'

'It is the greatest thing.'

'I don't say it isn't,' Audrey admitted. 'But I've been thinking a good deal about all this, and at last I've come to the conclusion that one thing isn't enough for me, not nearly enough. And I'm not going to be peculiar at any price. Neither a fanatic nor a monomaniac, nor anything like that.'

'You are in love,' asserted Rosamund.

'And what if I am? If you ask me, I think a girl who isn't in love ought to be somewhat ashamed of herself, or at least sorry for herself. And I am sorry for myself, because I am not in love. I wish I was. Why shouldn't I be? It must be lovely to be in love. If I was in love I shouldn't be *only* in love. You think you understand what girls are nowadays, but you don't. I didn't myself until just lately. But I'm beginning to. Girls were supposed to be only interested in one thing – in your time. Monomaniacs, that's what they had to be. You changed all that, or you're trying to change it, but you only mean women to be monomaniacs about something else. It isn't good enough. I want everything, and I'm going to get it – or have a good try for it. I'll never be a martyr if I can help it. And I believe I can help it. I believe I've got just enough common sense to save me from being a martyr – either to a husband or a house or family – or a cause. I want to have a husband and a house and a family, and a cause too. That'll be just about everything, won't it? And if you imagine I can't look after all of them at once, all I can say is I don't agree with you. Because I've got an idea I can. Supposing I had all these things, I fancy I could have a tiff with my husband and make it up, play with my children, alter a dress, change the furniture, tackle the servants, and go out to a meeting and perhaps have a difficulty with the police – all in one day. Only if I did get into trouble with the police I should pay the fine – you see. The police aren't going to have me altogether. Nobody is. Nobody, man or woman, is going to be able to boast that he's got me altogether. You think you're independent. But you aren't. We girls will show you what independence is.'

'You're a rather surprising young creature,' observed Rosamund with a casual air, unmoved. 'You're quite excited.'

'Yes. I surprise myself. But these things do come in bursts. I've noticed that before. They weren't clear when you began to talk. They're clear now.'

'Let me tell you this,' said Rosamund. 'A cause must have martyrs.'

'I don't see it,' Audrey protested. 'I should have thought common sense would be lots more useful than martyrs. And monomaniacs never do have common sense.'

'You're very young.'

'Is that meant for an insult, or is it just a statement?' Audrey laughed pleasantly.

And Rosamund laughed too.

'It's just a statement,' said she.

'Well, here's another statement,' said Audrey. 'You're very old. That's where I have the advantage of you. Still, tell me what I can do in your new campaign, and I'll do it if I can. But there isn't going to be any utterly – that's all.'

'I think the interval is over,' said Rosamund with finality. 'Perhaps we'd better adjourn.'

Anon., *The Home-Breakers*

This novel was published in 1913 as 'An anti-militant suffragist novel by a popular and well-known novelist who desires to
remain anonymous'. Its author, J. S. Stainton, appears,
however, to have disappeared into literary obscurity. In its
attack on militancy, the novel ponders the possible appeal the
movement might have to an apparently 'normal' woman and
shows the dangers it might bring to home, family and personal
happiness. In these two excerpts we can see, firstly, the threat
posed by Joan Campion to her own family and future in the
neglect of her son. Morality and marriage are also presented at
risk in the novel, when her absence from home facilitates the
manipulations of scheming Miss Devine, who seeks to steal
Joan's husband. In the second passage Elinor, the fanatical suffragette, is shown to reject her own happiness and desires when
she turns down Howorth's offer of marriage.

As he stepped back from the bedside, Giffard casually wondered
how Joan Campion had ever come to mother such a plain piece of
humanity, and he asked himself whether in his looks he favoured the
other parent, the ladies' doctor of Wimpole Street.

'Say, we haven't met before, have we?' inquired G. D. guilelessly.
'What do you do for a living? You look like a soldier. Are you one?'
Giffard shook his head.

'I'm only a civil servant. I've been out in Uganda for eleven years.'

'Oh, I say, how rippin'! And what yarns you could tell a chap,
couldn't you? Do tell me some!'

'Not to-night, old chap. You stop there for only ten minutes to get
warm; then off you go to your own bunk. Supposing you tell me a
little about yourself? Somebody told me you are at Rugby.'

'I am, thank goodness! *He* did that. Before we knew him it was
rotten, Mr. Giffard, really. My mater had no money worth speakin'
about. At least it wouldn't run to a public school, and I was just
about being turned down to a beastly office, from which I should
have done a bunk at the earliest opportunity. Then he came on the
scene – Mr. Campion, I mean – and now there's Rugby and all this!
If only the mater –'

At this point, to Giffard's incredible dismay, G. D.'s gallant,
chirpy voice suddenly broke, and a sob choked in his throat.

'Steady, old chap,' said Giffard, sitting down on the front of the bed – 'steady! Breaking down like that won't mend anything – never did yet. Did it now?' he added, appealing to what was most manly in the boy.

'I know I'm a rotter to blub, but I can't help it. It's all this bally stuff about Votes for Women! Oh, couldn't all that rot be stopped somehow, Mr. Giffard? It's doing such a lot of harm everywhere. Even at Rugger the chaps have got to know about my mater, and they rag me no end! If that was all, I shouldn't so much mind it. But *he* hates it too; and yet she won't stop! Can't anything be done to make her stop?'

'I don't think we'd better discuss it, my boy – do you?' observed Giffard as, with a good deal of unnecessary noise, he pulled out one of the drawers in the tallboys chest.

'But, hang it all, Mr. Gifford, my mater isn't that sort of woman, really! She's so awf'ly good-lookin' and rippin' in every way. You'd never think, lookin' at her, that she was a bloomin' Suffragette, would you now? Why don't they get hold of their own sort – the old maids and the frumps – and keep to them and leave a chap's mater alone?'

Giffard could not forbear a smile, though his heart was sore for the lad's evident distress.

'Then he's such an awf'ly good sort, and it's hateful for him. It isn't fair, either. That's what I say, Mr. Giffard. To take as much from him as we've done and go on in that bally way! He's so good about everything too! He says I can have two chaps here for the "long' – chaps whose father and mother are in South America and who'd have had to be boarded out at some beastly tutoring place and do holiday tasks, if *he* hadn't come to the rescue. But now they're comin' here instead. Then there's Jessy! She was awf'ly ill when she came to us. She had got used up – nursing, or something – and now see how well she is and what a fine time she has! And *he* pays for it all! It's hard lines on him. I say again it isn't fair –'

The boy was brought to a standstill by the sudden opening of the door and the appearance of Campion.

'What isn't fair, and what are you doing here at this time of night, you rascal?' he inquired, with an attempt at severity which didn't in the least deceive G. D.

'Oh, just something Mr. Giffard and I were jawin' about, and I'm goin' to bed, pater, really, I'm goin' now –'

He slipped from the bed and, as he passed Campion, he pushed a warm moist hand into his.

Campion stooped and kissed him.

'Good-night, my lad. Sleep sound. And don't let me catch you out of bed at eleven o'clock another night! Your mother has gone to bed. You will see her in the morning.'

'Right-o,' said the boy. 'Good-night, Mr. Giffard, and thank you for the warm.'

He closed the door and pattered away, while Campion laughed a trifle queerly.

'I dare say you'll think you have dropped into an odd kind of menagerie, Giffie,' he said as soon as G. D. was gone. 'Leave that stuff and come down and have a pipe and a drink. The night's young yet.'

. . .

'There is the gong, and here comes my son. Well, Guy? –'

Her wide, beautiful mouth quivered and Giffard was surprised to see the affectionate abandon of the meeting between G. D. and his mother.

The figure, attired in a flannel shirt and tweed jacket, simply flew to her arms and was clasped there with a joy there was no mistaking.

Giffard turned away with an odd tightening of his heartstrings, and he began to understand, partially at least, the infatuation of Dick Campion, which on the previous evening had been a complete enigma to him.

Magnificently dowered with gifts both of body and of mind this woman undoubtedly was. As woman, wife and mother she appeared to be without a flaw. How was it possible, then, to account for her strange secession from the normal grooves in which undoubtedly her spirit and her heart could be at home? In her was to be found every instinct of womanhood and gentlehood, yet she was avowedly a leader of the wild women, justifying to her own conscience and heart even 'red ruin and the breaking-up of laws.'

As a psychological study, she interested Giffard immensely. It was a far more subtle and alluring study than that presented by the same problem in his sister's life.

Had Giffard spoken out with brutal frankness his own secret conviction concerning Elinor, it would not have been found to differ in essence from the coarse jibe of the man in the street who tells the advocate of Votes for Women to 'go out and git a husbin'!'

A few minutes later Miss Devine appeared, looking not quite so radiant in the morning as she had done last evening, and last of all came Campion.

It displeased Giffard profoundly that Mrs. Campion did not take the head of her own table, but relegated that position to Miss Devine, who occupied it as her right.

. . .

Howorth did not say good-bye to Elinor with the others, he simply took up his hat and followed her out into the sunshine of Piccadilly.

'Will you give me another half-hour of your time?' he asked, as they stood just half a moment under the colonnade.

She looked at him in rather a startled way.

'I thought of walking back to the flat. You can walk with me if you like.'

'Not that way. Let us go west and have tea in Kensington Gardens and see whether we can come up with Peter Pan.'

She smiled faintly, and her eyes were still dangerously soft. Few women can witness the marriage of those dear to them without some inward emotion, and Elinor was more shaken by the event than she could have imagined possible.

So they turned together, then Howorth, imagining that she looked tired, hailed a taxi and put her in. They drove to the Albert Gate, then entering the Park, walked in a slanting direction towards the Gardens. They were more deserted than usual, the majority of their devotees, the children of the rich, had already been sent to mountain or sea. Howorth had no difficulty in finding a quite remote spot under a spreading tree, where they were quite out of hearing or sight.

'It's only four o'clock. Would you like tea now, or shall we sit down for a little?'

'Oh, there is no hurry for tea after a "Ritz" luncheon she said lightly. 'We can sit down if you like.'

'You looked tired,' he hazarded, and could not keep the thrill of tenderness from his voice.

Elinor was fully conscious of it, and the colour fluttered fitfully in her face, which, in spite of its somewhat worn look, seemed to Howorth the most beautiful as well as the dearest in the world.

All trace of self, almost all trace of earthliness, seemed to have been purged away; it had the serene and lofty look we see on the faces of those who are inspired by the noblest purpose.

Certainly Elinor Giffard entertained the highest possible conception of the Women's Cause; to her it was a religion, nothing less.

'London can be very beautiful in summer. What city in the world could offer anything like this in its very heart?' she said presently.

'It *is* beautiful,' answered Howorth, as he drew in his chair so that he faced her. When her eyes came back from following the flight of a bird in the sapphire sky and rested on his face, she knew what was coming.

'Don't,' she said hurriedly. 'Please don't; it isn't any use.'

'I love you, Elinor. I've loved you since the first day I saw you. You are the first woman I have ever wanted, or cared to look at twice. You know what I have to offer. It is a whole-hearted devotion. Please let your heart speak. If there is one responsive chord in it, let it be heard.'

Her distress was acute.

'I am so sorry, but it is quite impossible!'

'There is only one thing which makes it impossible,' he said steadily. 'And that, I hope, does not exist.'

'Oh, there you are wrong; there are many reasons, most, if not all, of them quite insurmountable. I shall never marry. I am pledged to the Cause. I am not one of those who are keen to-day and slack to-morrow; I've given myself to it. I mean to see it through.'

'Don't, Elinor! It isn't worth while. Did you see the light on Ted's face and hers at the altar today? That is the thing which makes life glorious.'

'Spoken so like a man,' she said, but her voice was very unsteady. 'I don't blame you for your outlook. It is part of you and will always be, and I like you so much that I'm sorry to give you pain, but it is quite impossible.'

'Why?' he persisted.

'I have told you. I will never marry. I am one of the women who has only room in her life for one thing. I have given myself to it absolutely. Ted's word "obsessed" is the right one. There is no room in my life for you or for any man.'

'I refuse to take that answer. There is only one answer I will take. If you look me in the face and say that you don't care for me, that you never could care, then I'll go away, but not unless.'

It was a few seconds before she faced him, and then her face had grown as white as the chiffon at her throat.

'You try me very much. It is not quite fair. I have been frank with you, but apparently you do not believe. I do *not* care. I shall never care in that way for any man, and further, I don't mean to marry. Even when we get the victory there will be so much to do educating our women for the new rôle they are going to play. I shall be needed.'

Howorth pushed back his chair and rose, for her words had the final sound.

'Then there is absolutely no hope?'

'None. I am sorry. I pray you may find someone who will make you happy yet. Do you mind going now? No, I don't want tea. I shall just make my way back alone. I should prefer it.'

He raised his hat gravely, and walked away, not offering even to touch her hand. Elinor sat quite still on the chair where he had left her, looking for a long, long time into the green heart of the gardens sacred to childhood. Here and there a mite in white fluttered against the green of the trees, the child of some happy, careless woman whose ears were closed to the call.

Elinor Giffard had suffered many things for the Cause, against some of which her whole soul had revolted. But to-day she had made the last sacrifice. She had lied for it. For she loved John Howorth, and had had the strength to send him away.

Howorth walked the whole distance back to his hotel, a bitterly disappointed man. When he reached Trafalgar Square he found that an immense crowd had gathered, and that there were evidences of a disturbance of some kind. Pushing his way through the throng, he found that it was Sylvia Pankhurst on the plinth of Nelson's column, holding forth to the multitude in no dubious terms.

The small, slim creature, wholly inspired by her own zeal and fire, easily carried a section of the crowd with her.

'If you are in sympathy with us, and I see by your faces that many of you are,' she cried, 'then follow me to Downing Street.'

She sprang down, waving the banner of the Union, and immediately the surging crowd closed about her and began to move towards Whitehall.

Howorth, fascinated, followed in its wake. Then the police intervened and there were some ugly moments. The hostile element in the mob began to hustle the women, and he observed some of them being badly used.

One had her bonnet torn off, and the pins had come out of her hair, and her face was bleeding. Howorth sprang forward, his innate manhood prompting him to rescue a woman in distress. But the police were before him, and presently she was marched off under arrest. Then quite close behind him Howorth heard a moan of distress, and turning swiftly, saw a small, slight, elderly woman clinging closely to the arm of a shabby old man with a thin, sad face.

'Oh, Walter!' she cried, 'that was our Aggie! To think we buried five and she's our last; but I wish we'd buried her too before this.'

It sounded like the verdict of England's motherhood on the Women's Cause.

L. Houseman, 'Woman This and Woman That'

In this poem Laurence Houseman, writer, critic, and member of the Men's League for Women's Suffrage parodies Kipling's well-known poem 'Tommy' to demonstrate the exclusion and exploitation of women.

We went up to Saint Stephen's with petitions year by year.
'Get out!' the politicians cried; 'we want no women here!'
M.P.'s behind the railings stood and laughed to see the fun.
And bold policemen knocked us down, because we would not run.

For it's woman this, and woman that, and 'Woman, go away!'
But it's 'Share and share alike, ma'am!' when the taxes are to pay!
When the taxes are to pay, my friends, the taxes are to pay
Oh, it's 'Please to pay up promptly!' when the taxes are to pay!

We went before a magistrate, who would not hear us speak;
To a drunken brute who beat his wife he only gave a week;
But we were sent to Holloway a calendar month or more
Because we dared, against his will, to knock at Asquith's door.

For it's woman this, and woman that, and 'Woman, wait outside!'
But it's 'Listen to the Ladies!' when it suits your Party's side;
When it suits your Party's side, my friends, when M.P.'s on the stump
And shaking in their shoes at how the cat is going to jump!

When women go to work for them the Government engage
To give them lots of contract jobs at a low, starvation wage;
But when it's men that they employ they always add a note –
'Fair wages must be paid' – because the men have got the vote.

> For it's woman this, and woman that, and 'Woman, learn your place!'
> But it's 'Help us, of your charity!' when trouble looms apace;
> When trouble comes apace, my friends, when trouble comes apace,
> Then it's 'Oh, for woman's charity!' to help and save the race!

You dress yourselves in uniforms to guard your native shores,
But those who make the uniforms do work as good as yours;
For the soldier bears the rifle, but the woman bears the race –
And that you'd find no trifle if you had to take her place!

> For it's woman this, and woman that, and 'Woman cannot fight!'
> But it's 'ministering angel' when the wounded come in sight;
> When the wounded come in sight, my friends, the wounded come in sight,
> It's a 'ministering angel' then who nurses day and night!

We may not be quite angels – had we been we should have flown! –
We are only human beings who have wants much like your own;
And if sometimes our conduct isn't all your fancy paints,
It wasn't man's example could have turned us into saints!

> For it's woman here, and woman there, and woman on the streets,
> And it's how they look at women, with most men that one meets;
> With most men that one meets, my friends, with most men that one meets –
> It's the way they look at women that keeps women on the streets!

You talk of sanitation, and temperance, and schools,
And you send your male inspectors to impose your man-made rules
'The woman's sphere's the home,' you say? Then prove it to our face:
Give us the vote, that we may make the home a happier place!

> For it's woman this, and woman that, and 'Woman, say your say!'
> But it's 'What's the woman up to?' when she tries to show the way;
> When she tries to show the way, my friends, when she tries to show the way –
> And the woman means to show it – that is why she's out today!

A. A. Wilson, 'An End'

From *Holloway Jingles* (1912). Like many other contributors to this volume of poetry, A. A. Wilson had been imprisoned in Holloway for window-smashing and had been on hunger strike. Her short poem explores the apparently conflicting demands of personal and political desires.

My heart is too much like the surging sea,
Thinking of self it hollows with distress;
Its climbing hills mount up in huge excess,
If then of life's bright hopes I think – and thee.

And yet I dread this tide monotony;
A birth, a growth, a death, of life I ask,
Whatever pangs, however hard the task,
A strife, a consummation let me see.

Biographical details

In this reference section I have tried to give a brief outline of each of the contributors. For the well-known figures from the campaign a wide range of biographical sources exist, and readers wishing to find out more about leading activists are directed towards Olive Banks's excellent *Biographical Dictionary of British Feminists*, volumes 1 and 2. Major novelists can be traced in the *Oxford Companion to English Literature*. For women writers the following are useful: Janet Todd, *Dictionary of British Women Writers* and P. and J. Schlueter, *An Encyclopedia of British Women Writers*. *Votes for Women* by Roger Fulford contains brief biographies of suffrage campaigners and *A Guid Cause: the women's suffrage movement in Scotland* by Leah Leneman provides details on Scottish suffragists. Finally the *Dictionary of National Biography*, *Who's Who* and *Who Was Who* are reliable sources of information about prominent people. Several of the writers included here are, however, not to be found in any of these biographical dictionaries. Some appear in the *Suffrage Annual and Women's Who's Who* of 1913, and the *Englishwoman's Yearbook* can also provide information, but the obscurity of many is testament both to the wide range of people interested in and writing about the suffrage cause and to the work that still has to be done by feminist historians and literary critics.

In each of the brief biographies that follow, I indicate one source of further reference, where possible.

Bennett, Arnold (1867–1931)
Novelist, born in Staffordshire, setting for his best-known novel, *Anna of the Five Towns*, 1902. From 1893 assistant editor, then editor of *Woman* periodical. Wrote wide range of novels, short

stories and plays. In 1911, in response to a questionnaire from *The New Age*, he gave suffrage his support, and was not antagonistic to militancy, although he believed it could at times be counter productive. In the 1920s published a series of articles on 'Our Women', arguing for women's professional training.
M. Drabble, *Arnold Bennett: a biography*, London, 1974

Billington-Greig, Teresa (1877–1964)
Born in Blackburn, the daughter of a shipping clerk, she ran away from home in her teens and became a school-teacher. Joined Manchester ILP, possibly through the influence of Emmeline Pankhurst, in 1903, and became involved in WSPU. By 1907 second London organiser, imprisoned in Holloway. That year she rebelled against Emmeline and Christabel's dominance of WSPU and their increasing alienation from ILP. Left, with Charlotte Despard and others, to form Women's Freedom League. In 1911 published *The Militant Suffrage Movement: emancipation in a hurry* attacking WSPU and Pankhursts. Also left WFL. Between 1946 and 1949 chair of Women for Westminster.
C. McPhee & A. Fitzgerald, *Non-Violent Militant: selected writings of Teresa Billingon-Greig*, London, 1987

Burton Baldry, Walter (1888–1940)
Educated King's College, London, Queen's, Oxford. Member of Stock Exchange, Director of Public Companies, editor and director *Fry's Magazine of Action and Outdoor Life* and from 1909 edited *Ousley's Magazine*. Author of poetry, epigrams, spoofs and parodies, including *From Hampstead to Holloway: the journey of a suffragette*.
Who Was Who, London, 1941

Chew, Ada Nield (1870–1945)
Suffragist and Trade Unionist. Born in North Staffordshire, the eldest daughter of thirteen children and daughter of farmer, left school aged eleven to look after home and children. In 1887 trained as a tailor and began work at Crewe factory. Came to public attention in 1894 through letters of a 'Crewe Factory Girl' in *Crewe Chronicle*, followed by four articles on life in the factory. Lost her job because of uproar and became active member of ILP. Joined the *Clarion* Propaganda Van in 1896 (where she met and married

George Chew). Gave birth to daughter and in 1900 became organiser for Women's Trade Union League. When NUWSS began to support Labour Party in 1912 became its organiser in Rossendale valley and travelled widely, with her daughter, speaking on suffrage. Also wrote series of sketches for *The Common Cause* and *The Accrington Observer*. During the war she became a member of the Women's International League for Peace and Freedom and, determined to achieve economic independence, began mail-order drapery business.

D. Nield Chew (ed.), *Ada Nield Chew: the life and writings of a working woman*, London, 1982

Collins, Mabel
A prolific novelist and fellow of the Theosophical Society. Published many essays on Theosophy and spiritualism, and co-wrote a novel, *Outlawed*, with Charlotte Despard.

Colmore, Gertrude (pseud.) (–1926)
Novelist and suffragette. Born Gertrude Renton, first married to H. A. Colmore-Dunn, a barrister, then, in 1901, Harold Baillie-Weaver, also a barrister but involved, like her, in Theosophy and animal rights, and an active member of Men's League for Women's Suffrage. An early member of WFL, active in speaking and demonstrating. Involved in pacifism during the war. Published a number of novels and short stories, and wrote *The Life of Emily Davison* published by The Women's Press in 1913. *The Times* obituary comments: 'Her gentle refined personality was reflected in these stories which won her an attached constituency of readers' (27 Nov. 1926).

A. Morley with L. Stanley, *The Life and Death of Emily Wilding Davison: a biographical detective story with Gertrude Colmore's 'The Life of Emily Davison'*, London, 1988

Crosby, Ernest Howard (1856–1907)
Author and social reformer, born into wealthy philanthropic family in New York. Through influence of Tolstoy's writings, became involved in social reform for single-tax programme, anti-militarism, industrial arbitration and settlement work. One of founders of Social Reform Club. Wrote number of books on ethical idealism and published volumes of poetry under influence of Walt Whitman.

Dictionary of American Biography, IV

Davison, Emily Wilding (1872–1913)

Suffragette and graduate of London University. Joined WSPU in 1906 and in 1909 gave up teaching to devote time to the cause. Took part in various demonstrations and deputations and from 1909 underwent series of prison sentences, including hunger-striking and forcible feeding. Came to wider attention through hosepipe incident in Strangeways prison in 1909. Involved in stone-throwing, window-breaking, setting fire to pillar boxes. In 1911 hid in hot-air shaft of House of Commons on three separate occasions. In June 1912 severely injured when jumping down an iron staircase in prison. In June 1913 ran in front of the King's horse in the Derby, fracturing her skull and dying without regaining consciousness. Her death, and elaborate funeral procession, brought wave of public sympathy to the cause.

A. Morley with L. Stanley, *The Life and Death of Emily Wilding Davison: a biographical detective story with Gertrude Colmore's 'The Life of Emily Davison'*, London, 1988

Despard, Charlotte (1844–1939)

Suffragist and radical. Born Charlotte French, she inherited family wealth when a young woman, and married the Radical Maximilian Despard in 1870. When her husband died in 1890 she found solace in mission work, became a vegetarian, and adopted the black lace mantilla which became her trademark. As a Poor Law Guardian in Lambeth from 1894, she was involved in Social Democratic Federation and ILP. Already committed to adult suffrage, she became a member of the WSPU in 1906, but a year later rejected the Pankhursts and formed WFL. During the war she was a member of the Women's Peace Council, and she stood unsuccessfully as a Labour candidate in 1918. The rest of her life was devoted to the Irish cause. She wrote ten novels, most extremely romantic, and her unusual dress and stern frailty made her a prominent figure in fiction about the suffrage movement.

A. Linklater, *An Unhusbanded Life: Charlotte Despard, Suffragette, Socialist, Sinn Feiner*, London, 1980

Emerson, Kathleen Maud

Born in Dublin, member of Irish Women's Franchise League and its secretary in 1911. Sentenced to two months' hard labour for window-breaking, London, March 1912, and fourteen days in

Dublin in November of that year. Heckled Winston Churchill and Lord Aberdeen at Dublin Horse Show and a public lecture over forcible feeding of Gladys Evans and Mary Leigh in 1912.
Suffrage Annual and Women's Who's Who 1913

Gore-Booth, Eva (1870–1926)

Poet, mystic, socialist and suffrage campaigner, born into an aristocratic family in Ireland. In 1896 she met Esther Roper, a graduate working for the political and economic emancipation of women in Manchester, who became her life-long companion. From 1897 she lived in Manchester, publishing poems but also involved in various women's labour organisations. Through her influence Christabel Pankhurst studied law and became a worker for the suffrage cause, but the friendship ended in 1905 when Christabel moved on to more militant activities. Forced through frequent illness to move to London in 1913, she became a pacifist during the war, and afterwards worked for prison reform. Her sister Constance, condemned to death for her part in the 1916 rebellion but later reprieved, became the first women elected to parliament in 1918, although as a Sinn Fein member didn't take up her seat.
G. Lewis, *Eva Gore-Booth and Esther Roper: a biography*, London, 1988

Grey, Laura

Contributor of a poem in *Holloway Jingles*. Little else is known about the writer although she was clearly a committed suffragette. She was arrested on several occasions, and gave evidence to the investigation by Brailsford and Murray into ill-treatment by the women's deputation to Parliament on Black Monday, November 1910, claiming she received fourteen bruises. Mentioned in accounts of prison life as running in the yard, playing the Duke in a performance of *The Merchant of Venice* and, at one point, looking 'bad, nails and fingers bluish'.
M. E. & M. D. Thompson, *They Couldn't Stop Us!*, Ipswich, 1957

Haig, Margaret (Lady Rhondda) (1883–1958)

The only daughter of a Welsh land and mine owner, later the Liberal MP Viscount Rhondda, she worked for her father and, after her marriage, became involved in militant suffrage activities through the WSPU and also wrote for *Votes for Women* and other newspapers.

In the First World War she almost drowned on the *Lusitania*. In the 1920s, recognised as a businesswoman and campaigner for equality, she helped found the Six Point Group and *Time and Tide*.
J. Alberti, *Beyond Suffrage*, London, 1989

Hamilton, Cicely (1827–1952)
Suffragist, playwright, actress, novelist and peace campaigner, and aware of a range of issues related to single women and the problems of economic independence. Attracting a certain amount of fame through her play *Diana of the Dobsons*, 1908, she was involved in suffrage campaigns from at least 1907. A popular speaker for the WSPU in its early days, she appeared to have joined the WFL by 1908. A member of the Women Writers' Suffrage League, she wrote the Pageant of Great Women for the Suffrage exhibition of 1910 and the popular play (with Christopher St John) *How the Vote was Won*. *Marriage as a Trade*, published in 1909, was an important analysis of the conditioning created by women's economic need to place themselves in the marriage market. After the war, she became a freelance journalist and a member of the Open the Door Council, formed to oppose protective legislation for women.
L. Whitelaw, *The Life and Rebellious Times of Cicely Hamilton: actress, writer, suffragist*, London, 1990

Houseman, Laurence (1865–1959)
Writer, poet, illustrator and art critic. Influenced by his sister Clemence, he became a member of the WSPU but left in 1914 to join the United Suffragists. Initially converted by Emmeline Pankhurst, he was active in the Men's League for Women's Suffrage and wrote plays and poetry for the cause. He fell out with the Pankhursts, however, over arson attacks and the slashing of the *Rokeby Venus*. Also active in homosexual politics for law reform.
Autobiography, *The Unexpected Years*, London, 1937

John, Mrs N. A.
A regular speaker at Glasgow WSPU meetings, imprisoned in Holloway in April 1912, and editor of *Holloway Jingles*.
L. Leneman, *A Guid Cause*, Aberdeen, 1991

Johnston, Sir Harry Hamilton (1858–1927)
A widely travelled diplomat, explorer, scientist, linguist, naturalist

and author of various blue books on Africa and histories of the British Empire, he used his twenty-six years of retirement to publish lighter novels. His wife, Lady Winifred, whom he married in 1896, was a member of the NUWSS and Vice-president in 1913 of the Littlehampton branch.

J. A. Casado, *Sir Harry Hamilton Johnston: a bio-bibliographical study*, Basle, 1977

Kenney, Annie (1879–1953)
A leading suffragette, born into a working-class background. Working in a mill from the age of ten, she was first influenced by the socialist writings of Robert Blatchford but was an immediate convert to suffrage on hearing Christabel Pankhurst speak in 1905. More or less adopted by the Pankhursts and, when sent to London as a WSPU organiser, by the Pethick-Lawrences, she remained loyal to the Pankhursts through all the internal strife, acting on Christabel's behalf and as a go-between when the latter left for Paris in 1912. Became seriously ill in 1913 when sentenced to eighteen months in prison and went on hunger and thirst strike. Married in 1920 and became involved in Theosophy.

O. Banks, *The Biographical Dictionary of British Feminists*, Vol. 1 *1800–1930*, Brighton, 1987

Lytton, Lady Constance (1869–1923)
A prominent suffragette, and second daughter to the Earl of Lytton. Her early life was constrained by ill-health and domestic duties with family but she was brought into WSPU through meeting Annie Kenney and Mrs Pethick-Lawrence. Initially doubtful about militancy, her first involvement was with prison reform. Disgusted with the special treatment she received because of her background when first arrested, she disguised herself as a working-class woman and was sent to prison for fourteen days and forcibly fed. In spite of ill-health maintained devotion to the cause and took part in window-breaking, but a stroke in 1912 left her partly paralysed. After the war, she sponsored the Marie Stopes birth control clinic.

O. Banks, *The Biographical Dictionary of British Feminists*, Vol. 1 *1800–1930*, Brighton, 1987

McPhun, Margaret Pollock
Press secretary of the WSPU in the West of Scotland, a member of

the Women's Liberal Association 1906–8, and, as a graduate of Glasgow University, Convener of the Scottish University Women's Suffrage Union 1909–10. Imprisoned in Holloway in 1912.
Suffrage Annual and Women's Who's Who 1913

Mitchell, Hannah (1871–1956)

Suffragette and socialist. As the daughter of a Derbyshire farmer, she was forced as a a child to look after other children and was bitter about the schooling denied to her but given to her brothers. Because of her antagonistic relationship with her mother, left home in 1885 then moved to Bolton, doing dressmaking and domestic work. Married Gibson Mitchell, a committed socialist, in 1895. From 1897, unhappy with the domestic aspects of married life, she began to take an interest in the ILP and suffrage and eventually became a WSPU organiser. This led, however, to a nervous breakdown in 1907. Disillusioned with the Pankhursts she became a member of the EFL for a time. A pacifist during the war, she was elected to Manchester City Council in 1924 and was involved in the ILP and local politics. O. Banks, *The Biographical Dictionary of British Feminists, Vol. 1 1800–1930*, Brighton, 1987

Pankhurst, Christabel (1880–1958)

Leading suffragette and the eldest of the family's five children. An attractive and charismatic speaker, and strong-willed force in the WSPU, Christabel became involved in suffrage politics through the influence of Eva Gore-Booth in 1901. Dissatisfied with the slow progress made after her mother founded the WSPU in 1903, she initiated programme of arrest from 1905. Gaining a First in her law degree but unable to gain access to a career there, she moved to London with her mother. Attempts at democracy within the WSPU were gradually abandoned under her influence but she was a powerful recruiter to the cause. From 1910 she encouraged, although did not initiate, militancy, but fled to Paris in 1912 to avoid arrest. Behind split with the Pethick-Lawrences in 1912. In that year published *The Great Scourge and How to End It*. At the outbreak of the First World War threw all her energies behind the war effort. Unsuccessful as a Parliamentary candidate in 1918, she turned her activities to the Second Adventist movement and lived in the United States from 1939 until her death. She remains a controversial figure for feminists and historians.

E. Sarah, 'Christabel Pankhurst: reclaiming her power' in D. Spender (ed.), *Feminist Theorists*, London, 1983

Pankhurst, Emmeline (1858–1928)
Founder of the WSPU and a leading suffragette. The daughter of manufacturers, from a radical background, she married Richard Pankhurst, a lawyer over twice her age and active in campaigning for suffrage, in 1879. In Manchester became involved in the ILP and was a Poor Law Guardian. On her husband's death, started a small shop and was offered registrarship. Founded the WSPU in 1903 and moved to London in 1907. From 1908 to 1914 repeatedly imprisoned, and often ill through hunger strikes, her apparent fragility combined with determination and tenacity made her an inspirational figure for many in the WSPU. She supported the war effort and in 1917 formed the Women's Party which was unsuccessful at the elections. By 1925 she had joined the Conservative Party.
Autobiography, *My Own Story*, London, 1914

Pankhurst, Sylvia (1882–1960)
Second of Mrs Pankhurst's five children, closest to her father, Sylvia had early successes in her career as an artist. Already in London through a scholarship at the Royal College of Art, she was involved in the early stages of the WSPU there, taking part in militancy and imprisoned many times. From 1905 she had a close relationship with the socialist Keir Hardie. Increasingly disillusioned with militancy and the WSPU's rejection of socialism, she devoted her energies to organising women in the East End of London and began to publish *The Workers' Dreadnought*, a paper for working-class women. The final break with her mother and sister came in 1912 but she continued to campaign for women's and adult suffrage. During the war she expressed her pacifism by forming the Women's Peace Army. Afterwards she became an advocate of Russian socialism and was imprisoned for five months for sedition. In 1927 she had a child by the Italian left-wing exile Silvio Corio but refused to marry. From 1936 onwards involved in the Ethiopian cause. Her history, *The Suffragette Movement*, 1931, offers a full account of the campaign and her family's role in it.
R. Pankhurst, *Sylvia Pankhurst, Artist and Crusader: an intimate portrait*, London, 1979

Pethick-Lawrence, Emmeline (1867–1954)

Leading suffragette. The daughter of a businessman, Emmeline Pethick first became involved in clubs for working-class girls in the 1890s. In 1901 she married Frederick Lawrence, a barrister, and they shared activities within the ILP. Initiated into the WSPU by Annie Kenney, she first became its treasurer but was then increasingly involved as a speaker and activist. In 1907 she launched *Votes for Women* with her husband, and their London home housed the WSPU offices. Frequently arrested and imprisoned, she was unhappy about the direction of suffrage militancy and in 1912 both she and her husband split with Christabel over violence, and were forced out of the organisation. In 1914 she joined the United Suffragists and during the war became a member of the Women's International League for Peace and Freedom, while her husband was a conscientious objector. She stood unsuccessfully for Parliament in 1918 and later became involved in campaigns for birth control, women's legal rights and the Six Point Group. Her husband was elected to Parliament in 1923 as a Labour candidate and later became secretary of State for Burma and India.
O. Banks, *The Biographical Dictionary of British Feminists*, Vol. 1 *1800–1930*, Brighton, 1987

Robins, Elizabeth (1862–1952)

Suffragette, actress and writer. Grew up in Ohio, and sent to Vassar to study medicine, but ran away to stage. Briefly married, but husband committed suicide. In London in 1880s made her acting name mainly by bringing Ibsen to the English stage, and also published novels under the pseudonym 'C. E. Raimond'. A member of the WSPU from the start, she played a leading role in the Actresses' Franchise League and was President of the Women Writers' Suffrage League. Her play of 1907, *Votes for Women!*, later became the novel *The Convert*. After the war she was a regular contributor to *Time and Tide* and wrote the feminist treatise *Ancilla's Share*. She was also a member of the Six Point Group.
Autobiography, *Both Sides of the Curtain*, London, 1940

Rock, Madeleine Caron

Poet, suffragette. Very little information. Arrested in 1910, and is described by *Votes for Women* as a poet, who 'sells the paper regularly on Chelmsford market day'. Appears to be the 'M.C.R.' of poem in *Holloway Jingles*. Author of *Or in the Grass*, 1914, and *On the Tree Top*, 1927.

Sharp, Evelyn (1869–1955)

Suffragette and writer. Earned her living by fiction and journalism, to her family's disapproval. Became a member of WSPU after being sent to cover a lecture by Elizabeth Robins. Wrote for various suffrage publications and was imprisoned on several occasions. She left the WSPU after the Pankhurst/Pethick-Lawrence split and became editor of *Votes for Women*. In 1914 she joined the United Suffragists and was also a founder of the Women's League for Peace and Freedom. A close friend of the scientist and suffragist Hertha Ayrton, she wrote her biography. In 1933 she married Henry Nevinson.

Autobiography, *Unfinished Adventure*, London, 1933

Sinclair, May (1863–1946)

Novelist and suffragette. Daughter of a ship owner who went bankrupt, she supported herself by her writing and published a number of novels, stories and other writings. Apparently non-militant, she belonged in 1908 to the WFL. A member of the Women Writers' Suffrage League and one of twelve vice-presidents for a time, she was also well acquainted with many of the leading literary figures of her time and with the avant-garde circles of imagists and vorticists. Her interest in psychoanalysis emerges in some of her more experimental works, and she coined the phrase 'stream-of-consciousness' in a 1908 review of Dorothy Richardson. Her pamphlet 'Feminism', published by the WWSL in 1912, was a refutation of Almroth Wright's attack on militants as hysterics.

T. E. M. Boll, *Miss May Sinclair: Novelist*, London, 1973

Smyth, Ethel (1858–1944)

Suffragette and composer. Began to make a name for herself as a composer in the 1890s, having persuaded her father through various acts of rebellion to be allowed to study music. Initially uninterested in suffrage, she was won over to the cause after hearing Emmeline Pankhurst speak, formed a close friendship with her, and decided to give up music for two years in order to devote herself to the campaign. Contributed to the movement through demonstrations and imprisonment but also wrote the 'March of the Women' and other songs. In

1912 she returned to music and to writing, publishing a series of memoirs over the years. Campaigned vigorously in support of women orchestra players and for women's place in music generally.
C. St John, *Ethel Smyth: a biography*, London, 1959

Swanwick, Helena (1864–1939)

Suffragist and journalist. Daughter of the artist Oswald Sickert, she studied economics at Girton, although her parents opposed her plans. Moved north after marriage to Frederick Swanwick, a maths lecturer, in 1888, and wrote reviews for the *Guardian*. From 1905 she was interested in the suffrage cause but not with the Pankhursts, and became editor of the NUWSS journal, *The Common Cause*. She resigned from this in 1912 when she wasn't given freedom to take the active stand she wished against the Pankhursts and militancy. A pacifist during the war, she helped form the Women's International League and was twice a member of the British delegation to the League of Nations.
J. Alberti, *Beyond Suffrage*, London, 1989

Thompson, Margaret Eleanor and Mary D.

Apart from their account of life in prison, little information available. Margaret was a member of the WSPU whereas Mary joined later, after belonging to the Constitutional Society. Margaret took part in speaking, pamphlet-writing and paper-selling, according to the *Suffrage Annual and Women's Who's Who* for 1913, and had been arrested for obstructing the police, window-breaking, and damage to property. There is no entry on Mary, who was at the time classical mistress at South Hampstead School for Girls.
Suffrage Annual and Women's Who's Who 1913

Ward, Augusta Mary (Mrs Humphry) (1851–1920)

Novelist and anti-suffragist. The granddaughter of Sir Thomas Arnold of Rugby, she was an active philanthropist and intellectual, supporting higher education for women and the place of women in the public services, but campaigning against the vote. An initiator of the letter signed by a number of women, 'An Appeal Against Women's Suffrage' in 1889 in *Nineteenth Century*, she was also influential in the Women's National Anti-Suffrage League. She appears to have believed women might be seen as 'ridiculous' in fighting for the vote and was particularly opposed to militancy. Her

most famous novel was *Robert Elsmere*, 1888, which was a huge success and provoked much debate at the time, but she wrote many other novels. She remained opposed to women's suffrage.
J. Sutherland, *Mrs Humphry Ward: eminent Victorian, pre-eminent Edwardian*, Oxford, 1990

Wells, Herbert George (1886–1946)
Novelist. The son of a tradesman, he published scientific romances, comic realist tales and social analyses in his fiction, which was only one part of his large and varied literary output. Involved with many of the radical causes of his day, Wells also questioned many of their ideas. His relationship with the Fabian Society was typical in this respect. Involved with various women with connections to suffrage, Wells supported women's rights in general although his depiction of sexual relationships caused some consternation at the time.
J. R. Hammond, *H. G. Wells: Interviews and recollections*, London, 1980

West, Rebecca (1892–1983)
Writer and suffragette. Born Cicely Isabel Fairfield, but changed her name after Ibsen heroine. Educated in Edinburgh but in trouble from age of fifteen because of her feminism. Attached herself to the WSPU and in 1907 wrote letter to *The Scotsman* protesting at degradation of women. In 1910 she won a place at the Academy of Dramatic Art but was soon writing for *The New Freewoman*, and *The Clarion*. By 1913 she had moved away from the WSPU position and disliked Christabel Pankhurst, although she still defended their tactics in print, writing satirical and outspoken pieces. In that year she also began a lengthy affair with H. G. Wells, to whom she bore a son. In the 1920s she was a contributor to *Time and Tide* and published a range of novels and articles through her long literary career.
V. Glendinning, *Rebecca West: a life*, London, 1987

Wilson, A. Agnes
Suffragette. Little information available. Was for some years secretary of Redhill Constitutional Suffrage Society, leaving that when the NUWSS condemned militancy. Arrested and imprisoned for window-breaking, given hard labour and went on hunger strike. Contributor to *Holloway Jingles*.
The Suffrage Annual and Women's Who's Who 1913

Zangwill, Edith Ayrton (1875–1945)

Suffragette and novelist. Daughter of an eminent electrical inventor, Professor W. E. Ayrton, and his first wife, Dr M. C. Ayrton, a medical pioneer, Edith Zangwill was also much influenced by her step-mother, Hertha Ayrton, a feminist, physicist and suffragist, active in militant movement and generous in contributions. Married Israel Zangwill, journalist, novelist and Zionist, in 1903, and brought him into the suffrage movement, where he appears to have become more prominent than his wife and a well-known speaker. She was active in the WWSL and published a number of novels. Both became increasingly critical of WSPU and later moved towards United Suffragists.

Bibliography

Primary source material

Anon., *The Home-Breakers* (London, 1913) [see Stainton, J. S.]

Bennett, Arnold, *The Lion's Share* (London, 1916)

Billington-Greig, Teresa, *The Militant Suffrage Movement: emancipation in a hurry* (London, n.d., *c.* 1911)

Burton Baldry, William, *From Hampstead to Holloway: the journey of a suffragette* (London, 1909)

Chew, Doris Nield (ed.), *Ada Nield Chew: the life and writings of a working woman* (London, 1982)

Colmore, Gertrude, *Suffragette Sally* (London, 1911) [rep. as *Suffragettes: a story of three women*,1984]

Colmore, Gertrude, *The Life of Emily Davison* (London, 1913) [rep. in Morley, A. with Stanley, L., *The Life and Death of Emily Wilding Davison*, 1988]

Colmore, Gertrude, *Mr Jones and the Governess and other stories* (London, 1913)

Despard, Charlotte & Collins, Mabel, *Outlawed* (London, n.d., *c.* 1908)

Gibson, Elizabeth, *From the Wilderness* (Hexham, 1910)

Gonne, Josephine, *Wails of the Weary* (Fawcett Library, n.d.)

Gore-Booth, Eva, *Collected Poems* (London, 1929)

Haig, Margaret, *This was My World* (London, 1933)

Hamilton, Cicely, *William – an Englishman* (London, 1919)

Houseman, Laurence, 'Women This and Women That' (WSPU, n.d.)

John, N. A. (ed.), *Holloway Jingles* (Glasgow, 1912)

Johnston, Sir Harry, *Mrs Warren's Daughter: a story of the suffrage movement* (London, 1920)

Kenney, Annie, *Memories of a Militant* (London, 1924)

Lytton, Constance, *Prisons and Prisoners* (London, 1914)

Mitchell, Hannah, *The Hard Way Up: the autobiography of Hannah Mitchell, suffragette and rebel* (London, 1968; 1977)

Mollwo, Adrienne, *A Fair Suffragette* (London, 1909)

Pethick-Lawrence, Emmeline, *My Part in a Changing World* (London, 1938)

Roberts, Kathleen, *Pages from the Diary of a Militant Suffragette* (Letchworth & London, 1911)

Roberts, Kathleen, *Some Pioneers and a Prison* (Letchworth & London, 1913)

Robins, Elizabeth, *The Convert* (London, 1907; 1980)

Rock, Madeleine Caron, *Or in the Grass* (London, 1914)

Sharp, Evelyn, *Rebel Women* (London, 1910; 1915)

Sinclair, May, *The Tree of Heaven* (London, 1917)

Smyth, Ethel, 'The March of the Women' (London, 1911)

Smyth, Ethel, *Female Pipings in Eden* (London, 1933)

Stainton, J. S., *The Home-Breakers: an anti-militant suffragist novel by a popular and well-known novelist who desires to remain anonymous* (London, 1913)

Swanwick, Helena, *I Have Been Young* (London, 1935)

Thompson, Margaret E. & Mary D., *They Couldn't Stop Us! Experiences of two (usually law-abiding) women in the years 1909–1913* (Ipswich, 1957)

Ward, Mary Augusta (Mrs Humphry), *Delia Blanchflower* (London, 1915)

Wells, Herbert George, *Ann Veronica* (London, 1909)

West, Rebecca, *The Judge* (London, 1922; 1980)

Zangwill, Edith, *The Call* (London, 1924)

Secondary sources

(Note: included in this bibliography are other primary texts not selected for inclusion in the volume)

Alberti, Johanna, *Beyond Suffrage: feminists in war and peace 1914–1928* (London, 1989)

Banks, Olive, *Faces of Feminism: a study of feminism as a social movement* (Oxford, 1981)

Banks, Olive, *The Biographical Dictionary of British Feminists, Vol.*

1 *1800–1930* (Brighton, 1987) and *Vol. 2: A Supplement 1900–1945* (Brighton, 1990)

Baylen, Joseph O. & Grossman, N. J., *The Biographical Dictionary of British Radicals* (London, 1979)

Beckett, Jane & Cherry, Deborah (eds) *The Edwardian Era* (London, 1987)

Benson, Stella, *Twenty* (London, 1918)

Blain, Virginia *et al.*, *The Feminist Companion to Literature in English* (London, 1990)

Boll, Theophilus E. M., *Miss May Sinclair, Novelist: a biographical and critical introduction* (Rutherford, New Jersey, 1973)

Byles, Joan Montgomery, 'Women's experience of World War One: suffragists, pacifists and poets', *Women's Studies International Forum*, 8: 5 (1985), pp. 473–87

Casado, James A., *Sir Harry Hamilton Johnston: a bio-bibliographical study* (Basle, 1977)

Castle, Barbara, *Sylvia and Christabel Pankhurst* (Harmondsworth, 1987)

Chew, Doris Nield, *Ada Nield Chew: the life and writings of a working woman* (London, 1982)

Collinge, Alice E., *Her Way and Three Other Plays* (London, 1923)

Daims, Diva, & Grimes, Janet, *Towards a Feminist Tradition: an annotated bibliography of novels in English by Women 1880–1920* (New York, 1982)

Doughan, David & Sanchez, Denise, *Feminist Periodicals 1855–1984* (Brighton, 1987)

Drabble, Margaret, *Arnold Bennett: a biography* (London, 1974)

Draper, Michael, *H. G. Wells* (London, 1987)

Durham, Martin, 'Suffrage and after: feminism in the early twentieth century', in Langan, M. & Schwarz, B. (eds), *Crisis in the British State* (London, 1985)

Elshtain, Jean Bethke, 'Feminist discourse and its discontents: language, power and meaning in feminist theory', in Keohane, N. *et al.* (eds), *Feminist Theory: a critique of ideology* (Chicago, 1982)

The Englishwoman's Yearbook (London, 1913)

Felski, Rita, *Beyond Feminist Aesthetics: feminist literature and social change* (Cambridge, Mass., 1989)

Fulford, Roger, *Votes for Women: the story of a struggle* (London, 1957)

Fuss, Diane, *Essentially Speaking: feminism, nature and difference* (London, 1989)

Gagnier, Regina, *Subjectivities: a history of self-representation in Britain 1832–1920* (New York & Oxford, 1991)

Gardiner, Juliet (ed.), *The New Woman* (London, 1993)

Garner, Les, *Stepping Stones to Women's Liberty: feminist ideas in the women's suffrage movement 1900–1918* (London, 1984)

Gawthorpe, Mary, *Votes for Men* (London, 1910)

Gibbons, Tom, *Rooms in the Darwin Hotel: studies in English literary criticism and ideas 1880–1920* (Nedlands, Western Australia, 1973)

Gilbert, Sandra M. & Gubar, Susan, *No Man's Land: the place of the woman writer in the twentieth century*, Vol. 1, *The War of the Words* (New Haven & London, 1988)

Glendinning, Victoria, *Rebecca West: a life* (London, 1987)

Green, Martin, *Dreams of Adventure, Deeds of Empire* (London, 1980)

Hamilton, Cicely, *Beware! A Warning to Suffragists* (London, n.d.)

Hamilton, Cicely, *Marriage as a Trade* (London, 1909; 1981)

Hamilton, Cicely, *A Pageant of Great Women* (Liverpool, 1912)

Hamilton, Cicely, *Life Errant* (London, 1935)

Hammond, J. R. *H. G. Wells: interviews and recollections* (London, 1980)

Harrison, Brian, *Separate Spheres: the opposition to women's suffrage in Britain* (London, 1978)

Harrison, Brian, *Peaceable Kingdom: stability and change in modern Britain* (Oxford, 1982)

Harrison, Brian, *Prudent Revolutionaries: portraits of British feminists between the wars* (Oxford, 1987)

Heape, Walter, *Sex Antagonism* (London, 1913)

Hepburn, James (ed.), *Arnold Bennett: the critical heritage* (London, 1981)

Hesketh, Phoebe, *My Aunt Edith* (London, 1966)

Holton, Sandra Stanley, *Feminism and Democracy: women's suffrage and reform politics in Britain 1900–1918* (Cambridge, 1986)

Holton, Sandra Stanley, '"In sorrowful wrath": suffrage militancy and the romantic feminism of Emmeline Pankhurst', in H. L. Smith (ed.), *British Feminism in the Twentieth Century* (Aldershot, 1990)

Houseman, Laurence, *Alice in Ganderland: a one act play* (London, 1911)

Houseman, Laurence, *The Unexpected Years* (London, 1937)

Hunter, Jefferson, *Edwardian Fiction* (Cambridge, Mass., 1982)

Hynes, Samuel, *The Edwardian Turn of Mind* (Princeton & London, 1968)

Keating, Peter *The Haunted Study: a social history of the English novel 1875–1914* (London, 1989)

Kent, Susan Kingsley, *Sex and Suffrage in Britain 1860–1914* (Princeton, 1987)

King, Elspeth, *The Scottish Women's Suffrage Movement* (Glasgow, 1978)

Leneman, Leah, *A Guid Cause: the women's suffrage movement in Scotland* (Aberdeen, 1991)

Lewis, Gifford, *Eva Gore-Booth and Esther Roper: a biography* (London, 1988)

Lewis, Jane (ed.), *Before the Vote was Won: arguments for and against women's suffrage* (New York & London, 1987)

Liddington, Jill, *The Life and Times of a Respectable Rebel: Selina Cooper* (London, 1984)

Liddington, Jill & Norris, Jill, *One Hand Tied Behind Us: the rise of the women's suffrage movement* (London, 1978)

Linklater, Andro, *An Unhusbanded Life: Charlotte Despard, Suffragette, Socialist, Sinn Feiner* (London, 1980)

MacKenzie, Midge, *Shoulder to Shoulder: a documentary* (London, 1975)

McPhee, Carol & Fitzgerald, Ann, *Non-Violent Militant: selected writings of Teresa Billington-Greig* (London, 1987)

Marcus, Jane (ed.), *Suffrage and the Pankhursts* (London & New York, 1987)

Marks, Elaine & de Courtivron, Isabelle, *New French Feminisms: an anthology* (Brighton, 1981)

Miller, George Noyes, *The Strike of a Sex* (London, 1891)

Mitchell, David, *The Fighting Pankhursts: a study in tenacity* (London, 1967)

Mitchell, David, *Queen Christabel: a biography of Christabel Pankhurst* (London, 1977)

Morley, Ann with Stanley, Liz, *The Life and Death of Emily Wilding Davison: a biographical detective story with Gertrude Colmore's 'The Life of Emily Davison'* (London, 1988)

Morris, Pam, *Literature and Feminism* (Oxford, 1993)

Mulford, Wendy, 'Socialist-feminist criticism: a case study, women's suffrage and literature, 1906–14' in P. Widdowson (ed.), *Re-reading English* (London, 1982)

Pankhurst, Christabel, *Unshackled* (London, 1959)

Pankhurst, Emmeline, *My Own Story* (London, 1914)

Pankhurst, Richard, *Sylvia Pankhurst, Artist and Crusader: an intimate portrait* (London, 1979)

Pankhurst, Sylvia, *Writ on Cold Slate* (London, 1922)

Pankhurst, Sylvia, *The Suffragette Movement: an intimate account of persons and ideals* (London, 1931)

Peterson, Linda, *Victorian Autobiography: the tradition of self-interpretation* (New Haven & London, 1986)

Pugh, Martin, *Women's Suffrage in Britain 1867–1928* (London, 1980)

R., A. J. (ed.), *The Suffrage Annual and Women's Who's Who* (London, 1913)

Raeburn, Antonia, *The Militant Suffragettes* (London, 1973)

Ramelson, Marian, *The Petticoat Rebellion: a century of struggle for women's rights* (London, 1972)

Ray, Gordon N., *H. G. Wells and Rebecca West* (London, 1974)

Rendall, Jane (ed.), *Equal or Different: women's politics 1800–1914* (Oxford, 1987)

Rich, Lieut. Col. C. E. F., *Recollections of a Prison Governor* (London, 1932)

Richardson, Mary, *Laugh a Defiance* (London, 1953)

Riley, Denise, *Am I That Name? Feminism and the category of 'women' in history* (London, 1988)

Robins, Elizabeth, *Both Sides of the Curtain* (London, 1940)

Romero, P. W., *E. Sylvia Pankhurst: portrait of a radical* (New Haven, 1987)

Rosen, Andrew, *Rise Up Women! the militant campaign of the Women's Social and Political Union* (London, 1974)

Roszack, Theodore, 'The hard and the soft: the force of feminism in modern times' in Roszack, T. & B. (eds), *Masculine/Feminine: readings in sexual mythology and the liberation of women* (New York, 1969)

Rover, Constance, *Women's Suffrage and Party Politics in Britain 1866–1914* (London, 1967)

Rubinstein, David, *Before the Suffragettes* (Brighton, 1986)

Sarah, Elizabeth, 'Christabel Pankhurst: reclaiming her power' in D. Spender (ed.), *Feminist Theorists: three centuries of women's intellectual tradition* (London, 1983)

Schlueter, Paul & Schlueter, Jane, *An Encyclopedia of British Women Writers* (New York, 1980)

Sharp, Evelyn, *Hertha Ayrton: a memoir* (London, 1926)

Sharp, Evelyn, *Unfinished Adventure* (London, 1933)

Sharratt, Bernard, *Reading Relations: structures of Literary Production: a dialectical text/book* (Brighton, 1982)

Showalter, Elaine, *A Literature of their Own: British women novelists from Bronte to Lessing* (London, 1977; 1982)

Showalter, Elaine, *Sexual Anarchy* (London, 1992)

St John, Christopher, *Ethel Smyth: a biography* (London, 1959)

Stern, Katherine, 'The war of the sexes in British fantasy literature of the suffragette era', *Critical Matrix*, 3 (1987), pp. 78–109

Strachey, Ray, *The Cause: a short history of the women's movement in Great Britain* (London, 1928; 1978)

Sutherland, John, *Mrs Humphry Ward: eminent Victorian, pre-eminent Edwardian* (Oxford, 1990)

Tickner, Lisa, *The Spectacle of Women: imagery of the suffrage campaign 1907–1914* (London, 1987)

Todd, Janet, *Dictionary of British Women Writers* (London, 1989)

Vicinus, Martha, *Independent Women: work and community for single women 1850–1920* (London, 1985)

Ward, Mrs Humphry, *The Testing of Diana Mallory* (London, 1910)

Watson, Norman, *Dundee Suffragettes* (Perth, 1990)

Whitelaw, Lis, *The Life and Rebellious Times of Cicely Hamilton: actress, writer, suffragist* (London, 1990)

Women's Press, *The Treatment of the Women's Deputations by the Metropolitan Police* (London, 1911)

Wright, Sir Almroth, *The Unexpurgated Case Against Women's Suffrage* (London, 1913)

Young, Frances E., *The War of the Sexes* (London, 1905)

Index